Understanding Marketing

MARK A. P. DAVIES

Loughborough University Business School

LONDON   NEW YORK   TORONTO   SYDNEY   TOKYO
SINGAPORE   MADRID   MEXICO CITY   MUNICH   PARIS

First published 1998 by
Prentice Hall Europe
Campus 400, Maylands Avenue
Hemel Hempstead
Hertfordshire, HP2 7EZ
A division of
Simon & Schuster International Group

© Prentice Hall 1998

Reprinted 1998

Typeset in 10/12pt Swift by
Hands Fotoset, Ratby, Leicester

Printed and bound in Great Britain by
Biddles Ltd, Guildford and King's Lynn

Library of Congress Cataloging-in-Publication Data

Davies, Mark A. P.
    Understanding marketing / Mark A. P. Davies.
        p.   cm.
    Includes bibliographical references and index.
    ISBN 0-13-490467-2
    1. Marketing.   I. Title.
    HF5415.D354   1997
    658.8–dc21   97-30765
                                                  CIP

British Library Cataloguing in Publication Data

A catalogue record for this book is available from
the British Library

ISBN 0-13-490467-2

2 3 4 5   02 01 00 99 98

Contents

CHAPTER ONE

Introduction to Marketing

Objectives

After studying this chapter, you should be able to:

1. Understand exactly what marketing is, clearly distinguishing it from simply promoting or selling.
2. Recognise the role that marketing can offer, both as a function and as a managerial philosophy in guiding future performance.
3. Appreciate the role of marketing as a dynamic activity, a continuous process rather than a static activity.
4. Recognise that customer orientation is not sufficient for a marketing orientation: also required is a competitor orientation and an ability to co-ordinate the resources of the firm.

Introduction to the marketing module

The first chapter of this module introduces the fundamentals of marketing and the reasons for studying the subject. We begin by explaining that the term 'marketing' is often confused with promotion or selling, and consequently why it is often undervalued or misinterpreted. The importance of marketing, both as a business function and as a managerial philosophy, is also explained. The nature of marketing as a dynamic process is discussed. Environmental features must be tracked for their likely effect on market performance.

In chapter 2, the influence and impact of the environment, together with internal factors on marketing decision-making, are examined. This is developed by discussing the marketing audit as part of marketing planning. Implementation, control and evaluation are discussed. There is a section on developing and sustaining appropriate competitive strategies.

Chapter 3 is a study of marketing research. Research is a prerequisite for ensuring that a firm focuses precisely on consumer needs. Some marketing research techniques are described, along with secondary and primary data collection methods.

The central goal of marketing is to focus on consumer needs. This requires effective targeting and marketing segmentation, together with a recognition that consumer needs are not the same for everyone. Targeting and segmentation are considered in chapter 4.

To gauge how consumers make purchase decisions, it is necessary to establish the psychological, social and environmental influences. These are considered in chapter 5, which elaborates on needs and motives.

Another aim of marketing is to improve profitability. Several empirical studies, described in chapter 1, provide evidence that there is a relationship between a sound commitment to marketing and financial success. Such a commitment requires an effective marketing strategy. This involves providing a suitable offering to consumers (that is, one in line with their expectations). Decisions must, therefore, be made on the marketing mix, the product, the price, the place (or distribution) and promotion. These are the subject of detailed study in chapter 6. The concept of integrated marketing is established, which requires a balanced combination of the marketing mix, with the individual elements reinforcing one another to provide a distinctive offering. Chapter 6 focuses particularly on new product development and deletion decisions.

Chapters 7–10 expand on further specific aspects of the marketing mix. Chapter 7 deals with pricing, and distribution management is dealt with in chapter 8. Chapter 9 discusses the role of advertising and sales promotion, and chapter 10 examines personal selling, public relations and direct mail.

Chapter 11 is about international marketing. The procedures involved when developing markets abroad are examined here. There is a particular emphasis on the extent to which the firm's strategy (or offerings) should be standardised (i.e. similar in foreign markets to the domestic market) or customised.

Finally, chapter 12 is devoted to the marketing of services, something of increasing importance in many nations.

1.1 What is marketing?

Journalists misinterpret it; pawnbrokers exploit it; drug dealers abuse it; politicians may give it a bad name or use it wisely. Does marketing have a shady image?

A major problem with marketing, in terms of understanding what it means, is its very name. A common misconception is that marketing is the same as 'trading' or 'dealing'. There are the unfortunate links with 'barrow boys', associated with 'making a fast buck', 'selling a fast one' and exploitation of the consumer.

Whilst it is fair to acknowledge that marketing does have a role to play in selling and trading, this is only a small part of its total function. Since marketing is supposed to make the selling process *easier*, 'exploitation of the consumer' is likely to be counterproductive, at least if some kind of *relationship* with the customer is to prevail.

The bad name associated with marketing may be more attributable to those that practise it, rather than the discipline itself. The same can be said of any profession: there is good and bad everywhere.

Let us examine a common definition of marketing. Marketing is about satisfying:

- **consumer needs** and
- **profitability**,
- **given your resources.**

The elements of this definition are emphasised because I want to expand on each part. We shall begin by examining *consumer needs*.

1.1.1 Meeting consumer needs

Maslow (1943) suggested that needs can be categorised along a hierarchy. This is represented by Figure 1.1, in which more basic needs (such as the need for survival; food and shelter) are satisfied first. This model suggests that once basic needs have been fulfilled, new, more refined or sophisticated needs are demanded, graduating from needs for affiliation and belonginess or love, to the need for self-esteem, and to self-fulfilment or self-actualisation.

The significance of Maslow's model is in applying it to different markets. A company should identify the kinds of needs most sought by its principal or target audience. In general, more sophisticated needs tend to be aimed at consumers who enjoy high standards of living. Expectations tend to be influenced more by cultural and economic forces than by products. Thus motor cars may be offered and promoted as a basic form of transport in India at a price the local market can afford, whereas in a more advanced economy, such as Western Europe, most consumers want something extra and are prepared to pay for it. Consider some recent car advertisements. Safety needs have become major issues in some markets, and the air bag has become a prominent feature in many campaigns. However, for many this is not enough. Today, the car has become a status symbol, and ownership of a particular make or model can signify one's social position or status in society. This is often demonstrated through the

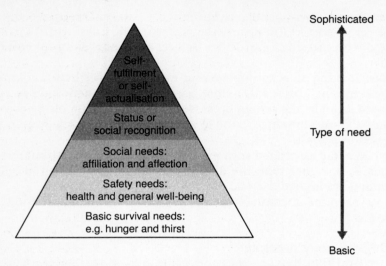

Figure 1.1 Hierarchy of needs, adapted from Maslow (1943)

performance of the car, or by the power shown through achievement, possibly achieved by creating high visual-impact commercials.

The need for self-actualisation merits some discussion. It is often recognised that money need not necessarily bring happiness. The final need in Maslow's hierarchy is self-fulfilment, or a sense of inner contentment and purpose – in short, feeling good about yourself and having a spiritual purpose in life. Thus the product should be an extension of your own personality. Since consumers are becoming more sophisticated in their needs, and because it is likely that self-actualisation can never be achieved completely, but is only a goal to strive towards, this need presents a challenge to marketers.

From a study of Maslow's hierarchy of needs it should be understood that needs arise to satisfy some kind of purpose or utility. Their purpose may be either:

- *rational* performance-related (based on some objective benefits), or
- *emotive* and/or irrational, based on fulfilling a psychological or social need, such as self-gratification.

Thus you might buy a new carpet because the old one has worn through, and decide on a particular brand because of its durability and ease of cleaning and maintenance (rational benefits). You might choose the colour to fit in with the existing decor, in which case the colour of the walls, curtains and furniture might be important: again, rational criteria. But you might be tempted to consider choosing a carpet for the drawing room on different criteria from your choice for the bedroom. Why? If you wish to impress your guests (need for social recognition), the chances are you will buy a better quality carpet for the room where your guests are most likely to see it. The choice of carpet for the drawing room is now determined by emotive needs.

When the need is emotive, an individual's feelings and attitudes are significant to marketers. Consider what you might do when you need to quench your thirst on a hot summer day. Your first decision (to satisfy the rational need of thirst-quenching) is to buy a drink. This decision is therefore made at the *product category level*. Your second decision is of more interest to the marketer. What *brand* of drink will you buy? A brand is defined as a distinctive product offering, which distinguishes it from competitive alternatives. There may be intense competition on the shop shelf. Why might you prefer Coca Cola to Pepsi-Cola or Fanta? When brands satisfy the majority of rational needs equally, emotive needs become more influential in brand choice.

It is likely that, at the brand level of decision-making, some brands stand out from the rest. Imagine a league table of your favourite sports clubs. Now visualise a similar table for soft drinks. Where do your preferences lie, and why? Interestingly enough, it may be that you have clear preferences, but you are not able to articulate the reason explicitly. If this is the case, then the basis of your brand preferences have probably been evaluated below the threshold of consciousness. Such is the power of marketing in developing powerful brand images to remind you of needs that you already had, but were perhaps not consciously aware of.

It is in retailing (and brand recognition in particular) that packaging plays a very important role. Most product manufacturers choose packaging that is distinctive and differentiates their product from that of competitors. Research has shown that, when consumers are asked to recall a product, they are more likely to think of the packaging than the product itself.

Brand preference for Coca Cola may be associated with a good matching of an advertisement to the life style and/or self-image of the consumer. For instance, the image created by a crowd of youngsters singing 'The Real Thing' or 'Coke is It!' may be enough to identify the catchphrase with youth or other pleasant feelings. Either the drinker *is* young or likes to *feel* young. Patronage is one path to group invitation and identity. In this way, the product may symbolise a particular youth culture. The fun-loving, sharing image conveyed by the advertisement may stimulate desire, so offering to satisfy the need for social acceptance.

But the success of Coca Cola (which has come a long way since its original objective in 1886 as a brain tonic to relieve nervous afflictions) cannot be attributed *solely* to clever advertising. There are now 300 million servings a day in over 155 countries – a true branding success, based in part on a superb strategy of licensing world-wide (to gain quick availability) combined with tapping into the relevant emotive needs of a global market.

A company must see needs from the consumers' viewpoint. For example, if a plastic dustbin is commonly used as a wine-making bin, then this is its purpose and it should be marketed accordingly. A classic failure to see needs from the consumers' viewpoint was made by Levi's in the 1970s, which harmed the famous red label of the *Levi's 501* brand. Diversifying into off-the-peg mix 'n' match suits told the core jeans buyer (age 15–24) something they did not want to hear: Levi's were their dad's jeans. This weakened the traditional brand values of youth life style, rebellion and freedom, as portrayed in the advertising.

Sometimes consumer usage patterns can indicate a lot about prevailing beliefs and offer insight into potential new markets. For example, a manufacturer of horse grooming products discovered that consumers were using their shampoos and conditioners on themselves instead of on their animals. Consumers believed that these protein-rich cosmetics would make their hair as glossy as a horse's mane. Analysis of consumer behaviour opened up a new market for the company.

1.1.2 How marketing affects profitability

Some might argue that marketing is overrated, or is not as effective as it is claimed to be. But generally, at least in the long term, profitability will suffer unless needs are identified and satisfied. Therefore, *there are financial incentives to practise effective marketing*.

Two cases will be examined to illustrate this:

1. A study by Wong, Saunders and Doyle (1988); and
2. An examination of the financial relationship of brand leaders and followers in the grocery market by Doyle (1989).

Saunders and Doyle (1988) examined the attitudes of US, UK and Japanese firms competing in the UK market for automobiles, hi-fi and machine tools. Japanese management was found to be more committed to long-term growth to dominate the market *at great sacrifice* in some cases, compared to US and the UK companies, which were content with short-term profits realised by steady growth.

The Japanese firms were very successful, although most of their products were in the middle to top end of the market and sold at premium prices (i.e. beyond the average price expected to confer prestige or a quality image). This indicates that if the right goods are made in line with consumer expectations, consumers will often return for more. This need not always reflect the cheapest prices. Figure 1.2 shows the cycle of virtue, developed by Saunders and Wong (1989). Finding out what consumers want involves researching their preferences in detail. This is the means of ensuring repeat patronage. For example, it would be wasteful if a complimentary bottle of champagne was given to *every* guest as standard policy in a premium priced hotel because some guests are likely to be teetotal.

A more recent example to demonstrate the opportunity for premium pricing is the Club World brand of British Airways. As customers, we do not always consider services as brands, but by identifying closely with the needs of the target

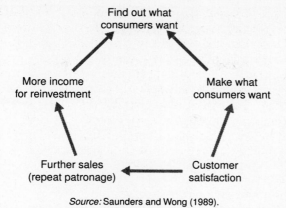

Find out what
consumers want

More income
for reinvestment

Make what
consumers want

Further sales
(repeat patronage)

Customer
satisfaction

Source: Saunders and Wong (1989).

Figure 1.2 The cycle of virtue

audience, BA have been able to offer different ranges of benefits at different prices. It is the package of benefits as a whole that conveys a distinctive brand identity (see Figure 1.3). Here improved features of the Club World brand (i.e. seating, lounges, lockers, comfort kits, menu options) offer collectively the generic benefit of extra comfort. The distinction between features and benefits needs to be appreciated. Features involve technical characteristics of the product or brand, which customers may not understand. Features, therefore, need to be turned into benefits by explaining how they can help consumers meet their needs in some way.

Studies undertaken in the 1990s suggest that American organisations are now more respected by top management, whereas respect for Japanese organisations has waned somewhat. Nevertheless, the attributes that cultivate respect have remained similar to those of the 1980s. Respect is still based on a commitment to developing a long-term strategy.

Doyle's study (1989) examined the financial relationship between brand leaders and followers. Doyle suggests that brand leaders are always the most profitable in their markets. A successful brand, which both retailers and consumers want to buy, achieves a high market share and is also the most profitable. The PIMS Study (Buzzell and Gale, 1987) demonstrated that, from a sample of 2,600 businesses across a diverse range of markets, those with a market share of 40 per cent generate three times the rate of return on investment compared with those with a share of 10 per cent. The relationship between market position and return on sales for UK grocery products is even more marked (see Table 1.1). Why is this relationship so striking?

Examine the data shown in Table 1.1 and Figure 1.4, then study the contributions in the text box. It should become clear that a fundamental objective of marketing is to dominate a position in a market, or at least establish a healthy

---

BRAND: BA Club World

Objective: To deliver passengers in the right frame of mind to do business.

Research: Track consumer feelings to support premium prices.

Product features (*with benefits*):

Comfort
Club World footrest and new seat designs, *with* built in *back supports.*
Separate lounges *away from crowds.*
Concorde – overhead lockers to *provide more space.*
To relieve jet lag, a comfort kit offers a cold eye compress, lip balm, face spray and rehydration gel.
Well being menu options and videos on how to *keep fresh.*

Convenience
Speedy route through security for *Premium* passengers.

Entertainments
More choice of viewing for Club World: eight channels.

Source: Adapted from British Airways (1993) *High Life*, May, 5–8.

Figure 1.3 Planning a brand

Table 1.1 Relationship between market position (rank) and net margin for UK grocery products

Rank	Net Margin %
1	17.9
2	2.8
3	−0.9
4	−5.9

Source: Doyle (1989)

market share (which is normally only reserved for a few brands in a given market category).

Explanations of financial performance of brand leaders

1. Successful brands (leaders) achieve higher customer loyalty. Unsuccessful brands (followers) suffer more from brand-switching. Peters

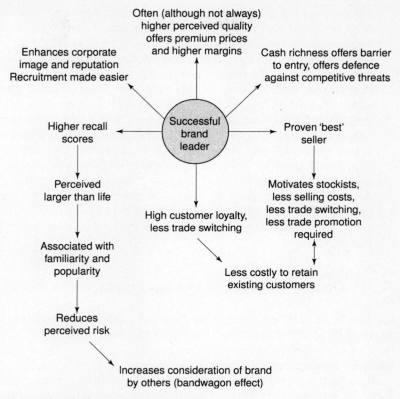

Figure 1.4 Implications of brand success

(1988) suggest it is six times as costly to win new customers as it is to retain existing ones.

2. This is partly due to the reactions of trade confidence in the brand. The trade is often reluctant to stock new brands if the existing leader satisfies the market. This in itself may act as a barrier to entry, but consider the additional incentives that may need to be offered in order to be considered for shelf space. Additional selling costs will be incurred by brand followers. Alpert, Kamins and Graham (1992) have shown that resellers also prefer leaders who are first in the market compared to those who are later followers.

3. Shelf space for followers is likely to be low and not located in premium positions. Strong leaders, with their financial strength, can prevent potential attacks by gaining privileged merchandising slots, as they are cash-rich and favoured by the trade.

4. Successful brands can often override adverse publicity, owing to their

prior strong loyalty attachments and financial strength. For example, despite initial bad publicity attracted when traces of benzene were found in some Perrier mineral water production, and BA's 'dirty tricks' campaign against Virgin Airlines, both Perrier and BA have bounced back and managed to reproduce their previous success.

5. Companies with strong brands, such as Mars, Glaxo, Shell and Cadbury, usually find recruiting personnel relatively easy.

6. It is likely that brand leaders are more likely to be purchased. They achieve higher recall scores with consumers (i.e. when consumers are asked to recall any brand names in a given product category, commonly used in advertising research). More remarkable is that the perceived size of brand leaders is exaggerated at the expense of followers (Figure 1.5). Since market leaders are considered greater than they actually are, and size is associated with famili- arity and popularity, brand leaders are considered less risky to purchase.

1.1.3 Finite resources act as a limiting factor in marketing

A decision has to be reached about what can and cannot be produced. Limited resources, both human and financial, may act as a barrier to entry.

Human resources

We have already indicated that successful brand manufacturers usually find recruitment easier than their less successful competitors. If firms have difficulty in recruiting quality talent, this can prove an obstacle to innovation, which is of prime importance to organisations seeking to be at the forefront of technology. But even firms in traditionally stable markets need to strive constantly for improvement in all their marketing operations to keep ahead of the pack. Consider a retail company that has difficulty in employing sales staff in its branches. If the sales staff are inadequately trained, or do not have the right qualities to deal with the public, then consumers will be dissatisfied with the service offered, and will probably buy elsewhere.

Activity

Record a recent experience you have had in retailing or marketing that left you dissatisfied. Account for your dissatisfaction, identify the cause and suggest possible solutions from the supplier's perspective to resolve the problem.

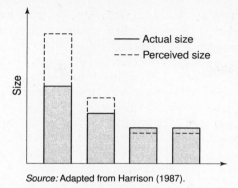

Source: Adapted from Harrison (1987).

Figure 1.5 Relationship of market share to perceived size

Financial resources

A limit on capital for reinvestment in plant and machinery for research and development, for market research or promotional budgets may impose severe restrictions on the way a company conducts its business. Whilst recognising that marketing professionals should be skilled in negotiating and justifying expenditure (which they may treat as an investment), additional money may not be forthcoming. Such restrictions need to be evaluated as part of the planning process when making marketing decisions.

Critics may refer to businesses which never spend money on marketing and still earn a profit. However, profits may not be maximised in this situation. For example, a frequent error made by companies is to underprice their goods or services based on a lack of customer research.

1.1.4 Marketing is a dynamic activity

Figure 1.6 illustrates the way that continuous investment in marketing is necessary to ensure success. Often, investment in marketing is *reactive*, when a company faces a problem such as a sales slump (point A). An outside consultant may be hired, only to be discharged when prosperous times come again (point B). If the firm does not learn from its original mistake, it may suffer again (point C). Of course, this is an extreme case, but one of the common features of many businesses is a lack of a concerted commitment to marketing. Not only must resources be available for marketing, but everyone within the firm should understand the basic philosophy of marketing in meeting the needs of its customers. Therefore, accountants who authorise spending, administrators who shape policy and personnel management who are responsible for recruitment and staff morale should all understand how a

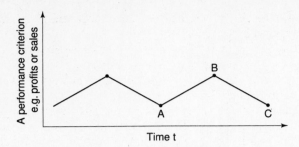

Figure 1.6 *Ad hoc* marketing investment

marketing philosophy can contribute to corporate objectives, and how they personally may contribute.

This requires a customer-centred focus throughout the whole organisation. In most cases, because consumers' needs change over time, the firm needs to adopt a proactive approach and be constantly aware of the environment and how underlying changes might impact on the business. A fuller explanation of why marketing must be dynamic is discussed in chapter 2.

1.2 A brief history of marketing

A study of the history of marketing indicates that a number of factors contributed to the reason why companies had to become more marketing-oriented.

1.2.1 Production orientation

Baker (1991) suggests that before the 1930s, production-oriented firms succeeded because there was an *excess of demand over supply*. This was in a period when companies concentrated on the manufacturing process, without researching consumers' needs prior to production. Henry Ford demonstrated his production orientation by promising customers that they could have any colour of Model T they wanted, so long as it was black. Once the competition offered a wider choice, Ford fell behind General Motors and has remained there ever since. The Sinclair C5 electric vehicle, the subject of this chapter's case study (pp. 19–30), is a more recent example of a failure to meet consumers' needs.

1.2.2 Sales orientation

Between 1930 and 1950 *the sales era* emerged, with its emphasis on hard, aggressive selling and promotions, *focusing on the needs of the seller.* Supply began to outstrip demand, partly due to the effects of the Depression and partly due to increased competition attracted by the market.

Extended distribution channels, with improved road and rail networks, meant that manufacturers were increasingly located farther away from their customers. This made it more difficult for them to judge what customers wanted, without their undertaking formal marketing research.

Greater access to *physical mobility* also brought a higher degree of *social mobility*, and sophistication increased with rising affluence. Consumers were ready to express their individual needs, exploring and demanding more choice. This meant there had to be a radical and rigorous analysis of what buyers required, and this called for increasingly *adaptive* management. In addition, various consumer groups emerged, e.g. the consumer movement brought about the Consumer Association. Publications on consumer protection and magazines such as *Which?* (which examine consumer accounts of alternative products) have in turn ensured producers listen to their customers in order to remain competitive.

1.2.3 The 1950s onwards: marketing orientation

A customer orientation is about planning customers' needs and researching markets continuously, so that what is produced reflects what the customer wants. Today, many successful companies ensure that top management are committed to developing an organisational culture to monitor continuously how their customers are treated. At Dixons (electrical retailers) and Marks & Spencer (clothing and food), for example, directors spend time in the stores, a practice that reflects how important marketing is to them.

According to Narver and Slater (1990), a customer orientation *alone* is not an adequate substitute for a market orientation, because it does not necessarily consider the competitive situation nor the co-ordination and sharing of resources with other departments. According to Narver and Slater, a market orientation involves three considerations, each with equal importance. These are represented by an equilateral triangle in Figure 1.7. These are customer orientation, competitor orientation and interfunctional co-ordination. After verifying these as sound constructs of a marketing orientation, they were tested to substantiate the claim that a marketing orientation has an effect on business profitability.

Customer orientation is the ability to create superior value for one's target customers continuously and requires an in-depth understanding of their current and future motives and needs (*ibid.*, p. 21).

Competitor orientation requires an understanding of the short- and long-term strengths, weaknesses, capabilities and strategies of current and key potential competitors (Aaker, 1988; Day and Wensley, 1988; Porter, 1980, 1985). This involves being responsive to competitive activity and planning for

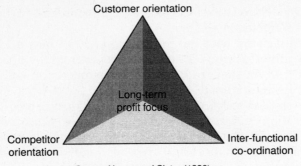

Figure 1.7 A market orientation

opportunities to create a competitive advantage. One of the characteristics of successful marketing is the ability to estimate the likely responses of competitors. Sustaining a competitive advantage is hard to achieve because competitors are not always predictable, partly because our knowledge of their capabilities is not as great as theirs! Sustaining a competitive advantage is illustrated in chapter 2.

Interfunctional co-ordination is the co-ordination of resources not only from the marketing department but from others too, in order to create superior value for target customers. This requires the marketing management to be both sensitive and responsive to the perceptions and needs of all other departments (Anderson, 1982).

Note that there is a danger in trying to assess whether a company is marketing-oriented or not by reference to its organisation chart alone. A marketing department is *not* marketing-oriented unless it follows correct procedures, such as investment in planning competitor surveillance and inter-action with other departments with whom it can develop opportunities *before* making decisions on markets. Conversely, a firm such as Marks & Spencer does not have a formal marketing department, but has developed an organisational culture and ethos which encourages employees to 'think marketing'. (See also chapter 2 on planning for environmental changes which enable marketing ideas to be implemented.)

An examination of the marketing era shows that consumers do not buy products for their own sake: they buy the core or generic needs that those products satisfy. Thus a television company provides the generic need of communication – a far broader concept than considering television simply as part of an entertainment medium. If it ignores the broader opportunities open to it, competitors are likely to exploit new technologies and become a threat. Remember that a successful product today may be in decline tomorrow. Hence, another indicator of marketing orientation is the extent to which a firm is committed to developing new products. (See chapter 5 for more details about how new products are developed.)

Determinants of a market orientation

Jaworski and Kohli (1993) consider a market orientation in terms of the way information is used, defined by the generation, dissemination and responsiveness of information at an organisation-wide level (i.e. not just the marketing department). Responsiveness is geared towards developing and executing plans. This can be interpreted as another way of measuring the market orientation which is compatible with Narver and Slater's (1990). In other words, effective management of information can offer the means by which customer orientation, competitor orientation and interfunctional co-ordination are achieved.

Jaworski and Kohli (1993) revealed several important determinants of a market orientation. Amongst these, they concluded that top management commitment to a marketing orientation was influential in gaining the same commitment from their employees. Thus top management acts as a role model for the rest of the workforce. Top management's reluctance to take risks had a negative effect on the organisation's responsiveness. This might be expected because they will influence less senior management to be more cautious and/or conservative about developing new products that meet changing consumer preferences.

Goal conflict between departments had a negative effect on intelligence dissemination and responsiveness. Thus where tension exists between departments, there is a lower likelihood of market information being shared. Jaworski and Kohli recommend training and cross-functional projects to overcome this problem. Cross-functional projects actively require the sharing of information between departments which enables employees to begin to understand each other's roles.

Organisations that reward employees on the basis of building customer relationships and satisfaction tend also to be more market-oriented. This is at the heart of internal marketing. Treating employees as a kind of 'internal customer', projecting a happy environment, makes people work harder and serve the customer better. The stark reality, however, is that some of the poorest paid workers are those who work closest to the customer – hardly the conditions to create self-motivation. Some companies have recognised this and reward their contact staff on the basis of positive customer feedback. Formal feedback can be obtained by using questionnaires. (Questionnaire design is discussed in chapter 3.)

Jaworski and Kohli also show a negative relationship between centralisation (in which decisions are mainly restricted to senior management) and market orientation. This suggests that it may be useful to 'empower' more junior employees to make decisions rather than to restrict all important decisions to senior management. This may make sense if we consider the role of the sales assistant who is closest to the customer. Senior management may have few opportunities to meet customers and so there is a risk that their perception of consumer needs may be at odds with what consumers really want.

Historical conclusion: consumers buy benefits

From an understanding of competitor orientation, companies must identify the products and markets that will meet the future needs of their customers. There is a risk that they may be too focused. For example, consumers do not buy filing cabinets, they buy a means of storage. With the rapid increase in information technology, manufacturers of filing cabinets might adapt to produce storage systems for floppy disks (Cannon, 1986).

You might initially categorise Parker Pens as being in the 'writing implements' business and therefore suggest that, as people write all year round, advertising should be constant. However, market analysis indicates that the vast majority of quality pens are not purchased by users, but by present givers. As the customer is not necessarily the consumer, Parker is actually in the *gift business*. Careful market analysis indicated the way the product should be marketed. Packaging was enhanced as a gift pack, and advertising was scheduled to reflect buying seasons, particularly Christmas. Pricing was geared to competitive gifts, not to other pens.

Defining a business too narrowly is referred to as *marketing myopia* (Levitt, 1960). You might consider that Black & Decker are in the electric drills business and that Revlon is engaged in cosmetics. These are examples of marketing myopia. Why? Because in each case the description has failed to consider the businesses as *solutions to problems*. Now consider the real benefits of Black & Decker products for drilling holes. A pocket laser at the right price, for example, could make a drill obsolete. The solution to the problem is about making holes. What about Revlon? They offer us hope! What about IBM? They understand the importance of providing generic benefits: they promote themselves as offering business solutions, not computer hardware.

The historical development and rationale of marketing for business success suggests that management has had to adapt to changes in its environment (e.g. infrastructure, increasing sophistication of wants by consumers, current domestic saturation of markets and global competition).

Therefore, a marketing orientation is a managerial development from a production and sales orientation, as a result of changing environmental conditions. Firms that monitor their changing environment are in a better position to retain control of their future. They can survive threats by taking advantage of opportunities ahead of the competition.

Questions for discussion

1.1   In what way is marketing different from selling?

1.2   How would you evaluate whether a company is mar

1.3   In what ways does your university or college seek t

1.4   Research the activities of one major organisation.
- What are their view of marketing?
- How do they compare to your own?

1.5a   Should marketing be restricted to the marketing department?

1.5b   Research the different types of activities, responsibilities and job titles of marketing management in different types of companies.

Evaluate those you consider most important and why.

Do job titles indicate the level of marketing responsibility? If not, why not?

Summary

The central focus of marketing is to satisfy consumer needs. Needs may be either rational or emotive. An examination of several household brand names (such as Levi's and Coca Cola) reveals that emotional response may have a significant part to play in their success.

A second aim of marketing is to ensure that a business is profitable. Two studies published in 1989, ranging from industrial goods to consumer groceries, suggest that there is a significant relationship between business success and investment and commitment to marketing. Doyle, in particular, concludes from a large survey of diverse businesses that there is a significant relationship between market share (relating to a firm's position as a leader or a follower in the market) and financial return. Explanations of the superior financial performance of brand leaders may be indicative of:

1. higher customer loyalty,
2. trade leverage and loyalty,
3. better treatment by the trade in terms of display and shelf allocations,
4. the ability to override adverse publicity,
5. the ability to attract and retain top talent,
6. a propensity to be considered for purchase, since brand recall is likely to be higher and perceived risk lower.

third aim of marketing is to make the best use of given resources. In this context, resources may act as a constraint. In some cases, a firm should forgo short-term costs for long-term investment. Treating marketing as an *ad hoc* activity, to be used only when things go wrong, indicates under-investment. Similarly, a workforce that is not educated about the role of marketing gives rise to an uncommitted organisation, unable to realise its true potential. For marketing to be a success, there must be commitment from everyone.

Marketing can be considered a development of managerial orientations, resulting from changing environmental conditions. As a result of an increasing surplus over demand in many markets, a production orientation, focusing on efficient manufacturing methods, is no longer viable. Neither is a sales orientation, focusing on the needs of the seller, because of consumers' greater sophistication and affluence. A customer orientation requires the adoption of marketing research before production starts, to provide offerings that meet consumer expectations more precisely. A marketing orientation will also monitor the competitive environment and recognise the value and contributions of other department within an organisation before making decisions in the planning of marketing resources.

Product-focused firms fail to view their products as providing benefits or offering solutions to problems. Without this strategic vision, products may become obsolete and the firm may not be able to survive. With sufficient planning, a firm can replace products to reflect the needs of the changing marketplace. This emphasises the dynamic nature of marketing.

In chapter 2, the concept of dynamism is developed by referring to the influence of the environment and how potential threats in the marketplace may be turned into opportunities by planning for environmental change.

To conclude this Introduction, read 'The Sinclair C5' case study and answer the following questions:

Q1.6 Was Sir Clive Sinclair production-oriented or market-oriented?

Q1.7 When developing new products, specific stages are required to focus more closely on consumer attitudes, perceptions, motives and behaviour. What stages were *not* conducted? Highlight the main problems which resulted.

Q1.8 Positioning is about establishing a central theme or image in the minds of the target audience. With respect to safety features, the C5 was wrongly positioned. Why?

Q1.9 For most customers the C5 was a risky concept. How could Sir Clive have reduced the 'perceived risk' associated with the purchase of the C5?

Q1.10 What alternative markets might have been developed for the C5?

Case study: The Sinclair C5 – an investigation into its development, launch and subsequent failure

ANDREW P. MARKS* *Paisley College of Technology, Glasgow*

Development

Sir Clive Sinclair is an electronics expert who achieved a number of 'world firsts' including the executive pocket calculator (1972) and the microvision pocket TV (1977).

The development of the C5 can be traced back to 1973 when Sir Clive pondered various ideas about electric vehicles within Sinclair Radionics Ltd. Various aspects were then considered, but there were no specific plans to develop a product to sell. At this time, other projects within the company took priority, and no further work was done on the electric vehicle concept.

As the world became more energy conscious in the 1970s, Sinclair felt even more strongly about an opportunity for an electric vehicle for personal use, and, in 1979, preliminary investigations were undertaken within the newly formed Sinclair Research Ltd, which designed and developed a range of personal computers including the very successful ZX Spectrum.

The vehicle was to carry one person, and was seen as a replacement for a moped, limited to urban use with a top speed of 30 mph [1] (p. 152).

Several different product layouts were examined and prototypes built, but this was solely to prove principles and not to develop a *specific* product. However, they were already thinking of launching a vehicle of some form in 1984, and during 1980 the product became more defined. It was to carry the housewife, the urban commuter or the youngster; its advantages over the moped would be that it offered greater safety, weather protection, economy and style – at a competitive target price of £500, based on the likely cost of such a vehicle compared with the competition, viz. the moped and the second car [1].

The specification of the vehicle was not backed by any market research, but instead was proposed by Sinclair and his team. In fact, the director of Sinclair's advertising agency commented that the C5 went through to the prototype stage purely on the convictions of Sir Clive [2].

A significant factor in development occurred in March 1980 when the government abolished motor tax on electric vehicles, which Sinclair

* Acknowledgements
I would like to thank Alan Leyshon, Senior Lecturer in Marketing at Paisley College of Technology, for advice during the preparation of this work. I would also like to thank I.D. Marks for his assistance in editing the final version.

saw as an indication of a growing appreciation for electric vehicles. More research was undertaken, and, by March 1982, a basic vehicle was completed, known as the C1. Development work continued within Sinclair Research Ltd until Sinclair Vehicles Ltd was established in 1984, funded by the sale of shares in Sinclair Research Ltd.

The vehicle body was handed over to Ogle Design to be professionally styled, but problems arose with a significant increase in body weight, and the project was withdrawn from it early in 1983.

At the same time, legislation was pending that could in effect introduce a new type of vehicle – *the electrically assisted pedal cycle*. The legislation was fairly clear-cut:

- two or three wheels with pedal propulsion;
- maximum weight of 40 or 60 kg depending on vehicle configuration;
- maximum motor continuously rated output, 200 and 250 watts, depending on vehicle configuration, and
- maximum powered speed 15 mph (24 kph).

In addition, the vehicle could be driven by anyone of 14 years of age and over. It did not require a licence, insurance or road tax. Furthermore, no helmet had to be worn [3].

Previous development work undertaken was applied to this newer concept, taking as the basis of the new design a recumbent cycle with two wheels at the back for stability. Thus the C5 was born.

The passing of the 'electrically assisted pedal cycle' legislation in August 1983 was the turning point for Sinclair, as he now thought he could create a market that had not previously existed. Development became more focused, and a specific product idea was now firmly rooted in his mind.

In autumn 1983, Sinclair placed a development contract with Lotus Cars Ltd, its task being to develop a C5 prototype and test it in conjunction with Sinclair Research. This would enable the vehicle to go from development to production, with particular attention being paid to safety aspects.

As the C5 was coming into the final stages of development, a manufacturer had to be found, and Hoover Ltd at Merthyr Tydfil was approached through the Welsh Development Agency. Hearing that Sinclair envisaged initial sales of 100,000 per annum rising to 500,000, agreement was reached by April 1984 with production commencing in the autumn. The C5 was to be sold by mail order, and therefore after assembly the vehicles were put into cardboard boxes and stockpiled at distribution centres at Hayes, Preston and Oxford.

The C5 was officially launched on 10 January 1985, at the Alexandra

Palace in London. The price was to be £399 (plus £29 delivery charge) and the C5 would come complete with an owner's handbook, battery charger and accessory catalogue.

Did the C5 Development follow the textbook seven stages to new-product development?

Idea generation – The C5 conception was essentially internal to the company, and was a 'technology-push' idea, as opposed to being 'demand-pull'. The most logical source of generating ideas is the consumers themselves. Even though no product existed that could be compared with the C5, the company could have undertaken market research to discover the opinions of potential customers about the vehicle.

Idea screening – This stage eliminates the unsuitable product ideas, but with Sinclair's project, there was no choice between different product areas. The only screening done seemed to be in terms of which concepts or models were considered better than the others. The idea approved by Sinclair was a one-seater vehicle replacing the moped. Several criteria should be checked against the new product to determine its feasibility, e.g. corporate fit, etc. However, in the case of the electric vehicle, the overwhelming criterion seemed to be the fact that Sir Clive himself believed the product would succeed, and that he could *create* a market.

Concept development and testing – The idea of the electric vehicle was elaborated into a product concept as a result of the preliminary study in 1979. Usually a company will put forward several different concepts and then gauge reaction from consumers before selecting one of them. Sinclair, however, decided that the concept would be of a small one-seater mode of transport designed to carry the housewife, etc. No feedback was sought from consumers.

It is important when developing a concept to define the core benefit proposition of the product, and, in fairness to Sinclair and his team, this they did do. The vehicle was to be silent, pollution-free, economic, and offer greater safety than a moped.

As for concept testing, there is no evidence to suggest any testing took place, so little indication was forthcoming in this early stage as to whether or not it was acceptable.

Business analysis – An economic analysis in terms of estimating sales figures was almost impossible for the electric vehicle, as there was no historical sale trends for comparable products. The only electric vehicles in Britain of any significant number were electric milk-floats, which hardly served as a basis for comparison!

Essentially, business analysis is break-even analysis, and one therefore needs sales estimates, as well as cost estimates, in order to determine possible profit. Sinclair could determine costs for development, manufacturing and marketing, but demand estimates would be very subjective.

One indication of possible demand were the figures for second-car ownership and mopeds. Department of Trade figures for 1978 showed that there were 17.6 million licensed vehicles in the UK, of which 1.2 million were mopeds and motor cycles. Also, 2.4 million households had a second car. Sinclair perceived the target market as being here and therefore based demand on these figures. However, a detailed business analysis could not be carried out, making the C5 development risky from the outset.

Product development and testing – This stage was the most exhaustive area to be carried out. Various shapes and layouts were developed and tested, with continued modification of all aspects of the vehicle. The major turning point that spurred on the product development was the legislation passed in 1983 which enabled Sinclair to develop a specific product from, i.e. the electrically assisted pedal cycle. This definitive model was also subjected to various rigorous tests, specifically under the Lotus contract.

Test marketing – There was no test marketing at all for the C5. Once the final product was decided on, it was prepared for national launch.

Commercialisation – The C5 was launched on the national market in January 1985, as opposed to a rolling launch.

Criticisms of the C5 experience

Having looked at the development of the C5, and knowing that the result of its launch was almost immediate failure, can we determine what factors contributed to that failure?

Development

The development of the C5 was, as already pointed out, very internal to the company, taking 'technology-push' to the extreme. The entire development seemed to progress on convictions of staff in the company, and not on external factors. Sinclair paid little or no attention to the marketing orientation of business.

A second criticism could be levelled at the absence of test marketing. NPD procedure says that test marketing reduces risks, and it seems that not carrying this out was a severe oversight on Sinclair's part. Test marketing could have given an indication of the limited future for the C5 as it stood, and perhaps the launch would never have taken place. If test marketing had indicated 'impending doom' for the C5, other market opportunities could have been sought, and the vehicle may have been a success elsewhere, e.g. in the leisure-related industry. Employing test marketing could also have eliminated teething problems, as Sinclair admitted, for example, that distribution arrangements had been a substantial contributing factor to the C5's problems [4].

Finally, some stages were not carried out very well; business analysis was subject to a lot of uncertainty, and thus was not as accurate as desired. Also, the concept development stage seemed very brief with few alternatives. Sinclair wanted the vehicle to be serious transport, and would view it as nothing else, even if a market may have existed elsewhere.

Badly defined market

The C5 was targeted towards 14-year-olds, the housewife for urban commuting, and generally anyone else who needed to get about. The company had no idea that this was the correct market; they simply thought that the C5 could 'fit' into this sort of market as new personal transport. In fact, the government legislation on the electrically assisted pedal cycle seemed to define the market for them. The C5 seemed to be targeted as a competitor to the moped and second car on this basis.

The root of the C5's problems was being presented as serious transport when it perhaps should have been marketed as an 'up-market' plaything [5]. Certainly, the limitations of the C5's performance did nothing to support it as being serious transport. Sinclair claimed a range of up to 20 miles on a fully charged battery, but, an investigation by the Consumers Association found that the C5 could only manage at most 14.2 miles, and that was on a flat surface with no stops. They found that for 'urban driving' incorporating hills, stopping and starting, etc., the range was only between 5 and 10 miles. Furthermore, in hilly areas, the driver had to pedal a lot due to the motor cutting out, and had to wait 15 minutes before it would start again [6].

A serious competitor to the second car? It seems rather that the C5 was hard work and of limited use.

Lack of market research

A major criticism has been the lack of market research undertaken. Sinclair went into the project 'blind', with no indication of success other than his own convictions. The only research done was presenting a prototype to 63 families in the A, B, C1, C2 groups in both suburban and town environments. The aim here, however, was product development in ensuring that controls were correctly placed [2].

Why is market research important? It is generally accepted that a company's health depends largely on its capacity to interpret the behaviour, attitudes and needs of the consumers who make up its market. In Sinclair's case, the firm did not know its market. It defined the target customer, but did no research as to whether these people would, in fact, want it.

Why, then, was there no research? There are several reasons; Sir Clive himself openly admitted that he does not believe in it, preferring rather to launch a new product for which demand is difficult to assess, and *creating* a new market [7]. This risky approach defies all the basic principles of marketing.

Secondly, Sinclair said that you cannot research an area where there is no comparable product in the market. *What he overlooked, however, is that you can research consumer attitudes and perceptions, to determine whether an opportunity exists.* Sinclair Vehicles must be criticised because, although it defined the market for its vehicle as being youngsters, commuters, etc., there was no research undertaken to see how these potential consumers perceived the C5 – i.e. did *they* consider it as serious transport or as an 'up-market' toy?

It would appear that trying to market a radically new product concept, with no idea of consumer attitudes towards it, was a rather risky route to take. Research may have shown the project no longer viable, and scrapping it would have saved a lot of money, as well as the company's reputation.

Safety and performance aspects

In terms of performance, it was found that the C5 did not meet the claims made. The range was lower than claimed, and it suffered power loss on upward gradients. The bulk of criticism, however, has been concern over safety. Sinclair maintained priority on safety throughout, and said that anyone who might have been concerned with safety was consulted, and full note was taken of all recommendations which might improve the safety of the vehicle [1] (p. 160).

Despite this emphasis, the Consumers Association ran its own tests on the C5 and came up with several criticisms:

1. The height of the C5 was such that the driver's body was directly at bumper height – likely to increase the chance of severe injury in a collision.
2. The driver was at a height to inhale exhaust fumes, and be hit by spray from other vehicles, affecting both the driver's performance and visibility.
3. The C5 was easily hidden behind other vehicles, making it vulnerable in heavy traffic.
4. The horn was ineffective.
5. The headlight beam was insufficient.
6. The low sitting position made dazzle from headlights an irritation.

The *external audit* consists of (1) the macro-environment, and (2) the company stakeholders, which include customers and the competitive environment. The *internal audit* includes an examination of marketing results split by products and markets, in terms of criteria such as sales turnover, profitability, market shares and costs. It also includes an analysis of the strategic direction of the firm, and so requires a review of objectives, segments of the market that have been targeted and appropriately positioned (see chapter 4 for more details), competitive advantages and *portfolio analysis* (the selection, investment and withdrawal of products from the overall business, treated more fully in chapter 6).

In the *external audit*, the macro-environment consists of politico-legal, economic, socio-cultural and technological forces since they are often considered as a given set of forces impacting on the organisation. They are sometimes referred to by the acronym PEST.

The second group of factors in the external audit refer to the *stakeholders*: groups that interact with the organisation and include customers or buyers, suppliers, distributors and competitors. In the internal audit, groups that interact within the organisation, and in particular within the marketing function such as different levels of marketing management, are important. They are accountable for a wide range of marketing decisions (e.g. distributors will set their own budgets for new products or advertising and will decide how to react to new or existing competitors adding to their product lines). Stakeholders can contribute significantly to the success (or failure) of marketing operations.

Finally, marketing management must identify and develop good working relationships with groups within the firm to make the best use of their *resources*. In a highly competitive firm, there may be competition not only with outsiders but also perhaps with subsidiaries of the parent firm. Internally, within a given division, marketing managers are responsible for how their appropriation is spent. They may need to seek approval from a number of important and critical decision-makers – financial accountants, engineers, administrative and production managers. Sometimes there is a separate director for Marketing and Sales within an organisation, and this is a cause of potential conflict. In large firms, typically offering multi-product ranges, there are likely to be several *brand managers*, each responsible for the management of a particular brand or range.

Since financial resources are finite, these managers necessarily *compete* with each other. The way they manage their relationships with other groups is therefore vitally important. Clearly, the art of marketing management is also a process of developing *political skills*, both inside and outside the organisation. It is not surprising that many recruitment advertisements for marketing posts expect first-class communication skills. Unfortunately, individual ambitions are often in conflict with corporate goals as a whole.

Thus groups both external to and within the organisation influence the future direction of an organisation (Table 2.1). This must be recognised in any planning process. The results of the audit can be used to conduct a SWOT appraisal (an acronym for strengths, weaknesses, opportunities and threats).

Table 2.1 Components of an audit

	Factors which influence performance at each level of the audit
External Audit	• Politico-legal, economic, socio-cultural and technological factors
	• External groups who interact with and influence the firm's ability to achieve its objectives. These groups are suppliers, buyers, competitors and customers
Internal Audit	• Marketing management
	• Other participants within an organisation who interact with marketing, e.g. finance, operations, personnel

From the audit, it is possible to identify the favourable and unfavourable conditions and market positions an organisation currently faces. These correspond to the company's strengths and weaknesses. Those conditions that are likely to arise in the future (i.e. beyond the current conditions facing an organisation) correspond to opportunities and threats. A SWOT appraisal (stage 2 of Figure 2.1) identifies the core strengths of the organisation vis-à-vis the competition and highlights other environmental opportunities and threats. (This is illustrated more fully in section 2.4.)

Management can then determine how far they need to proceed or progress to achieve their objectives (or goals of the organisation) and whether, in the light of this analysis, they need to modify their future goals or courses of action to achieve these goals (strategies). This is stage 3 of Figure 2.1, in which the future direction of the firm is reviewed and competitive strategy decided (section 2.3). Arising from this is how to implement the strategies recommended at stage 3. If a firm's audit suggests that there is a need for a premium product in a given market, how will management design, price, distribute and communicate a premium product? Decisions on implementation of these activities are described in chapters 6–10 respectively. Finally, an organisation needs to establish how it will evaluate whether its plans are being met by monitoring actual results against targets. Feedback is then fed into the next audit. In order for this planning process to be effective, senior management must be and be shown to be committed to it. Without this, cynicism on the part of less senior management will result in a low commitment to meeting the organisational objectives and goals.

Another problem in Britain historically has been an overemphasis on a *brand management system*, in which the managers responsible for the welfare of a brand were forced to get results in the short term because of the pressure for quick financial returns. Such a culture tends to undermine the pursual of longer-term strategies, which enable the firm to compete more effectively. One solution is to reward management that thinks – and acts – strategically. Thus evaluation should

not just be about comparing operating statistics such as sales a
weekly basis, but also about evaluating the strategic performan
timespan. Evaluation and control should consider not only the
criteria are evaluated (e.g. setting benchmarks based on excee
achievements) but also the timing and frequency of reviews.

The following sections review the external audit in more dctan,
the macro-environment (2.1) and the company stakeholders (2.2). Products and
markets are analysed at each level. Next, arising from the internal audit, is the
need to analyse alternative competitive strategies to achieve a differential
advantage (section 2.3). The SWOT appraisal is illustrated in more detail (2.4).
Details of how to achieve a competitive advantage and sustaining it are outlined
in sections 2.5 and 2.6 respectively.

2.1 The macro-environment

An ability and commitment to predicting changes in the macro-environment
ensure greater control over how marketing resources will be used in the future.
Since PEST factors may act as a *marketing constraint*, marketing management must
forecast the *direction* and *intensity* of change. Change may work in the company's
favour, or against it. Whatever the circumstances, there must be the *ability* and
aspiration to adapt. Returning to the dinosaur analogy, fossil records indicate that
prehistoric animals perished owing to their inability to adapt to their changing
environment. Organisations must always keep abreast of changes in the external
environment which will affect their future. Such environmental monitoring
allows them to identify future opportunities and threats in the market. Such a
process is called *environmental scanning*.

We shall now examine in detail the macro-environmental forces. These are
politico-legal, economic, socio-cultural and technological factors.

2.1.1 Politico-legal forces

The political, legal and regulatory forces of the environment are closely
interrelated. We, as members of organisations, might be encouraged to maintain
good relations with politicians to ensure they understand our viewpoint before
they pass legislation which affects our business. Organisations also need to be
well prepared for a change of government, since an incoming administration is
likely to introduce new policies and legislation. For example, it is not uncommon
for business executives to liaise with members of the opposition party to exchange
views on trade and industry. Healthy relationships can be established in this way.

Political influence may be significant in terms of legislation on trading (say,
whether to exercise liberal attitudes to free trade or impose protectionist
measures), pricing, fiscal policy, employment, health and safety at work practices

and product liability (regulating product safety). Government regulation can help to accelerate the growth of a market or protect old ones from competitors. One industry which is dependent on government policy is the environmental market. The market will be influenced by the standards imposed on air and water quality, control of toxic substances and recycling industrial waste. The three countries with the largest share of the world environmental market are the United States, Japan and Germany. They all have stringent environmental laws which can act as significant barriers to entry for firms wishing to trade in those countries, but which do not meet their exacting standards.

Governments and their agencies are big buyers in a number of strategic markets such as defence and transportation, and politicians can influence how much an agency purchases, and from whom. Finally, officials can help secure foreign markets with their influence.

Several legal forces are also important to marketing management. The following examples illustrate UK practice.

The Monopolies and Mergers Commission investigates situations which might act against the public interest, if at least a quarter of a good or service is supplied by a single organisation, or by a group of connected organisations. Large organisations which hold a monopoly over supply have been accused of setting unfairly high prices to consumers. This can arise when there is a lack of competition in the market.

A number of laws protect the consumer against unfair practices. These include the Food Act 1984 (regulating the description and purity of foodstuffs), the Trade Descriptions Act 1968 and the Sale of Goods Act 1979. These require that goods be fit for their intended purpose, and not designed to deceive the consumer. Other laws protect the consumer and the manufacturer. For example, the Trade Marks Act 1994 offers the chance to register smells, sounds, place names and three-dimensional shapes in the UK as trademarks. For example, Direct Line, the insurance company, a subsidiary of the Royal Bank of Scotland, registered its advertising jingle. The Act also closed the loophole which previously allowed counterfeit goods to be sold, providing they were described as 'fake'. However, despite the Act, the multi-million pound trade in 'lookalikes', retailer own brands that are packaged and presented to resemble closely the style of manufactured brands without trademarks, is likely to continue. A number of test cases can be expected to be decided in the courts. One difficulty for lawyers is to establish whether consumers genuinely mistake lookalikes for other brands, and to what extent this impinges on sales of the original brand. Another problem is how a lookalike should be defined.

The European Union
Strategic alliances are organised efforts by governments to seek common trading or economic policies, which aim to be mutually beneficial. The Single European Market, which came into effect in 1993, attempts to ensure that many of the traditional trade barriers between Member States are removed, by harmonising

standards. By removing statutory differences between Member States' requirements, an effective trading bloc of close to 400 million people has been created. To reflect its strength in world trade, it has been referred to as the 'United States of Europe'. Harmonisation of standards is related to:

- Professional services, such as teaching, accountancy and marketing,
- Product quality and safety standards (product liability),
- Food labelling, safety and hygiene standards.

Harmonisation of manufacturing standards across Member States provides greater opportunities for manufacturers of, say, pharmaceuticals or detergents to serve the entire European Union (EU) with a single set of production facilities. Furthermore, harmonisation of technical standards for components and sub-assemblies offers manufacturers a range of suppliers across the continent without breaking national regulations. Consumer opportunities arising from greater competition between supplies in the EU should bring a greater choice of products at lower prices (European Marketing Data and Statistics, 1996).

Case study: Apocalypse or paranoia?

During March 1996, a number of leading medical experts announced that there is circumstantial evidence of a link between consumption of beef infected by BSE, a fatal condition of cattle, and Creutzfeldt-Jacob disease, a disease of the human brain. Despite the lack of conclusive scientific proof, Britain appears preoccupied with the possible link.

Intensive farming methods have been blamed for the possible cause of BSE. This is likely to have arisen from infected cattle feed. Activities such as hormone injections have also been used to meet growing consumer expectations of cheap meat in quantity.

After years of speculation, followed by denial of any previous links, the British government was forced to act fast. Should it do nothing and suggest the link was media hype, intervene mildly or, at the extreme, destroy all cattle?

On 27 March 1996, the European Commission declared a worldwide ban on British beef exports. Thus the British were put in the strange position of being the only people allowed to eat it.

The government decided to slaughter cattle over 30 months old (the quality of which is normally allocated for pies and sausages). To what extent should compensation, if any, be offered to the British government and its farmers in recognition of the scale of the problem? Since the ban applies to all live cattle, slaughtered meat and their by-products, in pharmaceuticals and food additives, it has repercussions for many industries. Beef products, for instance, are used in lipstick and in gelatine. Compensation will only be granted on the basis of the UK government convincing the Commission there is no further health threat.

Cattle prices have slumped and have had a knock-on effect in the supermarkets, with more shelf space allocated to other meat products. Some supermarket authorities have described it as the food scare of the century. However, retail multiple chain stores were treating the problem in different ways. Several chains moved quickly to develop strategies for dealing with the problem. Most stores provided leaflets and lists of foods containing beef and derivatives. Tesco was planning to introduce source labelling for Scottish and Irish beef. The Cooperative Wholesale Society already included the country of origin on most fresh and frozen beef labelling. Iceland sourced its prime beef joints from South America, and was quick to point out that their own label frozen and chilled beef products do not contain any offal or mechanically recovered meat. Tesco informed shoppers that its suppliers adhered to strict government guidelines on feed, with additional random spot-checks made for reassurance. But some authorities predicted consumers would not distinguish between different types and origins of beef, thus creating a more global problem. Whilst Asda were introducing several price promotions on beef products, they also made available a list of beef-free products at customer service desks. In addition, many retailers were setting up special hotlines to deal with customer concerns. Some stores were reporting a surge in vegetarian sales.

Of the fast food chains McDonalds reacted fastest in issuing a statement that British beef would be taken off their menus in the interests of consumer confidence. Burger King followed suit very quickly. Then Birds Eye announced they were no longer producing beefburgers made from British beef.

Meanwhile the demand for beef has also slumped in other EU countries, despite assurances of its origin.

Sources: Adapted from Andrew Don, 'Industry Urged to Work Together on Beef Scare', *Supermarketing*, 29 March 1996, p. 4; Andrew Don, 'Retailers Take Action as BSE Crisis Hits the Meat Counter', *Supermarketing*, 29 March 1996, p. 5.

Q2.1 What markets are likely to prosper from the alleged link between Creutzfeld-Jacob disease and British beef?

Q2.2 How might beef from other countries be affected?

Q2.3 To what extent are the policies of the retail multiples appropriate? Explain your answer.

2.1.2 Economic forces

How many times have you heard the state of the economy being used as an explanation of the state of a market? You only have to pick up a newspaper and read the business section to appreciate the significance of the economy for market performance. For example, the UK housing market has been depressed over the last seven years with sporadic signs of recovery appearing in 1997 as a protracted recession comes to an end.

The reason why the economy affects markets is because the state of the economy is directly or indirectly related to the level of *buyer power* (or propensity to buy) within markets. And in so many markets, the demand in one market is *derived* from another (for example, sales of car batteries depend on sales of cars). Buyer power is reflected in the ability to buy, based on *disposable income* (or after-tax income) of individuals, the use of credit and a *willingness to spend*. Figure 2.2 summarises the main factors affecting buyer power.

Significance of factors affecting buying power

Disposable income is affected by the state of the economy. In an economic downturn or recession, total consumer spending will fall and unemployment will rise. Consumer spending may fall simply due to lack of *business confidence* (such as the threat of job losses). For some markets, demand will be worse hit by a recession. It is likely that the demand for essentials will be upheld, whilst 'luxury' or 'discretionary' markets will be adversely affected. Examples of discretionary markets include household goods and services, leisure and personal goods.

The converse applies when consumer confidence is high, typically in a *boom economy*. Under such conditions, luxury goods are in demand. In a recession, the demand for products serving basic utilitarian needs will be upheld.

Another economic problem is *inflation*. This is the cumulative effect of price increases over time, which reduces the real value of money in terms of purchasing

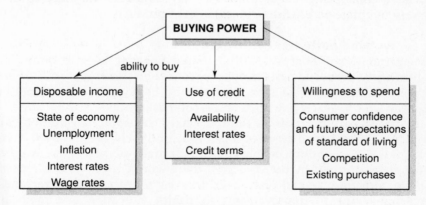

Figure 2.2 Factors affecting buying power

power (i.e. consumers can only buy less, given the same amount of money at face value in the future). The government may tackle inflation in a number of ways, including imposing wage restraints or wage freezes on industry or the public sector. It might increase interest rates, a move designed to curb inflation by reducing consumer spending. Although higher interest rates might tackle inflation sufficiently, this policy can have a detrimental effect on investment in both industrial and consumer markets, so timing is critical.

The *availability of credit* opens up new markets for consumer durables. Many products such as motor cars for personal use are commonly bought on credit finance deals, so the withdrawal of such finance options can shrink the market. In the UK recession of 1990–94, many car manufacturers offered interest-free credit options to absorb slack demand in the consumer market. Clearly, credit terms and interest rates will affect ultimate demand.

The *willingness to spend* depends on future consumer confidence. If consumers fear they will lose their jobs, perhaps because of fierce competition from abroad, their spending will be restricted. If domestic industry fears a downturn, investment is often cut back, so industrial markets are reduced and domestic industry becomes uncompetitive.

When seeking expansion overseas, suitable export markets must be found. One indicator of good prospects is the potential market size. One influence here is the complementary nature of goods, i.e. how ownership of one good influences the purchase of other, related goods. For example, television owners are likely to purchase video recorders. Ownership data can therefore be used as an indicator of demand for such products. The value of this can be demonstrated when considering exporting to foreign markets. Foreign markets whose economies are closely linked to the domestic market are most likely to be in need of, and spend money on, products similar to those that are popular in the domestic market. By comparing relative standards of living on the basis of an index combining a series of consumer durables purchases, it is possible to forecast the demand for other associated products. Such data are also useful for identifying saturation in markets and price points for various grades of products.

Working patterns

As the population of Europe is ageing, there will be far fewer working people in the future and more and more people dependent on state support. The European Commission has projected that there will be 113.5 million pensioners in the European Union, nearly one third of the population.

A similar pattern exists in the UK, where there were 16 million full-time workers in 1988, a figure expected to fall to 12 million in the year 2000. According to Handy (1989), 10 million people in the UK have already reached retirement age. Handy estimates that by the year 2025 there will be more people retired than working. There are several reasons for this. First, average life expectancies are increasing owing to improvements in health education and medical care. Secondly, many in work are retiring younger than earlier generations. Thirdly, most European governments now expect a permanent level of what is deemed 'acceptable unemployment'.

The birthrate in many European nations has also declined. Contributory factors include delayed marriages, the rise in two family incomes and the cost of bringing up children.

There are some marked differences in population trends between Member States of the European Union. Whilst France and Italy's percentage of over 65s is projected to grow by 7.5 per cent and 9 per cent respectively between 1993 and 2000, the corresponding percentage for Sweden is estimated to drop by 7 per cent (European Marketing Data and Statistics, 1996, Tables 0221 and 0223).

The effects of an increasing non-working population will impose greater demands on the state for adequate social security, healthcare and provision in retirement. Concern over whether the state will be able to meet these needs will encourage some consumers to seek alternative arrangements for their future needs. This offers opportunities for organisations to offer private health insurance and pension plans.

With fewer working people supporting an increasingly large number of elderly, a greater emphasis will be placed on *labour-saving devices*, so markets will expand in DIY and self-service retailing. Packaging technologists, for example, should consider how packaging can reduce labour costs (by reducing material handling or economising in stacking and storage).

2.1.3 Socio-cultural forces

The cultural and social aspects of the environment affect how and why we live and behave as we do. These aspects include education, religious beliefs, diet, clothing and housing, and how we view marriage and the family. Although these changes may be evolutionary rather than revolutionary, they are significant for marketing management. It is likely that specific groups will be more affected than others, and in different ways. (This is the rationale for segmentation as a marketing technique, a topic discussed in chapter 4.) We have already noted the effects of changes in demographics on working patterns. The shift towards an ageing population in Western economies offers the opportunity for new markets meeting the needs of mature citizens. As a given population lives longer, the demand for leisure and entertainment facilities for this group should grow.

Household numbers, size and two family incomes

In Europe, the relatively affluent period of the past twenty years has been accompanied by a gradual increase in the number of households, and a corresponding reduction in their size. One factor behind the growth in European households has been the sharp increase in the numbers of divorced and separated people. One-person households are most common in Sweden, West Germany, Norway, Denmark and Finland, with the UK lagging behind with about 25 per cent of single-member households. Household size has fallen for a number of reasons.

With greater job opportunities for women over the last thirty years, working women are tending to delay marriage and have fewer children. The emergence of the career woman has required a re-examination of how several markets are targeted. For example, trends in smaller family sizes affect requirements of packaging size. Recently, there has been more shelf space allocated in supermarkets to smaller units of pre-packed food, including frozen meals and cereals. Traditional demographic features such as social class (based on the income of the head of the household) have been criticised by social scientists for their dubious predictive value on buyer potential. In an age in which two family incomes are common, social class becomes less useful as an indicator. An increase in the number of working women is reflected by shopping trends in terms of one-stop shopping and extended opening hours. The legalisation of Sunday trading in the UK is evidence of this. Other markets have prospered by offering time-saving devices to the increasingly convenience-oriented shopper – for example, sandwich bars and fast food outlets, home shopping and automatic teller machines outside banks and large supermarkets. This in turn has opened up new opportunities in packaging, such as vacuum packing to prolong food freshness. In manufacturing, awareness of time utility has opened up new markets for microwaves, video recorders, dishwashers and freezers. In the service market, there is greater demand for childcare centres, dry cleaners and financial services. In the grocery market, there has been a marked increase in the sales of pre-prepared convenience foods. This has led to the need for innovative packaging that is suitable for microwaves.

Acceptance of credit and attitudes towards risk

The social stigma associated with using credit has changed since the 1960s. Credit facilities often encourage consumers to spend on high-outlay items. Recently, however, there may have been a marginal swing away from this in the UK, in part, because many home-owners are tied to negative equity (in which the current market value of their homes is less than their mortgage).

The attitude to risk when buying many products is influenced by both culture and life style and should be considered carefully before making commitments in marketing. Consider the difference between the Americans and the British when it comes to managing their money. There are strong incentives for Americans to use savings as a long-term investment because they are more likely to pay for their children's education. Consequently, they tend to invest in riskier investments, such as shares, compared to their British counterparts, even though their savings as a proportion of their wealth is much lower than in Britain. The British tend to use their savings for 'rainy day' money, short-term cash to cover holidays, a new car or an unforeseen emergency. Building societies appear to provide the security the British need.

Environmentalism

Many consumers are becoming more environmentally aware and conscious of the way in which resources are consumed. This is an area of marketing that is having a dramatic effect on labelling and packaging decisions. Consumer demand for environmentally friendly products requires a complete rethink of the way products and packaging are produced. Typical 'environmental' claims now include recyclable and biodegradable packaging and ozone-friendly and additive-free contents. Anita Roddick of the Body Shop (a UK cosmetics company) was one of the first to identify the demand for cosmetic products which have not been tested on animals, and has exploited a flourishing business opportunity. The importance of environmental ('green') marketing is further demonstrated by organically grown (free from artificial chemicals) fruit and vegetables and schemes designed to cut waste. Survey research has shown that <u>some</u> consumers are willing to pay for 'green' products. Although 'greening' of a company's products or operations does cost money, many organisations realise that these costs are necessary if they are to stay in business. There is an increasing trend for larger companies to reduce the number of their suppliers whilst demanding good environmental track records from those they retain.

Ethical and 'caring' marketing for the 1990s?

Whilst the 1980s was labelled a decade of self-gratification and self-interest, the 1990s is associated with a shift towards ethical practices and 'politically correct' behaviour. Machiette and Roy (1994) suggest that there is an increasing consumer awareness of ethical practices in marketing vis-à-vis what is marketed (the product or service), how it is made and distributed, and at whom it is targeted. They argue that organisations that respond positively to these socio-cultural shifts can gain a competitive advantage over those who do not. The level of commitment to social responsibility is likely to be directed by commercial values. This in turn will be influenced by the nature of the product, the target group and the corporate culture (i.e. what is considered acceptable within an organisation). A company involved in promoting alcohol on inner city hoardings should answer to a higher sense of social responsibility because of the risks associated with the potential abuse in its consumption, particularly by vulnerable groups such as minors. Some organisations are applying ethical standards to all their business partners, including suppliers. In Europe, for example, IKEA (the Swedish furniture store) recently decided not to sell carpets unless they could be certified as made without the use of child labour. A new group uniting charities and a German rug importer recently launched a trademark, 'Rugmark', the first 'human rights' label to indicate products made without the use of child labour. Few firms are tackling human rights issues, despite a significant number of consumers showing strong enough feelings to boycott firms whose ethical standards are dubious. Human rights could become a more significant issue as many multinationals are moving into more Third World countries and contracting out an increasing volume of their production to low-wage countries in order to cut costs.

2.1.4 Technological forces and the information revolution

The greatest impact in marketing in the next twenty years is likely to come from information technology (IT). Advances in technology in general are responsible for many innovations which render existing products obsolete. Consider the graduation from the electronic typewriter to the word processor, or the move from slide rules to pocket calculators. The pace of technological change is responsible for shortening the *life cycles* of many products. There is a greater need than ever to track and pinpoint environmental changes that may affect business. Even the strongest brands are under threat in tomorrow's markets. For example, the prestigious *Wall Street Journal* provides its readers with important business information worldwide. Today, electronic information systems offer up-to-the-minute business data for busy executives who do not have the time to read traditional journals. These electronic systems are posing a threat to the future of the journals.

The revolution in the way information is handled and transmitted has had a number of effects, both negative and positive. It has arguably brought about higher levels of structural unemployment. For example, many clerical jobs in banking have disappeared with the increasing availability and use of information technology, such as automatic teller machines.

Perceptions of job insecurity are attributable, in part, to the impact created by technological change. It is said to be responsible for the slow growth of some consumer markets. But there are also many advantages. The decrease in the 'information float' (the time information spends between travelling through different channels), is responsible for a greater level of customer service in many cases, e.g. electronic mail offers a much speedier form of communication than a hand-written letter.

Another example is the use of bar coding on packaging, which eliminates the need for individual pricing of goods. This has led to improvements in stock control and the accuracy of marketing information.

Figure 2.3 outlines some of the main advantages of improved databases with advances in IT. How this is designed, stored and retrieved enables more effective decisions to be made. This has enabled better forecasts in projecting the individual market value placed on each customer over their expected life (life values) and a greater control and evaluation over investment decisions. Consequently, marketing will need to be *increasingly accountable* for what is spent and why, justifying our actions to other decision-makers (e.g. finance, general management). For example, a retailer can now use scanner data at the check-out, combined with your personal details, which are provided when you complete an application for a store card. Purchase information collected might include what you purchased, with whom, when and where, and can be matched to personal details such as age and where you live. Past histories of shopping behaviour enable patterns to emerge. These can be tied in with more effective promotional offers. For example, offers can be mailed to your home address (or offered at the

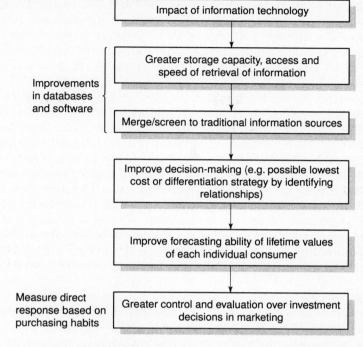

Figure 2.3 How information technology improvements can improve accountability of the marketing function

check-out) at the time when you are most likely to be in the market for the good. If you are not using a store or counter as often as in the past, reminders or incentives can be issued.

2.2 The company stakeholders and the competitive environment

Top European managers agree that the biggest challenges facing their businesses are competition and the pressure on costs. Marketing management must identify and nurture resourceful relationships with groups that interact with their organisation as part of its business activity. These will influence the relative ease with which an organisation can compete. The relative numbers and size of each particular group will determine their negotiating or bargaining power (Porter, 1980). In essence, because these groups can be co-operative or confrontational, the environment in which they operate is sometimes referred to as competitive. For example, having few buyers in a market and many suppliers improves the bargaining power of the buyers. In the UK grocery market, about 70 per cent of the market is blocked to manufacturers unless they can sell to the large retail supermarket chains. Conscious of this, supermarket management is able to obtain better deals, impose constraints such as exclusivity of supply and determine rigorous specifications. This behaviour reflects the laws of supply and demand economics and is just as relevant to other groups, such as competitors and customers.

The performance of an organisation is influenced by the structure of the industry in which it operates. To understand why some industries such as pharmaceuticals and soft drinks have traditionally sustained higher long-run profits compared to others such as coal and steel, it is necessary to examine those factors that affect the intensity of competition. These influence the relative attractiveness of entering (or leaving) one market compared with another. These are: the threat of new entrants and of substitutes, the bargaining power of buyers and of suppliers, and the nature of competitors within the industry (Porter, 1980). In general, when any combination of these is intense, a warning signal is given that industrial performance is likely to be squeezed and ambitious financial and marketing objectives (such as a high return on working capital or healthy margins or sales volumes and strong market share) might be difficult to achieve.

The threat of new entrants is determined by barriers to entry. In some industries, such as pharmaceuticals, there are massive research and development costs, in which the lead-time between researching a breakthrough wonder-drug and getting it licensed for the market may take decades: an effective barrier to entry. Hence, higher margins should be expected for those currently successful in the market. Another barrier that affects the number of suppliers is 'technological know-how'. In the linoleum industry, for example, manufacture is a trade secret, restricting the number of plants to just four in the world.

Another barrier to entry is access to distribution. Ninety-five per cent of rough or uncut diamonds from Russia have traditionally been traded through a Central Selling Organisation (CSO), run by De Beers in London. This allows De Beers to control distribution and sales, and hence prices, to a few selective traders who can only buy on De Beers' terms and conditions.

If members of the CSO are tempted to bypass De Beers and sell their stock independently, they are likely to be barred from future purchases at CSO 'sights', thereby restricting their main supply. Unsurprisingly, this allows the price of diamond jewellery, the main end-use, to sustain extremely high profit margins (Gooding, Harding and Lloyd, 1995). This illustrates how the bargaining power of suppliers can influence the nature of price and distribution decisions. The threat of substitutes can also be demonstrated by the diamond market. Although diamond is the hardest natural substance known, a number of innovations have been successfully implemented to mirror the properties of a diamond. 'Yttrium aluminium garnet' is one synthetic stone that is difficult to distinguish from a diamond with the naked eye. But sold at a fraction of the price of a real diamond, the strategy is obvious.

Although one potential threat to the fortune of De Beers is the secondhand market for diamonds (because if it became significant, it would lead to a price war), the strapline used in promotional literature – 'A Diamond is Forever' – has discouraged their purchase and so has helped to sustain a steady demand for 'new' diamond jewellery.

The threat of substitutes can be reduced by building up switching costs. These can be psychological rather than physical. The advertising agency Howell Hendry Chaldicott Lury reckon that sustaining a unique selling proposition (i.e. based on unique physical attributes) is more difficult today than ever before because of ease of imitation, facilitated by technological change. Thus motor cars will increasingly need to create brand personalities to sustain a distinguishable offering. A recent Peugeot campaign for the 406 demonstrates this clearly with an emotional campaign aimed at raising the status of the driver (from an ordinary person to that of a distinguished hero), with no product benefits demonstrated whatsoever. Ford have followed suit with an emotional campaign promoting their popular Escort, focusing on the life style of the user rather than demonstrating the features of the car.

In terms of industry competitors, a firm that can offer a unique hard-to-copy benefit is likely to be associated with less intense rivalry. Evidence suggests that the use of emotion in promotions, if carefully employed, is harder to copy than making rational, informative claims.

In markets that are increasingly commoditised (i.e. little difference is perceived between different brands) there is a greater tendency for someone to cut prices. This often leads to an increasingly hostile competitive environment in which marginal suppliers are likely to be squeezed out of the market unless they can survive by developing niches, aimed at a more focused group of consumers.

2.3 Monitoring competitive strategies

Porter's analysis of competitive forces illustrates that marketing management need to collect data on competitive objectives or aims, their strategies or means of achieving these objectives, and their response patterns. In this way analysis of their strengths and weaknesses can be made. Since the market has already been acknowledged to be dynamic, competitive activities will change over time as buyers and suppliers enter and leave the industry, substitutes are developed and the intensity of competition changes, so requiring a regular monitoring and review of competitive performance.

As part of the competitor audit, only key factors considered to be critical to the success of an industry in question should be used for rating the firm against the main competitors in the industry. These *critical success factors* are determined by managerial judgement. One way of doing this is to consider how best to achieve the maximum advantage over a competitor with the minimum of effort. Effort might be measured in terms of management time or financial resources. Critical factors may relate to particular functions, such as the ability to offer a product to the quality the consumer wants in the right quantity at the right time. This may require a sufficient production capacity and tooling and production know-how to meet the demand to order. Alternatively, functions may be financially oriented (e.g. the cashflow of a firm may be vital to invest in new technologies sufficient to remain competitive) or marketing capability (e.g. ability to develop new products successfully). They may alternatively relate to general competence levels (e.g. ability to recruit and retain management). These can be expressed as a capability profile, as a record or summary of relative strengths and weaknesses. Once the factors have been identified, a suitable rating scale for each factor can be made, ranging from 1 (very poor) to 5 (excellent) (refer to Figure 2.4). From this, it would appear that competitor B is better than our organisation at responding to changes in marketing, but less able to produce it (compared to ourselves, in which we score highly). This might suggest an opportunity to join forces to market a product in a joint venture, in which the strengths of each company are shared. One factor which might discourage B from co-operating is their relative strengths over us in technical innovation. They might be concerned that we will 'poach' some of their technical ideas when we have greater access to their information. Such problems require a trade-off analysis of relative strengths and weaknesses in deciding the future action of the company. On the face of it, our future marketing capability appears to be weak compared to B's, and we need to improve if we are to remain

Critical success factors*	Your company					Competitor A					Competitor B				
	1	2	3	4	5	1	2	3	4	5	1	2	3	4	5
Quality and reputation of branding				●				●					●		
Flexibility to meet market changes in production			●					●				●			
Flexibility to meet market changes in marketing	●							●						●	
Trade leverage				●			●					●			
Technical innovation	●							●						●	

* These are not exhaustive, merely illustrative.

Figure 2.4 A competitor profile analysis

competitive. The only distinctive relative advantage is in trade leverage and this is probably achieved by relatively stronger branding.

After reviewing this, an organisation can exploit its competitive weaknesses, especially when compared to the macro-environmental forces.

2.4 SWOT analysis: a planning tool to cope with the changing environment (PEST factors and stakeholders)

Since changing environmental conditions are inevitable, it is necessary for organisations to plan ahead. A *SWOT appraisal* examines the existing favourable and unfavourable conditions (respective *strengths* and *weaknesses* and future external *opportunities* and *threats*) beyond the current position facing the firm (see Figure 2.5).

To identify strengths and weaknesses, an internal examination of the firm's position is made, based on performance factors *relative* to the competition, and these are then matched to opportunities and threats in the macro-environment and stakeholder analysis. Thus, although information from the competitive audit

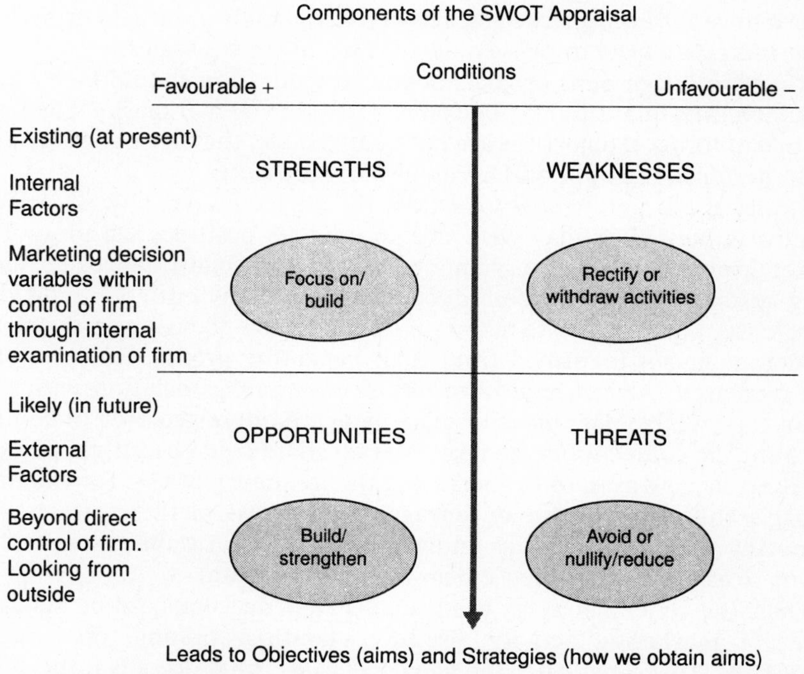

Components of the SWOT Appraisal

	Conditions	
	Favourable +	Unfavourable −
Existing (at present) Internal Factors	STRENGTHS	WEAKNESSES
Marketing decision variables within control of firm through internal examination of firm	*Focus on/ build*	*Rectify or withdraw activities*
Likely (in future) External Factors	OPPORTUNITIES	THREATS
Beyond direct control of firm. Looking from outside	*Build/ strengthen*	*Avoid or nullify/reduce*

Leads to Objectives (aims) and Strategies (how we obtain aims)

Figure 2.5 A SWOT appraisal (with corrective decision-making circled)

may help identify competitors' major weaknesses, it may not always be possible to exploit them owing to restrictions in the wider environment.

Performance factors to consider include:

- turnover,
- profit and market share for each product/brand for each market segment,
- company and market trends,
- company profile analysis.

An appraisal of product decisions (such as the quality and range on offer), pricing, distribution decisions and policy, and levels of promotional support should also be made relative to competitors. Annual reports of multinational competitors can offer insight into the importance of each market to the group as a whole by the relative amount of space devoted to each market. Competitors may be identified within different market sectors, for example, airlines may begin to compete with trains for short distances where flights are keenly priced.

After conducting a competitive audit and SWOT analysis, it should be easier to identify areas of key potential *competitive advantage*. Interpreting the results also offers guidance in the revision of marketing in the firm. This is because weaknesses and strengths are identified by comparing objectives to actual performance for each marketing activity. A shortfall in targets or performance might indicate a need to revise objectives or future strategies.

The *objectives* or aims or goals of your organisation should be both realistic (attainable) and quantifiable (for example, to increase market share by 10 per cent within 6 months). If objectives are not quantifiable, they are not easily measured and so performance appraisal becomes more difficult.

Strategies are simply how to achieve the objectives (i.e. how we arrive at the objectives). Your firm may wish to maintain its position, withdraw from the market, grow or dominate a segment. Thus firms in mature markets, faced with rising costs of getting their products stocked in new outlets, might decide to adopt a 'stay put' decision to maintain their position, focusing on their core skills and competencies identified from their capability profile. For example, BMW have increased their volume through a consistent association with executive saloon cars, whilst Mars plc (chocolate bars) are interested only in being first in the countline confectionery market. Market share could be improved by finding new users or new uses, or by increasing the frequency of use. For example, both Kellogg's and Nabisco have encouraged greater use of their cereals (Kellogg's promoting their cornflakes as an evening snack, and Nabisco persuading consumers to eat more Shredded Wheat per user occasion).

Once the general strategy has been decided, decisions can be taken on each aspect of marketing activity; product planning, pricing, distribution and promotions. This constitutes the *marketing plan*. The process is rather like going on a journey. The objective is to set your goal (say, the destination is London), and your strategy is how to get there. There are many options: motorway if the fastest route is required; minor roads for a scenic route. The plan is made up of the details of the map, i.e. how to get their specifically.

Typical decisions on product planning might involve:

- retaining products in which there is steady growth (increasing revenues);
- retaining those products bearing a positive contribution to fixed costs;
- withdrawing from products which:
  - promise too little cash for future projects,
  - increase risks excessively,
  - encourage competitive retaliation,
  - affect sales of other products in the existing range ('cannibalisation').

A firm may decide to reduce investment on certain products (e.g. rationalisation of a product line, or reduction in marketing support) because they are no longer profitable to the firm. Typically, these will be products in declining markets. A crucial decision in rationalising resources and products from the firm is the impact on other sales. Thus, some industrial buyers would expect a full range of products.

Q2.4 Read the case study 'Hong Kong and its Hotel Infrastructure' and develop a SWOT analysis for the Hong Kong hotel industry. You should use a presentation like that outlined in Figure 2.5.

Case study: Hong Kong and its Hotel Infrastructure

Hong Kong is a major centre in Asia for the hotel industry, with several major international chains and head offices. Its location has helped it to become a centre for hotel management, investment and development expertise, with markets, standards and quality of staffing that are of the best in the world.

Although tourism is the second most important foreign currency earner for Hong Kong after textiles and garments, the hotel industry that serves it is restricted in supply for several reasons.

One factor that determines the competitiveness of the industry is the country's infrastructure and labour force. Owing to high inflation, wage rates in the hotel industry have risen alarmingly. Attracting labour to hotel work from better paid occupations elsewhere in a country of near full employment is difficult. Importing labour from elsewhere may provide a solution, but the government has only approved a small proportion of hoteliers for taking foreign labour. Thus labour shortages have hindered growth, despite the increasing year-on demand for hotels from visitors. Growth of visitors increased by 170 per cent between 1984 and 1993. China will also have an increasing role in Hong Kong tourism development. Since March 1993 the mainland Chinese have been able to use their own currency in Hong Kong. Unfortunately, customs have not kept pace with tourist traffic, causing delays for passengers, late departures and even missed connections. Nevertheless the fast-increasing economic growth of other Asian countries and its supporting infrastructure suggest a bright future for the tourism industry and the hotel industry. Supporting industries which stimulate travel are the multinational corporations of Asia, involved in construction, finance and property. Services account for over 70 per cent of Hong Kong's GDP, with the closest local rival being Singapore. Despite this supporting industry bringing in business travellers, corporate travel and entertainment budgets have been reduced in recent years, causing many executives to seek less expensive accommodation.

Despite labour shortages in Hong Kong, those who have been trained in the Hong Kong hotel trade are keenly sought elsewhere. For example, there has been a steady influx of trained hotel managers to Indonesia, where demand exceeds supply and this is likely to increase in the future.

What brings visitors to Hong Kong depends on the nationality. In Europe and the United States, the Chinese culture and 'East meets West' theme is promoted. In 1993, 54 per cent of all visitors had been before.

Source: Adapted from F. Go, R. Pine and R. Yu (1994) 'Hong Kong: Sustaining Competitive Advantage in Asia's Hotel Industry', *The Cornell H.R.A. Quarterly*, 35, 5 (October), 50–61.

2.5 Strategies for competitive advantage

Exploiting competition can best be achieved with a knowledge of the options open to the firm.

2.5.1 Achieving competitive advantage

According to Porter, competitive advantage can be achieved by offering the lowest delivered cost to the customer (cost leadership) or by offering superior perceived value to customers, which requires offering a unique dimension that is valued by customers (differentiation). Both these strategies can be confined to a narrow segment of a market (a focus strategy) or offered across the market to a range of segments. Thus there are four generic strategies (see Figure 2.6).

A firm intending to use cost leadership aims to achieve the lowest cost position. By focusing on cost-cutting across a range of business activities, it is possible to achieve higher profits.

Management can identify where the best sources of competitive advantage arise by examining their value chain.

Management should examine their value chain to identify the best opportunities for competitive advantage. The value chain is made up of the required activities a firm performs in the course of its business (Porter, 1985). Thus primary activities include design, production, marketing, distribution and servicing of their products. Support activities, such as purchasing, technology, human resource management, accounting, finance and quality management, support any or all of the primary activities. By examining each value-creating activity, superior skills or resources relative to the competition can be identified which may be developed to create a low cost or differentiated position.

2.5.2 Creating cost leadership

Cost leadership can be achieved by economies of scale, in which production costs per unit can be reduced with longer production runs arising from increasing volume to full capacity (assuming it meets demand). Research and development costs can also be spread over more units under higher volume.

The philosophy and activity of total quality management (TQM) attempts to achieve quality at every point along the value chain, with the effect of reducing errors in faulty products first time. Thus, improving the design of PCs reduces the need for costly call-outs in maintenance and repairs. Studies have shown benefits in cost reduction, although the main objective of TQM is constant reliability of a

Competitive advantage

		Lower cost	Differentiation
Competitive scope	**Broad target**	Cost leadership	Differentiation
	Narrow target	Cost focus	Focused differentiation

Source: Porter, M. (1990),
Competitive Advantage of Nations, p. 39.

Figure 2.6 Generic strategies

quality product and an ongoing commitment to constant improvements from everyone involved. In the medium to long term, greater loyalty arising from outstanding reputation for reliability is likely to increase demand, which can improve economies of scale in production. The Boston Consultant Group have suggested that costs are reduced on average by 15–20 per cent each time cumulative output is doubled because there is a tendency for people to learn how to make efficiencies through experience.

Examining the relationships of channel members and deintegrating can help reduce costs. Daewoo considerably reduces its costs by not having a commission-earning salesforce.

2.6 Sustaining a differential advantage

This can be achieved by identifying those characteristics or resources within the value chain that customers consider important. With improvements in technology, it is quicker and easier to imitate successful products in the market, so sustaining a differential advantage is becoming more difficult. Slater (1996) suggests that it is all about continuously offering superior value – value being the difference between the benefits customers gain from using a product and the costs they incur in finding, acquiring and using it. The means of achieving longer-term comparative advantages include creating goods that are difficult to copy. These can be achieved by taking out a patent (which legally restricts imitation for a fixed number of years). Another way firms sustain their advantage is to anticipate where the competition is coming from. The major challenge here is determining the *moving target*, because competitors are continuously improving the value they give. The main factors that serve to offer a sustainable advantage are shown in Figure 2.7.

Firms can exploit growing opportunities and defend market positions on the basis of quality, service, low cost, speed, innovation and ability to learn. Although higher quality competitors tend to enjoy greater loyalty and lower costs, as

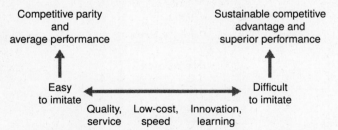

Reprinted by permission of the publisher from S.F. Slater, 'The Challenge of Sustaining Competitive Advantage', *Industrial Marketing Management*, 25, 79–86. Copyright 1996 by Elsevier Science Inc.

Figure 2.7 Capabilities and competitive advantage

buyers' expectations of quality have risen, so offering quality has become more of a necessity simply to compete on equal terms with other competitors. In other words, a lack of quality is a 'hygiene' factor which reduces loyalty. To achieve a consistent service, employees need to be motivated and customer satisfaction monitored both internally and outside the organisation. By thoroughly understanding the vital business processes that are necessary to deliver customer value it is possible to reduce some operations to cut costs. Only 10–20 per cent of expenses may be directly generated by activities that produce customer value, so many businesses have shed their workforces to reduce their operations in line with this (downsizing).

Speed includes the time it takes to get a new idea developed to the market. Time to market is reducing, requiring greater demands on organisations. The time it takes to develop a new car has been reduced from 5 years to under 3 years. Speed also includes the time it takes from receiving the customers' order to delivering it. This is an area where many companies are slack and complacent. A final dimension of time is the speed it takes to solve customer problems. Dissatisfaction arising from poor customer service is likely to erode loyalty.

Innovation is a necessary requirement in technological markets. At 3M, which has built up an enviable long-term performance, products less than 5 years old account for more than 25 per cent of sales. In order to encourage innovation, the ethos of an organisation must reward champions and tolerate market failures that occur in spite of sound business planning.

Organisations also need to encourage a continuous learning culture. This must involve stakeholders in the product development process and benchmarking (making comparisons against the best practices of the competition on a systematic basis).

On the basis of one or several of these in combination, a distinctive personality can be established for the organisation as a whole or for a range of brands, which can help sustain competitive advantage.

Case study: 'That'll be the Daewoo'

The Korean company Daewoo is a $8.4 billion Seoul-based ship-building and electronics conglomerate, which is also one of Asia's biggest firms. Despite its size, its origins are surprisingly recent. It was founded in 1967 by Kim Woo Chong with three associates and $18,000 of capital.

Daewoo cars arrived in Europe in April 1995 with some fresh sales techniques (no dealerships, no salesmen). They instigated the most successful launch in the history of British mass motoring, with the aim of obtaining 1 per cent market share. By March 1996 it had reached that goal. In a European market that was sluggish during 1995, Korean manufacturers doubled their share, in which established Korean makers, Hyundai and Kia, had also improved sales.

Whilst the Europeans have improved the quality of their cars and cut costs, the Koreans can afford to drop prices with less restrictive import controls than their Japanese competitors which are currently set at 10 per cent of the market. Consequently, during 1995, the Japanese manufacturers, such as Toyota, Mazda and Nissan have lost sales.

Despite the Japanese believing they have the edge in advanced technology over their Korean competitors, the Japanese are lobbying behind the scenes for a relaxation of European controls or tighter controls on Korean exports to Europe. British manufacturers have great difficulty in selling cars either in Korea (due to problems in setting up distribution networks and the abnormally high tariffs and taxes) whereas in Japan, land and labour is scarce and, expensive for manufacture, and loyalty is entrenched to home-made motors.

Daewoo's ambitions are to enter the US by 1997 with bargain-based cars selling in mass merchandisers such as Sears and Kmart, with estimated sales at 100,000 units per year. They are currently investing in plants in Eastern Europe, where labour is cheap, for export to Britain. Plants and distribution deals are also planned for Russia, India, China, Iran and the Philippines. However, feedback on the Korean-based Kia and Hyundai has been disappointing in the States, suggesting improvements required in customer satisfaction and perceived quality. One commentator suggested Korean cars have an image problem there, although there are benefits to be claimed in becoming established in the American market.

The demand for cars in the States attracts volume producers. The intensified competition attracted by the huge demand for cars in the States, presents a challenge to any volume producer. This competition also encourages constant refinement. Whilst there is always room for a better mouse-trap, the demand based on affordability will come mostly from the emerging economies of the former Soviet Union and other Eastern Bloc areas, India and South America. The costs of production and marketing are generally lower in these countries. A recent success has been the agreement to sell its cars to the government in Moscow, designed for a state-run taxi service.

Source: Adapted from T.L. Stanley (1995) 'Who the Heck is Daewoo?', *Brandweek*, 25 September, 36, 36, pp. 24–5; and J. Walters (1996) 'Korea Tailgates the Japanese'. *The Observer*, 17 March, p. 8.

Q2.5 Why is Daewoo successful in European markets, and will this necessarily follow in the US?

Q2.6 Is Daewoo likely to achieve a sustainable competitive advantage?

Summary

After reading this chapter you should understand that marketing is not simply about satisfying needs, but about *maintaining* them. Marketing managers must gain more control over future events by investing in marketing planning. This is because the environment within which we all operate is constantly changing. A particular feature of great importance is the *macro-environment*, which consists of economic, socio-cultural, technological and politico-legal forces. These are often considered as 'given' constraints, so we must prepare for their potential impact on our organisations. Each of these forces will have a bearing on how we decide what new products to make, what to move out of, what prices to charge, what distribution channels to use and what promotional programmes to implement.

It should be recognised that these macro-environmental forces affect, through change, the relative power of our trading partners; our buyers, suppliers, competitors and even our customers. Greater social and geographical mobility, combined with higher educational levels, and a greater standard of living has brought about a more discerning consumer. The manufacturer who offers no choice should beware. At a more refined level, it is also necessary to nurture relationships with our business colleagues internally, to ensure future resources are aimed at a common corporate goal rather than simply fostering self-interest.

This chapter has focused on the macro-environmental forces. Economic forces include the general economic conditions, the value of labour, disposable and discretionary income, business confidence, credit availability and a willingness to spend. All these factors can be influenced by government economic policy. Socio-cultural forces include societal attitudes to work and leisure, education and health, diet and environmentalism, family values and religion. Technological forces involve the way new processes and products improve our standard of living, and in turn shape our expectations of the future. Amongst those most relevant currently is the information revolution – the way information is handled and transmitted, and the role of bio-technology. Politico-legal forces include the changing nature of stakeholder policies and the legal and regulatory structure. These forces require the tracking of government policy and stability (since this affects tenure, leading to change) and legislation on anything that might affect our business. One of the effects of the Single European Market has been to harmonise legislation across national boundaries of Member States to improve their trading opportunities. Any marketer in a participating country should keep abreast of such legislation.

A SWOT analysis enables a company to examine critically the effects of the environment on its current situation and to improve its decision-making with respect to future planning and objective setting. By identifying current strengths and weaknesses, and future threats and opportunities it is possible to chart gaps in the market and prepare better for aggressive competition. It is simply a tool to aid future planning.

References

Dibb, S., Simkin, L., Pride, W.M. and Ferrell, O.C. (1991) *Marketing: Concepts and Strategies*, European edn. London: Houghton Mifflin.

European Marketing Data and Statistics (1996) 31st edn. London: Euromonitor.

Gooding, K., Harding, J. and Lloyd, J. (1995) 'Diamond Cartel Cuts up Rough', *Financial Times*, 24 August, p. 17.

Handy, C. (1989). *The Age of Unreason*. London: Hutchinson Business.

Machiette, B. and Roy, A. (1994) 'Sensitive Groups and Social Issues, Are You Marketing Correct?', *Journal of Consumer Marketing*, 11, 4, 55–64.

Porter, M. (1980) *Competitive Strategy*. New York: The Free Press.

Porter, M. (1985) *Competitive Advantage*. New York: The Free Press.

Porter, M. (1990) *The Competitive Advantage of Nations*. Houndsmills, Basingstoke: The Macmillan Press, p. 39.

Slater, S.F. (1996) 'The Challenge of Sustaining Competitive Advantage', *Industrial Marketing Management*, 25, 79–86.

Summers, D. (1996) 'Brands at Bay', *Financial Times*, 7 March, p. 16.

CHAPTER THREE

Marketing Research

Objectives

After studying this chapter, you should:

1. Appreciate why marketing research is important for effective marketing.
2. Know what the main research methods are.
3. Understand the rudiments of a cost-effective marketing research plan.
4. Know the procedures of good practice for questionnaire design.

Introduction: defining and interpreting the marketing problem

Marketing research is undertaken in order to improve decision-making in marketing. Therefore, it is usually done to help solve marketing problems. Before data collection can begin it is important to define clearly the boundaries of the marketing problem. This may require discussion amongst marketing management, researchers and outside consultants. This is an important stage because failure to recognise a problem means it is unlikely to be redressed.

Ideally, data should be collected from the market rather than from management, who may be blinkered by the pains they have taken to develop what they believe is the perfect product. Consider McDonalds Golden Arches. They have over 14,000 outlets in 72 countries, so you would expect them to be competent in marketing – researching the needs of the market before producing. However, even they make mistakes. Remember the McPloughmans? The cheese, salad and pickle

statistical tests are inconclusive, leaving judgement on decision-making to the skill of the manager. Decisions are facilitated by a clear report on the research findings and recommendations. For instance, in the previous example, research might reveal that price increases were the only reason for the fall in demand, so management knows it must refine its pricing policies.

In some circumstances research questions are more appropriate than hypotheses if the nature of the research enquiry is to find out more about boundaries of the marketing problem. Such studies are referred to as exploratory.

The first section of this chapter provides an overview of how marketing research can help improve decisions in the marketing mix. The main types of data are next discussed: *primary* and *secondary* research, and the *ad hoc* versus *continuous* approach. We then examine how to make marketing research cost-effective by adopting a systematic plan of data collection. Existing data should be used first, before embarking on commissioned or *ad hoc* research to solve a specific problem. Options for data collection are also matched to research objectives, whether prioritised on cost, time or quality (degree of accuracy of research) required. The chapter concludes with more details of the report stage.

3.1 Refining the marketing mix

Marketing research is:

> the objective gathering, recording, analysis and retrieval of data
> relating to the marketing of goods and services for problem solving
> and improvements in decision-making and control.

Research can be used to improve decisions on pricing, products, communications such as advertising and sales promotion, or distribution.

3.1.1 Pricing research

In chapter 6, we examine how consumers might react differently to products across different price ranges. The identification and recognition of different price elasticities of demand might enable the firm to segment the market, using separate offerings at different price levels. This is an application of *pricing research*. Sometimes firms conduct surveys to find out what their customers feel about their prices. One application of this is to assess whether it is possible for the firm to charge more. Sometimes price points are so sensitive that it is best to leave them alone. With increasing prices for raw materials, it is often better to reduce the *size* of product offered to the market. A key element in the success of this approach is whether customers notice the difference. Competitive supplier monitoring of prices is required to keep a check on market considerations. The recommendations of any pricing research should consider both market and cost requirements, and should tie in with profit projections.

3.1.2 Product testing

Product testing is one stage of new product development, discussed in chapter 6. Product testing includes concept testing the basic idea or application on potential consumers, screening and test-marketing. Product testing is also important for established brands to assess and monitor their current positioning. Product testing might include pack testing either to ensure that the material is strong enough to support the product in distribution, handling, stacking and storage, or in terms of ensuring the pack conveys an appropriate brand image. For example *Interbrew* faced a positioning problem with its famous Stella Artois brand. Consumer research, based on attitudes, concluded that too much modernising of the packaging had damaged the brand heritage. The date of the brewery's origins could be mistaken for a production number, and the chevron symbol hardly reinforced the pedigree of the lager. Its heritage was restored by revamping the bottle and the surface design of the label. This was integrated with physical distribution and advertising to provide a co-ordinated campaign. For instance, not only the bottles but crates and vehicles were redesigned. Over 2 per cent share was gained in less than 12 months.

This example demonstrates the importance of attention to detail, which may have profound effects on overall performance.

3.1.3 Advertising research

Advertising research is a multi-million pound business and deserves special research treatment. Typically, for a campaign, advertising is tested before it is broadcast (*pre-testing*) and also measured after the campaign has started (*post-testing*). Pre-testing ads involves showing mock-ups of commercials (sometimes using a story-board with a sound track) to prospects and testing their:

- levels of awareness,
- product interest,
- reactions to the ads or the product,
- understanding,
- inclination to purchase.

Post-testing may compare attitude change between before and after public exposure; this also includes sales tests. *Media research* aims to obtain the best package of media *classes* (e.g. whether to use television or radio, say) and within each class, specific *vehicles* (say, a choice between *The Daily Telegraph* or *The Times* to advertise a business product). Research can also be applied to sales promotions, public relations and the personal selling function, of course. Figure 3.3 shows how IBM evaluate their marketing support, using a questionnaire. In this example, customers' perceptions of their salesforce are assessed, including their

Your marketing support

Please give your evaluation of your satisfaction with the following aspects of your IBM marketing support.

7 Their knowledge of you and your industry?

Very satisfied	Satisfied	Neither satisfied nor dissatisfied	Dissatisfied	Very dissatisfied	No Experience
☐	☒	☐	☐	☐	☐

Comments and suggestions for improvements: _____

_____

_____

8 Their knowledge of your I/S strategy, objectives and applications?

Very satisfied	Satisfied	Neither satisfied nor dissatisfied	Dissatisfied	Very dissatisfied	No Experience
☐	☐	☒	☐	☐	☐

Comments and suggestions for improvements: _____

_____

_____

9 Their knowledge of IBM products and services?

Very satisfied	Satisfied	Neither satisfied nor dissatisfied	Dissatisfied	Very dissatisfied	No Experience
☐	☐	☐	☒	☐	☐

Comments and suggestions for improvements:_____

_____

_____

10 Their ability to combine products and services into solutions which meet your needs?

Very satisfied	Satisfied	Neither satisfied nor dissatisfied	Dissatisfied	Very dissatisfied	No Experience
☒	☐	☐	☐	☐	☐

Comments and suggestions for improvements:_____

_____

_____

11 Their responsiveness to your needs and requests?

Very satisfied	Satisfied	Neither satisfied nor dissatisfied	Dissatisfied	Very dissatisfied	No Experience
☐	☐	☐	☒	☐	☐

Comments and suggestions for improvements:_____

_____

_____

Figure 3.3 IBM questionnaire (Reproduced with permission of IBM)

information systems strategy, empathy and responsiveness to customers. IBM can use this information to run special training courses to ensure total consumer satisfaction.

Suppose a respondent scored as indicated by the crosses from questions 7 to 11. If scores are assigned to each box ranging from +2 (very satisfied) to −2 (dissatisfied), then the overall score is +1+0−1+2−1=+1 and the average score for each question =1/5=0.2, which provides an aggregate image over a possible range from +2 to −2, so clearly there would be some room for improvement.

3.1.4 Distribution research

Distribution research involves investigating channel design research, including supplier requirements, customer service research and site location research. For example, the location of a new supermarket site is critical for success. Selection would require an analysis of:

- the demographic mix of proposed sites,
- parking facilities,
- access to main roads and traffic flow patterns,
- property prices,
- compatibility with other stores in the area, to assess the degree of direct competition.

Even a small business such as a launderette which is expanding needs to take these factors into account: catchment area, from which potential custom will be derived, the percentage of people who are likely to be in need of public washing and/or drying facilities and relative convenience of the site location of the launderette compared to others nearby. Whilst a busy road might improve awareness of the location, a lack of parking space would probably deter drivers from using it.

3.2 Types of data used in marketing research

Figure 3.4 shows a classification of data types.

3.2.1 Secondary data

Imagine you have to do some competitive analysis. It makes sense to start with existing data – *secondary data*, which have already been published. You might use data from within your firm (*internal data*) or *external data* (obtained from outside sources). Where would you start? You might begin by examining records of

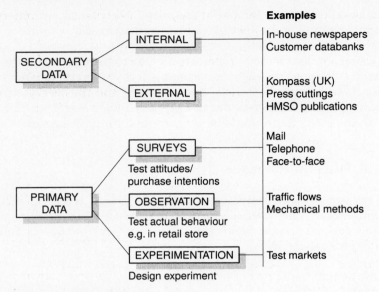

Figure 3.4 Data collection methods

databases and company file information within your department. Consulting colleagues might indicate further sources of information. Your company library (if there is one) is a good place to search. It is likely that external data will not be in a readily usable form. Such data may be costly to obtain and interpret, and should be used only after first consulting internal data. Examples of external data include names and addresses of competitors (which can be found in Kompass UK), and government statistics such as *Economic and Social Trends*, published by HMSO. These can be useful for forecasting projections of industry demand or sales of a total market, but further work needs to be done to make an estimate of competitive sales. Published accounts, audited data, commissioned data available on subscription and trade association statistics can all help. A variety of private firms also offer reports on specific markets: *Keynote Reports* is an example. Another source of information about competitors is press cutting agencies, who collect information about nominated companies from published sources. Collecting secondary data is called *desk research*. The skill of a desk researcher is largely in knowing whom to contact to obtain the relevant data. Desk research involves all possible business contacts, such as suppliers, buyers and sales staff.

3.2.2 Primary data

If secondary data are not available or are incomplete, *primary data* may be required. Surveys, observation and experimentation are all alternative forms of primary data, as shown in Figure 3.4. Primary data material may be collected by *survey* to solve a particular problem.

Survey research includes interviewing, either by post, telephone or personal interview. *Surveys* such as usage and attitude tests are sometimes used to evaluate products on the market. Examples are shown in Figures 3.5 and 3.6 for a manufacturer wanting to know more about how consumers feel about a new product. Figure 3.5 shows part of a questionnaire written for an adult audience.

Date: Code:

Identity No.
1
2
3
4
5

PLEASE COMPLETE THIS QUESTIONNAIRE AFTER YOU HAVE EATEN THE PRODUCT

Name: _____

Address:_____

Name of product trial: _____

Please give your answers either by placing a tick ✓ in the box, or by writing in the answer in your own words where necessary.

Q1   First, what if anything, did you particularly like about this brand?
PLEASE WRITE IN YOUR ANSWER BELOW

_____
_____
_____
_____
_____

Q2   What, if anything, did you particularly dislike about this brand?
PLEASE WRITE IN YOUR ANSWER BELOW

_____
_____
_____
_____
_____

Q3   Which of these statements best describes your overall opinion of this brand?

                                        PLEASE TICK <u>ONE</u> BOX ONLY

I liked it a lot .... ☐ 1

I liked it a little .... ☐ 2

No feelings either way .... ☐ 3

I disliked it a little .... ☐ 4

I disliked it a lot............................ ☐ 5

Figure 3.5 Typical product test using self-completion questionnaire designed for adults

BRAND X

Children's Questionnaire

| DUP (1–8) |
| CC2 (10) |
| V2 (11) |

NAME:

INTERVIEWER TRANSFER:

PLEASE ANSWER THESE QUESTIONS AFTER YOU HAVE EATEN
BRAND X

ANSWER THE FIRST 2 QUESTIONS BY WRITING IN YOUR
ANSWER

IDENTITY NO:
1
2
3
4

Q.1 First, what did you like about this brand?
WRITE IN YOUR ANSWER BELOW

_____

_____

_____

_____

_____

Q.2 What didn't you like about this brand?
WRITE IN YOUR ANSWER BELOW

_____

_____

_____

_____

_____

Figure 3.6 Typical product test designed for children

PLEASE ANSWER THESE QUESTIONS AFTER YOU HAVE EATEN THE PRODUCT.
ANSWER EACH QUESTION BY PUTTING A TICK IN THE BOX
NEXT TO THE ANSWER YOU AGREE WITH MOST

Interviewer code:
Identity No:
1
2
3
4
5

Q.3   How much did you LIKE this brand?

I liked it a lot .... ☐ 😀 1

I liked it a little bit .... ☐ 🙂 2

No feelings either way .... ☐ 😐 3

I didn't like it very much .... ☐ 🙁 4

I didn't like it at all.............................. ☐ ☹️ 5

Q.4   How much did you like the LOOK of this brand?

It looked very nice............................... ☐ 😀 1

It looked quite nice.............................. ☐ 🙂 2

No feelings either way .... ☐ 😐 3

It didn't look very nice .... ☐ 🙁 4

I didn't look nice at all .... ☐ ☹️ 5

Q.5   What did you think of the COLOUR of this brand?

I liked the colour a lot .... ☐ 😀 1

I liked the colour a little bit.................. ☐ 🙂 2

No feelings either way .... ☐ 😐 3

I didn't like the colour very much .... ☐ 🙁 4

I didn't like the colour at all .... ☐ ☹️ 5

Questions 3–5 in Figure 3.6 are presented more visually to attract a child's attention. This is achieved with the use of large font size and pictures of faces. Every research technique must be designed for a specific target audience. Secondly, presentation and layout can be as important as content (i.e. what is asked) in terms of encouraging a reasonable response rate.

This survey is a self-completion version. In this case, the questionnaire was left with the respondents to complete in their own time (in the home) and collected a few days later. Questions 3–5 in Figure 3.6 ask about the overall preference, the overall appearance and colour of the new brand in question. Further questions might be added, such as the product consistency or texture, and its taste and sweetness, which can also be evaluated using a pre-selected range of alternative responses or boxes. Since the design of these questions does not allow respondents to describe their feelings in their own words, these are collectively referred to as *closed questions*. Such information provides the manufacturer with the means to analyse the comparative brand strengths and weaknesses, with the aim of making product improvements. This can be achieved by providing a mean score from 1 to 5 for each attitudinal statement used in the questionnaire. Such a technique is a means of *quantitative research* because numbers can be assigned to the results. For example, if 40 per cent of respondents thought the brand was 'too sweet' and another 30 per cent felt it was 'a little too sweet', this would suggest a reduction in the sugar content, so saving the manufacturer money *and* satisfying consumer needs more precisely. Further questions may be designed to identify how consumers use the product (i.e. as a snack, as a dessert, after meals or at other particular times of the day).

Questions 1 and 2 in Figures 3.5 and 3.6 are called *open-ended* or *open response* questions because they allow each respondent to reply individually rather than according to pre-determined responses. The responses to open-ended questions may be varied and different for many respondents, and difficulty may be experienced in classifying or coding them for quantification. In many cases, such responses may be significant without the need for coding. As an extreme example, consider someone who responds adversely to a brand of cat food, claiming that her cat had died after eating it. Such a dramatic response would require examination – even if *just one* respondent said this – because a single adverse response of this kind is enough to cause a public scare if widely publicised. The point to remember is that quantifying responses should *not* be the *only* basis on which to make recommendations.

Business sense is also important when interpreting the more *qualitative* responses. These often provide insight and explanation into *why* the quantitative data arise, such as the nature of purchase behaviour, and attitudes to and feelings about a product. It may be used to explain who the best targets are for new products or merchandising displays. Research conducted by Riley and Blanchard (1996) indicates that a certain group of male shoppers, labelled 'magpies' are more experimental than women, and are thus more prone to brand-switching and to try new products. Riley and Blanchard argue that men, who account for 20 per cent of shoppers, are more visually and spatially aware than women and suggest that store environments must provide adequate space and time to explore aisles, with intolerance shown for jumbled or unclear fixtures. They do, however, add that classifying consumers into typologies or different groups can encourage static thinking since people within these groups do not always act in consistent ways.

Surveys can also be conducted to track purchase intentions of competitive products. This could be achieved by post, telephone or face-to-face interview. Which would you choose? The answer depends on your objectives.

If you are working to a tight research budget, you would normally choose post. If the primary objective is high accuracy, face-to-face interviewing is probably more appropriate, since it enables you to gain more control. This is because any anxieties or misunderstanding by the respondents can be quickly identified and handled through interaction. This flexibility is not available with post, and contributes to the comparatively high non-response rate, making it less accurate. Telephone surveys are intermediate between cost and accuracy, offering a quick reply if a tight deadline is the most important objective. There is a fine trade-off between quality, cost and time when considering which method of data collection to use. Whilst face-to-face interviewing is the most expensive (because a visit is often required to meet the respondents and this takes up more time) it provides the greatest control of all three survey methods. The advantage over telephone is that you can see the person you are interviewing and use your presence to gain better rapport. Additional findings can also be detected from non-verbal behaviour, which can be used to improve the response (e.g. if the respondent looks tired during an interview, a short break may be recommended). Often in commercial surveys, a complementary mixture of methods can be used to enhance response rates. For example, the telephone may be used in advance of sending out a mail survey to prepare targeted respondents and inform them about its purpose and timing. Telephone may also be used to follow up non-responses to a mail survey.

According to Summers (1995), technology is changing the way data are collected, so that the use of the telephone is likely to increase. Instead of using interviewers to conduct field surveys, most face-to-face interviews are likely to be assisted by computer. Along with computer-assisted telephone interviewing, interviewers can tap answers directly into a computer package, so reducing processing time and improving accuracy. It is also possible to check on the computer what time an interview was conducted, and to use satellite technology to check where the interview took place and verify expense claims. Speech recognition by computers will eliminate the need for interviewers for some types of telephone surveys. The use of videophones, which allow you to see the face of the receiver, will help to improve rapport.

An alternative form of primary data is *observation*. A retail organisation, for instance, might be interested to know the number of people entering their stores (store traffic) compared to the number of purchasers. When Halfords (motor car and cycle accessories store) discovered the purchaser/store traffic ratio was lower than expected, they switched from self-service to personal assistance. Observation can also be conducted remotely. For example, concealed cameras capture shoppers' non-verbal behaviour, such as eye movement and 'jockeying' from one queue to another, say, at a check-out. Such information provides an opportunity for retailers to ascertain the shopping route norm. It also allows them to redesign displays and evaluate their queuing systems.

The final method of collecting primary data is by *experimentation*. Sometimes direct mail is tested by sending out two versions in which one version varies by a single dimension, e.g. an added price offer or a different appeal. These are referred to as split-run tests. When different permutations of a similar offering are tested on different groups (*treatments*) this form of trial and error is called experimentation. If the variable being tested is different levels of incentive offers, this is called the independent variable. Performance criteria such as sales or enquiries might be the dependent variable – if you wanted to assess the impact of different incentives on sales or enquiries. If you are assessing the effects of an incentive on enquiries or sales, you would need a control group (a target not offered an incentive) to measure the difference in responses between the control and the treatment groups. Experimentation is therefore oriented to establishing and measuring causal relationships between the variables under study.

Test marketing, an application of experimentation, gives an opportunity for manufacturers to 'try out' different marketing mixes in separate test sites to refine their offerings before making a full-scale launch. Sometimes test marketing is conducted on established products, in order to alert management to unsuspected problems (or opportunities) associated with a product. For example, Stamford Marketing Consultants discovered that many purchasers of a new snack food placed the packages into their shopping trolleys upside down. Since the package was not designed for this, an unusual amount of compacting of the contents occurred and consumers were dissatisfied. A redesigned package allowed a successful introduction.

3.3 Continuous research

Continuous data may be collected on an ongoing basis, either internally or externally by commercial organisations and sold to others. Examples of external secondary data sold to others are *consumer panels* and *retail audits* provided by such agencies as A.C. Nielsen, IRI, Sofrès of France and GFK of Germany. An example of a consumer panel database is provided in Table 3.1.

Data from a consumer panel allow a firm to monitor the shopping behaviour of panel members, who agree to record specific purchases, often in a diary or more recently with self-scanning equipment to keep an electronic record of their purchases. Panel number 70261 refers to one consumer in the Scotland area and brand 080 refers to a particular brand of tomato ketchup, the product of study in

Table 3.1 Example of consumer panel of shoppers: sauces and ketchup

Panel List of purchases by continuous reporters
Product field: Sauces and ketchups
Period: 104 w/e 3rd January 19XX
Area: Scotland

Panel number	Purchase	Brand	Size	Outlet	Offer code	Quantity	Price paid	Nominal weight	Age Wife	House size	Social class	Child –16	Wife status
70261	7944	080	020	6232	00	1	26.5	1	3	05	C2	1	2
	7947	080	020	2412	00	3	22.0	1	3	05	C2	1	2
	8035	080	020	2412	00	1	25.0	1	3	05	C2	1	2
	8041	080	020	2412	00	1	23.0	1	3	05	C2	1	2
70273	7916	390	020	7012	00	1	16.0	1	5	02	E	0	0
	7951	390	020	7012	00	1	25.0	1	5	02	E	0	0
	8012	390	020	6522	00	1	27.0	1	5	02	E	0	0
	8033	390	020	6522	00	1	26.5	1	5	02	E	0	0
	8036	470	010	6522	00	1	23.5	1	5	02	E	0	0
	8043	390	020	6522	00	1	30.0	1	5	02	E	0	0
70279	8008	080	120	7012	00	1	27.5	1	5	02	C2	0	0
	8012	450	010	7012	00	1	21.5	1	5	02	C2	0	0
	8013	790	090	7012	00	1	43.0	1	5	02	C2	0	0
	8014	080	020	7012	00	1	27.5	1	5	02	C2	0	0
	8040	450	030	6812	00	1	25.5	1	5	02	C2	0	0
	8044	480	030	7012	00	1	35.0	1	5	02	C2	0	0
	8050	480	030	6522	00	1	35.0	1	5	02	C2	0	0
	8101	080	020	6522	00	1	32.0	1	5	02	C2	0	0
70305	7905	050	030	6522	00	1	35.0	1	2	03	D	1	1
	7909	050	010	6522	00	1	25.0	1	2	03	D	1	1
		450	010	6522	00	1	18.5	1	2	03	D	1	1
	7910	450	010	6522	00	1	18.5	1	2	03	D	1	1
		050	010	6522	00	1	19.5	1	2	03	D	1	1
	7912	488	030	3012	00	1	18.5	1	2	03	D	1	1
	7913	050	010	6522	00	1	26.0	1	2	03	D	1	1
	7915	450	010	6522	00	1	18.5	1	2	03	D	1	1
		488	030	6522	00	1	19.5	1	2	03	D	1	1
	7917	488	030	6522	00	1	32.0	1	2	03	D	1	1
	7918	488	030	6522	00	1	26.0	1	2	03	D	1	1
	7921	450	010	6522	00	1	19.5	1	2	03	D	1	1
		450	010	6522	00	1	18.5	1	2	03	D	1	1
	7923	050	010	6522	00	1	18.0	1	2	03	D	1	1
	7925	050	010	3012	00	1	18.0	1	2	03	D	1	1
		450	010	3012	00	1	19.0	1	2	03	D	1	1
	7929	050	010	6522	00	1	18.0	1	2	03	D	1	1
		450	010	6522	00	1	19.0	1	2	03	D	1	1
	7932	050	010	6522	00	1	19.0	1	2	03	D	1	1
		450	010	6522	00	1	18.0	1	2	03	D	1	1
	7939	050	010	6522	00	1	19.0	1	2	03	D	1	1
		450	010	6522	00	1	19.0	1	2	03	D	1	1
	7943	480	010	2414	00	1	26.0	1	2	03	D	1	1
	7944	050	010	3012	00	1	20.0	1	2	03	D	1	1
		450	010	3012	00	1	20.0	1	2	03	D	1	1

this record. Notice that the researcher has specific marketing data details (pack size, outlet, price offers given by offer code) and demographic information (age, house size, social class, number of children in household and working status of wife). All data are allocated to a number of predetermined categories and allocated a code. For example, wife status is allocated a code from 0 to 2 according to whether each panel member is working full-time, working part-time or is a full-time housewife. Panel data can be useful to ascertain brand loyalty for a given product, store loyalty and likelihood of brand-switching behaviour for different incentive offers and price ranges. It could also be used for targeting offers which are most likely to be accepted by particular groups.

Retail audits are a way of collecting continuous data on stock records for specific retail groups. Before the introduction of electronic point of sale (EPOS) technology, records were kept at periodic intervals to evaluate the sales for each brand between the intervals. Stock turnover is useful to retailers because they want to know which brands are most popular. Again, the effectiveness of in-store incentives can be identified by measuring the effects between before and after the offers have been redeemed. Improvements in information technology over recent years enables stock records to be maintained minute by minute as goods leave the store. This is achieved by scanning the barcodes at the point of sale. Using the data collected from the EPOS, a retailer can evaluate the success of in-house incentive offers much more quickly. Moreover, the response time to collect data from other retailers is shortened, so improving the service to subscribers. A summary of what consumer panels and retail audits can offer is given in Table 3.2.

Table 3.2 Comparison of market analysis information offered by retail or trade audits and consumer panels

	Trade audits	Consumer panels
Total market	Certain outlets	Certain consumer types
Consumer purchases	yes	yes
Brand shares	yes	yes
Trade selling price	yes	yes
Promotions (on pack)	yes	yes
Trade purchases	yes	no
Distribution	yes	no
Display	yes	no
Consumer demographics	yes*	yes
Type of retail outlet	yes	yes
Brand-switching	yes*	yes
Media exposure of consumers	no	yes

* for store card holders

3.4 *Ad hoc* research

This is research conducted for a special purpose, so it is primary data.

3.4.1 Trends in using research agencies

Recent trends suggest that continuous research of fast-moving consumer goods is becoming a smaller part of the overall industry with regular tracking services and *ad hoc* qualitative studies becoming more important (*Economist*, 1995). For example, psychographics research is being refined to examine the rate of consumer acceptance of new technologies. A new values and lifestyle consumer profile, iVALS, is being designed to examine the attitudes, preferences and behaviours of users of the Internet and online services. Early results indicate differences between users and non-users are based more on knowledge and education than on income, with implications for new means of targeting (Heath, 1996). Tracking involves monitoring changing consumer reaction to brands, advertising and corporate images. Another trend is that clients are becoming more sophisticated in requiring customised studies for interpreting consumer behaviour. Whereas research agencies were once allocated the role of providing the facts, they are increasingly being asked to provide strategic insight into the planning of new products, i.e. *ad hoc* research. A.C. Nielson have connected their computers to some of their biggest clients and have even shifted some of their equipment into their offices (e.g. Kraft and Unilever) to build more stable partnerships as clients want more interpretation of data.

In section 3.1 research was discussed that might improve decisions in the marketing mix. Section 3.4.2 focuses on an example of this as *ad hoc* research. Thus *ad hoc* research is not restricted to packaging, but can be applied to pricing, distribution or promotional decisions.

3.4.2 Packaging research

Packaging can either serve to enhance communications such as image or product positioning, or provide functional performance standards. Thus positioning research might identify that:

- glass conveys freshness (particularly for jams and yogurts);
- colours can represent favourable associations such as green conveying natural products;
- size can offer added value (such as the extra packing in Easter eggs, the gift wrapping of premium food hampers or the false bottoms of fireworks);
- shape (such as flat, oval, blow-moulded bottles) can offer excellent size impression.

The key to enhancing positioning is to identify those values and/or attributes that are both salient and discriminating, and to use packaging in a way that can reinforce those that are considered to give most competitive advantage. In computers, it might be modernity and user-friendliness, for beers it might be heritage. In some segments, for example blind consumers, the needs are very specific, such as offering braille messages around the rims of containers, especially for hazardous substances.

Packaging research which tests communication objectives includes focus group research, the *tachistoscope*, and projective imagery tests. Research into functional objectives includes pseudo-product test designs. Attitudinal scaling techniques can be used to test both kinds of objective.

3.4.3 Communication objectives

To communicate competitively, the pack must create an awareness in-store. The average shopper scans each pack across a counter in about 0.2 seconds, so the pack must be distinctive and attractive. Also, the message on the pack must be clear, relevant and easy to understand, without requiring extensive effort to decide:

- what it is,
- what it can be used for, or its conditions of use,
- how it is made (if relevant, as in foodstuffs).

Research tests into targeting/general attitudes/preferences

Focus groups
Small sample groups of different demographic profiles discuss their feelings about a new pack design. They might be shown the pack design for 5 minutes and asked for instant recall. Additional questions may be asked:

- Would you be prepared to buy it?
- If not, who would buy it?
- Where would you buy it?
- How might it be improved?

Impact/Awareness
The *tachistoscope* tests visual reception of the packaging. The tachistoscope is a slide projector, which enables stimuli such as packaging graphics to be presented under varying conditions of speed and illumination. The tester can find the speed at which a message is received. It is possible to assess the rate at which packaging information is conveyed, and therefore provides a measure of visual impact and awareness.

Understanding

For radically new product concepts intended to satisfy a latent demand, it is critical that the pack communicates what it is/how it can be used/who it is for. The *projective imagery test* finds out what respondents feel would be in the packet, and who would buy it.

3.4.4 Functional objectives

Pseudo-product test design

Suppliers, consumers and distributors can be provided with two packs (with no brand names/visual cues on them), and asked for their preferred choice.

Post-experience preferences

For established brands in the market, these groups may be asked if they have experienced any problems with their packaging. For example, packaging of own-label tea might be tested by asking the following questions:

- Is it easy to open?
- Does the packaging tear on opening?
- Does it pour easily?
- Does the freshness of the product remain after opening?
- Does the packaging remain intact after repeated usage?
- What are the problems experienced?
- What are the recommendations for improvement?

These questions should not be evaluated in isolation, but relative to the brand leader, and other national brands of standing.

Problems with interpretation

Respondents may need to be probed, especially if they provide over-evaluative information, such as 'great – nice – I like it'. This information is not specific, and is therefore difficult to use as a basis of decision-making. Probing can provide a salient battery of attributes, which can then be quantified. For example, a consumer may believe the packaging is sophisticated because of its gold colour. A useful measurement technique is to use a form of attitudinal scaling which can measure both communication and functional objectives of packaging.

The *semantic differential scale* uses a series of bipolar adjectives. Both image and functional attributes can be tested. For example, pack A, compared to pack B is:

	+3	+2	+1	−1	−2	−3	
Special	—	—	—	—	—	—	Ordinary
Exciting	—	—	—	—	—	—	Boring
Dull	—	—	—	—	—	—	Bright
Hard to use	—	—	—	—	—	—	Easy to use

This can indicate the relative strengths and weaknesses of particular pack designs. It provides an overall index of packaging effectiveness, using the aggregate scores of each respondent. A frequency diagram can then be produced (Figure 3.7). The results indicate that improvements are required since more people are dissatisfied than satisfied.

An alternative use of the semantic differential scale is to measure the means of each factor for every respondent. This allows you to identify specific strengths and weaknesses. In the aggregate analysis the overall index may be satisfactory, but ratings of specific criteria may not be. Therefore, both measures of analysis are necessary and should be compared to the main competitors. It should be noted that attitude scales are widely used on a variety of research problems, not just packaging research.

Trade-off techniques such as *conjoint analysis* can also be used to identify preferences in combinations of offerings. For example, respondents might be asked to rank various combinations of price levels, pack sizes and promotional offers. This may be done by comparing criteria pairwise, or by simultaneously rating a suitable array of combinations of criteria, designed by a software package. This technique is called the *full profile method*. Consider a toothpaste manufacturer wanting to establish the best combination of pack sizes, offers and price points. Tests might use showcards of combinations such as in Figure 3.8.

Consumers rank each combination. Various computer packages then attribute utilities or levels of importance to each criterion and combination of criteria. The most appropriate combination can then be made to consumers, based on their preferences.

Q3.1 A toy manufacturer designs toys for two different age ranges: young children aged between 2–3 years of age and for company executives. For each group, explain the types of primary research techniques you might use in order to provide information on usage and attitudes.

Hint: What difficulties might you encounter in collecting your data?

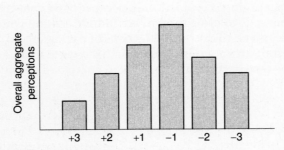

Figure 3.7 Frequency diagram of aggregate scores

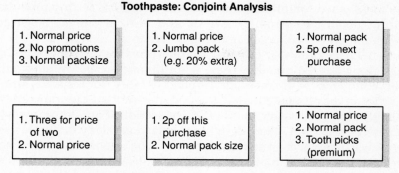

Figure 3.8 Showcards offering combinations of criteria for a brand of toothpaste

Q3.2 Management recognises that socio-cultural factors can have a significant impact on the demand for toys. Why? Describe the kinds of socio-cultural information you might require.

3.5 Further applications: questionnaire design

Since the survey is one of the most popular forms of data collection, it is important for you to understand how questionnaires should be designed. Well-designed questionnaires increase response rates due to improved interviewer rapport. Nevertheless, social changes are causing some problems. The effects of rising crime, together with the increasing numbers of women in the workforce, has contributed to the increasing non-response rate as more people refuse or are not available for interview. Another contributory factor is that the public are becoming increasingly tired of filling in questionnaires and becoming more cynical about the underlying motives of market researchers, which is not helped by sales made under the guise of market research. Professional market researchers tend to adhere to an ethical code of conduct which forbids this practice. It is in their interests because unethical practices damage the industry as a whole.

Successful questionnaire design involves establishing a rapport with respondents, since one of the main difficulties is *non-response*. You need to establish the purpose of the questionnaire without necessarily compromising client confidentiality. Offering an incentive such as a report on the results helps. Moreover, the *structure*, *layout* and *content* of the questionnaire often needs to be pre-tested on a small sample of the target audience in order that adjustments can be made to enhance comprehension. Remember you are setting up a dialogue with future potential customers. Words and phrases should be structured logically, but also be familiar, clear and unambiguous.

Figure 3.9 lists a number of pertinent questions that should be considered when designing a questionnaire. These will influence response rates, either in terms of ability or willingness to respond. Ability to respond requires a consideration of the respondent's background, clarity of the questions and logical sequencing. Before reading on, look at the first section of questions involving the respondent's background. When designing a questionnaire you should use these questions to ensure you can answer yes to them. You might think about how you might resolve any negative replies here. For example, the second question may be overcome by a simple explanation of terms or by simplifying the jargon, for in question 1 the subject-matter may be a more fundamental problem. It might indicate that there are more appropriately qualified respondents to answer questions on particular subjects. For example, if a father of a family is the person who normally shops in the supermarket, then it is he who should be asked questions about shopping habits, not his wife.

Companies spend vast amounts of money on asking respondents questions about their attitudes towards past events, which requires them to stretch beyond their memories. For example, it is of little use asking customers about their attitudes towards, say, the quality of a sales response to their telephone enquiries about mundane products if these enquiries were made about six weeks earlier. The author had great difficulty in offering an accurate response on a scale from 1 to 10. So you should be careful when interpreting responses which require great details about past events or issues. Where respondents are required to stretch their imagination, they are likely to opt for middle-of-the-road scores (say between 4 and 7 from a scale of 1–10), which may not reflect their true feelings at the time of the event. Such research is over-analysed and wasteful, yet the company I was referring to is a brand leader in financial services! This demonstrates the importance of good design in data collection, which makes interpretation easier.

Questions 5–9 in Figure 3.9 ask you to consider clarity when designing questionnaires. If you have answered yes to any of these questions, you have a problem. If the questions you are asking do not make sense, or are ambiguous in some way, you lose credibility as an expert of your subject, and response rates will fall. A clearly worded questionnaire gives the respondent confidence in you, and consequently your questionnaire is more likely to be answered.

Sometimes questions are double-edged; that is, they can be interpreted in two ways. For example, you should never start a question with a negative because it can be interpreted on two levels. For instance, the question: Can't you read the labels on this product? could be answered 'yes' to indicate 'I can't read them' or 'yes' to indicate 'yes ... I can read them' as a signal of condemnation to the question. Negative questions also pre-judge the respondent's view – they are weighted in favour of a negative reply. Thus any analysis of results arising from negative questions would be flawed.

CONSIDER RESPONDENT'S BACKGROUND

1. Does the respondent have appropriate knowledge about the subject?
2. Does the respondent understand the technical jargon in a question?
3. Is the respondent likely to be able to remember pertinent facts about a past event or issue?
4. Is the respondent the most apt person to answer questions on a particular subject/topic/decision?

CONSIDER CLARITY

5. Is the question grammatically correct?
6. Are the words ambiguous or do they hold more than one meaning or context?
7. Can a question be interpreted in more than one way?
8. Are two or more questions asked at the same time?
9. Are there hidden agendas in the question?

LOGICAL SEQUENCING

10. Does the order of the results affect the quality of responses?

PERTINENT QUESTIONS INFLUENCING WILLINGNESS TO ANSWER

11. Are there favoured times of the year/week/day when a particular category of respondent is more likely to answer?
12. Are any questions considered sensitive or embarrassing to one's social or psychological standing?
13. Are any questions considered controversial?
14. Are any questions considered confidential?
15. Are any questions considered trite or unnecessary?

Figure 3.9 Pertinent questions in designing questionnaires

Ability to answer can be tested through pre-testing or piloting your first draft of a questionnaire to a small percentage of your sample respondents. Feedback will enable you to refine the questionnaire. Questions 11–15 refer to issues that will affect the willingness to answer. When a respondent is most busy, time is valuable and answering questionnaires will take a low priority. The art is to research when respondents are least busy and most receptive to answering. Respondents are also less willing to answer questions they feel threaten their social status or good character. Consequently, people are more liable to lie about issues relating to their politics, sexual habits and orientation, church-going and charity-giving. They may be loathe to talk about personal issues such as income or their age. If such issues are required for segmentation purposes they can be asked for in age and income bands and presented at the end of the questionnaire (since asking them at the beginning might discourage further response). Other questions may be considered unnecessary or confidential (such as your business). If this is a probable reaction by respondents, you should prepare yourself by justifying the reason for asking such questions.

3.5.1 Structuring the questionnaire

Assume you are the manufacturer of a radio clock alarm and want to design a new, improved product for the consumer. Typically, you will need to find out if consumers are currently satisfied with the products they already have. But this presumes that consumers already own a travel radio and alarm clock. Existing owners may vary in their attitudes from non-owners. Such information might be commercially beneficial to you when designing your new product.

It helps to build the core structure of the questionnaire by using a *flowchart* diagram. Therefore, the initial core structure of your usage and attitude survey might be that shown in Figure 3.10.

Start with a closed question on ownership. Further questions depend on this answer. Note that the questions are *filtered*, depending on ownership. This is to ensure that groups of respondents answer relevant questions only. There is no

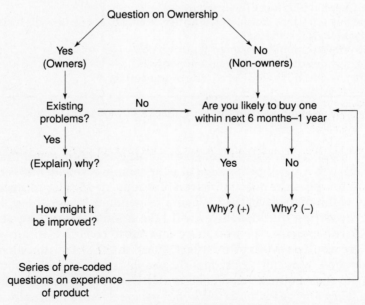

3.10 Flowchart structure of questionnaire design, illustrating the use of filter questions

point in asking non-owners about existing problems. To ensure the interviewer (or reader) does not miss any questions, procedures must be used to clarify the route of the questionnaire. Instructions directed at the interviewer are normally in capital letters and for respondents in lower case. Arrows or different coloured sections are used to clarify the route of the questionnaire, once the questions have been coded. Eight questions are identified in Figure 3.11.

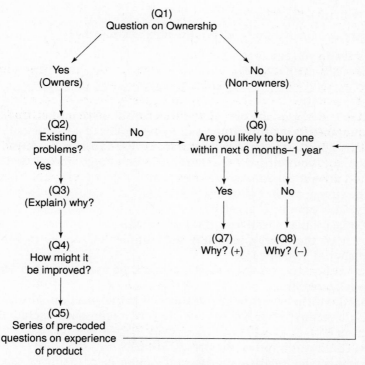

Figure 3.11 Questionnaire showing eight questions logically structured

The questionnaire can now be refined/elaborated to include specific questions, such as:

Q1 Do you own a travel radio and alarm clock?
IF YES, GO TO Q2. IF NO, GO TO Q6. [*Notice filter question here*]

Q2 Do you experience any problems with it?
IF YES, GO TO Q3. IF NO, GO TO Q6.

Q3 Explain what these problems are.
[*PROBE, IF NECESSARY*]

Q4 How might your travel radio alarm clock be improved?

Q5 Using a phrase from Show Card A, rate the importance of the following factors in your ideal travel radio/clock alarm.
(i) Sound quality
(ii) Colour
(iii) Convenience for travelling
(iv) Station variety
(v) Price
(vi) Outlets available

Q6 Are you likely to buy within the next six months?

Q7 Why do you say that?
-8 [PROBE, IF NECESSARY]

Q3.3 Consider a questionnaire aimed at the organisational market. Imagine you are a components manufacturer, supplying aerials to portable radio manufacturers. What data might be useful in designing a new product?

Q3.4 Read the questionnaire and findings on 'Where to go in Anytown' (Figure 3.12) and answer the following questions:
1. Is the survey consumer or organisational?
   Why? To whom is it targeted?
2. What is/are the objective(s) of the research?
3. Page 1 of the survey indicates the number of replies to the survey mailshot of 1,500 people.
   What alternative research methods might be used to achieve the objective(s) (stated in 2)?
4. What do you believe to be the weaknesses in the questionnaire structure?
5. Are there any other factors which you might have included under Section 6?
6. How could you improve the presentation?
7. What are the relative merits and demerits of using a face-to-face interview instead of a mailshot?
8. How do you think the data were used?

3.6 The marketing research plan of how data are collected

Usually you will need to initiate several marketing research projects before you can make recommendations from the results. This requires good planning to prioritise the procedures in data collection, so enabling you to achieve cost-effectiveness. A typical sequence of events is illustrated in Figure 3.13.

If information already exists which is appropriate to your needs in solving a given problem, then it should be used before undertaking primary research because it is far cheaper. If the information is accessible in-house, it makes sense for you to use this first. If not, your skill in knowing where to access the data externally, and in what form, is important. The danger in this desk research is that the information may not be in a form that is directly relevant to solve your problem, you may need to break it down into more manageable units.

Data may be obtainable at an affordable price from syndicated surveys, compiled by commercial organisations, who effectively share their data with many decision-makers. The decision to use primary data in the field will depend on how relevant and accessible secondary data are, their accuracy and your objectives, in terms of cost, time and accuracy. If you need highly accurate results, then primary research can be conducted, particularly if you are not working to

---

Figure 3.12 Anywhere questionnaire

---

c/o The Secretary, Anyplace Aisle, Anytown, Anywhere, 1XY ZAB

January 19 . .

To: The Manager

Dear Sir or Madam

We would like to introduce you to fifteen new places to take your customers, representing a wide range of interests and activities.

We are organising a one-day workshop during the first half of April 19 . . at the splendid venue of Anytown, in Anywhere. Here you will find representatives from each of these fifteen top attractions eager to discover how they can help you and ready to answer your queries. There will also be entertainment and refreshments laid on.

We would be grateful if you would complete the enclosed quick-tick questionnaire and return it (no stamp needed) to:
The 'Where to Go in Anywhere' Group, FREEPOST, Box No XYZ, Anytown, 1XY ZAB whilst indicating your interest in attending the April workshop.

Yours faithfully

Sir Somebody
Marketing Manager

QUICK-TICK QUESTIONNAIRE

Please complete and return to: The 'Where to Go Anywhere' Group, FREEPOST, Anyplace Aisle, Anytown, 1XY ZAB – no stamp is needed

1. Does your company organise trips?   OFTEN ☐   OCCASIONALLY ☐   NEVER ☐

2. Does your company get asked for advice or information on places to visit?
    OFTEN ☐   OCCASIONALLY ☐   NEVER ☐

3. How many attractions would usually comprise a day's outing?
    1 ☐   2 ☐   3 ☐   Other (please state) ....

4. If more than one attraction is visited in a day would they usually be
    similar ☐   or different ☐   to each other?

5. Which do you find your customers prefer?
    Famous attractions ☐   New attractions ☐
    Unusual attractions ☐   Other (please state) ....

6. What factors affect most your decision on which attraction to choose or recommend for an organised trip?

	Very Important	Considered	Not Important
Size	☐	☐	☐
Opening hours	☐	☐	☐
Travel distance	☐	☐	☐
Location	☐	☐	☐
Quality of roads on route	☐	☐	☐
Type of group wanting trip	☐	☐	☐
Visited before	☐	☐	☐
Not visited before	☐	☐	☐
Restaurant / tearoom facilities	☐	☐	☐
Gift shop	☐	☐	☐
Number activities available	☐	☐	☐
Weather-dependent	☐	☐	☐
Cost of entrance	☐	☐	☐
Guided tours	☐	☐	☐
Near town / shopping centre	☐	☐	☐

7. Any additional comments ....
....

I would like to receive FURTHER DETAILS on the April WORKSHOP

NAME ....   POSITION ....

COMPANY NAME ....

ADDRESS

THANK YOU FOR YOUR TIME

business. The path to success is knowing the audience. Without this, any business will fail.

Extending this idea to a specific commercial example, Tom Smith's, a Norwich company which makes Christmas crackers, must select jokes to suit their target audience. This means considering who might be at the Christmas lunch. Some might be offended by sexism or racism, or jokes involving slang, so the message must be kept very clean. This example illustrates how the target audience has implications for how the product is offered, which will ultimately affect the way it is *positioned*. Product positioning is how the consumer perceives and assesses the product, and is often evaluated relative to the competition. The target consumer must include both the purchaser and the user (or recipient of the message), since satisfaction from both may affect future demand for the brand. But since it is difficult to predict (and control) who will be present at the Christmas lunch, Tom Smith's cannot afford to segment the market. When the target market is difficult to define and measure, it is usually best to position the product with a broad appeal for a mass market. Tom Smith's treat and position their jokes (a core part of their product's offering) at the level that will be acceptable to everyone.

Conversely, when the target is clearly defined, steps can be taken to ensure a product is directed at a particular segment of the market. Sometimes this can be communicated by explaining for whom a product is NOT intended. For instance, Priority Holidays are designed for youngish couples who want to relax away from the pressures of bringing up a family. In their brochure, holidays are described as for those '. . . who are able, or want to travel without children', in which accommodation is contracted exclusively to guarantee a 'child-free' holiday.

4.2 Conditions for segmentation

4.2.1 Segmentation and mass marketing

Organisations have a choice in the way they approach their target market. They can offer a single marketing mix to everyone, using the *undifferentiated* approach (sometimes called the *total market* or *mass market* approach), in which case, everyone would be considered to have similar needs and wants. This means that a standard product or service is offered, using one price level, one method of distribution and one way of communicating its range of benefits.

Alternatively, the organisation may feel that the needs and wants of specific groups of consumers can best be served by providing different offerings or *marketing mixes*. When there is a specialist rather than universal demand for a particular offering, *segmentation* appears a practical alternative. In practice there are few offerings demanded by a mass market. Washing water might be considered a mass market, but contrast this with trying to make a success of producing a universal shoe. Apart from not fitting most people, shoes are bought for a variety of reasons, some of which are more to do with fashion status than fit and comfort. *Segmentation* serves to deal in a practical way with *the identity of distinctive groups of consumers*. Within each segment, each member holds similar or *homogeneous* characteristics, needs or wants within the market. Members between each segment who hold different characteristics, needs or wants are said to display *heterogeneous* behaviour.

> Market segmentation is therefore the process by which consumers in markets with some heterogeneity can be classified in to smaller, more similar homogeneous markets.

4.2.2 Criteria for effective segmentation

The decision to segment or not will depend on a combination of factors. Apart from being sensitive to end-user wants, the size, structure and resources of your company are important considerations.

Generally, segmentation has an advantage over mass marketing because it allows a firm to focus more rigorously on the detailed demands of a specific group of consumers. Spreading too many resources over the divergent needs of a mass market may be counter-productive. If the overall market size is large, a smaller company with fewer resources might best be able to focus on a *niche market* rather than attempt to spread its scarce resources over an extensive market coverage. The investment required to reach and communicate to mass markets arises from the need to offer both extensive distribution channels and promotion respectively. If, for example, a company is too small to make an offering available to a whole market, segmentation might be conducted geographically, serving the needs of a locality or region rather than national or international needs (in which there is global demand). Alternatively segments can be commercially viable by specialising in a single product line such as the retailer Tie Rack. Overall, small market size calls for a mass market approach, whereas niche opportunities increase as the market becomes larger.

If the market is particularly fragmented or complex (e.g. food sauces) there is an opportunity for smaller players to reach smaller, specific segments. For example, chilli sauce has a limited market. If a firm has a low market share in an overall market, a good opportunity for growth is to identify a niche market since, as we suggested in chapter 1, it would be difficult for brand followers to compete with brand leaders possessing price leadership. However owing to higher production runs and/or larger bulk orders, mass marketing can provide better economies of scale compared with companies operating in niche markets.

Finally, if the competition is intense, it can be avoided by identifying an alternative, characterised by little or no competition. The Japanese, for example, initially penetrated the UK with television sets by entering the hitherto under-exploited miniaturised television market. With a foothold in the market, they

Table 4.1 To segment or not to segment

Factor	Mass	←──→	Niche
End-user wants	Similar	1 2 3 4 5	Different
Product market size	Small	1 2 3 4 5	Large
Product market structure	Simple	1 2 3 4 5	Complex
Market share	High	1 2 3 4 5	Low
Resources of company	High	1 2 3 4 5	Low
Scale economies	Yes	1 2 3 4 5	No

were then able to grow steadily. Since there is a combination of factors to consider in deciding to segment or not, a profile analysis such as Table 4.1 should be used.

Table 4.1 offers guidance on whether a product should be offered to a mass market (i.e. no segmentation), or to a niche or segment of the market. The guide shows several market and company factors. By examining each product against each factor, it is possible to determine whether each product should be aimed at a niche or a mass market. To illustrate, if you were a manufacturer and scored 1 or 2 for most product factors, this would suggest not to segment but to direct your product at everyone. A score of 4 or 5 would indicate opportunities for focusing your attention at particular segments of the market.

The next section demonstrates how to use segmentation effectively.

4.3 Segmentation strategies

Once you have decided segmentation is appropriate for your circumstances, the next stage is to ascertain which segmentation strategy to adopt. There are two segmentation strategies. These are the *multi-segment approach* and the *concentration approach*. Each is featured in Figure 4.1, along with mass marketing (described in the previous section).

4.3.1 The multi-segment strategy

This is selecting and targeting more than one segment, each with its own distinctive marketing mix. For example, different brands of a make of car such as Vauxhall might be distinguished according to the specific performance needs matched by income. Figure 4.1 might represent a range of Vauxhall products, identifying the likely target audience for each segment as shown on the following page. A typical target market for segment 1 is clearly those on limited incomes, e.g. young couples. Whilst segments 2 and 3 might be more appropriately designed for the car fleet market, the prestige model in segment 3 is more likely to be tailored for the senior manager, whereas an Astra or Vectra might be a 'typical' sales representative's car. You might consider this a generalisation, but

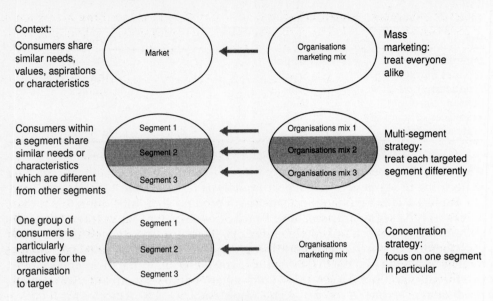

Figure 4.1 Alternative segmentation strategies

Segment	Brand offerings	Target	Typical Brand
1	'Standard products', functional only, with 'no frills'	Young couples	Corsa
2	Standard company car	Junior/middle management	Astra or Vectra
3	Prestige car	Senior management	Carlton/Senator

this is a feature of segmenting markets. Not everyone fits neatly into a market segment.

4.3.2 Comparing segmentation strategies

If your organisation has limited resources, it might pick a concentration strategy, focusing its resources on a single segment only. Rolls-Royce is a classic example. Since the market is barred to most people by cost, control over the marketing mix to reach the right audience has to be carefully implemented. Who are these privileged people? They are likely to be wealthy entrepreneurs. Research indicates they can be reached most effectively by promoting at performing arts, such as operas (in which 50 per cent of social class A, representing senior management or top professional status, regularly congregate). (Social class is examined in a later section.)

You should now be in a position to understand clearly the differences between mass marketing, a multi-segment strategy and a concentration segmentation strategy. Consider now the potential risks of using either segmentation strategy. The main problem in using the multi-segment approach is that lower priced segments might be associated with higher priced segments. Consumers traditionally targeted in the higher priced segments might bestow lower quality on the company, inferring lower brand quality and a trading down. This is one reason why some manufacturers do not promote their name on their brands or in advertising. The rule is that *segments should not be allowed to mix*. Several years ago Parker Pens broke this rule, and the company name was harmed when they offered a low-priced pen. Had they allocated this product to the Third World under a different name, or used separate distribution channels, members of different segments would not have come in to close contact.

The problems with the concentration strategy approach are more obvious. Although a company with limited resources or special expertise might be concentrated in one segment, there is danger of over-reliance on one brand. What if the brand loses its market appeal, or a competitor outperforms it? What if the advance of technology renders it obsolete?

Earlier in the discussion we noted that different segments can be distinguished on the basis of characteristics, attitudes or values held on products, services, ideas or other stimuli or behaviour. The next section demonstrates the varied ways by which segments may be distinguished. These may be applicable to either *consumer* or *organisational* markets. The relationship between consumer and organisation markets is shown in Figure 4.2.

The main distinction is that, in consumer markets, the purchaser benefits individually from consumption, whereas in organisational markets, the buyer, who is often a professional, buys on behalf of the organisation for its well-being. The distinction can sometimes be very fine. For example, a householder may buy a home computer for personal development, intellectual stimulation or as a 'fun' toy for the children. These are all *consumer* markets. If the reason for buying was to compute spreadsheets and help with the accounts as part of a family business, it is *organisational*. Asking the reason for buying is an effective way of distinguishing between consumer and organisational markets. Although there is some overlap in the way segments can be distinguished between consumer and organisational markets, there may also be differences.

4.4 Segmentation for consumer marketing

There are a number of standard demographic features used to segment consumer

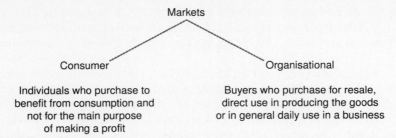

Figure 4.2 The distinction between consumer and organisational buying behaviour

markets. These include age, sex, race, religion, family life cycle, social class and socio-economic grouping or grade. We shall now examine each of these in detail.

4.4.1 Age

Tour operators recognise the varying needs of different age groups and offer varied packages accordingly. Compare, for example, the sensual intimacy of a Buddies holiday brochure with that of Saga, in which happiness is extensively featured. Radio stations focus on a particular age group to decide what music to play. The choice of music on BBC Radio 1 is said to be geared to the 18–35 year age range, whereas BBC Radio 2 is designed for a more mature audience.

Although age can be used as a means for distinguishing between the needs of different groups or segments, it must be used with caution. A report by Mintel, entitled 'The Over 50s' (1989), an Executive Summary, discovered that media portrayals of this group as mature citizens was often resented. The report elaborates that a significant number in this group find life more satisfying than when they were younger.

Many people in late middle-age consider this to be a time for 'selfish' spending and a chance to indulge themselves with a clear conscience, particularly when they do not have to worry about family responsibilities. For example, this age group spends a lot of time and money on their appearance. Although there is a large market to tap, those seeking to design services and communicate propositions aimed at this age group must be careful. Members of this group are unlikely to spend money impulsively, despite the absence of mortgage commitments. Moschis, an American professor of marketing, indicated that marketers need to offer marketing offerings that are stimulated by the *cognitive ages* of individuals, not their chronological ages. Cognitive age refers to how old a person feels. In practical terms, if a 55-year-old man perceives himself as 15 years younger, then he should be targeted with products designed at his perceived age group rather than his chronological age. If you refer to the advertisement for Saga holidays (Figure 4.3), you will see that it uses cognitive age as an emotional appeal.

Figure 4.3 Saga holiday advertisement
(Reproduced with permission of Saga Holidays Ltd)

4.4.2 Sex

Physical differences between the sexes will explain why some products and services are more appropriate for either one of the sexes. Convention can also be important. Although unisex clothes exist, there is a convention about what is acceptable, in terms of the choice open to either sex. According to Jowell *et al.*, (1992), how people feel about sharing workloads between the sexes is not always reflected in their behaviour. In a survey conducted in 1991, 76 per cent of respondents believed household shopping should be shared equally, and 58 per cent believed making the evening meal should be shared equally, but only 47 per cent and 20 per cent respectively actually shared these tasks equally. Although there is a trend towards a greater equality in task-sharing, some tasks are still predominantly performed by one sex. In general, men are expected to repair household equipment, whereas women are expected to do the bulk of the washing and ironing (*British Social Attitudes*, 1987). Sexual stereotyping has been reinforced by marketing. The person most often featured in advertisements of household products for the kitchen is still a woman. In some cases, this stereotyping is highly functional. For example, reliability is often emphasised in car ads designed for women. Although they buy similar cars to men, many women may lack repair skills or feel less confident about maintenance.

4.4.3 Race

Each race has its own cultural identity. Marketers must therefore research what is specifically acceptable, tolerable and intolerable when designing marketing mixes for different races. For example, in Moslem countries, how people dress is far more restrictive than in the West. Tourists visiting these countries should be wary of wearing short skirts or even leggings, since they are likely to offend.

4.4.4 Family life cycle

People's financial circumstances and needs will vary according to their marital status and their stage in developing or managing a family (age and number of children). Jain (1975) reviewed specific stages when these circumstances change, which can be used for targeting particular kinds of products (see also Worcester and Downham, 1988). These stages may be condensed into:

- the bachelor stage,
- newly married,
- married with child-rearing,
- older married with dependent children,
- empty nest I (no children living at home, but family head still working),

- empty nest II (family head retired),
- solitary survivor (in work, later retired).

The relationship between family life cycle (FLC) and excess income over expenditure is shown in Figure 4.4. It is one dimension of the FLC affecting market affinity for goods. This particular example refers to a typical career couple, in which the wife does not return to work after child-rearing. Study the relationship carefully and decide how this might be useful for targeting products, e.g. furniture.

The surplus of income after paying for basic necessities (food, clothing and shelter) is called *discretionary income*. It is most useful as a dimension of an individual's buying power for luxury items. This includes entertainment, holidays, cars, education, electrical and domestic appliances and furniture.

Consider the left-hand side of Figure 4.4. A single home owner with a recent mortgage may have little discretionary income. Although incomes may be appreciating for families with children (middle of Figure 4.4), expenses will be incurred for child-rearing products. The furniture manufacturer may target practical, 'no frills', self-assembly furniture at these groups, irrespective of income. For households whose children have left home, discretionary income

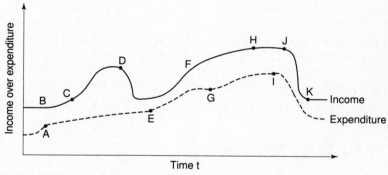

Key
A Rising costs of living with initial mortgage
B Singles with career prospects
C Dual income of newly married, both earning, no kids (i.e. DINKIES – double income, no kids)
D Spouse ceases work for child rearing
E Expenses rise on rearing first child
F Rising income reflects promising career ahead
G Second child and/or possible house move to accommodate larger family size incurs extra expense
H Income peaks in fifties
I Falling expenditure reflects offspring leaving home and/or mortgage paid off
J Retirement, after which income may fall significantly
K May be dependent on occupational pension and/or investments/savings

Figure 4.4 Significant stages in the family life cycle, with possible effects of income over expenditure

may be more plentiful. Many maturer families at this stage of the FLC would want and can afford luxury furniture, possibly customised rather than ready-made. Although income is likely to fall significantly in retirement (right-hand side of Figure 4.4), an individual's wealth will depend on how much reliance there is on the state pension compared with a private pension.

One of the limitations in using the FLC is that changing demographic patterns are requiring the general shape of the model to be constantly revised. The incidence of rising divorce rates, single-parent households and women in the workforce, common throughout Europe, suggest that care must be taken in modifying and interpreting the FLC for a given market.

4.4.5 Social class

Historical records reflect the persistent prevalence of social class in affecting behavioural norms. For example, in recounting the sinking of the *Titanic* in 1912, historians noted that the wealthier customers of the upper decks were given priority treatment in evacuation, whereas those in the lower decks were considered last. Indeed, most of the survivors were wealthy.

Social class, *social grade* or *socio-economic grouping* is a multifactorial measure, determined by the occupation of the chief earner in the household rather than a previous reference to the income of the head of the household. This revision is important because head or owner of a household may not be the chief income-earner. For example, the incidence of negative equity of some mortgagees restricts both geographical and social mobility, and these are sometimes considered to be related to social class or grade. Classes are commonly graded A–E (See Table 4.2). It is most effective as a segmentation tool when people

Table 4.2 Social class or grade as defined by National Readership Survey

Grade	% of families	Description	Typical examples
A	3	Senior managerial or professional	Company director, lawyer or doctor
B	10	Middle managerial or of professional status	Bank manager of smaller branch, university lecturer
C1	24	Junior managerial or clerical/ general white-collar work	Office clerk
C2	30	Skilled working class	Plumber
D	25	Unskilled working class	Taxi driver
E	8	Unemployed, students and retired dependent on state pension	—

within a class share similar values and display similar behaviour to a product. Share ownership, for example, is still predominantly held by the professional classes (ABs), but the privatisation issues did attract a number of C2s, who were effectively targeted.

One of the dangers in using social class for segmentation purposes is to assume that class reflects spending power. It need not be. Consider the limited discretionary income of many ABs after they have paid for the privileges of private education for their children and perhaps a large mortgage at high interest rates. The discretionary income of a skilled plumber (C2) working in London might well be more than that of a bank manager (social class B) working in a small rural town.

O'Brien and Ford (1988) have also identified many other anomalies which distort any relationship between class and discretionary income, including:

- inherited wealth,
- two family incomes,
- the 'unofficial' economy,
- significant overtime payments,
- other unearned income (e.g. investments).

Using social class is also problematic:

- in luxury or discretionary markets
- in markets in which there are no significant divisions in society,
- where the divisions are so extreme that the potential middle market may be limited.

For example, in Brazil, there is an upper class and a lower class but no middle class. By contrast, Australia provides manufacturers with an effective mass market with 95 per cent belonging to the middle class. The rule is that a market with significant lack of a middle class is not a suitable target for many luxury products. If social class cannot be used to assess the likely affinity to certain products and markets, (i.e. it fails to discriminate on these grounds) other techniques, such as using ACORN, might be more effective.

4.4.6 Location based variables

ACORN

Recently, (A) (C)lassification (O)f (R)esidential (N)eighbourhoods has been used to classify people's behaviour and attitudes according to where they live and what they live in. House purchase is often the biggest single expense of a household budget, so people will usually buy according to what they can afford. The type of house (size and age) will to some extent dictate life style, which will in turn relate to family life cycle to some degree. The strength of ACORN is that *it is a combination of several indices*. It is sometimes labelled under the broad umbrella of *geo-demographics. Postcodes* can be used to determine housing stock and life styles – they are often employed in mail-shotting for better targeting. For example, a person living in a Victorian terrace in Surbiton may want different things in life from someone living in a block of flats in Hackney, East London.

Spatial (or geographic) segmentation

Consumers may be classified in their needs according to geographical area. Geographical segmentation is one of the considerations of international marketing, since cultures vary. Even within countries, variations abound. There may be physical reasons for choosing geographical segmentation. For instance, cars in the northernmost states of the United States must be fitted with heaters, those in the South with ventilators.

Retail supermarket chains need to alter their ranges of merchandise to suit local store differences in their consumer profiles. This might be analysed on a geographical basis. Hart and Davies (1996) have suggested how expansion into non-core ranges (e.g. clothes and entertainment) will not only be store-specific, but category by store-specific, and will have implications for positioning.

4.4.7 Psychographics or life styles

This identifies the living patterns of individuals as expressed by their *activities*, *interests* and *opinions*. Advertising agencies often devise their own psychographic profiles of consumers. For example, personality traits and attitudes might be used to split up consumers into segments on the basis of their needs for *achievement* and *control* over others. Activities might be used to separate groups on the basis of whether their life is *centred on themselves*, or for the *good of other people*, and whether their interests are predominantly family, home or job related.

VALS 2 is a psychographic profile made up of values, attitudes and lifestyles, developed and revised by SRI International. Several of these groups can be classified as either outer-directed or inner-directed. Outer-directed groups are those whose purchase behaviour is driven by how they feel others will evaluate them, usually on the basis of what they own, in which possessions serve as symbols of status. *Achievers* are relatively wealthy and motivated by status. Inner-directed groups base their decisions about what possessions can do for them, unconcerned about others. Several groups are considered to be principle-oriented, in which behaviour is influenced by strong beliefs. These may arise either from a belief in responsibility, integrity, knowledge and maturity (the *fulfilleds*), or a belief in traditional institutions. If tradition has a powerful influence on behaviour, such as the Church and the role of the family, these consumers are classified as *believers*. In the latter case, purchasing behaviour is predictable, buying well-known, domestic brands. Groups can also be classified according to their need for variety-seeking behaviour and/or physical energy. Thus *experiencers*, who tend to be young and active in sports, are said to be a good outlet for targeting new markets and brands, but loyalty may be lower than for other groups. *Makers* are also relatively active, but do not buy goods for status but as a means for creating other things. Their motives for purchasing are more influenced by activities which they feel are worthwhile pursuing to enhance their quality of life. The TAG Heuer advertisement (Figure 4.5) appeals to achievers who are striving for success. It also appeals to experiencers who are young at heart, needing a challenge and enjoying a sense of adventure. The target audience is likely to have drive and ambition with high energy levels.

Some of the major labels common to many psychographic profiles are:

- *The experimentalists* or *experiencers*: These are willing to buy new things. Advertising can appeal to this group by encouraging trial purchases and offering new benefits not previously satisfied.
- *The moral right*: These are radicalists attempting to change others. They can be an important group, in so far as they open up new markets.
- *The popularists*: To achieve approval, this group copies the habits of the mainstream. They are easily influenced by peer group pressure, so endorsements might be a good marketing stimulant.

The problems in using psychographics include:

- The practical difficulty in measuring consumers within different profiles (since attitudes and opinions are mental rather than strictly observable).
- The tendency to straitjacket consumers when, in fact, consumers have highly complex personalities, and whose interests and opinions may change with different marketing situations. For example, an individual might react rather negatively to shopping for mundane, everyday items, become excited when shopping for products relevant to a hobby, and yet act conservatively when shopping for financial services. The same consumer may therefore be willing to *accept risks* and plunge into the latest hi-fi (to suit a hobby) only to be *risk-averse* when buying a private pension plan. Clearly, the danger in using a psychographic approach is over-reliance on stereotyping personalities.
- Another problem is whether they are stable over time. The yuppie of the 1980s, for instance, is no longer in vogue.

4.4.8 Benefit segmentation

Some segmentation variables are causal rather than descriptive. When the benefit sought, or reason for buying, is used to discriminate between consumers, this is

4.5 Segmentation for organisational markets

Whilst some of the segmentation variables useful to consumer markets are also applicable to organisational markets, there are several differences. Demographics relevant to organisational markets include:

- geographic location (because some industries, such as shipbuilding, tend to be regionally concentrated);
- primary business or industry (often referred to as a *standard industrial classification*, SIC);
- size (in terms of numbers of employees or some performance criterion such as sales);
- type of buying situation.

SIC numbers were developed to classify organisations systematically according to their particular type of business service or product manufactured. Data from various publications are available from the Central Statistical Office. They can also be obtained from some commercial databases such as Jordan's FAME (Financial Analysis Made Easy). Using FAME, information is arranged in the form of a tree diagram, starting with the most general divisions covering a broad range of industries, which is successively refined into narrower divisions covering more specific industries. For example, sales of carbonated soft drinks can be found by first accessing food, drink and tobacco from a more general division on the database (Figure 4.6). Each general division is allocated a SIC number (in the case of food, drink and tobacco, 4.2) and this can be further subdivided into sub-codes, such as for soft drinks (coded 42.8). In turn, this can be further split into mineral waters and soft drinks (code 4283.1) and fruit and vegetable juices (code 4283.2). Often the SIC code is researched to identify associated industries which at first hand would not have been considered as requiring similar needs.

SIC codes can be used with other commercial data to evaluate the potential market size of an organisational market. It is possible to extract financial information from FAME, such as sales turnover, for each business under each SIC code. By identifying the SIC numbers of the industries that buy a firm's output, it is possible to identify the number of firms that might be buyers, both nationally and locally. Names, addresses and telephone numbers of executives can be traced from suitable business-to-business directories such as *Kompass*, which is available in most libraries. These names can be matched to each SIC code.

Estimating potential business opportunities from published annual sales (either from a suitable directory or database such as FAME) has its limitations, in so far as records are historical and so do not necessarily account for future trends. To confirm or deny the attraction of a market, future demand can be estimated by contacting a sample of the companies found in the directory. Possible agenda during an interview might include company trends, economic factors, obstacles

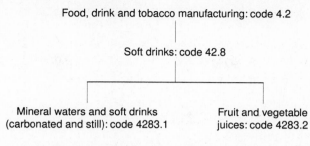

Source: Jordan's Software and Information Solutions, Jordan's Ltd, Bristol.

Figure 4.6 SIC classification for soft drinks

to growth, major competitive trends and likely future prospects. An important skill in interviewing in industrial markets is knowing whom to ask questions because each contributor holds different amounts of influence in purchase decisions, according to their levels of responsibility and organisational status.

Another feature of organisational markets is how the usage rate is allocated amongst firms in the industry. In many cases, demand may be heavily skewed towards a few firms. *Pareto analysis* is sometimes used to describe this pattern, in which 80 per cent of sales are derived from 20 per cent of companies. Prioritising such key accounts is a necessary part of marketing. Size of companies or regional concentration may provide an insight into prioritising the potential accounts. Behavioural segmentation in terms of identifying light and heavy buyers is also relevant in the organisational market.

Another organisational segmentation variable is the *type of buying situation*. This is explained more thoroughly in chapter 5. It is sufficient here to understand that the buying decision-making unit may comprise a single individual or multiple sources of influence. For example, when a company buys a significant piece of processing equipment, the decision might be influenced by the buyer, the production manager, the technical manager, production operatives and the financial director. If there are multiple sources, their priorities have to be identified and targeted accordingly. The type of buying situation also includes the level of experience of the purchaser with the product or service. When industrial purchasers are buying goods for the first time, the marketing task facing the seller is far greater than that of a straight rebuy situation. That is why, for industrial purchases, the selling task requires an investment in planning to get to know the individual decision-makers, together with the products of the firm.

Example of segmenting for both consumer and organisational markets: Figure 4.7 is a map of a fictitious town, and Table 4.4 shows how areas on the map would be selected for targeting: lawnmowers for the general consumer market, larger lawnmowers or lawnmowers for the organisational market.

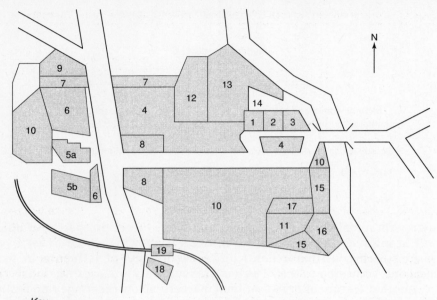

Key

1. Car park
2. School
3. Hospital
4. Central business district
5a. Factories
5b. Industrial estate
6. Council estate
7. Modern flats
8. Victorian terraced
9. Modern terraced
10. Older semi-detached houses
11. Proposed area for building development
12. Modern semi-detached houses
13. Farmland
14. New building site in operation
   (3-bedroom semi-detached houses)
15. Older detached (pre-1950)
16. Modern detached (post-1950)
17. Bungalows (modern)
18. Gurubury Brewery
19. Station

Figure 4.7 Town map

Q4.1 Select areas on the map which you feel are suitable for targeting the following products:

(a) Double glazing,
(b) Home improvements.

Indicate any other segmentation variables (apart from location) which might be relevant together with the likely targets.

Table 4.4 How lawnmowers might be segmented, with typical target markets

Item	Segmentation variable(s)	Reasons	Targeting
Lawnmowers for general consumer market	1. ACORN: housing type of postcode	Owners of property in areas with gardens	Non-flat households 8–10 12 15–17
Lawnmowers for general consumer market	2. Behavioural	Replacement market	Find out expected life and obtain/buy purchase lists to identify individual households
Larger lawnmowers	Benefits	Either appropriate for larger gardens or sit-on mowers	Likely to be up-market, residential areas e.g. 15–17
Lawnmowers for organisational markets	Standard Industrial Classification (SIC)	Particular business needs	Industrial Estates, also owners of farms (e.g. 13)

4.6 Complex segmentation

So far we have examined segmentation variables *in isolation* to aid understanding. In practice, markets are often complex so that the type of variables already considered (e.g. sex, age, social class) are not effective for discriminating between groups in isolation, but only in *some combination*. When more than one segmentation variable is combined to divide up market segments, this is referred to as *complex* or *multivariable* segmentation.

To illustrate how complex segmentation works, imagine that a supplier of credit finance has identified three relevant segmentation variables from which to design a segmentation strategy. These are the status of people based on their occupied property (which may be divided up into either outright owned, mortgaged or tenant property), their annual household income (less than £20,000, £20,000–40,000 and over £40,000) and their use of credit (classified as light, moderate and heavy users). Figure 4.8 illustrates the potential 27 different segments open to the credit supplier. Should the supplier choose a multi-segment strategy, offering 27 different marketing mixes to each segment? This is unlikely to be profitable and would increase costs – some segments might be difficult to reach, or too small to be profitable. The choice of segments to target will therefore be selective. Figure 4.8 shows a shaded box as one segment, the high earnings, outright owned, heavy user of credit, which has been targeted as the most important segment. As a general rule, the credit supplier would keep on adding prioritised segments with their own marketing mixes until the costs of target

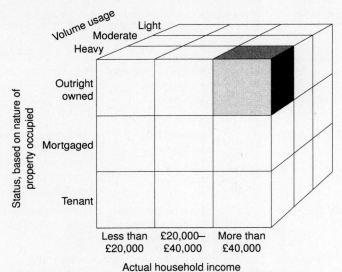

Figure 4.8 Complex or multi-variable segmentation

penetration outweigh the benefits. You might consider other ways of segmentation in the market for credit finance.

Q4.2 Table 4.5 represents an adult survey conducted by a market research agency. Using complex segmentation, they have categorised consumer feelings about the effects of sugar, fat and food additives in different foodstuffs according to sex and age.
(a) On the basis of the results for sugar, what managerial actions might be taken by a food manufacturer?
(b) Suggest whether fat and food additives should be segmented, and if so, how, using the data in Table 4.5.

Table 4.5 Which food is most likely to causedamage to our health?

| | Men | | | | | Women | | | | |
Age	15–24	25–34	35–44	45–54	55+	15–24	25–34	35–44	45–54	55+
Sugar %	14	19	19	20	31	10	13	11	17	24
Fat %	37	45	31	32	22	42	35	40	38	25
Food additives %	18	23	17	19	17	24	54	45	21	19

BUPA EssentialCare provides all the essential benefits you expect from private health care, like hospital charges and specialists' fees for in-patient and day-case treatment. What it doesn't cover are the less essential costs, such as the relatively small amount (around £50) that you'd pay for an initial private consultation with a specialist. And that's why we can keep BUPA EssentialCare subscriptions so low.

And because EssentialCare comes from BUPA, Britain's leading independent health care organisation for over 45 years, you can be sure it's been designed to provide the right kind of cover for your needs – at a price that's right.

It's reassuring to know that, should you need treatment, BUPA EssentialCare provides you with:

- Prompt private hospital admission when it suits you
- The convenience of over 800 BUPA Participating Hospitals for you to choose from
- The comfort of private accommodation, usually with colour TV, telephone and en suite bathroom, where family and friends can visit when you want
- The kind of individual care and attention that helps ensure your speedy recovery

There's no overall limit to the amount or number of claims you can make for each person in any one year.

And all this can be yours at a very affordable price.

Source: Undated BUPA EssentialCare brochure.

With BUPACare you can choose the level of cover that's right for you. And, whichever level you choose, you know you can always count on prompt private treatment, from your initial appointment with a specialist, right through to hospital treatment and after-care, if you need it.

And because BUPACare comes from BUPA, Britain's leading independent health care organisation for over 45 years, you can be sure it's been designed to provide the best choice of cover for your needs.

It's reassuring to know that, should you need treatment, BUPACare provides you with:

- Prompt private treatment when it suits you

- A choice of specialist to treat you personally, from initial consultation to after-care.
- The convenience of nearly 900 BUPA Participating Hospitals to choose from
- The comfort of private accommodation, usually with colour TV, telephone and en suite bathroom, where family and friends can visit when you want
- The individual care and attention that helps ensure your speedy recovery
- Flexible cover for hospital and out-patient treatment, with no waiting period
- Emergency cover and medical assistance, including repatriation where necessary, whenever you travel abroad

There's no overall limit to the amount or number of claims you can make for each person in any one year.

Source: Undated BUPACare brochure.

Figures 4.9a and b BUPA publicity (Reproduced with permission of BUPA)

4.7 Positioning

This is about creating the kind of identity that an organisation (or its brands) wishes to be associated with. Consumers tend to hold mental pictures or images of brands, products or services, in relation to each other. If you can imagine a league table of brands for a particular product category of your choice, it suggests you have a reasonably clear view of how you perceive each brand. If you find this task difficult, perhaps there is no clear leader or winner according to your assessment criteria, whatever they might be. It could be that several brands are considered equal, suggesting that the positioning of each brand is unclear, ambiguous or simply a repetition of another. If you are a typical member of the target audience, this would suggest the owners of these brands may have a positioning problem, because they have failed to establish perceived superiority to be associated with their brands. It is important to realise that perceptions may be markedly different from the objective qualities of any brand, which could be verified by scientific testing.

4.7.1 Positioning content

Positioning is an essential part of brand management. To gain more control of brand image, it is useful for us to know how consumers form opinions about products and services. Their assessment of brands are based on a combination of perceptions about what brands can do. Olson and Reynolds (1993) have classified how these perceptions may be structured into:

1. Product *attributes* or characteristics, such as the mildness of Fairy Liquid (washing-up detergent).
2. *Benefits* or *consequences* of using a product, such as Fairy Liquid is gentle on the hands, so keeps them tender and soft.
3. *Values* that the product helps to satisfy or achieve, i.e. the symbolic meaning derived from taking out extra life assurance might be 'peace of mind'.

Collectively, Olson and Reynolds refer to this as a knowledge structure of consumers. If this knowledge structure can be identified for different brands by all consumers of the target market, an organisation can identify its strengths and weaknesses relative to its competitors. This information would indicate what identity an organisation could aspire to, if effective communications are implemented. Hence positioning content is about *what* to position a brand with.

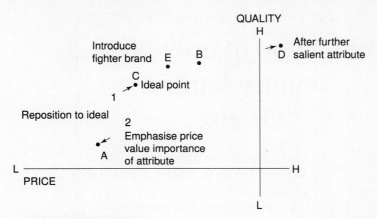

Figure 4.11 Perceptual map

although it should be realised that it is not sufficient to be well positioned to be successful in the market. For instance, a well-positioned brand may suffer from poor awareness, limited distribution channels, or a poor sales force, thus limiting sales.

In Figure 4.11, the firm is positioned on the basis of low or high price and low or high (perceived) quality on the perceptual map. The firm can choose to reposition itself from its own current positioning (A) to the ideal point, perhaps by altering the physical characteristics or qualities of the product. It could also attempt to shift the ideal position closer to A, by emphasising the importance of price as an attribute. In the latter case, communications have made improvements in product quality seem redundant. Alternative strategies would be to add a third salient attribute D, such as in the case of Radion washing powder, which was promoted on the basis of providing a pleasant smelling benefit. Hitherto, this benefit or consequence had not been used in advertising washing powders. Sometimes firms introduce *fighter brands* such as that positioned at E. With this strategy, the competitor B will be undecided whether to move closer to the ideal on lower price (towards A) or settle nearer to the new fighter brand. If B moves towards A, it could find that the fighter brand takes most of its sales. If it attacks the fighter brand, brand A is unharmed. The competitor may, of course, reposition itself directly at the consumers' ideal position, in which case A is in trouble.

A classic example of how market dominance can be overcome or reduced using positioning, was given by Avis, in 1962 (see Figure 4.12). Avis decided to use a 'No. 2 spot' to their advantage. At that time, Avis were way behind Hertz in the rental car market and close to the No. 3 spot, held by National. By referring to the No. 2 spot to gain empathy and understanding, through trying harder, Avis positioned themselves closer to Hertz (assimilation) and distanced themselves

When you're only No.2, you try harder. Or else.

Little fish have to keep moving all of the time. The big ones never stop picking on them.

Avis knows all about the problems of little fish.

We're only No.2 in rent a cars. We'd be swallowed up if we didn't try harder.

Avis can't afford to relax

There's no rest for us.

We're always emptying ashtrays. Making sure gas tanks are full before we rent our cars. Seeing that the batteries are full of life. Checking our windshield wipers.

And the cars we rent out can't be anything less than spanking new Plymouths.

And since we're not the big fish, you won't feel like a sardine when you come to our counter.

We're not jammed with customers.

In 1962. Avis lost $5 million. Then they told America they were the underdog. Who could resist? It was the David & Goliath legend on wheels. In 1965, Avis secured a profit of $5 million. And made Hertz wince. This is what good newspaper advertising can achieve. It is compelling, informative, and it works. Rent this page, and drive your point home.

PEOPLE READ NEWS-PAPERS

Source: Permission granted from Avis Europe Ltd, Bracknell.

Figure 4.12 Avis advertisement

further from National (contrast).

Thus 'we're only No. 2' brings the No. 1 position to the minds of the reader, not No. 3. The ability to move a brand closer to another is called *assimilation*, and to dissociate from another is called *contrast theory*. To make decision-making easier, consumers will seek to remove shades of grey and so perceive two brands as more similar than they are (assimilation) or further apart than they really are (contrast).

Sometimes this *assimilation-contrast theory* can be used to reposition between *product categories* rather than *brands*. Thus the Sony cassette deck is being assimilated with the quality of the compact CDs in Figure 4.13. As you can appreciate from these examples, repositioning may be achieved by refining the communications rather than the physical quality of a product. It need not always require changing the product itself at all.

Summary

Targeting, segmentation and positioning are closely related marketing techniques. There are few opportunities for successful mass marketing because most markets comprise members whose characteristics, needs or aspirations vary sufficiently to make provision of distinct offerings to smaller groups or segments necessary. Members of a segment will have similar needs, characteristics or aspirations, but be different from members of other segments. Once you have identified segments, a segmentation strategy needs to be developed. This can either be through a multi-segment strategy or a concentrated approach. A multi-segment strategy requires targeting two or more segments with distinctive marketing mixes. Great care has to be taken to ensure that segments are not in close contact with each other, since different price value offerings should be geared to each segment. When adopting this strategy, you should use separate distribution channels and different brand names.

With a concentrated approach, you would focus all your resources on providing an offering to a solitary segment. The danger is that you might over-rely on one segment, should your consumers' tastes change within that segment, so close vigilance is necessary.

For either of these strategies, you need to decide which segments to target. Targets must be reachable, accessible, identifiable and profitable. Niche markets or segments are more likely than mass marketing when the market size is large, market share and resources are low, market structure is fragmented or complex and the competitive intensity is high.

Consumer segmentation can be based on consumer characteristics such as demographics, geographical location, life styles, benefits and consumer purchasing patterns. Segmentation for organisations may include geographical location, size, SIC number, benefits and purchase behaviour. Consumer demographics include age, sex, race, family life cycle, social class and ACORN. You should consider cognitive age, if segmenting by age; and net income after accounting for expenses related to family and housing positions if using family life cycle. Social class relates to the income earner of the household, but you should not use it as a bold indicator of disposable income.

Geographical segmentation might be based on differences in terrain, climate and cultural diversity accounting for different needs. Often advertisers consider attitudes, opinions and activities when segmenting markets, conveying interests and life styles.

In the organisational market, you might consider behavioural usage patterns, because there are a smaller number of buyers, whose units of purchase may be

Figure 4.13 Sony advertisement

comparatively high, requiring prioritised targeting.

You should recognise that complex segmentation is a more realistic way of segmenting markets, using several tools in combination, such as several geo-demographic measures. These are becoming more sophisticated with improvements in database technology and networking. Complex segmentation allows you to provide a more precise offering.

After deciding on how your market will be segmented, the next stage is to decide on positioning. Positioning should be viewed from how your consumers *perceive* your offerings, which is not necessarily the same as *you* might think.

You should recognise two aspects to the art of positioning, *content* and *process*, which need to be unified. Positioning content involves examining all the ways the product could be positioned. This includes attributes (or characteristics), benefits (or consequences of consumption) and values or life's goals. In turn, attributes can be concrete (verifiable by test evidence and objective) or abstract (not possible to verify and subjective). Benefits can be functional (performance-related) or psychosocial (driven by what you feel personally or socially contrived). Values may be instrumental (preferred ways to behaving) and terminal (preferred way of being). Attributes can be determined by using the Kelly Repertory Grid. Salient, discriminating attributes or benefits, based on perhaps attitudinal ratings, can be used to identify:

1. a firm's product position on the map,
2. its main competitor's position,
3. the ideal or referent point (the preferred positioning of most consumers).

Strategies or processes can then be designed to bring a product's position nearer the ideal point. Alternatively, the ideal point can be shifted by using effective communications, justifying and emphasising the importance of benefits in favour of your product. It is also possible to add further salient attributes not hitherto used in communications, or to introduce a fighter brand to weaken the competition.

Positioning to a segment can sometimes be achieved by the very *absence* of attributes rather than inclusion or emphasis. It is also possible to enable consumers to associate two brands (or products) close to each other which are objectively quite different (assimilation) or vice versa (contrast). Targeting, segmentation and positioning, the basic tools of marketing, enable us to meet consumer needs more precisely. In order for us to offer appropriate offerings to our target segments, it is necessary to understand the factors that underlie consumer behaviour. This is the subject of the next chapter.

References

British Social Attitudes (1987), Aldershot: Dartmouth, p. 102.

Hart, C. and Davies, M.A.P. (1996) 'Consumer Perceptions of Non-food Assortments: An empirical study', *Journal of Marketing Management*, 12, 297–312.

Jain, S.C. (1975) 'Life Cycle Revisited: Applications in Consumer Research', Proceedings of the 5th Annual Conference of the Association for Consumer Research.

Jowell, R., Brook, L., Prior, G. and Taylor, B. (1992/3) *Social and Community Planning Research*, SCPR. Aldershot: Dartmouth.

Marketing (1986) 'What Makes a Lifestyle?', p. 24.

Mintel (1989) 'The Over 50s' (An Executive Summary).

O'Brien, S. and Ford, R. (1988) 'Can We at Last Say Goodbye to Social Class?', *Journal of the Market Research Society*, 30, 3, 289–332.

Olson, J.C. and Reynolds, T.J. (1983), *Understanding Consumers' Cognitive Structures: Implications for Marketing Strategy in Advertising and Consumer Psychology*, Volume 1, ed. Larry Percy and Arch Woodside. Lexington, MA: Lexington Books, pp. 77–90.

Worcester, R.M. and Downham, J. (1988) *Consumer Market Research Handbook*, 3rd edition. Maidenhead: McGraw-Hill.

CHAPTER FIVE

Consumer and Organisational Buyer Behaviour

Objectives

After studying this chapter, you should be able to:

1. Understand why consumer behaviour is important.
2. Recognise the main stages in the buying process.
3. Identify and understand how psychological and environmental factors influence buyer behaviour.
4. Understand what the motives are of different categories of shoppers, and offer different marketing programmes for each.
5. Distinguish between consumer and organisational markets.
6. Distinguish between the different types of organisational markets.
7. Understand the significant differences between both markets when making purchasing decisions.

Introduction

Why is stamp collecting no longer a popular hobby in Britain? Why do people switch from a particular brand of photographic film if they are happy with its performance? Why was a hotel worker sacked for turning on a central heating switch despite his shivering customers? Why do the British appear to favour cars with manual gearboxes instead of automatics? Why do supermarkets wash potatoes and then cover them in peat before selling them to customers? Why do department stores place mirrors near to lifts and escalators? Why does the

Meridian Bank Group sometimes make employees prepare deposit slips wearing spectacles smeared with Vaseline and count money with three fingers taped together?

The answers to these questions all reflect the growing importance of consumer behaviour. Consumer behaviour affects our daily lives. We cannot ignore it. Our hobbies (whether stamp collecting, photography or something else), our choice of car, our shopping activity, where we choose to eat out, the clothes we wear, the bank we patronise – all these decisions are influenced by consumer behaviour. Consumer behaviour is the study of how we, as consumers, behave. But it is not just overt behaviour that is important. Equally significant is the mental and *psychological* aspects which precede overt behaviour. This includes our perceptions and feelings, motives and personality, together with *environmental* aspects, such as family and peer group influence. In order for marketing management to gain more control over how their consumers behave, it is necessary to make predictions about how they behave.

Management can only make accurate predictions if they have a knowledge of how these psychological and environmental aspects affect purchase behaviour. By reading this chapter, you should be in a better position to predict future behaviour. The answers to the questions in the opening paragraph offer some clues as to how we might proceed.

A solution to the first question indicates the *dynamic* nature of consumer behaviour. Stamp collecting once flourished because of the enthusiasm displayed by youngsters, who then continued the hobby later in life. With the pervasiveness of modern technology, in the form of computer games and toys, stamp collecting now appears less exciting. This is also an example of how technological factors influence market demand, which we examined in chapter 2. We cannot afford to ignore the dynamics of consumer behaviour.

The second question is the basis of a popular examination theme: *Why does behaviour not always reflect attitudes?* Consumers may try another brand of film simply for a change (i.e. they become involved in *novelty-seeking behaviour*), or another brand may be on special offer to encourage trial purchase. Sometimes free film is offered for the cost of processing. Deals such as free samples are an example of *operant conditioning*. Offering an up-front reward has the expectation of future patronage with the promoted brand, providing there is satisfaction with it. *Scratch tests* used by perfumery companies in magazine advertising also use operant conditioning in the same way. There are many other reasons for possible brand-switching behaviour. For example, advice from a friend or sales assistant may persuade us to try a new brand. Such distractions at point-of-sale action are known as *situational factors*, influencing purchase behaviour.

Next, why are manual gearboxes, which are more difficult to drive than automatics, preferred in Britain? This seems to reflect British values, since Americans and Continental Europeans prefer automatics. It is an indication of a cultural quirk. *Culture* is a blueprint for a society: it reflects our basic norms, conventions and value systems, and ultimately affects our behaviour. An extreme viewpoint would be to accept that we are all trapped within our own cultures. One authority on the subject suggests that the British need to feel in control over their driving and are more at ease with what they are used to – the traditional manual gearbox. Such quirks are obviously important to car manufacturers when targeting a specific market.

For some religions, beliefs and customs may be particularly strong. For example, Jews may be penalised for offending the custom of working on the Sabbath, which is strictly holy for Orthodox Jews. In one case, a hotel worker was sacked for turning on a central heating switch, despite his customers shivering. This was a kosher hotel, and switching on a heater amounted to breaking the Sabbath rule. What this example demonstrates is that marketing people must be sensitive to the beliefs and customs of such groups if they are to be successful in doing business with them. Clearly, opening up for trading on the Sabbath in an orthodox Jewish area is likely to be met with resistance.

Have you decided yet why potatoes are treated in washed peat? The answer lies in how our *perceptions* affect our behaviour. Covering potatoes in peat conveys the perceptual effect of freshness, since we are more inclined to believe they have recently been picked, when in reality they might have been in storage for some time. Freshness is associated with a covering of soil. The key is for marketing to identify *positive associations* with stimuli. Supermarket retailers are here exploiting the *time proximity* principle. This principle states that certain activities tend to be associated together (around the same time).

Queuing for lifts has been a major problem for multi-storey department stores. By placing mirrors strategically at locations near queuing areas, the *perceived time* of waiting is reduced, since patrons pass the time looking at themselves, paying attention to grooming.

Consumers, of course, come in all shapes and sizes. Some are less fortunate than others and have disabilities such as arthritis. The old are particularly vulnerable, and need special treatment. The Meridian Bank Group, an innovator in staff training, uses *role play techniques*, to help their staff understand and appreciate how difficult it is for such groups to make simple banking transactions. Hence the Vaseline-smeared spectacles, simulating poor vision, and the taped fingers, giving an indication of the difficulties faced by those with arthritis.

Having considered the importance of consumer behaviour on our lives, it is necessary to examine some of the major influences in how consumers buy. The main factors in influencing buyer behaviour are examined, classified by environmental and individual influences. The stages in the purchasing decision process are then described. A central feature of this is the choice criteria consumers use in evaluation. Finally, the differences in the reasons for buying in the decision-making units and in the evaluation processes are explained for both consumer and organisational markets.

We start by examining a simple relationship between a stimulus and response in order to explain how consumers behave.

5.1 The stimulus–response model

The stimulus–response relationship is shown in Figure 5.1. *Stimuli* generate sensory inputs such as things we see and hear, touch, feel and smell. *Responses* are the resulting mental and/or physical reactions of individuals who are influenced by stimuli. Responses, of course, may be *mental*, or in the form of *overt behaviour*, as suggested in the introduction. Stimuli may be marketing or non-marketing oriented.

Q5.1 Make a list of all the marketing stimuli and responses you can think of. Read no further until you have done this. It should take 10–15 minutes.

A third category of variables, *intervening variables*, need to be understood. These include such features as culture, personality and group influence. Intervening variables are those factors that influence how the stimulus affects the response (see Figure 5.2). For example, an advertisement showing a scantily clad woman selling sun cream might be acceptable in one culture, but not in another. The culture might therefore influence the overall attitudes towards a product. Another factor is *group influence*, relating to social groups of people whose members share some common interest or purpose. They may have considerable influence on others. For example, a Women's Rights Group might protest against the advertisement just described, and so influence the actions of others. The decision by students to wear denim jeans to college may be influenced by what other people are wearing, and in particular their friends and peer groups, rather than reflecting the wearer's true personality. Where group influences are particularly strong, they can be exploited in marketing. For example, the intimacy of door-to-door selling, combined with strong group influence has been largely responsible for the success of party selling such as Tupperware (plastic kitchen containers) and Ann Summers lingerie.

Both responses and intervening variables can be recategorised as environmental and psychological or individual influences. The definitions of each are given in Table 5.1.

Culture and sub-culture, social class, group influences and situational factors are listed as environmental influences on consumer behaviour. Culture, group influences and situational factors have already been considered in this chapter. Social class was explained in detail in chapter 4. Psychological influences include our personality, self concept, learning, memory systems and our attitudes.

STIMULUS ━━━━━━▶ RESPONSE

Figure 5.1 Stimulus–response relationship

Table 5.1 Environmental and psychological/individual influences on consumer behaviour

Environmental influences

Culture: Is the blueprint that reflects norms, conventions and value systems for a given society.

Subculture: Is a segment of a given culture, e.g. a teenage or university student subculture might aspire to the latest fashions, music and vogue magazines.

Social class: In the UK, this is determined by the occupation of the chief earner of the household.

Group influences: Reference groups are social groups who are collections of people who share some common interest and purpose. They can exert considerable influence on others, e.g. denim jeans in universities appear to be the standard outfit for students. Other influences include the family and opinion leaders, particularly in influencing new product adoption.

Situational factors: A variety of situational factors affect buyer behaviour. In the store situation, this might include the presence of neighbours or sales assistants giving advice, in-store decor and 'atmospherics', and out-of-stock situations.

Individual characteristics:

Personality	Is a person's unique psychological make-up of traits or identifiable characteristics which, in combination, influence the way a person is likely to respond to various stimuli.
Self concept	How an individual views himself or herself.
Learning and memory	The consumer learns to build up brand or store loyalty for those goods which have satisfied in the past and switch from those in which experience has been unpleasant.
Attitudes	Measure the readiness to act in a particular way to a stimulus according to prior knowledge and feelings.
Motives	Is a reason for action directed towards achieving a desirable goal.

5.2 Psychological influences

5.2.1 Personality

The way we respond to day-to-day activities reflects our underlying *personalities*. In a classroom, for example, each student will have a *unique blend of traits* or combination of identifiable characteristics. The way in which we behave generally is influenced by a combination of innate characteristics and experience including our physique, intelligence, occupational training and social and cultural pursuits. Although it is very likely several people will share similar individual traits, the *combination* each has is unique to that individual. This explains why some people will find a comedian funny, whereas others don't (read the

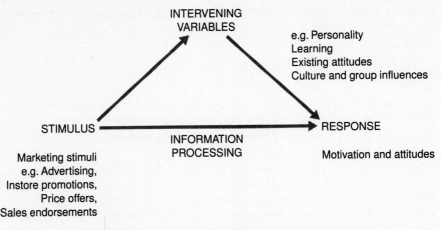

Figure 5.2 Intervening variables between stimulus and response

introductory example used in chapter 4). Trying to segment on the basis of personality profiles is difficult because although individual traits can be measured it is difficult to predict behaviour from unique combinations of them. Nevertheless, general personality profiles are built up for the purposes of psychographics or life styles segmentation, which were described in chapter 4. Certain traits have been used for assessing the suitability of recruits for marketing posts, e.g. the need for commitment, empathy and self-motivation are often asked for in sales positions.

5.2.2 Self-concept

Self-concept is how an individual views himself or herself, and influences the way we purchase in many markets. For items that offer a chance for us to express ourselves, self-concept can be important. Such *'conspicuous consumption goods'* might include our choice of beer we drink in a pub, the clothes we wear, our brand of watch, the car we choose to drive. The image of ourselves that we wish to create is exploited by advertisers when goods are displayed as *indices of power* or *social status*. Totems or social badges may be idolised such as a Gucci bag, a Rolex watch or a Mercedes car.

5.2.3 Learning and memory

A knowledge of how *learning* and *memory* operate is important to encourage favourable associations with certain stimuli, and to reduce the probability of

For example, if a brand is technically superior to the competition but is not accepted in the marketplace, consumers might have difficulty in understanding its benefits (i.e. evaluation of alternatives is perhaps difficult). For example, several makes of video recorder appear to be over-technical and over-elaborate for their purpose, with complex instructions.

You will return to this kind of problem later in the case study titled 'Freezecare'.

5.3.1 Problem recognition

The stages in the purchasing decision process can now be described in detail. Imagine you are in a state of tension between an ideal situation and an actual situation. This is called *problem recognition*. Applying this to ownership of goods (or lack of them) you are only likely to be aroused to take action if a sufficiently large discrepancy exists. You might feel sufficiently envious of your neighbour's new car to start acquiring marketing information on cars, for instance. This is the next stage – internal search.

5.3.2 Internal and external search

Internal search would involve you making a quick and largely unconscious review of your memory for stored information and experiences. Your attitudes and prior beliefs would form the basis of this stored information which you would draw upon to make brand preferences. If a sufficiently strong brand preference exists, a routine purchase occurs. It is likely, in the case of buying cars, that your internal search will not provide sufficient information about different makes of car, or indeed how to evaluate them, because you do not buy cars frequently and because of the high outlay involved. You will therefore be motivated to pursue *external search*. Marketing stimuli would include comments from dealers and friends, publicity and possibly test drives. You would then process this information by integrating it with your existing knowledge and experiences to derive meaning from it. That is why advertising managers are interested in finding out about what we, as consumers, already think. They can then predict our likely reactions to marketing stimuli. An illustration is the potential for lucrative profits that marketers can acquire by developing apparently simple product ideas. Imagine a certain liquid refreshment. Whilst it can be sold, targeted to 'yuppies' (young, upwardly mobile people in executive status), it can also be sold 'on tap' for a nominal price. What is it? Marketers have identified that a vast number of consumers believe that branded mineral waters are healthier than municipal tap water, and have presented high-priced offerings, with advertising to reinforce these beliefs. Their beliefs are not necessarily supported by available data; there are few government standards for bottled water, and in some cases sellers get their water from municipal suppliers and then give it extra treatment. Despite this, there has been a growth in the United States of about 500 per cent in bottled mineral waters between 1978 and 1988 (Loudon and Della Bitta, 1993).

5.3.3 Evaluation

The next stage leading to purchasing is the *evaluation phase*. Consumers may or may not use information from marketing stimuli on which to make their judgements, depending on whether they are motivated and have the ability to do so (Petty and Cacioppo, 1984). If they are not motivated, or are not able to use information presented (perhaps because it is too difficult to understand), they may use source effects as the basis of evaluation (such as what they feel about any endorser used, their perceptions of the attraction of the packaging, or the brand name or price as a cue of quality).

If consumers are sufficiently motivated and have the ability to use information from marketing stimuli, then the evaluation phase would involve you comparing the information gained in the search for alternative products to the product-judging criteria or standards you consider important. Using a multi-attribute model, you might consider that safety, 'looks' and performance are the most important criteria (called *salient beliefs*) and allocate them a score of +1, +3 and +2 respectively. In other words, 'looks' are the most important consideration to you in car purchasing, followed by performance, then safety. Next, you would evaluate each brand considered for purchase in terms of how well you considered it to achieve each salient belief. The range might be from +3 to −3, say. If you ranked safety as +2, 'looks' as +2 and performance as −1 for brand 'X', you would end up with a weighted score of +2 +6 −2 = 6. This would represent your overall attitude score towards brand X. In other words, the overall score A_0 is equivalent to the total brand scores $\Sigma b_i e_i$, in which each brand score is the evaluation score for each criterion (e_i) weighted by its perceived strength (b_i) (see Table 5.3).

The higher your overall attitude to the brand, the more probable it is that you are going to buy it. You might ponder on this and suggest that you do not usually calculate sums in your head when comparing/evaluating different brands. However, it is likely that you would use an approximate mental process when

Table 5.3 Calculating your attitude to a brand of car (brand X)

Salient beliefs or criteria	Strength of beliefs or criteria (b_i)	Evaluation score (e_i)	Brand score ($b_i e_i$)
Safety	+1	+2	+2
'Looks'	+3	+2	+6
Performance	+2	−1	−2

Overall attitude score, A_0 = +6

evaluating high involvement items (items that could incur a considerable loss to you, should you make a poor selection), although you may not allocate such precise scores to the beliefs and evaluation scores. (For a more detailed account of how consumers process labelling and packaging information, see Davies and Wright (1994).) Sometimes more heuristic methods are used such as screening out those brands which do not meet certain criteria or which convey specific negative attitudes.

5.3.4 Post-purchase evaluation

The final stage after purchase is called *post-purchase evaluation*. This is an important stage, because for many products the goal of marketers is to gain consumer loyalty.

If you have negative attitudes about a recent car purchase, it might be because you have subsequently seen competitive information, raising doubts about your purchase. Such a state is called *cognitive dissonance* (see Festinger, 1957) because your thoughts (cognitions) about the brand are not in line with your behaviour (since you have recently purchased it). This state of tension needs resolving. For some products when this happens, you might rationalise that the purchase was not very important anyway, suggesting you have little to lose having made a bad decision. This is unlikely for a car purchase (since outlay is relatively high) so you might screen out negative information about your product and collect and process only positive information (by paying particular attention to current commercials of the brand), thus supporting your original purchase. Alternatively, you might rationalise that competitive information, in conflict with your purchasing decision, comes from an unreliable source, or that the criteria used for comparison against your brand are not important to you. Any of these techniques will reduce cognitive dissonance, and so improve the chances of future loyalty.

That is why car manufacturers attempt to maintain relationships with their customers after a sale by circulating magazines with news about the latest products and offer owners the opportunity of joining exclusive car clubs, making the customer feel important.

Now read the case study Freezecare and answer the questions that follow.

Case study: Freezecare

Freezecare, a leading manufacturer of home freezers, suffered a gradual erosion of market share during 1992 to 1996.

Marketing research studies for the brand leader conducted with purchases over this period show a high degree of customer satisfaction with the product and with service provided by the distributors. Advertising was increased by 20% in 1994–5 with no apparent effect on sales. During the period 1992–96 market share decreased from 35.2 per cent to 29.6 per cent. All major competitors had increased their shares very slightly.

As Marketing Director of Freezecare, you must diagnose the cause of share erosion. You are already aware that home freezers represent a major purchase for consumers, involving an extended search, covering several weeks from problem recognition to the purchase decision. You have the results of a buyer intention study conducted in 1996 which are similar to previous findings. The study consists of a cross-section of consumers, indicating the following brand preferences among consumers who indicate they intend to purchase a home freezer within the next six months.

Consumer Brand Preference

Brand	Preference
Freezecare	39.5%
Brand X	21.3%
Brand Y	15.5%
Brand Z	12.6%
Others	11.1%

You have now scheduled a meeting with the marketing research director of the company. Possible research projects will be discussed at this meeting to identify the company's problem.

Q5.2(a) How do you interpret the discrepancy between market share held by Freezecare and consumer preferences for home freezer brands? At what stages of the buyer decision might there be a problem?

Q5.2(b) Which marketing variables are most likely to be the source of Freezecare's decline?

5.4 Consumer and organisational marketing

This section focuses on organisational markets. So far we have discussed buyer behaviour from the perspective of the individual or consumer. But purchase decisions can also improve the prospects of organisations as we briefly discussed in chapter 3.

Negotiating skills (as a buyer or as a seller) can be improved with a knowledge of the different motives between buyers in consumer markets and organisational markets. We begin by distinguishing between these two markets.

5.4.1 Reasons for buying

As suggested in chapter 4, buyers of products or services can be classified according to the *reason for buying*. You may recall that if you were to buy a computer for personal use and home entertainment so you or your children can gain direct benefits for themselves (e.g. pleasure, intellectual stimulation, etc.), then this is a *consumer market*. Alternatively, if you were intending to run a business from home, this becomes *organisational marketing*, since benefits are a means to an end: providing commercial advantage. Similarly, if you run a company and order 250 microcomputers or a computer network say, with the intention of building sophisticated databases or improving stock-ordering systems, this is clearly an advantage to your organisation rather than to you directly. Table 5.4 summarises the relationship between derived benefit from buying and type of market.

The second distinction involves the *type of buyer*. If you are buying a microcomputer for your children to play with, you are not purchasing as a professional buyer would. For a start, you would be unlikely to have the depth of market knowledge, expertise or responsibility that a professional purchasing officer would need to prepare large purchasing contracts. The *technical expertise* required of professional buyers can be appreciated by comparing advertisements of similar products in the commercial press with those intended for a mass market for consumers. You might compare the language used in your technical or specialist journals at work with that used for advertisements in daily newspapers. What does this tell you about the intended target audience for each? It is likely that the specialist journals will use far more technical language. This would not be successful if used in a daily newspaper.

5.4.2 Buyers in organisational markets

Having established the distinction between consumer and organisational markets, why is it important to identify buyers in organisational (or business to

Table 5.4 Reason for purchase in consumer and organisational markets

	Consumer	Organisational
	Microcomputer for home use	*Microcomputers for organisational use*
Possible benefits	Enjoyment or intellectual pleasure	For improvement of management systems
Motive	Self-gratification/ indulgence	To improve the firm's corporate goals, such as standing in the marketplace, efficiency or profitability

business) markets? You may recall from chapter 4 that generally there are *fewer buyers* in the organisational markets, so they can be traced more easily. Indeed, there is much to be gained by doing so, because a smaller number usually account for most of the demand. A whole market segment in the consumer market may be worth far less than a single customer in the industrial market. One consequence of this is that forecasting the demand for products intended for the organisational market becomes particularly important. The text box shows how potential demand can be estimated for dust control equipment.

Primary research conducted to assess market potential for dust control equipment

This requires an assessment of the demand by various businesses of various sizes and product/market portfolios who are in need of such equipment. An early stage on the research involves identifying the main decision-makers for dust control equipment. They can then be asked questions about their types of dust problems. Further research might identify (a) any site area where dust fumes or toxins are generated (b) the type of dust generated at work (c) the existence of any current dust control or extraction equipment (d) perceptions of the type of model which best matches the current model used by the company, and (e) the likelihood of any anticipated requirement for dust control equipment within the future, and when.

The principle of Pareto analysis, based on the relative importance of customers, has been adapted for managerial situations. In organisational buying, a large number of sales are sometimes attributable to a relatively small proportion of customers, sometimes referred to as the 80:20 rule (Figure 5.4).

Why does this pattern occur? Consider an organisation such as the Ford Motor Company. It is likely to purchase thousands of tyres at any time, so one order is far more significant than a single purchase in the consumer market. Whilst not all organisational markets are characterised by such heavy buying, those that are provide a profitable way for segmenting the market on the basis of past purchases as outlined in chapter 4. In other words heavy buyers should be prioritised for special treatment.

5.4.3 Who is involved in the decision-making process?

Another distinction between consumer and organisational markets is the *number of decision-makers involved* in influencing the purchasing process. If you were involved in buying microcomputers in the organisational market, your scale of

precise and thorough – relating not only to purchase price but cost of usage as well.

5.4.6 Summary of the purchasing steps involved in organisational markets

The stages in the purchasing function, the activities associated with each stage together with the likely decision-makers is shown in Table 5.5.

Remember, it is important to identify the decision influencers at the various stages of the buying decision.

5.4.7 Relationship marketing and financial performance

This section examines the differences between suppliers who are allowed *long-term relationships* with their buyers and those who are offered *transactional* approaches with their buyers. These contrasting approaches towards buyer seller relationships are shown in Table 5.6.

Table 5.5 Purchasing activities and decision-makers for different stages in organisational markets

Stage	Explanation of activity	Possible decision-makers
Problem recognition	An organisational need requires filling	Initiators, e.g. marketers
*Develop specifications	Decide what will solve problem/ fill need at acceptable cost	A decision-making unit may include discussion with: Influencers (e.g. Marketing/Design Engineers) Users Administrators
Search	Identify supplier list	Buyers, but Finance may authorise budget
Evaluation (*Complex vendor ratings)	Screen alternative suppliers based on specifications. Select on basis of a desirable quality and low cost	Buyers and possibly others
Purchase	Includes terms of purchase (credit, maintenance agreements)	Decider, e.g. Purchasing Director
Post-purchase	Compare performance to expectations in specifications. Users offer feedback to revise future specifications. Availability of spare parts may also be influential	Users/shop floor workers

*Stages additional to consumer market.

Table 5.6 Contrasting styles of business between transactional approaches and long-term relationships between buyers and suppliers

	Transactional approach	Long-term relationship
Supplier sourcing:	Extensive, and reaped to exploit separate opportunities	Selective, and nurtured to develop loyalties over the long term
Contract of exchange	Each contract is treated as a separate process	Each contract is treated as a part of the previous: as a continuous process of exchange

The transactional approach is a traditional approach to supplier sourcing, in which each buying opportunity is treated as a separate business decision. Owing to both buyer and supplier wishing to take advantage of each opportunity, it is likely buyers will choose from several suppliers, in which loyalty will not be a dominant feature in the negotiations. Consequently, a number of suppliers may be used. In contrast, a buyer may plan ahead with the purpose of developing an ongoing relationship with a few select suppliers. Each buying opportunity is treated as part of a continuous process, in which the relationship between buyer and seller grows. New business may arise from the relationship which would not be possible under a transactional approach.

The impact of relationship marketing on financial performance has been studied by Kalwani and Narayandas (1995). Their research indicated that suppliers experiencing long-term relationships with their buyers enjoyed greater sales, better rates of return on investment and lower stockholding costs, but suffered from lower gross margins in comparison to a matched sample of suppliers experiencing a transactional approach with their buyers. The lower gross margins may be explained by the downward pressure on prices brought about by buyers (who are in a relatively strong position with their suppliers). Suppliers may aspire to such relationships because it offers more security in future sales. Such suppliers are likely to invest heavily in aiming to please their customers.

Those suppliers enjoying long-term relationships with greater rates of return on their investment can be explained by cost reductions in their selling and administrative expenses arising from lower customer turnover, and greater customer satisfaction, leading to lower service costs such as trouble-shooting.

The lower stockholding costs associated with long-term relationships can be explained by more reliable forecasting (arising from greater stability in demand patterns) in contrast to the relative uncertainty of future business generated from a transactional approach. A summary of the impact of these relationships upon financial performance is recorded in Table 5.7.

Long-term relationships are not always best for organisations. Considerable inertia may exist in some markets, in which buyers may face a lack of choice in seeking alternative suppliers or vice versa. A purchaser may face considerable

Table 5.7 Impact of the relationship practice on financial performance of suppliers

Financial performance measure	Transactional approach	Long-term relationship
Gross margin	Higher	Lower
Sales	Lower	Higher
Rate of return on investment	Lower	Higher
Stockholding costs	Higher	Lower

Source: Adapted from Kalwani and Narayandas (1995).

switching costs in breaking away from an established supplier. These include considerable effort screening potential new suppliers, developing new contracts, developing trust in the relationship and confidence in the capabilities of the new supplier. Collectively these costs may deter an organisation from switching, even though it may hold reservations about its relationship with its current partners.

5.5 Different organisational markets

Organisational markets may also be subdivided according to the purchasing environment. Imagine you are buying goods for the purpose of making something of commercial value, or for use in commercial operations. These are classified as *producer markets*. So if you are buying computer hardware appliances in a producer market, their demand is *derived*, i.e. dependent upon the number of computers sold.

An example of a producer market is Nutrasweet, a non-fattening sweetener, 180 times as sweet as sugar, sold in bulk to food manufacturers, who in turn use it in the production of soft drinks and cereals.

If you were embarking on purchasing goods with the intention of reselling through a distributor, this would be a *reseller market*. All retailers, as distributors, buy with the aim of reselling, and so are purchasing in reseller markets. A key objective of manufacturers is to persuade retailers that their goods can complement the retailer's existing range of stocks. An example of a reseller market is Geest Industries, who buy fresh fruit and vegetables from farmers and small traders with the aim of reselling it.

Government markets reflect social demands bought by national and local governments, providing the public with education, water, energy, national defence, road systems, street lighting and health care services. For companies such as British Aerospace, the government may be the only customer.

Other organisations have charitable, educational, community or other *not-for-profit goals*, referred to as *institutional markets*. Examples include museums, universities, libraries, churches and hospitals. Charities often rely on *volunteers* or unpaid staff to provide services. In essence, there may be three target markets:

donors to attract money, *volunteers* and *users* of their services (those in need). Therefore, the marketing of charities and other institutional markets can be quite complex. Clearly it is important to identify these different types of organisational markets, because each may have a different set of *motives*.

The importance of what is offered will vary between consumer and organisational markets. *Personal selling* may be more important in some organisational markets where *interaction* is necessary to overcome technical *objections* and to explain the *complex* workings of technical products. If there is a heavy concentration of buyers, it makes sense to invest in personal selling to manage relationships. It would not be cost effective for sales people to target each potential individual in the consumer market, whose order value may be relatively very small. *Advertising* is more likely to be used to reach such large groups in the consumer market.

Q5.3 Make comparative judgements between producer and consumer markets on the basis of the criteria shown in Table 5.8. You should consider your answers as *general* responses, relative to each market. (For example, you may consider that the average order value of producer markets is relatively higher than for consumer markets.)

Q5.4 Read the case study on Carlton Valves. What are the problems in this producer market? Suggest ways they may be tackled.

Table 5.8 Comparison of purchasing influences between producer/industrial and consumer markets

Factor	Producer/industrial market	Consumer market
Importance of purchase		
Average value of each purchase		
Number of buyers in market		
Importance of *each* purchase in relation to the total market		
Risk and professionalism of purchasers		
Number of people influential in the buying decision		
Extent of rational buyer behaviour		
Type of demand – derived or direct		
Influences on marketing mix		
Degree of mass advertising		
Importance of packaging graphics		
Importance of personal selling		
Importance of functional attributes relating to products		

Case study: Carlton Actuator Stop Valves

Carlton Valves is a small company, located in old-fashioned premises in the north-west of England. They have produced high-quality stop valves for the last 50 years. Stop valves are designed to hold and control the transportation and storage of liquids of various viscosity, including hazardous substances such as fuming acids and toxic cocktails.

The management team comprises three directors and a Divisional Managing Director. There is a Sales Director, a Finance Director and a Director of Production.

Although the production process is predominantly batch production for mainstream customers, about 10 per cent of sales turnover is derived from *ad hoc* enquiries, mostly requiring a customised service. Some of these customers also require advice on new applications, which are then made to order. Currently no charge is made for this advice on design. Although this activity conforms to their business brochures, in so far as they claim to be able to supply any fitting of actuator valve, of any quantity, of any diameter, the stark fact is that jobbing production takes up more management time in troubleshooting, such as chasing up orders, and ordering spare parts from subcontractors, and consequently affects the bottom line of the financial statement. Although gross margins are better on customised products, net margins are lower than for many items made by batch production (despite the additional stockholding costs, since batches are often made to stock). The lower net margins arise from accounting for production overheads, administration and management time. One problem associated with producing one-off items is that the set-up time in setting the shopfloor machinery is costly, compared to batch production, normally associated with a single set-up for a long production run, making it more economic. However, production problems also exist with batches. Finished work can end up in storage, taking up valuable space, and work-in-progress may deteriorate if left unfinished in the yard. Some batches tend to generate more than the average number of defects, which ultimately slows delivery of finished items to customers.

Currently, any marketing is *ad hoc* and decisions tend to be reactive, as problems arise. A constant source of conflict is the daily disagreements between the Sales Director and Production Control. The Sales Director, Casper Wanamaker, requests orders on the shopfloor are prioritised in terms of importance of customer, whilst the production department tends to allocate production according to the most economic batch runs based on their resources at the time.

Carlton obtain business in several ways – they have a small budget of less than £40,000 for trade advertisements, and this generates some new enquiries. Leads are followed up by the Sales Manager. Existing customers tend to recommend Carlton to other customers, who in turn contact Carlton direct. They also attend exhibitions, which offer valuable feedback on competitive behaviour.

Over 50 per cent of Carlton's business arises from the chemical, petroleum and pharmaceutical industry. The Sales Director spends most of his time with key accounts in these industries.

Carlton have experimented in developing markets overseas. Many enquiries in Europe have not been converted into sales because prices are considered unreasonable.

The Managing Director is concerned by the increasing competitive threats from the Far East and Eastern Europe, who are able to undercut UK manufacturers by up to 30 per cent on certain valves. He is also concerned about the recent drop in profitability, and is considering hiring a marketing manager to generate new business. The Sales Director feels they must first investigate *who* their most profitable customers are. The Production Director is not convinced that some jobbing items are justified purely on the basis of satisfying very important customers.

Q5.5 How would you proceed and what advice would you offer?

Summary

Consumer behaviour is important to marketers because it affects our daily lives. It is a complex process, consisting of both observed behaviour (as we view it) and precursors to it, such as the mental processes of motives, attitudes and perceptions. These latter psychological influences, along with environmental components can be exploited by marketing. With a knowledge of these influences on consumers, various stimuli are presented or manipulated to influence future behaviour. For example, advertising messages can be used to influence attitude change. Sometimes marketing is less effective, owing to consumer exposure to too many competing stimuli (such as competitive advertisements), so there is a danger of confusion or even memory relapse. Marketers can attend to this by rehearsing exposures in a number of ways, by presenting vivid pictures or concrete images.

Consumer behaviour is also dynamic, highlighting the significance of a changing marketplace. Marketers cannot afford to ignore it.

The main stages in the buying process are problem recognition, search, evaluation, purchase and post-purchase evaluation. When deriving meaning from stimuli, consumers integrate their existing knowledge with new information that is actively searched for. Then an evaluation can be made. Remember the multi-attribute model. Evaluation is often based on weighting the ranked criteria, considered important to judge alternative brands, by each brand's ability to achieve them. The sum is then derived. The multi-attribute utility model assumes the brand with the highest score is the most preferred.

Favourable associations with a brand take the consumer one step closer to purchase. But marketers must also ensure that positive attitudes that help create a purchase are maintained at the post-purchase stage for many markets. If there is dissonance between attitudes and resulting behaviour, it must be resolved. This can be achieved by developing relationships with customers (e.g. by sending product literature). In many circumstances, it is more cost-effective to retain existing customers than to attract new ones.

Environmental influences include culture, group influences, and situational factors such as distractions at point-of-sale. The way we, as individuals, respond to both environmental and psychological influences reflects our basic personality traits. Shopping profiles have been classified according to one of several motives: rational value, empathy, sentiment/good citizenship, entertainment and convenience. These are called the economic, personalised, ethical, recreational/social and apathetic shopper respectively.

Buyers in the organisational market vary from those in the consumer market in several respects. There are relatively few organisational buyers, and their orders tend to be of higher value. Since these markets tend to be more technically oriented, accurate targeting with personal selling is a popular activity. Personal selling allows interaction and feedback, of vital importance when managing relationships with groups of powerful, professionally motivated buyers. Buying tends to be more systematic in the organisational market, often involving a multidisciplinary team of accountants, engineers and marketing staff, who may at various stages of the buying process, become more or less involved. The complexity is usually managed by outlining detailed specifications for what is considered appropriate to solve a particular problem, and following this up with a rigorous screening and evaluation phase called vendor rating. Price, as one criterion analysed in vendor rating, has a wider definition in the organisational market: it includes not only the purchase price but an examination of costs of production in using each product.

Alternatively, instead of treating each purchase decision separately, buyers may wish to gain longer-term relationships with some of their suppliers. Suppliers may gain significant financial benefits in increased sales, reduced stockholding costs and an improved rate of return on their investment.

In the consumer market, decisions may not rest on rational criteria alone. Advertising is a cost-effective way of communicating to these consumers who tend to be individually far less significant in terms of buyer power.

Organisational markets can be split up in to producer, reseller, governmental and institutional markets. The demand within each market is derived, requiring efficient forecasting systems to track demand. The ability to identify the different organisational markets is important because each has a different set of motives.

Producers and reseller markets are interested in the commercial value of the product, whereas the last two may consider social objectives more seriously.

References

Cannon, T. (1986) *Basic Marketing*. London: Cassell, 183–4.

Davies, M.A.P. and Wright, L.W. (1994) 'The Importance of Labelling Examined in Food Marketing', *European Journal of Marketing*, 28, 2, 57–67.

Dibb, S., Simkin, L., Pride, W.M. and Ferrell, O.C. (1994) *Marketing Concepts and Strategies*. London: Houghton Mifflin, 101.

Engel, J.E., Blackwell, R.D. and Miniard, P.W. (1993) *Consumer Behavior*. Chicago, IL: The Dryden Press.

Festinger, L. (1957) *A Theory of Cognitive Dissonance*. Evanston, IL: Row, Peterson.

Kalwani, M.U. and Narayandas, N. (1995) 'Long-term Manufacturer–Supplier Relationships: Do they pay off for supplier firms?', *Journal of Marketing*, 59, January, 1–16.

Loudon, D. and Della-Bitta, A.J. (1993) *Consumer Behavior, Concepts and Applications*, 4th edn. Maidenhead: McGraw-Hill.

Petty, R.E. and Cacioppo, J.T. (1984) 'Source Factors and the Elaboration Likelihood Model of Persuasion', *Advances in Consumer Research*, 11, 668–72.

Stone, G.P. (1954) 'City Shoppers and Urban Identification: Observations on the social psychology of city life', *American Journal of Sociology*, 60, 36–45.

CHAPTER SIX

Managing the Product in the Marketing Mix

Objectives

After studying this chapter, you should be able to:

1. Understand the key significance of a 'balanced' or integrated marketing mix in exchange relationships.
2. Appreciate how the product life cycle affects the type of marketing mix offered.
3. Understand why new products are required, and how they might be developed.
4. Plan for the future cash implications of new and established products.

Introduction

Although some earlier work is consolidated and reinforced here, a number of concepts are developed further. The material in this chapter is fundamental to *marketing strategy* and so requires your thorough understanding.

6.1 Managing the marketing mix

The marketing mix involves making decisions on the four Ps (product, place, price and promotion). The marketing mix must convey the desired *brand* or *product signals* and *messages*, focusing on the needs of the *target audience*. This is shown in Figure 6.1.

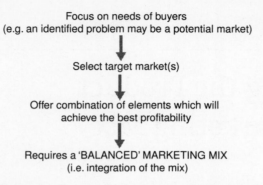

Figure 6.1 How marketing strategy is developed

Different 'offerings' or combinations of product features, prices, place (distribution policies) and promotion are aimed at different groups, in recognition of their distinct needs. This is the basis of marketing strategy. In the following chapters, individual strategies are discussed for each function of the marketing mix. Price and distribution are discussed in chapters 7–8. Marketing communications are examined in chapters 9 and 10. When developing a suitable strategy we use an appropriate marketing mix, which offer a combination of benefits designed to cater for the needs of the target audience.

Consider as an example the vast choice of universities which potential undergraduate students have. Several universities usually offer similar courses, so what makes an individual one special? Research conducted by Davies, Preston and Wilson (1992) suggests an important influence in undergraduate choice may be the distance of each university from the student's home. A favoured university should not be so near that parents can watch their every move, but not too far away that it would make the journey unbearably long to visit home (say, for Sunday lunch). However, this benefit is of little use unless the 'right course' is offered in the first place. The course is the key or 'core product' which the university can 'package' with secondary or supportive benefits, called the augmented product (see Figure 6.2). In an increasingly competitive market it is the ability to offer appropriate supporting benefits that may distinguish a successful product, in demand, from an unsuccessful one.

As improvements in technology enable competitors to copy the core benefits of products quickly the significance of getting the supporting benefits right for the target market should be appreciated. Most products on the market fail to distinguish themselves sufficiently to sustain a competitive advantage. This is often because supportive benefits of a product have been overlooked. In contrast, a university offering ample car parking space, campus accommodation, purpose-built buildings and varied sports facilities might influence overall choice when two or more courses are perceived to be virtually identical.

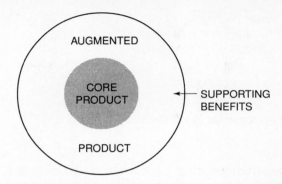

Figure 6.2 Relationship of core product to supporting benefits

Now consider another example. If you pay a premium price to choose a familiar airline (say, American Airlines, United Airlines or British Airways) to fly to New York for a holiday instead of using an unfamiliar carrier, what does that indicate about the values you place on service? Probably quite a lot. It would suggest that you consider service (whether in the form of extra comfort, cleanliness, friendliness or even security) as more valued than the extra premium you are paying, which could run in to hundreds of pounds. Although the 'core product' involves the destination from Heathrow to New York, say, in a relatively quick time, the augmented product, sold at a premium, is gauged by your perceived quality in service (such as extra seat space, offering more comfort or perhaps by reliability and peace of mind in flying with a well-known brand name). When an airline prices its products, it has to ensure enough demand to reach break-even, yet at the same time avoid a poor image by cutting prices too low. A mixture of *price* and *non-price factors* influence perceived quality. Non-price factors include mix factors not attracting custom by relying on price, such as the quality and use of advertising (see Figure 6.3).

Consider the delicate balance in the way the offering is perceived by manipulating marketing mix elements. If there is too much advertising, there may be over-full demand and, with only a finite capacity of seats on any one flight, a likelihood of complaints. Cutting prices too far might damage quality perceptions. Therefore all aspects of the product must be mutually supported. When brand managers steer their brands to ensure each decision on the marketing mix reinforces every other, this is referred to as a '*balanced*' or '*integrated*' mix.

Now apply this rule to a particular product. Consider an appropriate 'balanced' mix for a cheap, throw-away watch (say purchase price £8, designed to have a working life of 5 years). Who would stock it? How would it be packaged? What about after-sales service? What might be the reason for the purchase?

It is likely that the product would have little symbolic value and be based on utility. I once bought such a watch at an airport as a distress or emergency

Figure 6.3 Price and non-price factors in the marketing mix

purchase because I had forgotten to bring my normal watch with me. In this context, the throw-away watch is acting as a *convenience product*. How might this affect stockists? Availability is important, so many outlets should stock it; this is called *intensive distribution*. My purchase was enclosed in a blister pack displayed on a wall rack – hardly luxurious, but certainly functional. After-sales was non-existent. The producers could hardly support after-sales with such a low purchase price. Also, since it has a fixed life, after-sales would be unnecessary.

When all elements of the marketing mix reinforce each other, the total effectiveness on the brand is greatly improved over and beyond the combined effectiveness of elements if they were isolated. Thus, a successful company with a prestigious reputation for well-made products and strong branding will normally find it easier to introduce new products associated with its name than an unknown company of moderate standing. The same can be said for reputable stores offering new merchandise. Such an effect is sometimes referred to as the 2 + 2 = 5 effect, or *synergy*, in which the overall combination is greater than the sum of the isolated parts.

Davidson (1972) distinguishes two ways in which marketing offerings may be developed; by *market-led marketing*, starting with the needs of the market and by *asset-led marketing*, in which company assets are considered as the starting point. With asset-led marketing, payback return on the original investment is usually quicker because, by attempting to make best use of what the company already has, the investment is comparatively low. Notice that asset-led marketing is *not* the same as production orientation, described in chapter 1. Asset-led marketing is being marketing-oriented with the resources you already have. It is still focusing on the needs of the customer, but the risk is lower because initial investment is based on how the company can make better use of its existing resources whilst satisfying consumer needs. With production orientation, needs are not researched and customer focus is lost. The distinction between market-led marketing and asset-led marketing is indicated in Table 6.1.

An example of asset-led marketing is demonstrated by Bic, manufacturers of low-quality, low-unit cost, disposable razors, diversifying from pen manufacturing using their plastic technology. This product offers convenience to the consumer.

Read the case study 'The Chips are Down' and answer the subsequent

Table 6.1 Market-led and asset-led marketing

	Market-led marketing	**Asset-led marketing**
Start point	The market	Company assets
Risk	High	Lowish
Investment	High	Low
Payback	Typically 3–5 years	1–2 years

Source: Adapted from Davidson (1972).

questions, assuming the role of the Marketing Director of Crackle-Pop. Present your answer to (a) in the form of a checklist of problems with contributory reasons/explanations.

Part (b) requires a list of objectives, designed to tackle each problem identified in Part (a). This case study provides an example of what can go wrong if there is an imbalanced marketing mix. A secondary objective of the case is to enable you to appreciate how marketing must interact effectively with other departmental functions (such as finance and production) in order to be successful. It therefore reinforces the role of integrated marketing.

Case study: The chips are down

At the Annual General Meeting, the Chairman of Crackle-Pop, a leading manufacturer of crisps in the UK, remained cautious about expanding into new flavours, shapes and package sizes (see the data presented in Appendix 6.1).

Consumer tests in which the consumer could see the package and identify the brand revealed that this product was regarded as old-fashioned and dull, appealing to people over 45 who purchased them in pubs. One director quipped that they would go down well with some brown ale! By comparison, a leading competitor, Tastee Tips, was described as having a younger, modern image, appealing to children, teenagers and young housewives who would purchase the product in grocery outlets and confectioners. Only 40 per cent of retail outlets stocked more than one brand.

Tastee Tips had invested enormously since 1991 in capital equipment designed to be less labour-intensive. The new machinery installed meant that production runs were less likely to be held up, so enabling lower costs per unit to be passed on to the trade. This, together with new packaging technology, encouraged retailers to display the Tastee Tips brand. Shelf life of Tastee Tips had been improved, allowing extension to areas previously not covered, giving the brand national distribution. Trade dissatisfaction with Crackle-Pop, by contrast, meant that confectioner, tobacconist, newsagents began to destock. Tastee Tips are also offered in new film packs, providing better visibility of the product at point of sale.

To promote selling in (the task of selling to the trade or middleman before the ultimate consumer market), the management of Tastee Tips offered a wide variety of schemes designated to maintain wholesaler interest in the brand. Crackle-Pop, however, was only offering discounts to warehouses buying ten cases at a time (minimum order quantity).

The media expenditure for both companies is shown in Appendix 6.2 and a user profile in Appendix 6.3. Presently, the price of each brand has remained similar but Crackle-Pop reckon extra advertising would require increasing their price 1p above the standard pack price of Tastee Tips. Moreover, the firm was unlikely to break-even if a major investment programme was pursued although this was based on forecasted sales.

Q6.1 (a) You are the Marketing Director of Crackle-Pop. Present a case to your Chairperson, summarising current problems facing Crackle-Pop as if they were being presented to the remaining Board of Directors.

(b) The Financial Director has been critical of your Department in the past and suggests there is little money available for future investment. Suggest possible options open to the Marketing Department.

Appendix 6.1 Market share percentage of crisp market by company brand, 1992–93

| | Company/Brand name | |
Date	Crackle Pop	Tastee Tips
1988	15	0
1989	40	1
1990	50	14
1991	57	22
1992	61	27
1993	55	36

Appendix 6.2 Media expenditure by company

Medium	Crackle Pop	Tastee Tips
TV	£555,000	£1,500,000
Press	£ 75,000	£ 10,000
Billboards	£240,000	£ 220,000

Appendix 6.3 User profile of crisp market (%)

Age range	Crackle Pop	Tastee Tips	Heavy users of crisps (10+ per month)
15–24	12.2	24.2	27.9
25–34	11.3	18.5	21.0
35–44	23.5	17.3	17.3
45–54	32.0	15.9	17.1
55–64	20.2	13.2	10.8
65+	0.8	10.9	5.9
Socio-economic class			
AB	9.4	20.4	8.7
C1	18.9	21.2	15.4
C2	22.5	28.2	40.3
D	34.8	16.5	33.7
E	14.4	13.7	1.9
Sex			
Male	50.6	41.0	44.0
Female	49.4	59.0	56.0
	100.0	100.0	100.0

Q6.2 'The Marketing Mix' in the text box is a sentence completion exercise. Fill in the blanks, using the list of words below. Use each word once only.

Personal Selling	Synergy
Mass	Exclusive
Quality	Industrial
Consumer	Luxuries
Finance	Intensive
Reliability	High
Research	Boom
Low	Slump
Under	Over

The marketing mix

A marketing mix must be designed with its target in mind. Without it, a mix has no value.

Consistency of the mix
Getting one aspect of the mix 'right', such as high prices designed for exclusive, high-income groups, might be one step towards success, but is not sufficient alone. Getting all aspects right (product, place and promotion) will reinforce each other, offering _____ .
   A premium priced product, designed for an exclusive market, needs its image reinforcing by selecting exclusive distribution channels and perhaps better than average customer service.

Rules of the marketing mix

1. *Ensure there is a target market*
   _____ will indicate if there is a specific need for particular performance specifications.
   Promote that which is needed, distribute that which is required (based on sales forecasts).
2. *Communicate the right message to each target audience*
   Advertising a price reduction will not necessarily convince existing customers to re-purchase what they considered to be a(n) _____ product. However it may be deliberate policy if the firm is attempting to widen the market, say to _____ appeal.
3. *Be sensitive to the quality/value association in the promotional mix*
   The 'value' spent in packaging and/or advertising, together with customer service, should reflect the _____ expected in that market. For example, an expensive perfume is unlikely to sell well in a shabby brown box with plain cellophane glued to it. Equally, a high quality product is wasted if sales assistance is considered rude or indifferent since the company image is adversely affected.
4. *Be sensitive to the quality/value association in distribution*
   The distribution policy selected should be based on the required image expected at point-of-sale to the end-user. For example, there is little point in spending millions in creating an advertising image for a well-made product if the *agent* or *distributor* is careless in transit, or the quality packaging designed to reinforce the exclusive image is damaged at point-of-sale. Clearly the manufacturer should take time to screen carefully more selective and prudent distributors.

5. *Assess the balance between under/over-servicing*
   Price is often reflected by quality but sometimes quality is reflected by price, e.g. management training. Some marketers make the mistake of ___ pricing markets in which there is healthy demand and sustainable premium pricing. For example, at the luxury end of the car market, in some cases there are three-year waiting lists. Over-servicing the needs and expectations of the target audience may cost the firm revenue, but so too can under-servicing (e.g. cutting short on customer service such as dealer networks, trained sales advisers, frequent stockouts, late deliveries and poor packaging).
   Promotional schemes should be geared to the type of market.

6. *Promote that which is readily available*
   Something that is mass advertised should be available to everyone in most retail outlets (i.e. ___ distribution). Alternative promotions should be used for goods that are not reachable or affordable for most people. For example, Rolls-Royce Motors use sponsorship.

7. *Promotions should be geared to customer expectations*
   If and when a product is advertised with profound claims, the product (benefits) should live up to those expectations when used by consumers.

8. *The relative importance of each marketing mix element will depend upon the intensity of price elasticity of demand governing the market situation*
   This may explain why the prices of postcards, swimsuits, etc., may be increased the nearer you are to a holiday resort or tourist spot, especially in the peak season. It also depends upon the type of market. (See chapter 5 on consumer versus organisational markets.)

9. *Consider your existing heritage*
   ___ quality products can be launched as a platform for cheaper versions in the future. The reverse, to trade-up and gain higher margins, is more difficult to justify. Consider why.

10. *Trade according to the economic situation*
    In _____ times, the market potential for ____ and premium priced products is usually higher. In recessions, major markets often trade down. In the UK recessions of the late 1970s/early 1980s, and late 1980s/early 1990s, advertising budgets were sharply reduced as manufacturers rationalised and looked for productivity improvements.

11. *Be aware of non-price factors in organisational markets*
    The Purchasing Officer may adopt conservatism and loyalty against price cutting, due to the inherent risks involved in

switching sources of supply (e.g. uncertainty as to delivery and quality performance standards). The risk is influenced by the level of expenditure, where even minor adaptations to meet consumer needs might become a hedge against aggressive price competition. For example, a warranty reduces buyer risk. Smaller organisational markets may, however, be more sensitive toward price.

In government markets, potential suppliers will be invited to tender only if their products or services can be shown to satisfy objective performance tests. This indicates the relative importance of non-price factors in these markets.

Integration can therefore:

    (a) Satisfy the intended target audience.

    (b) Build and sustain a competitive advantage.

Further differences between producer (industrial) and consumer markets

For manufactured parts in producer markets which have fewer uses, there may be *fewer buyers*. However, each *purchase order* may be *very high*, indicating the *importance of every buyer*. The *Pareto Rule* suggests that perhaps 80 per cent of *industrial market value is accounted for by 20 per cent of customers* so it is important that these are identified specifically.

Relationship of buyer behaviour on the marketing mix

Mass marketing techniques (advertising, widespread distribution channels) are clearly inappropriate for many _____ markets. Instead, _____ is important, particularly if the product is very technical. Items of high unit value also carry a *greater degree of price flexibility* (e.g. credit leasing, discounting and after-sales service).

Furthermore, the *rational behaviour of the industrial buyers* means that *performance factors are critical*, whereas those resting on psychological components (e.g. packaging graphics) are less appropriate. Remember: in _____ markets, the buyer is more likely to purchase impulsively.

6.2 The product life cycle

In chapter 2, we outlined the dynamics of a changing marketplace. One outcome of this is the way product demand will change over time. You can probably remember several examples of products which were successful but are now no longer available in the market. The reality is that virtually every product currently available will become obsolete in the future, making a strong case for *new product development* (see section 6.3). Marketers have followed the performance of products over their market life, called the *product life cycle* (PLC), and have identified five main stages. These are *pre-launch, introduction, growth, maturity* and *decline*. As a product moves through its life cycle, objectives and strategies relating to the marketing mix will need to be re-assessed and possibly changed to adapt to new forms of competition. By appreciating the typical progress of a product through its life cycle, we are better able to maintain profitable products and drop unprofitable ones. This section begins by examining each stage of the life cycle, and the implications for marketing management adopting suitable strategies at each stage.

6.2.1 The pre-launch stage

The pre-launch stage occurs prior to the introduction of a product on the market. Since there are no sales at this stage, and costs could be considerable (such as research and development and commercialisation costs), profits are well below zero. Because of the financial risk involved, it is necessary to project future returns over the life cycle of the product and assess the payback time (the time it takes to pay back the original investment). Owing to the uncertainty of market success (only about 10 per cent of new products are commercial successes) a series of probabilities are sometimes attached to different scenarios, projecting the optimistic and pessimistic rewards. If it is decided to enter the market, it is important the new product has the backing of everyone involved. Without this commitment, it is unlikely to succeed.

6.2.2 The introduction stage

Once a decision has been reached to launch the product and it appears on the market, this is called the introduction stage. This and the following stages are illustrated in Figure 6.4.

The immediate marketing objective is to persuade stockists to try out the new product. If the product is from a well-known company, strong in branding, this is relatively easy compared to an unknown one, who may have to offer substantial incentives to gain shelf space (see chapter 9 on trade promotions). Furthermore, there is always the possibility that the new product is not accepted by consumers. This possibility can be reduced by communicating the benefits of it (over the existing competition, if any) since these benefits may be unfamiliar. Informative advertising is also useful to emphasise where the new product can be found, if this is not obvious. This is most applicable to shopping and speciality goods, which are not extensively distributed.

If the product being launched is radically new (compared to introducing a new brand), there will be little or no competition to start with. The firm therefore has a head start in attempting to gain market acceptance as quickly as possible, but the necessary costs in advertising, publicity, sales promotions and distribution will mean that profits are still negative.

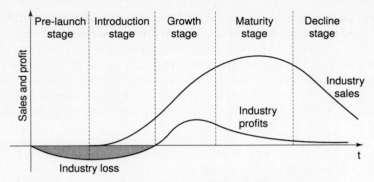

Figure 6.4 The stages of the classic product life cycle model

Pricing may be deliberately high to absorb some of those costs quickly, and to attract the innovator and early adopter segments of the market – opinion leaders who are willing to try the latest products and experiment in contrast to the typical mainstream consumer who may be more concerned about the price. When prices are intentionally high at the introductory stage of the life cycle, it is known as *price skimming* and when intentionally low to capture high sales, it is referred to as *penetration pricing*. (Refer also to section 7.1, pp. 187–93.)

6.2.3 The growth stage

If there is significant market acceptance, sales will rise rapidly (probably at an accelerating rate), profits will begin to emerge, reach a peak and then start to decline. This is the mark of the growth stage, characterised by products with a high price–earnings ratio. The growth stage is critical to a product's survival because competitive reactions to its success during this period will affect its life expectancy. It is possible that early success will attract intensive competition in the market and, at this stage, profits will start to erode because of the need to increase promotional expenses and possibly cut prices to retain loyalty. Promotions can help differentiate a product from the competition by helping to give it a brand personality.

6.2.4 The maturity stage

At the maturity stage, the sales curve peaks to a plateau, then starts to decline, with profits continuing to fall. This stage is typified by intense competition, in which weaker brands are eliminated from the market. During this period, many buyers will be well informed about the benefits and functions of the product.

Apart from using promotions and advertising to remind and reinforce the benefits of a given product, an alternative option is to improve the product to extend its life. Figure 6.5 demonstrates product extension strategies. Product extension need not necessarily involve development of radical new ideas arising from an invention, but will more likely be an adaptation of a current product (see Table 6.2). When inventions are commercially developed, or existing products are modified to improve the benefits offered to consumers, they are known as innovations.

Thus when Mars introduced M and M's in 1988 to compete head-on with Rowntree's Smarties (chocolate beans), a new, blue-coloured Smartie was introduced to rejuvenate interest and regain Rowntree's lost share. Rowntree counteracted with market development to attract older children, by presenting computer graphics in their advertising. Similarly, the sales of Reckitt & Colman's Dettol (a liquid antiseptic) were reducing by around 2 per cent per annum owing to the new competition of new pre-packed sterile items offered to its sizeable hospital market. Reckitt & Colman counteracted this by developing a range extension including Dettol Bubble Bath and a Dettol kitchen cleaner, both for

Table 6.2 Types of new product

Inventive	Unique products for which there is *a real need not being met by an existing product*, for example, a cancer drug or a product to rejuvenate body skin. Another example is the telephone.
Adaptation	Significantly different variations on existing products, for example, calculators with a memory. Another variation is changes in packs, styles, designs or colours. For example, a company can appear to be more environmentally friendly by converting to non-CFC plastics (less harmful to the ozone layer).
Imitative (me-too)	Products copied from competition. Often highly competitive markets. For example the Tesco supermarket chain launched a new spread called 'Unbelievable' in direct competition with Van de Bergh's 'I can't believe it's not butter'.

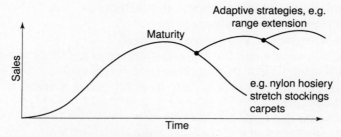

Figure 6.5 Product extension strategies

household use. The kitchen cleaner was a response to publicity given to listeria and salmonella poisoning. In each case, Reckitt & Colman capitalised on the brand heritage of the parent family brand (Dettol) and retained the sword symbol, conveying trust and confidence.

6.2.5 Decline stage

If there is total market saturation for a product, there may be little choice but to remove a product from the market. Rapidly falling sales, typical of the decline stage, may reflect this. Only products should be retained which:

(a) offer a positive contribution towards fixed costs;
(b) remain compatible with the remainder of the range offered.

At this stage, the remaining products will appeal to a different group of people from those at earlier stages of the life cycle, requiring a different marketing mix. Late adopters to the market will probably be more motivated by bargains and so price appeals may predominate. In some cases, an entire distribution channel may be eliminated if it does not contribute sufficient profits. Advertising expenditure is now at a minimum.

The objective is to reap the cash benefits of such products to reinvest for future new products, so there is always a steady balance of products across the life cycle in the firm's portfolio.

Q6.3 Figure 6.6 shows a product life cycle. Use the diagram to answer the following questions:
  (a) Where do sales begin to take off? Mark point A where sales begin to increase at an increasing rate.
  (b) Where do sales begin to fall off? Mark point B where sales begin to increase at a decreasing rate.
  (c) Mark point C, the plateau of sales. What decisions should be made here?
  (d) Separate the stages into phases of:
  (i) launch, (ii) growth, (iii) maturity, (iv) decline.
  (e) When is profit likely to develop?
  (f) When are costs likely to exceed revenues?
  (g) Explain at what stages the following strategies are likely to happen
      (i) sales promotions to encourage trial purchase
      (ii) high advertising expenditure to differentiate a brand from the competition
      (iii) product deletion
      (iv) range extension

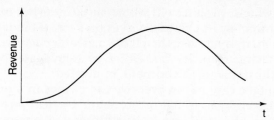

Figure 6.6 A typical product life cycle

Using the product life cycle in practice

The PLC theory suggests that if management can identify the stages a product has reached in the life cycle, this would indicate possible marketing strategies (i.e. how the marketing mix might be implemented). In practice, management will experience difficulties in identifying when a product is likely to move on to the next stage of the life cycle. Relying on projections of historical sales and profits (from which the PLC is derived) may offer guidance as to future courses of action to follow, but it cannot prescribe the best course of action, if used in isolation. There is a danger management may miss important changes in the market.

Understanding the current position facing a product, and how to proceed, requires identifying the underlying influences of market demand, their probabilities of occurring, and the effects of these influences on the product must be estimated. This requires considerable managerial judgement and intuition, beyond the scope and function of a single model. Contributing to these influences are the current environmental factors that impede or accelerate progress.

The stark reality is that few products follow the classic or typical 'S'-shaped life cycle curve, as outlined in most marketing textbooks. Consider fads, characterised by explosive growth, followed by an equally rapid decline with little or no maturity stage of significance. Examples of products classified as fads that for a relatively short time were extremely popular were the Hoola Hoop and the Rubic Cube. Conversely, some products that have been well branded have remained in the maturity stage for decades. Examples include Kit-Kat, Mars Bars and Guinness.

The life cycle theory does not offer recommended times to help management in identifying each stage of the life cycle. For that, management must consider the buying characteristics of their market and their competitive position. For example, some industrial durable or consumer durable products are easily prone to saturation. Consider the replacement sales for a bell foundry: these are somewhat limited by the durability of the product – bells can survive a millennium! Under such circumstances, sales may be largely restricted to repairs and maintenance. In other markets, such as fast-moving consumer goods, repeat patronage on a frequent basis may be necessary for survival, in which competitive activity may influence managerial decisions rather more than a product life cycle.

Indeed, the general pattern which a product will follow can be more influenced by the commitment given to it than by its current market position. If management believes in a product and *wants* it to succeed, then it has a greater chance of doing so. For example, a brand facing maturity can either be rejuvenated with an injection of managerial enthusiasm and investment, or deleted.

Management must also take care not to over-react to swings in a product's fortunes. If sales are influenced by seasonal or economic cyclical factors, the turning point on the product life cycle may be misinterpreted. Seasonal data involve significant differences in purchases that follow in certain months of the year on a regular basis. For example, ice-cream sales are low in winter, high in summer.

Cyclical activity involves long-term economic trends spanning several years, which increase sales during periods of high economic growth (or boom times) and conversely decrease rapidly when faced with a slump or recession. In projecting three months' sales data of ice-cream, a strong seasonal component which increases sales by 50 per cent might be concealed. The true picture of the underlying trend, adjusted for seasonal variation, might paint a different picture, such as a slowly declining market.

Longer-term projections of historical sales data may also be misinterpreted if cyclical activity is not accounted for. In boom times the sales of many discretionary and luxury markets improve; conversely, in a recession they contract. Unless seasonalities and cyclical activities are accounted for when determining sales trends, the performances of products will not be analysed properly and mistakes will be made in the implementation of marketing mix strategies.

Assuming management is able to identify the various stages on the life cycle for its product mix, another problem facing management is to decide how quickly to implement a new strategy as a product turns from one stage to another. The theory would suggest that implementation is immediate, because no transitional stages are described, but this is both impractical and impossible. For example, it is not possible to convert from an extensive distribution network to a more selective one overnight by virtue of the product turning into maturity! Perhaps it is best to interpret the stages of the PLC as a continuum, requiring slow evolutionary changes in strategies as a product moves gradually from one stage to the next. This appears a more realistic model from which to work.

6.3 The stages in new product development

Why do so many new products fail? As we discussed in chapter 1, prior market research into consumer needs is vital before embarking on large-scale production. Yet most new products fail because of a lack of investment in research, as demonstrated by the failure of the Sinclair C5. New products vary in their degree of novelty from those which already exist. Most new products are adaptations or improved modifications of existing products. Almost all new cars, for instance, are modifications on style and performance from previous models. Even a pack revamp to reposition a product could be considered a new product. However, the risk in consumer acceptance is still great.

At the pre-launch stage of the life cycle, before a product is introduced, we need to consider six phases of new product development. These are idea generation or *ideation, screening, business analysis, product development, test marketing* and *commercialisation*. A product may be dropped at any stage along the way to commercialisation.

6.3.1 Ideation

Ideation is usually managed by developing systematic approaches to generating new product ideas. Sometimes project teams involving different layers of management across different functional disciplines are encouraged to stimulate ideas through brainstorming. We can also identify latent needs by asking our buyers, distributors, sales staff or customers what problems they experience with our products currently on the market. Many entrepreneurs have become successful this way. Some firms such as 3M and Hewlett Packard encourage ideation by devoting a percentage of employee time (at certain grades and disciplines) for developing new ideas on a regular basis.

6.3.2 Screening

Those ideas considered to have potential are then screened for compatibility with organisational objectives, resources, buyer needs, production, marketing know-how and environmental fit. Some ideas may be tested for consumer reaction at this phase, known as concept tests. Concept tests are important for ascertaining the most appropriate benefits/appeals to meet the needs of the specific target market.

6.3.3 Business analysis

Those options that are successfully screened are then analysed for their ability to contribute towards profitability. This requires a thorough business analysis to forecast demand. Another aspect is to assure the new product idea will be financially viable. A break-even analysis is conducted (i.e. a projection is calculated as to how many sales are required to cover all costs associated with the project, including research and development). Only if forecasted demand exceeds the break-even point, will the project be estimated to be profitable.

Also important is an assurance that the intended new product will not take sales away from the existing product portfolio. When sales of a new brand affect the existing range adversely, this is known as *brand cannibalisation*.

6.3.4 Product development

Product development is the next phase. We need to ensure it is technically feasible to produce our new product at a low enough cost to make the final price reasonable. At this stage, we need to develop the idea or concept into a fully working model or *prototype*. We can then test the prototype on consumers to assess its positioning in terms of tangible and intangible attributes associated with it (i.e. as perceived by consumers). In particular, consumer response to the product and how they might use it are of paramount importance. Where state-of-the-art technology is important, such as the competitive field of designing racing bikes, expert opinion may be critical. Giant Bikes (UK Ltd), for example, use top professional cyclists to help design improvements, including the design that won an Olympic Gold for Chris Boardman in Barcelona.

6.3.5 Test marketing

Test marketing involves introducing the new product to a restricted market area to determine the reactions of buyers before launching to the total target market. A restricted launch in a natural setting offers us the chance to get things right without the expensive embarrassment of trying to correct a nation-wide blunder.

Test markets may also be used to experiment with different aspects of the marketing mix. For example, price sensitivity could be tested by offering different price points in two different test areas, keeping other mix elements constant. Some marketers believe test marketing can be counterproductive, because it provides the competition with too much information about future plans. For this reason, some marketers use *simulated test markets* geared to, say, particular promotions such as trial offers in participating stores. Respondents use the product at home and are then asked a series of questions about the new product, from which subsequent positioning decisions may be made. Alternatively, the manufacturer's brand may be shown with competing brands during a slide presentation and questions asked. This offers the advantage over normal test marketing in that competitors are not aware of the new launch. Test markets may be run in the future using virtual reality.

Although test marketing has been traditionally associated with testing at the final product stage, Burke (1996) suggests that advances in computer graphics and 3-D modelling offer to bring simulated test marketing to the earlier stages of marketing planning, such as in improving the screening of new ideas. This can be achieved by allowing the marketer to create the atmosphere of a store environment (with products stocked on shelves) on a computer screen. This is referred to as a virtual store (since it attempts to mirror the reality of the market). Software now exists which offers the shopper the opportunity to view a virtual store from all angles (including marketing stimuli such as ads, packaging, etc.). Consumers can shop by picking up packages and purchasing goods by touching various images on the screen. In turn (without the consumer knowing) a computer can record the amount of time a consumer spends shopping in each product category, aisle, the type of products purchased and how the consumer moves about the store.

By altering the store layout and variables (e.g. brands stocked, prices, promotional offers) information can be gained on what merchandise to stock, how much to stock and where it should be stocked. According to Burke (1996), this technique is far more flexible and cheaper than traditional simulated test marketing since little cost is incurred in redesigning the store layout electronically.

6.3.6 Commercialisation

The final stage in new product development is called the commercialisation phase. Plans for a full-scale launch are now fine-tuned, estimating demand and refining the marketing mix in line with the results from the test marketing stage.

6.4 Managing the cash resources of the product mix

NPD is important since, like a football team, no product has a divine, everlasting privilege to reign supreme. Hence the requirements for continual reinvestment for the needs of tomorrow. The dynamics of the marketplace and the increasing progress of competitors indicate that firms need continually to innovate and develop new products. But in chapter 1, you may recall that a constraint on a marketing orientation was the limit of its own resources. Realistically, most marketing activities cost money; the NPD process is no exception. Various models have been designed to offer guidance on how a portfolio or range of products can be managed to ensure there are sufficient funds available to continue NPD in to the future.

The Boston Consulting Group (BCG) has developed a model for guiding which new and established products should receive future investment in the development of new products. This is known as the growth share model or portfolio matrix. For a given range of products of a company, there will be some that soak up more cash than they generate (cash users) and some that will generate more cash. It is necessary for marketing management to identify these in order to establish a complementary balance of products in the product mix (i.e. total range of products offered). Incidentally, this examination is also part of the auditing which should be conducted as part of a final SWOT analysis in marketing planning (see chapter 2).

Products may be classified into four categories according to (i) their relative market share (compared to their major competitor), and (ii) their rate of market growth. In each case these are classified as high or low, giving a 2 × 2 matrix (see Figure 6.7). Before the individual categories are explained (stars, cash cows,

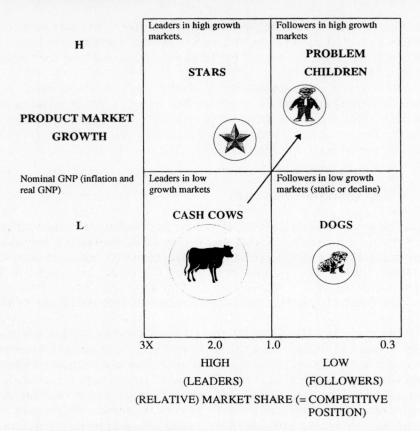

Source: Adapted from G. S. Day (1977), 'Diagnosing the Product Portfolio' *Journal of Marketing*, April, 30–1.

Figure 6.7 The strategic sequence of the growth share matrix

problem children, dogs) the main three assumptions of the BCG matrix are outlined. The first assumption of the model is that an appropriate cash balance is the ultimate, or at least a major objective, of NPD. The next two assumptions are important because they help define the categories. The second assumption is that market share is associated with returns on investment. Market leaders are considered to generate higher margins and enjoy lower costs (cost leadership). Several factors account for this. Market leaders are associated with quality management. They will have learnt over time, through superior knowledge, how to reduce costs in their supply chain from sourcing to customer delivery. With their superior brand recognition they hold a strong bargaining position with their buyers and suppliers, and are able to lead with often higher prices. In contrast, a brand follower may suffer from high rates of brand-switching, so requiring more investment directed to selling and promotions, both to distributors and consumers. In other words, followers have weaker trade leverage.

Analysis should be conducted at both a product and a strategic business unit level (for a range of products competing within the same business). Thus a business is designated as a leader (or follower) according to whether it is in a superior (or inferior) position relative to its major competitor, in which relative market share:

$$= \frac{\text{market share of business under analysis}}{\text{market share of largest competitor}}$$

The third assumption of the model is that the market growth is associated with marketing expenditure. High market growth is recognised to attract competitors, so extra funds are needed to erect barriers to entry from would-be entrants or to build or defend market position. Conversely, in a low-growth market, less cash on a *pro rata* basis is needed to defend share because competition is less intense, with many leaving the market as it becomes less attractive. This market growth is sometimes considered as a proxy for the product life cycle stage.

The four categories based on this model are known as problem children, stars, cash cows and dogs. The basic idea is to have a sufficient number of cash cows in the portfolio (since they offer a surplus of cash) which can be used to inject cash selectively into some of the more promising problem children (which tend to absorb cash because they are low share products during high market growth). Cash cows offer a surplus of cash because they are leaders (enjoying high margins) in low-growth markets (less intensive competitive rivalry). The pattern of the typical product development as the market grows and wanes in the life cycle is for some problem children to build share by gaining a disproportionate number of new users and grow successively into stars of the future, from which will develop future revenue-generating products (i.e. cash cows). The timing of the injection of funding is critical to ensure that a company does not become overburdened with too many problem children (which cannot be adequately funded by insufficient cash cows). Dogs, towards the end of the life cycle, are poor contributors to funds and a decision must be reached on when they should be withdrawn from the market. Dogs can be harvested to gain some residual cash based on their established reputation in the market. Since many consumers of dog products will be bargain hunters, rewards are limited to the supplier. The net cash flow implications for each category are shown in Table 6.3. When the firm is faced with many problem children or dogs, these are warning signals for the future. A firm might decide to drop out of a market if faced with an uncertain future, especially if the risk/reward ratio of converting problem children into stars is too great. Faced with lack of funds but a belief in a product area, an option would be to license the technology.

How is the growth matrix constructed? Each product is represented in the model (Figure 6.7) by a circle centred at the relative share and current market

Table 6.3 Cash implications for items categorised by Boston Share Growth Model

Item	Relative market share	Cash generated	Explanation	Cash used	Explanation	Net cash effect	
Star	High	++	Advantages of experience in market and strong trade leverage	High – –	Expenditure increased to reduce competitor attraction to market	0	
Cash cow	High	++	Advantages of experience in market and strong trade leverage	Low –	Competitors leaving market, with expenditure reduced	+	Extra/surplus cash used to support other growth areas
Problem child	Low	+	Trade more uncertain about future prospects of product so reluctant to stock it, or require strong incentives	High – –	Expenditure increased for selected items	–	Negative cash flow
Dog	Low	+	Little or no investment	Low –		0	

Source: Based on G. S. Day, 'Diagnosing the Product Portfolios', *Journal of Marketing* (1977), 41, 29–38, and Y. Wind and H. J. Claycamp, 'Planning Product Line Strategy: A matrix approach', *Journal of Marketing* (1976), 40, 2–9.

growth rate. The size of each circle is proportionate to the sales revenue. The matrix is divided into four quadrants. The horizontal line is set at nominal GNP growth (i.e. inflation plus growth in GNP). As a rule of thumb, this is often set around 10 per cent annually. Thus, markets growing more than 10 per cent p.a. are considered high growth markets, whereas those growing less than 10 per cent p.a. are considered low growth markets. A vertical line is placed at a relative share of 1, which is the dividing line of a market leadership position. In Figure 6.7, the firm is likely to have sufficient resources to meet the cash demands of the problem children. The position of the cash cow suggests it has about twice the share of its nearest competitor.

Whilst the BCG Matrix is still used as a tool for making portfolio decisions, it is only a guide. Some critics have questioned its versatility because a cash balance is not the only criterion on which product decisions are made. Firms may be cash-rich and capital can be raised in many ways, such as equity capital, asset-stripping or by increasing the debt/equity ratio. It also tends to ignore risks in supply continuity and technological changes, and does not consider other strengths of the business apart from market growth.

(*Note*: Multiple choice questions 6.12–6.14 can be used to assess the understanding of the Boston Share Growth Model.)

6.5 Choosing amongst alternative growth strategies

New product development is only one of several strategies a firm can pursue in the pursuit of growth. A firm could also choose to increase sales in current markets with existing products: this might be achieved by improving or expanding the salesforce or by aggressive advertising. This is called market penetration and is less risky than NPD because the firm can build on its existing knowledge base of current products and markets. If a firm decides to expand into new markets (market development) uncertainties arise over market acceptance (e.g. socio-cultural factors in chapter 2). Thus firms such as Kellogg's have had difficulty in expanding into new markets such as India because cold cereal products at breakfast are not generally accepted. Published market research statistics, taken from some foreign markets, may be unreliable or incomplete, for making sound judgements on market potential. However, if opportunities are limited in the current market (perhaps owing to market saturation), then a firm may have no option but to expand through one of the more risky strategies: market development, NPD or diversification. Diversification is the most risky because the firm moves in to both new markets and products.

Over-zealous diversification can sometimes lead to financial problems if a firm expands too quickly. The problems faced by the advertising empire of Saatchi and Saatchi in the early 1990s after moving into management consultancy were attributed, in part, to its moving away from its core business in which it excelled (i.e. offering advertising solutions to its clients). Despite caution required when

PRODUCT

	Present	New
Present	Market penetration	Product development
New	Market development	Diversification

Source: Ansoff (1957).

Figure 6.8 The Ansoff matrix

adopting diversification strategies, it can provide tremendous payoffs for those willing to accept some business risk. In some technological markets, such as the virtual reality market (see case study) a firm may have little option but to seek new directions for growth, in order to establish barriers to entry or defend a market position. Alternative strategic growth options open to firms are shown in Figure 6.8.

Case study: Virtuality

By wearing a special headset (head-mounted display, or HMD) it is possible to experience a computer-generated three-dimensional world. Instead of visualising a 2-D image from a computer screen, the image appears everywhere. This experience is known as virtual reality (VR). It is an industry that is evolving rapidly. A survey by *Cyber Edge Journal* stated that in 1993, 56 per cent of VR professionals had fewer than two years' experience.

Virtuality Group Plc, with subsidiaries in the UK, US and Japan, is the leading supplier of VR systems and software in the Location Based Entertainment Market with an estimated 75 per cent global market share. Location Based Entertainment is an out-of-home centre in which people may be attracted to the leisure services offered, such as at theme parks and family entertainment centres. Virtuality's systems have been installed not only in amusement arcades, but in retail outlets, cafés, bars, theatres, cinemas, museums, clubs and even cruise liners. Any high foot-traffic area could be a potential market.

In May 1993, Virtuality signed a licensing agreement with Sega of Japan for use in their interactive game centres and arcades, fifty of which are planned to open by the year 2000. The first model was demonstrated at an amusement machine exhibition in Japan in October. In the home VR market, Virtuality has a licensing agreement with Takara, in which it has customised a head-mounted display suitable for use as a personal viewing device. Licensing offers an opportunity for strategic partners to share in the technological know-how of Virtuality, but under the terms and conditions agreed between both partners. Licensing offers Virtuality not only development fees but future royalties (a kind of commission) on sales. Licensing achieves quick market expansion by forging links with suitable strategic partners, who can often offer strong established distribution channels.

Despite a recent cyclical downturn in the out-of-home entertainment business, the future of Virtuality appears bright. Innovation and product development are improving the quality of VR technology and making it more affordable as new consumer markets are sought. For example, new head-mounted displays are 20 per cent the weight of previous models. Also, the improving price/performance ratio of VR-capable computing is increasing the demand in the home market. Demand is set to grow with rising consumer expectations of their graphics requirements, as the Internet becomes progressively more integrated with 3-D images and VR environments.

Virtuality is now focusing on exploiting its higher margin industrial applications. Many industrial applications generate higher margins because of customised specifications required to match client needs. It is building relationships leading to further licensing agreements. A wide variety of applications are possible, as town planners, architects, interior designers and property developers are finding uses for it. Car, ship and airline manufacturers have used VR to test ergonomic factors in the early design stages.

A growth market for the VR technology is in the advertising, marketing and promotions market (AMP). Since 1994, graphics have improved at lower costs, offering great opportunities for adding the logo of a company to a VR system, and in the emerging market of education and training. For example, Kawasaki use VR technology to simulate motorcycle dangers and hazards as teaching aids in their driving schools throughout Japan.

Virtuality also provides a range of software, which it sells for entertainment and industrial applications. Applications include sports simulation and medical training. Today, the company is a leading developer of VR software and has systems in more than forty countries and an estimated 50 million people have played its games.

Source: Virtuality Group Plc, Annual Report and Accounts, 1994 and interim report and news releases, 1996.

Q6.4 What are the main markets available to (a) organisational purchasers, and (b) consumers?

Q6.5 How might the organisational market be segmented?

Q6.6 Using the Ansoff matrix, classify the growth strategies of virtuality by market penetration, market development, NPD and diversification.

Q6.7 What are the advantages of licensing to strategic partners?

Summary

Managing the marketing mix involves presenting a suitable offering of perceived utility to a target market. There must be a suitable strategy for product, price, distribution and communications. A key concept in designing the mix elements is to ensure they are balanced or integrated, i.e. elements reinforce each other in support of a specific intended offering. Marketing management must also recognise that a range of supportive benefits may prove crucial in gaining a differentiating point from intense competition. This might include service elements rather than tangible attributes only.

There are two ways marketing offerings which can be made: one is market-led, the other focuses on what the firm already has, but at the same time addressing the needs of the consumer. The asset-led method offers lower risk and payback return is typically quicker owing to a lower initial investment.

In managing the progress of products on the market, marketers can use the product life cycle model as a tool to identify at what stages there should be a particular emphasis on specific aspects of the marketing mix. The stages of the life cycle are pre-launch, introduction, growth, maturity and decline.

At the introduction stage, consumers learn about the benefits, uses and availability of a new product, a stage enhanced by trial samples and advertising. It is not until the growth stage that a firm typically enjoys a return on its original investment, and profits will depend, amongst other things, on the speed at which there is consumer acceptance and competitive retaliation and entry into the market. The firm can build barriers to entry by developing a distinctive character or personality for its brand. Nevertheless profits should be expected to slip as competitors share in the market following. At the maturity stage, sales begin to flatten out then start to decline, owing to saturation or changing consumer tastes.

The firm may decide to extend product life through new product development, which need not be a radical innovation but simply a range extension, or by gearing the product at new market segments (market development). Otherwise, communications will take the form of reminding consumers of the benefits, offering reassurance. Some competitors will now have left the market, and marketing expenses may be reduced, so offering a cash surplus to the firm. During decline, products will be divested. It is important to recognise that a healthy firm will be characterised by a balanced portfolio of products across the different stages of the life cycle, since products in the introduction and growth stages can be financed only by cash reaped at later stages. A firm without such a balance will find it difficult to fund new products.

New product development is required to meet the changing needs of the marketplace. Many new products fail owing to a lack of marketing research into consumer needs.

At the pre-launch stage of new products, there are six stages of development: ideation, screening, business analysis, product development, test marketing and commercialisation. Ideation involves the systematic process of generating ideas, which are then screened for market compatibility and range fit. Business analysis comes next. This involves forecasting demand, costs and profits. A working model or prototype is then developed and tested for market reaction, and costed to estimate a likely market price. Next, the new product is test-marketed in a limited area to enable flexibility in any late changes that are deemed necessary. The last stage, commercialisation, involves fine-tuning the results of the test market to prepare sufficiently for a full-scale launch.

Marketing management needs to ensure they have sufficient cash resources to fund future new and established products. One method that offers guidance on this is the Boston growth share model. Management needs to ensure it has sufficient cash-generating products to fund new products, which currently might soak up a lot of cash but which are regarded as an investment as successful revenue-earners in the future.

Finally, NPD is one of four growth strategies open to a firm. Alternatively, a firm could penetrate the market (with existing products in existing markets), develop new markets with existing products or diversify (seek new products in new markets). When existing sales with current products and markets become established, it is likely a firm will need to consider either market development, NPD or diversification.

References

Ansoff, H.I. (1957) 'Strategies for Diversification', *Harvard Business Review* (September–October), 113–24.

Burke, R.R. (1996) 'Virtual Shopping: Breakthrough in Marketing Research', *Harvard Business Review* (March–April), 120–31.

Cannon, T. (1986) *Basic Marketing*, 2nd edn. London: Cassell.

Davidson, J.H. (1972) *Offensive Marketing*. London: Cassell.

Davies, M., Preston, D. and Wilson, J. (1992) 'Not-for-Profit Services: A Case of University Student Accommodation', *European Journal of Marketing*, 26, 12, 56–71.

Day, G.S. (1977) 'Diagnosing the Product Portfolio', *Journal of Marketing* (April), 29–38.

CHAPTER SEVEN

Pricing

Objectives

After studying this chapter, you should be able to:

1. Understand the main determinants in making pricing decisions, including costs and market influences.
2. Recognise the factors which affect the price elasticity of demand of products.
3. Understand pricing tactics/options available.
4. Appreciate why, under special circumstances, firms may price under cost.

Introduction

Although pricing is the only element of the marketing mix generating revenue (the remainder: product, place and promotions, involving expenditure), the setting of prices for products and services isn't simply a financial formula based on covering costs. Consider for a moment the hundreds of prices set by different hotel chains.

Some chains will target affluent consumers, who may consider price less important compared to lavish surroundings and prompt and friendly service. Hotels located near airports (such as Holiday Inns) may target airline crews and tourists. Here the customer base may be relatively more price-sensitive. Other hotels may offer standard services to a different clientele at budget prices (e.g. Motel Six in the US). Prices may also vary according to season. Price incentives may be more frequently offered in off-peak times, in order to fill order books. Discounts may be offered for block bookings (such as to tour operators who provide regular, repeat business, or to large families who are privileged with concessions). Thus pricing can be used to achieve a number of business objectives: market targeting, positioning or simply to achieve financial goals.

Clearly, pricing can be a highly complex, yet critical aspect of a company's offering. This chapter examines some of the tasks facing those who are responsible for price-setting. In particular, price-setting requires the ability to *integrate* marketing and financial objectives (Figure 7.1). Marketing objectives will be about monitoring the nature of competition and the demand function to ensure that targeted segments believe prices charged are *value for money*. Note that making pricing decisions arising from competitive prices alone is not sufficient; examining consumer positioning is also important. Financial objectives will consider *costing methods*, since prices should cover costs for most situations. In a later section, some situations will be examined when for tactical reasons pricing is set not to cover costs.

7.1 Nature of demand

When considering changing prices it is necessary to assess how this will affect demand. A useful starting point is to determine the price elasticity of demand.

One easy way to determine whether the market is *price-elastic* or *inelastic* is to examine the *demand* function, a slope of demand measuring the quantities Q demanded for given price levels P. Figure 7.2 shows a price-inelastic demand curve.

Price elasticity of demand is the relationship of the change in quantity demanded with price movements or changes in prices. The ratio of price elasticity is therefore $E = \Delta Q / \Delta P$, in which E = elasticity, Δ = change and Q and P are quantity demanded and price respectively. When $E = 1$, the demand function is said to be

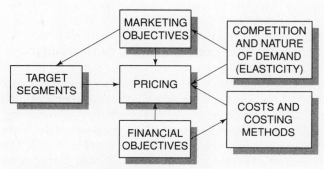

Figure 7.1 Determinants of pricing

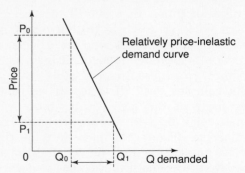

Figure 7.2 Market showing inelastic demand

perfectly elastic. This is when a change in quantity demanded (say, a decrease) is exactly proportional to a change in prices (an increase). This relationship is important to producers and suppliers in deciding whether to charge higher prices to their customers when faced with increasing costs (e.g. raw materials or overheads).

By forecasting future elasticity, a firm is able to decide whether it is appropriate to pass on any cost increases to its customers and if so, by how much. If the market is expected to react adversely to a price increase, the firm may decide to bear some of the cost itself.

In Figure 7.2, the demand curve is forecast to be inelastic, where $E < 1$, i.e. the quantity demanded will change less than a proportional decrease in price. If a firm was considering a price cut from P_0 to P_1, perhaps to prevent the entry of a competitive product, the quantity demanded would not rise in the same proportion (i.e. the extra quantity demanded arising from cheaper prices would only be from Q_0 to Q_1). Since $\Delta P > \Delta Q$, it might be wise for the firm to consider an alternative strategy. Usually in inelastic markets, such as that depicted in Figure 7.2, it is more sensible for firms to sustain higher prices. Price-cutting activity is usually ineffective in inelastic markets, whereas in very elastic markets it can shift demand and may be essential to remain competitive.

7.1.1 Factors affecting price elasticity of demand

What affects the elasticity of markets? Table 7.1 offers you some indicators. The first contributory factor is the market structure (i.e. the number and intensity of competitive suppliers). If there are a large number of competitors offering similar perceptions of value, then prices are likely to be fiercely competitive, since a price increase by any one would result in a loss in its market share. When the supermarket multiples started offering cut-price petrol, this forced some of the major oil companies to rethink their pricing strategies. As this extra competition

Table 7.1 Factors affecting price elasticity

Factor	Relative elastic markets	Relative inelastic markets
1. Number and intensity of competitive suppliers	Large numbers Similar size and power All prices set near to competition or market price	Few in number Hold variations in power Largest set prices; others tend to follow
2. Number of buyers	Relatively few	Many
3. Knowledge/information held about market		
(i) Price points	Familiarity	Unfamiliarity
(ii) Cost of suppliers	Familiarity	Unfamiliarity
4. Degree of necessity	Discretionary Subservient needs, e.g. luxuries	Core needs, e.g. emergency items due to circumstances (breakdown service on motorway)
5. Degree of comparability	Commodities Established products	Customised services and products New products

caused some petrol stations to close, others decided to match local competitors on price (e.g. Esso announced their Price Watch Scheme as a means of retaliation. As they extol, quite extraordinary!) Thus price changes often arise owing to changes in competitive practices. Similarly BT submitted to charging phone calls to the nearest second when Mercury entered the market and advertised the fact that 'some companies' (strongly implying BT) charged to the nearest unit. BT have responded by targeting particular services. They have recently used members of the public to emphasise the value of their long distance calls in their advertising.

Where there are relatively few suppliers or, at the extreme, a single supplier or monopoly exists, prices can be raised to meet excess demand over supply. Monopolies are not common because they are considered against the public interest and may be referred to the Monopolies and Mergers Commission. However, unofficial monopolies can exist by nature of the market structure and dispersion of customers. Some supermarkets have been accused of charging more for fruit and vegetables to inner city residents relative to out-of-town shoppers. Local supermarkets in inner city areas may hold a captive market over some inner city residents who are less affluent and less mobile (especially if they are not car owners) than their out-of-town neighbours. Since inner city residents are more likely to have unhealthy eating habits, wastage of fresh produce is higher, contributing to higher costs, which may be passed on to the customer. Thus price need not reflect quality.

Secondly, the number of buyers will also affect demand and prices. For example, car prices vary significantly across the year. The most popular time to buy a car is in August because many want the new registration plate. Since demand is high, sales staff are able to pitch at higher prices, whereas sales just before August, especially for old models that need shifting from forecourts, can sometimes be bought at bargain prices. Similarly, cars still in the showroom during the New Year are less in demand because they are being replaced by newer models. This is another good time for the buyer.

The third contributory factor influencing elasticity is the level of knowledge held by consumers or industrial buyers. If consumers are *familiar with price points*, i.e. points at which a given product is *expected* to be priced, then they are more likely to be sensitive to pricing. There may be a range of price points which are considered acceptable to different segments of the market (called the '*zone*' or '*latitude of acceptance*'). Above this zone is a *ceiling price*, which is considered poor value for money, and below it a *floor price* (the minimum price considered feasible to retain credibility) below which consumers would associate inferior quality. The zone of acceptance for a particular consumer of fast-moving consumer items might be represented by Figure 7.3, in which perceptions of price points might be allocated for several stores. These perceptions will vary for both different consumers and products, so it is the general consensus of consumer perceptions that will be of most interest to retailers when setting prices. Consumers are more likely to be aware of the prices of fast moving consumer goods (fmcgs), which are purchased on a regular basis, than for consumer durables, which are less often purchased.

The prices of some fmcgs are so well known that retailers call them KVIs (known value items). Consequently KVIs are more likely to be price-elastic than less frequently purchased items. Examples of KVIs include sugar, salt and margarine. It is important to ensure that the pricing of these items is keen to

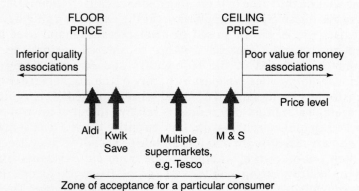

Figure 7.3 The zone of acceptance

promote *store traffic* and encourage *loyalty* to the store. Similarly, if the cost curves of the supplier are known, consumers are better equipped to question the price.

A fourth contributory factor influencing elasticity is the *degree of necessity during the purchase occasion* associated with the goods. Business people exploit this in many ways, e.g. the prices of buckets and spades increase the nearer they are sold to beaches. In recessionary times, when consumers are attempting to 'tighten their belts', the market for discretionary goods (associated with discretionary needs) falls, (e.g. snack foods such as crisps, biscuits), but the demand for basic needs is largely upheld. Emergency items, such as *unsought goods*, might sustain a high mark-up, such as funerals and locksmith services.

A fifth contributory factor influencing elasticity is *degree of comparability* (see Figure 7.4). Goods may be classified according to their ability to be differentiated and their ability to sustain high margins.

Similar products with little scope for differentiation, such as most commodity items (usually those that appear to be visibly physically similar), cannot afford the luxury of high mark-ups because the costs associated with brand-switching might be devastating. But a brand that is suitably differentiated from all competing options offers more flexibility to raise prices above the norm. For example, Stella Artois, a premium lager, is advertised as 'reassuringly expensive' to support customer perceptions of quality values. Using a pre-emptive association of quality (i.e. being first in the market to use it) prevents it being copied by competitors. Ghosh (1994) discusses how perceptions of value for money vary in a retail context. Products such as dried fruits might be priced as ingredients and displayed next to cake mixtures (as a commodity), or repackaged and displayed alongside health foods as a nutritional snack with a higher price tag. When the store sells fruits alongside other snacks, the price of those other snacks influences consumer perceptions of a fair price. This contextual effect is a means of exploiting added value. Note that degree of comparability is not the same as the second contributory factor: familiarity of price points. Occasionally, commodity

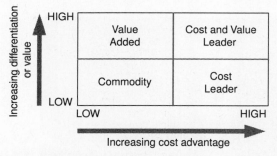

Adaptation permitted by the publisher of M. Christopher, S. Majaro and M. McDonald, *Strategy: A Guide to marketing for senior executives,* Gower Business Enterprise Series, 1989.

Figure 7.4 The competitive options

items can be transformed into *shopping goods* (which are keenly sought by name) because of strong branding, which distinguishes them above the crowd of 'me-toos' or imitations in the market. An example would be 'Newman's Own' Italian salad garnish, sold in supermarkets. There are many examples in other product fields. Cosmetics are generally difficult to compare unless sampled and so many rely heavily on the packaging to convey a distinctive identity and price to indicate quality; in combination these can offer value added. Services requiring a high degree of customisation, such as those offered by garden designers, and in particular services with good track records in which consumers require a specific outcome such as legal services, can be suitably differentiated to command high prices.

In technical markets, degree of comparability may be difficult, offering scope for higher margins. It is unlikely that members of the general public would have the technical knowledge or expertise necessary to evaluate the objective quality of one brand of motor car against another. It is for this reason that price and branding are two of the most important marketing tools in the trading of cars. It is critical that car manufacturers achieve an appropriate price/quality value positioning for their different market segments. Whilst price supports a quality position, it can also unnecessarily restrict the total market unless carefully handled. One of the dilemmas facing prestigious brands such as Mercedes or BMW is how to extend market size without alienating existing customers, since existing customers wish to be perceived as prestigious and exclusive (associated with owning these brands). Figure 7.5 'Brand is Better' shows how BMW, using its existing brand strength, attempts to persuade non-users to consider a second-hand BMW as preferential to a new, but less prestigious, brand of car. Mercedes have also advertised their cars to target this new segment but using a slightly different message.

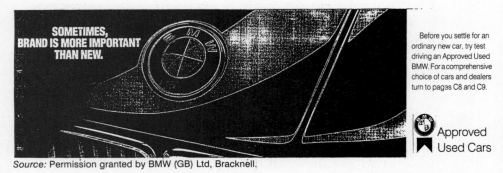

SOMETIMES, BRAND IS MORE IMPORTANT THAN NEW.

Before you settle for an ordinary new car, try test driving an Approved Used BMW. For a comprehensive choice of cars and dealers turn to pages C8 and C9.

Approved Used Cars

Source: Permission granted by BMW (GB) Ltd, Bracknell.

Figure 7.5 Raising salience of the brand by targeting new category users: secondhand BMW purchasers

Another dimension affecting comparability is the degree of novelty associated with the market or the product. When a new product is launched, the firm has to decide how to gain market acceptance. The vast majority of consumers would be hesitant about rushing in to buy a radically new product. They may prefer to wait and test market reaction by those who can afford and are willing to take more risk (called the 'innovators'). They are responsible for the fortunes of many new markets because their acceptance of or reluctance to buy a new product will influence the rate of adoption (or failure!) in the mass market. The question is: whom does the firm target? Prices can be skimmed to appeal to the exclusive values associated with the innovators, and providing there is little competition, high margins can be gained. In later stages of the *product life cycle*, the price can be reduced as competition increases, to adapt pricing for the mass market. The alternative strategy is to *penetrate* the mass market as quickly as possible with low prices, with the objective of gaining high volume sales. In highly technological markets such as pharmaceuticals, a skimming strategy offers the chance to recoup some of the original investment early on and shorten the payback period (the time it takes to recoup the total, original investment). In a market with much potential competition, consumers are more likely to be price-sensitive, and a penetration strategy might be more appropriate. You can justify a price decrease far more easily than an increase, so skimming offers relatively more flexibility to change future prices in line with the market or competitive activity.

Determination of price elasticity of demand suggests that a market orientation towards pricing is a critical component. Central to this orientation is the concept of customer value, so price cannot be separated from an analysis of quality. This is why firms examine price/quality relationships when setting prices. But quality is multidimensional, and needs to be clarified to the customer to ensure justification of prices. One method of linking price to quality is through communicating value for money.

7.2 Communicating value for money to the customer

Products priced higher than competitive levels (especially in business-to-business markets) may still be linked to customer value but may need to be justified by the skill of the sales staff. Many organisational purchases are triggered by the commercial values derived from their purchase over their working life. The net effect of this will involve how such purchases reduce costs and increase revenues. For example, a computer hardware system might have an asking price in excess of competitive quotations. On closer examination, it is revealed that it is more economical over its estimated working life because it is easier to install, implement and train staff, and maintenance costs may be negligible. The total costs arising from rival products may indicate they are not the best buys.

How might value for money be measured?

AT & T, the leader in the US telecommunications industry, measures the satisfaction of its customers relative to that of its competitors' customers for a number of activities. This is achieved by a customer value added index (CVA), which is:

$$CVA = \frac{AT \& T \quad WWPF\ Score}{WWPF\ Score\ of\ customers\ from\ major\ competitor} \times 100$$

WWPF refers to *Worth What Paid For*, i.e. it measures perceived value for money. The results are then compared to standard benchmarks from which decisions are made. For example, if the index is 110 or more, then AT & T would be considered world class, if it dips below 82, it is considered a serious weakness, which might call for possible divestment of the activity under evaluation. Experience has shown that the index is a good predictor of revenue share for the company in its many market segments, with share being highly correlated with the index.

7.3 How costs are defined

Financial objectives must also be accounted for when determining pricing. You might expect a firm to cover its costs, but what does this mean? A variety of costing methods may be used when attributing costs to consumers. Simplistically, costs may be divided into *fixed costs* (those that exist *regardless of production*) and *variable costs* (those that *vary according to production*). The way that these costs, in part or in full, are passed on to consumers determines the costing system adopted. The method of *full cost recovery* attempts to recoup the *total costs* involved. A danger here is that unit costs may be determined on the basis of forecasted sales. If forecasts are optimistic (actual sales are less than expected) then the fixed costs will be spread over fewer sold units, bearing a higher cost per unit.

Consider, for example, a product of which your firm has estimated to sell 100,000 units. Imagine the fixed cost to be £25,000 and the variable costs to be £1 per unit. The cost per unit = £1.25 or (£125,000/100,000), assuming you sell everything. At a selling price of £1.50 each, you (as the supplier) would be rewarded with a mark-up of 25p each. But if sales were dramatically lower, perhaps only 25,000 units, then the cost per unit = £50,000/25,000 = £2 per unit. A selling price of £1.50 would now incur a loss of 50p per unit.

In some situations, recovering full or total costs is ineffective. The firm instead may decide to claim only variable or *marginal costs*, or perhaps expect a contribution towards fixed costs. Airline seats and hotel rooms may be priced accordingly, to make some contribution towards fixed costs instead of being left vacant. The largest discounts on airline tickets are therefore for those seats still available near to take-off. This explains why the price of airline tickets varies throughout the day for what appears to be a similar service – it is a reflection of the supply/demand equation.

7.4 Integration of marketing and financial objectives

For most situations, a firm needs to price within a range which not only encourages customer acceptance (within the 'latitude of acceptance' or range of discretion) but also covers costs. There is another floor price to consider: that which is unacceptable to the producer. The range of discretion or acceptance will vary according to the price elasticity of the market, as shown in Figure 7.6.

For relatively inelastic markets, there is likely to be a wider range of price points to cater for different segments of the markets, some of whose needs can be met by achieving differentiation through added value or by effective positioning based on *non-price factors*. These non-price factors might include customer service, advertising, personal selling or packaging quality, but there are many others. Such a wide range of price points will offer a relatively wide range of acceptance. Contrastingly, in more elastic markets, there will be a relatively narrow range of discretion from which firms can select prices. In many cases, pricing may be a dominant issue in customer behaviour, dictated by the actions of competitors. Tracking market prices is therefore necessary, but many strategies are still open to firms. With rising prices, firms may decide to reduce margins and bear the costs themselves, or seek new ways of reducing costs, such as better supplier sourcing, or value analysis (seeking to eradicate unnecessary costs in manufacture or assembly). In some cases it may be possible to desensitise customers to price, perhaps by retargeting at niche markets. Two pricing techniques illustrate how market demand for a product can affect its financial viability: target pricing and transfer pricing.

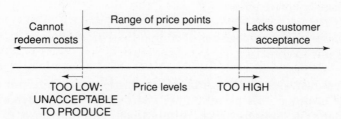

Figure 7.6 Acceptable prices determined by both financial and marketing objectives

7.4.1 Target pricing

Market acceptance of a product is sometimes heavily influenced by price. If this happens, price should be decided at the earliest stages of product design based on consumer research, rather than designing a product to match product specifications required, and then costing and subsequently pricing it. The danger in the latter case is that specifications may be over-elaborate for the needs of the market, and prices may need to be reduced to achieve sufficient demand at a price point which is no longer profitable. Using target pricing, the materials, functions and the finish of a product are strongly influenced by prices aimed to match the needs of specific market segments rather than price being determined by the product specification. Olympus cameras are priced using target pricing (Mitchell, 1996).

7.4.2 Transfer pricing

Sometimes a firm is in a position to sell on both the open market and to other divisions within a group. Should the firm sell internally to its other divisions at the same prices as externally (i.e. what the market will bear), or should it consider to price at cost, or somewhere between the two? Figure 7.7 shows two subsidiaries, S_1 and S_2, requiring supplies from its parent manufacturer, M. The solution should depend on good business practice. If the order books are healthy and full, then the manufacturer cannot afford to sell to its subsidiaries at less than market price, unless there is excess capacity. If demand is slack, pricing at *cost plus* (between market price and cost price) will offer some contribution towards fixed costs and so seems a sensible solution.

7.5 Pricing tactics

7.5.1 Identifying key price points

From the section on pricing, you should recognise that the latitude of acceptance for setting prices is an important concept. Significant changes in elasticities can be determined from key price points by:

(a) preparing price comparisons of competitive products,
(b) using this to construct a *price/volume chart*.

Figure 7.8 demonstrates the importance of elasticity for determining an optimum pricing formula. This price/volume chart indicates the dynamics of changes in demand at various price differentials beyond those of three competitive motor insurance quotes. The key price points are at 7 and 9 units above the competitive prices. The optimum price differential is 7 units above the

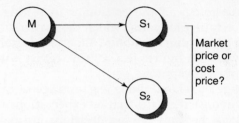

Figure 7.7 The transfer pricing problem

competition. This is because the firm can price its motor insurance up to 7 units more than the average of its three main rivals without losing much market share (since the demand curve A is relatively flat and inelastic up to price point 7). However, a further 1 unit of price differentials (from 7 to 8 units) generates a fall in market share from 15 per cent to about 10 per cent. Along any price point depicted by curve B, the demand for the service falls proportionately more than a corresponding increase in price. Beyond the 9 point mark the curve again flattens (at C), perhaps reflecting a hard core of loyal supporters. If the firm wished to pursue a policy of high prices, it might decide to improve non-price factors such as service or image dimensions to alter the demand curve at B (i.e. make it more inelastic). If this is not achieved, it may be prudent to price at the differential point of seven units.

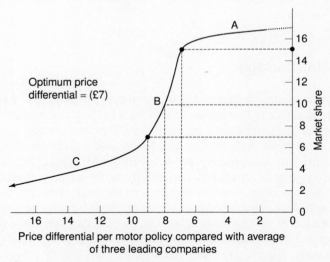

Figure 7.8 Price elasticities at varying differentials

Much will depend on the psychology of the consumer in setting prices. Shopkeepers know that there are certain price points which they can use to make their products and services *appear* good value for money. Shoes, for instance, are often priced at 1 point just below round figures (e.g. £29.99, rather than £30). Using such tactics is known as *psychological pricing*.

When setting prices for a range of related items (e.g. a range of cars) it is important to ensure price levels are consistent with market expectations *across the range*. This is known as *team pricing*, because pricing decisions are not set in isolation, but in relation to a series of other goods. Team pricing offers the chance to offer a range of prices for different market segments in order to maximise profits. Clearly, a luxurious car would be expected to hold a much higher price than a mid-range one, and so pricing in this market can offer indications of quality as a positioning tool.

7.5.2 Price bundling

Car manufacturers often attempt to raise the overall prices of cars by offering a number of separately priced extras, not all of which are optional. In many cases the cost of these extras can be a considerable percentage of the overall cost of the car.

Daewoo uses comparative advertising to emphasise its price bundling policy which absorbs those extras as part of its inclusive pricing, compared to the separately priced options of its rivals (Figure 7.9).

Daewoo thus illustrates that it is even better value than consumers might have first thought by highlighting the price differential in the final row of the ad.

7.5.3 Tactical pricing

A common problem facing marketers is to stimulate trial purchase of a good. You may feel it is only reasonable that consumers will stick to their main brand if they are satisfied with it. Pricing can be used tactically as a 'foot in the door' technique to lure consumers away from their loyalty, e.g. Tesco uses a mixture of new deal pricing (targeted on many convenience products frequently purchased), multi-saver prices (when buying in quantity) and other more *ad hoc*, special price reductions. *Loss leaders* are often used by retailers to increase store traffic in the hope that patrons will buy other goods on impulse, from which the profit will more than offset the losses on the loss leader. Cut-price cigarettes are a popular loss leader with confectioners, tobacconists and newsagents (CTNs). *Bait pricing* uses a similar rationale. Nightclubs frequently display low entry prices prominently to lure customers inside, but decline to mention high bar prices. *Price*

USE THE

DAEWOOPRICE

APPROACH TO FIND THE REAL
COST OF BUYING AND SERVICING A NEW CAR:

	Daewoo Nexia 1.5 GLXi 5dr	Ford Escort 1.4 L 5dr	Vauxhall Astra 1.4 LS Hi-Tq 5dr	Nissan Almera 1.4 GX 5dr	Fiat Brava 1.4 SX 5dr	You Fill In
LIST PRICE	£10,495	£11,410	£11,795	£11,495	£11,194	
Delivery	included	£470	£475	£465	£450	
12 months Road Tax	included	£140	£140	£140	£140	
3 year Servicing	included (up to 60,000 miles)	£225.67	£295.37	£446.65	£426.50	
3 year Comprehensive Warranty	included	£410	£276	included	£459	
3 years Total AA Cover	included	with warranty	with warranty	£220	with warranty	
Electronic ABS	included	£365	£625	n/a	£724	
Driver's Airbag	included	included	included	included	included	
Engine Immobiliser	included	included	included	included	included	
Metallic Paint	included	£230	£225	£225	£206	
Air Conditioning	included	n/a	n/a	£1,445	n/a	
DAEWOOPRICE	£10,495	£13,250	£13,831	£14,436	£13,599	
Vs Nexia 1.5 GLXi 5dr	–	+26%	+31%	+37%	+29%	

The Daewooprice approach lets you work out the real cost of buying and running your car. Use our table to calculate the real cost of any car you may be interested in. All prices are correct at 15.10.96, and please note that the warranties listed do not necessarily provide the same levels of cover. We phoned 3 competitor dealerships for each car to obtain our figures. Although you may get a discount on other cars it depends on your haggling skills. Daewoo's fixed prices range from £8,795 to £12,995, and with our independent part exchange valuation system, there's never been a better time to have your car assessed. For more information call 0800 666 222. The real cost of buying a new car? That'll be the Daewooprice.

 DAEWOO

Figure 7.9 Daewoo advertisement using comparative price (Reproduced with permission of Duckworth Finn Gribb Waters, advertising agency of Daewoo)

offers, credit by instalment and *deferred payment schemes* are other methods designed to capture the attention of the price-sensitive consumer.

7.5.4 Differential pricing

When the same service or product is offered at different prices to different groups of customers, this is known as *differential pricing*. Tactically, this method is useful when the demand changes according to different times of the day. During week-days, the price of the same journey by National Railways will vary according to whether it is in peak or off-peak times, serving commuter traffic and tourists respectively. The price of a ticket from Newcastle to London is cheaper if purchased in Newcastle than a ticket bought in London to make the return journey, reflecting the price sensitivity or elasticity of different market segments. What may surprise you even more is that you can buy a first class ticket on some train journeys at only a nominal rate above the standard class fare, compared to the full fare required if purchased from a station ticket office. This last example serves to illustrate the flexibility required in any pricing formula (and is similar to the airline seats problem used in an earlier section).

There is another reason for charging different rates to different groups of customers. Some customers can be distinguished on the basis of their profitability by the amount of attention and service provided to them. Thus financial institutions might charge for the servicing of some current account customers (which traditionally contribute little to profit). Those targeted might be those who make frequent transactions (so incurring more management time) and those whose account values fall below a particular figure (say £1,000). This makes sense because without such a system, more profitable customers are subsidising the service. If these less profitable customers move their accounts elsewhere, the firm is unlikely to be harmed. This is an example of demarketing, if this is the ultimate intention.

7.6 Deciding the intensity and speed of price changes

A price change may be considered necessary in the face of changing fortunes in costs of production or distribution, or changing demand patterns. When a decision is made to change prices, tactical decisions must be made about their intensity and speed of implementation. Prices can either be changed by the full amount in one stage or alternatively implemented in steps. In the latter case management may decide to use the price steps to assess the best price point to maximise profitability. Alternatively, implementing the price rise immediately is more likely to invoke hostile reaction, especially if it is considered unjustified. Hence, it is a wise practice to inform customers of price increase *before* implementation, and to try to justify it, if customer relationships are to be valued.

Management must also consider the speed at which a price change is implemented. If it is in response to competitor moves, it may be possible to follow competitors' increases slowly (and so gain more empathy with the customer than by reacting quickly). However, a quick price reaction is sometimes necessary to improve profit margins or to contribute to sunk costs (costs already spent based on business contracts already made). For example, the scare associated with British beef during March 1996 has wiped millions in value off farmers' incomes, and has resulted in sharp price reductions and special offers on meat products in supermarkets.

Q7.1 Conduct a pricing survey on consumers who normally do the household shopping. Find out if they can remember the prices they paid for different types of goods, and if not, the extent to which they make errors. The survey should be conducted within 24 hours of shopping. You could use a list such as the following product categories:

- washing up powder
- regular shampoo
- cereal products (this could be further subdivided by category)
- cooking oil
- soft drinks
- books
- pre-recorded musical tapes or CDs

Are there any patterns of price awareness that are common to most consumers? Are there significant differences between product categories? Are there differences between manufacturer and store brands? Account for these differences.

Q7.2 Monitor the pricing behaviour of a product of your choice that is currently on special offer. Examine the moves of competitive products in the same category. Can you account for the differences in price between brands (a) when on offer, (b) when there is no offer?

Case study: Direct Line Insurance

Prior to the 1990s, sales in the motor insurance industry were mainly made through high street retailers, in which brokers acted as intermediaries. Commissions typically ranged between 10 and 25 per cent of annual premiums. There was an opportunity for selling insurance policies through direct marketing.

Financed by the Royal Bank of Scotland, Direct Line set up the first direct marketing operation in 1985 to reach customers directly and bypass the broker. The potential for keener prices was there, with no commission charges, and a move away from a high street presence to a great reliance on the telephone. It was a popular move. By 1994, Direct Line was the UK's largest private motor insurer. Quotes might be as much as 20 per cent lower than the best quotes available from traditional brokers.

The acquisition costs of setting up a direct marketing operation are expensive. There is advertising and additional staff required to replace the brokers. Staff also need to be trained in both product and telephone selling techniques. But payback is returned on this investment by the additional loyalty achieved through exploiting the advantage of direct marketing.

Whereas traditional insurers retain customers for around two years, Direct Line's estimated loyalty is about eight years. Loyalty is achieved through both price and service. Some insurers have attempted to improve their retention rates by offering discounts based on the number of years of custom. This is in addition to the no-claims discounts drivers are entitled to.

By cutting premiums, there is a grave danger that margins will be eroded. Direct Line were therefore careful to position their advertising and their product to appeal to consumers who historically have low risks in claiming. These were considered to be sensible, family car drivers and mature drivers. They did not sell to owners of powerful cars or to those living in inner city areas associated with high crime statistics. In addition they offered preferential discounts for no claims beyond those of competitive insurers.

Many insurers have tried to emulate the success of Direct Line. With intensified competition, it is becoming progressively harder.

Sources: Adapted from G. Holmes and A. Sugden (1992) 'What Makes that Little Red Telephone Ring?', *Accountancy*, November, 32–4.

Q7.3 What factors influence the pricing of motor insurance? Which are the most critical for success and why?

Q7.4 Is there a potential market for targeting motor insurance at high risk groups? If so, how would the marketing mix need to change from the current operations at Direct Line?

Summary

Price-setting requires the ability to integrate marketing and financial objectives. Marketing objectives (such as achieving market share) require the establishment of what price levels are acceptable to consumers and how these vary across different price points. This reaction to price movements (price elasticity) will indicate whether price or non-price factors should predominate in the marketing mix.

For relatively elastic markets, in which consumers are particularly sensitive to price, price-cutting may be used. In relatively inelastic markets, non-price factors may be more effective as a purchase motive.

There are several indicators of how elastic a market is likely to be. If there are many suppliers of a similar size within a given market, the market is likely to be relatively elastic, unless products can be differentiated. Otherwise one market price will tend to predominate. Consumer familiarity with price points or costs of suppliers, discretionary needs of consumers and commodity or established products would also tend to suggest elastic markets.

For relatively inelastic markets there are likely to be fewer suppliers, the largest of which command sufficient respect to set their own prices. Consumers of such markets tend not to be familiar with price points. Typical products and services include emergency items, customised offerings and new items not yet established in the market. Central to the market orientation of pricing is the gauging and communication of consumer value.

Financial objectives include covering costs, although this raises the issue of whether only variable or total costs are covered. To ensure full cost recovery requires an accurate forecasting of sales, from which unit costs are based.

For many situations, a firm needs to cover its costs, yet price at a point which is acceptable to its targeted segments. It follows that key price points need to be identified before a range of acceptable prices can be ascertained.

There are many instances in which pricing is used tactically to counter awkward situations and achieve specific marketing or financial objectives. These include transfer pricing, skimming and penetration pricing, team pricing, loss leaders, bait pricing and differential pricing. Some of these require a conscious effort to price under cost. You should be familiar with these techniques and why they are used. In the case of new product launches, a range of price points can be chosen between the limits of penetration pricing (lowest possible price, designed to achieve high volume sales objectives) and skimming pricing (in which the highest possible price is charged to a segment in the market most prepared to pay for it, designed to achieve high margin objectives).

References

Christopher, M., Majaro, S. and McDonald, M. (1989) *Strategy: A guide to marketing for senior executives*, Aldershot: Gower Business Enterprise Series.

Ghosh, A. (1994) *Retail Management*, 2nd edn. Sidcup: Harcourt Brace.

Mitchell, A. (1996) 'The Price is Right', *Marketing Business* (May), 32–4.

Nagle, T. (1987) *The Strategy and Tactics of Pricing*. Englewood Cliffs, NJ: Prentice Hall International.

CHAPTER EIGHT

Distribution

Objectives

After studying this chapter, you should be able to:

1. Understand the key decisions involved in distribution management.
2. Make decisions on the number of levels in the distribution channel and the number (or intensity) of retail outlets.
3. Distinguish between different types of distribution channel members, including direct channels and vertical marketing systems.
4. Understand the impact of the relative power of channel members in the distribution chain and the strategic options for branding.

Introduction

The management of the distribution function, including supply chain management, involves managing the sourcing of organisational resources upstream from suppliers and distributing resources downstream to customers. Figure 8.1 shows the stakeholder or channel members in the chain or channel of distribution from source or supplier to eventual consumer or end-user. How does channel management help the consumer? The aim is to provide a reliable and responsive service to meet customer orders with a guaranteed delivery date in the right quantity, at the required level of quality. In achieving a given level of customer service, there is a trade-off between the customer objectives of time, quality and

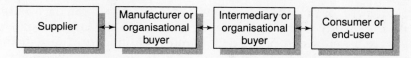

Figure 8.1 Stakeholder analysis of total supply chain management

accessibility and the cost to the supplier or distributor, which may ultimately be passed onto the customer in the form of higher prices.

Since there are often many members in the channel from source to point-of-sale (Figure 8.1), it is the job of distribution management to co-ordinate the supply chain to ensure that problems are avoided or alleviated. Typical problems involve differences in perceptions between different channel members. The result can be conflict, which then requires resolving. Several examples of conflict within the channel follow, and some solutions are offered.

This chapter examines some critical areas of distribution management. The following sections discuss the importance of distribution management and the role of middlemen, as they ultimately influence the length of the channel. This is followed by a section on the growing importance of direct marketing. We then examine how intensely distributed a product should be. Different types of channel members are described and the advantages of vertically integrated marketing systems considered. This is followed by an investigation of how branding strategies should be adapted to power changes between channel members, including alternative strategies such as category management.

8.1 The importance of distribution and supply chain management

Distribution management often needs to balance the limited resources it faces, based on the conflicting demands of its channel members. A typical problem involves achieving the optimum stock of goods on hand at any time. Note that if stocks are held for long periods, a firm loses money, associated with the costs tied up with capital that could be used elsewhere, insurance on stocks held and other allied costs, such as increased likelihood of damage, pilfering and/or obsolescence. Therefore, finance seeks minimal stocks on hand, whereas the marketers would be very wary of potential lost sales and perhaps termination of a client's business caused by a stock-out. The goal is to achieve sufficient stocks to meet a variety of customer requirements without incurring unnecessary costs. This may be the job of production control. But sometimes there is a source of conflict between production control, who schedule production resources on the basis of the most economic production-runs, and the sales department, who wish the needs of a very important client to be met first (so disrupting the most 'efficient' resource scheduling designed by production control).

Procurement, or the study of organisational purchases, can have a dramatic effect on the quality of the final product and can be the largest single cost if suppliers are unreliable or fail to deliver consistent quality requirements. The concept of total quality management, to educate suppliers and other channel members in developing a problem-preventation mentality, can help a company offer consistent reliability and quality products that are envied by competitors (Oakland and Porter, 1995).

Christopher (1994) suggests the main strategy of supply chain management is to offer maximum flexibility in meeting customer requirements for a range of products, in any quantity, without incurring significant costs. The key is to be responsive to consumer demand by analysing and reducing the time it takes between receiving orders and eventual supply. Information technology in retailing has helped link the point of sale or consumption with the point of supply to trigger fast reaction-times to meet changing consumer demand. Another trend in industrial markets is for organisations to modularise their products, in which the final finish of the product is postponed until orders are made, whereupon partly finished work is completed to specification. This offers greater flexibility in meeting customer service levels at reduced costs (because stocks are not held for long periods). For example, Rank Xerox hold stocks only as work-in-progress, and work is completed only when orders are raised.

Costs can be dramatically reduced by examining alternative supply chains. For example, two suppliers offering similar prices and quality of raw materials may turn out to have different cost implications for the firm if one produces with less wastage in manufacture. It might also be possible to make or import goods from abroad where there is a pool of readily available labour which is relatively cheaper than manufacture. Also, the ability to innovate and respond to changes in the market is dramatically influenced by supplier and distributor relationships. Sometimes these relationships can take the form of agreements between one supplier and a distributor, leading to barriers to entry for the competition. This is more likely to happen if some members neglect the importance of their channels of distribution, or do not respect the value of their partners in the distribution chain.

Despite Mars having launched a brand extension with their ice-cream product in the early 1990s (which coincidentally broadened the appeal of ice-cream to adults) the success of this brand has been limited by weak distribution. Walls, as the major player in the market, has a stranglehold on ice-cream distribution by offering small shopkeepers freezer cabinets free – on condition that they stock only Walls ice-creams. Even with Mars' substantial advertising spend, their poor distribution has resulted in their failing to establish sufficient retail space, allowing competitors the opportunity to respond with new products and technical innovation. Despite the fact that Walls were referred to the Monopolies and Mergers Commission for their influence on retailers' purchases of ice-cream, Mars appeared to misread the importance of distribution.

From chapter 1, you will recall that the importance of marketing is increased as organisations target consumers who are geographically distant from the point of manufacture (or supply). This is not only because it is more difficult to ascertain consumer needs, as the point of manufacture is increasingly distant from the market, but also because organisations must consider the most cost-effective ways of reaching consumers who may be geographically dispersed. Decisions include whether merchandise will be sent by the company or via middlemen (or intermediaries), in what form it will be sent, and how it will be stocked, stored, handled and packaged. Many of these decisions are interrelated and management must integrate the functions to provide a desired rate of customer service at a minimal cost.

Consider the role of a chemicals manufacturer, with products designed for carpet cleaning. Management has to decide the best way to present the product to the consumer. How would you approach this? You might start by identifying who the users are. Typically, these are home owners and tenants (a domestic market), industrial users, such as offices and shops, and institutional users, such as schools and hospitals. To assess market size, you might consider how often the product is used. In the industrial and institutional markets, the cleaner is likely to be purchased to serve heavily carpeted areas (owing to the higher incidence of floor traffic). This enables the distribution manager to consider appropriate pack sizes. It is likely that the household purchaser will buy household cleaners over the counter, which are designed to clean standard-sized carpets in homes, whereas bulk purchases may be necessary in the industrial and institutional markets.

You need to research whether the targeted organisations use their own staff to do the job or hire on a contract basis (in which case, questions arise concerning the ease of supplying labour with the product, and even dispensers). Consumers, whoever they are, should be able to buy the product or service when they want it, with the minimum of effort and with easy accessibility.

Other decisions relate to how the product is made up (in concentrated or diluted form before its destination). This is important since delivery of concentrate reduces transportation costs (less bulk) but raises a potential problem of training authorised users to dilute a potentially hazardous product. Advice at point of sale may add perceived value to the core product, so enhancing the manufacturer's position. You should also appreciate that the nature of the product will affect decisions on stocking policies, storage and handling. Some products do not keep well under certain conditions and are highly perishable, so requiring strict controls, such as monitoring the air conditions and who is authorised to use them. Clearly, distribution management has a broad function in enhancing marketing effectiveness.

8.1.1 Deciding the length of the distribution chain

The route from product or service supplier to the consumer is called a *channel of distribution*, or distribution chain. How short or long do you think it should be for a given product or service? The answer lies in how useful middlemen or intermediaries are for the given product. An *intermediary* (or distributor) is an organisation or individual that links the supplier of goods and services to the end-consumer. Wholesalers and retailers are typical intermediaries for consumer markets (see Figure 8.2).

By using intermediaries, the number of total transactions required to serve the end market is substantially reduced. Consider two distribution chains servicing electrical goods (a) without a wholesaler, and (b) with a wholesaler (Figure 8.3). In case (a) the number of deliveries or routes covered if each of the two electrical manufacturers dealt separately with each retailer is eight, whereas in case (b) the number of deliveries is reduced by 25 per cent to six. The channel in (b) is more efficient because the inclusion of a wholesaler offers the chance to deal with both manufacturers and retailers. In practice, there are many more manufacturers and retailers in most markets than are shown here, so the potential for reducing distribution costs is much higher.

Similarly, retailers as intermediaries can reduce the number of transaction costs between manufacturers and ultimate customers, but using intermediaries is not always required, nor indeed useful. In the case of a highly perishable product, a manufacturer might prefer to send the product *direct* to the end-user (using the smallest possible distribution chain). A wide range of products may help make direct distribution and selling more cost-effective. In contrast, unless a producer offering only a single line reaps high margins, the cost of direct distribution might be commercially unfeasible. You should recognise that intermediaries serve a number of functions. Since wholesalers purchase in large unit sizes, they can *break bulk* into saleable units that are more manageable for retailers. Wholesalers and retailers will also hold inventory for their immediate

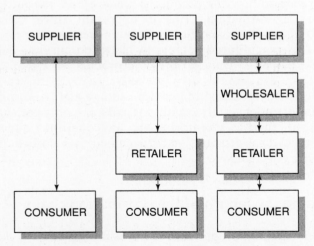

Figure 8.2 Distribution channel options, with choice of intermediaries

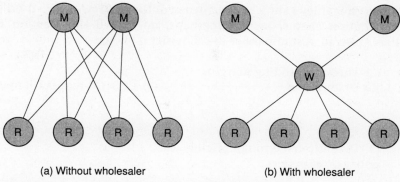

(a) Without wholesaler   (b) With wholesaler

Figure 8.3 How intermediaries can reduce delivery costs

customers. It is likely that most wholesalers will carry a range or *assortment* of different brands, offering the customer choice, as well as offering specialist *technical advice*. Indeed, manufacturers should screen their stockists to ensure they offer the right kind of advice to their customers. Because intermediaries are closer to the end-consumer than the manufacturer, they can often offer invaluable *market feedback* on trade and competitor reaction. Some intermediaries also offer tailor-made services for their trading partners, so creating *added value*. For example, in the building trade, stair fixtures and fittings such as nosings and coving may be cut to size (fabricated), so improving supplier/customer relationships. Intermediaries may also *improve cash flow* to their trading partners by extending *credit facilities*.

Why might a firm make changes to its distribution chain? The answer may lie in a change of strategic direction perhaps reflecting increased competition.

'Sugar turns sour to the middlemen'

Recently, Dixons, the nation-wide retail chain, announced that they needed to remain competitive with the invasion of COSTCO, a discount warehouse entering the retail market for computers. Dixons were concerned that their margins might fall, so they obliged Alan Sugar of Amstrad, their current supplier, to reduce prices. The carrot for Amstrad was anticipated to be large-scale distribution. Amstrad replied by opening up their own business directly available to the consumer, selling at factory prices with fast delivery and with the promise of a 30 day refund if dissatisfied. The advantages to Amstrad Business Direct are:

- No costs involved in providing extra service to middlemen such as advertising costs.
- Total control over terms of sale, including a dedication to service such as a permanent hotline to cater for maintenance, repairs and enquiries.

Although Stanley Kalms, the Chairman of Dixons, had asserted his power in the distribution chains, he had (perhaps) misjudged the reaction from his supplier, Amstrad. A summary of the activities is shown:

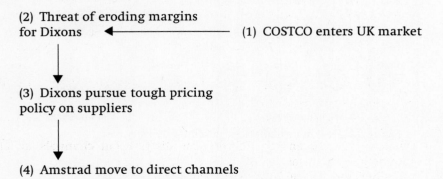

(2) Threat of eroding margins for Dixons

(1) COSTCO enters UK market

(3) Dixons pursue tough pricing policy on suppliers

(4) Amstrad move to direct channels

The example shows that changes in the terms and conditions of one business partner (be it a buyer, supplier or influencer) can affect all others within the distribution chain.

Alternatively, it may be technology that drives the length of the channel. The following case in the travel industry illustrates this point.

Case study: Travel business moving more direct

The travel industry is using new distribution channels thanks to improvements in technology. Traditional on-line systems used by travel agents are notoriously slow. To check availability of flights or packages, agents have had to rely on filtering through each individual tour operator's reservation system using Viewdata terminals. It is not unknown that checking availability of a popular destination, say to the Algarve in August, might take up to an hour.

What is needed is a rapid scanning technology that can respond to queries about what is available on a particular date by consolidating information from all the tour operators. Thomas Cook has recently introduced this system for its telesales operations.

Alternatively, new channels are being exploited. For example, Thomas Cook have installed several multimedia kiosks in National Westminster branches. Self-service, touch-screen terminals allow customers to browse through multi-media information about holidays and talk to sales staff using a video-telephone link. Teletext is popular with late bookers. Whereas teletext accounted for 3 per cent of Airtours' late bookings in 1992, it accounted for 20 per cent in 1995. Another channel set to expand is the Internet. Flight schedules, access to hotels and car rental agencies can be made. Reservations can be made on line and tickets delivered through travel agents or by post.

Some airlines are experimenting with ticketless travel by offering plastic cards bought at the airline, which reduces the need to pay commission to travel agents. Another approach is to use electronic ticket machines in hotel lobbies and airports that can print out tickets that have been reserved by telephone. All these are examples of direct marketing.

Source: Adapted from Vanessa Houlder, 'Plenty of New Departures', *Financial Times*, 10 August 1995, p. 10.

Q8.1 What are the advantages of the new distribution channels to (a) the suppliers, (b) the consumers?
Q8.2 What business do you believe the travel market is in?
Q8.3 Will the traditional travel agent survive as a result of the technological changes? Explain your answer.

8.1.2 The growing importance of direct marketing channels

Direct marketing is the non-personal communication and distribution by producers or suppliers direct to their consumers. Without using intermediaries, direct marketing offers direct suppliers greater control in building up a close contact with their consumers to encourage loyalty. Direct marketing is becoming of increasing importance as retailers increasingly seek new strategies for cutting costs.

Direct marketing does not include personal, face-to-face selling (explained in chapter 10), but does include home shopping techniques such as mail order and direct response (off-the-page selling or advertising using freephone numbers) and telemarketing (inbound and outbound). It also includes the use of interactive electronic media. Each of these is explained. The main benefits and limitations of home shopping are then discussed.

Mail order involves reaching customers through the post or increasingly at work, with catalogues or brochures. The 'average' consumer is recognised to be female, and of average income and education, married with children and a credit user. The market is dominated by Great Universal, Freemans and Littlewoods, who collectively hold over 70 per cent of the market. However, different catalogues under each company are targeted at different price segments of customers under the guise of different names. It is important to segment the market because about 20 per cent of all catalogue users make up 60 per cent of sales. Next have responded to this problem by charging for their life-style oriented *Next Directory* since whilst only about 2 per cent of owners make ultimate purchases if catalogues are free, between 5 and 15 per cent buy something if there is a cover charge. Another way of tackling the low response rate is by very selective screening of databases. Thus Johnson Fry, the construction and financial services group, offer a magazine of investment products aimed at millionaires who have over £500,000 to invest.

Advertising designed to encourage a direct response by telephone or reply coupon allows marketing management to measure the direct effectiveness of advertising in terms of number of enquiries and enquiries to sales. It may underscore the total effectiveness of advertising since no scheme has yet been evolved for measuring the indirect effects of advertising precisely (see chapter 9 for more details). Direct response advertising can exceed targets and cause logistical problems in meeting quick responses to telephone enquiries. If this happens, it can harm the credibility of a company, so forecasting demand from direct response is critical. When customers are proactive in ringing a company for further information, this is known as inbound telemarketing. A common obstacle is that consumers have difficulty in remembering the number off-air.

A freefone number (often recognised as an 0800 number) is sometimes continued with words or numbers associated with the advertised brand, such as 0800 000 850 for the Volvo 850 or 0800 28 28 20 (tu-weet-tu-weet-tu-o!) for the Royal Guardian Direct Insurance which features an owl as part of its brand mark (the silent but visual part of its brand identity). These so-called 'designer' telephone numbers are likely to increase in the future as telemarketing grows.

When dealing with inbound requests, a common irritation for consumers is to be left waiting for a response. Voice processing equipment can be used to encourage the user to stay on line. By pressing options on a touch-tone telephone, voice processing can distinguish between urgent and non-urgent options in order to reduce the queue-time at busy periods. In this way staff can send out literature at less hectic moments and improve customer service, without incurring excessive costs in increasing manpower.

Outbound telemarketing refers to direct contact by the company. In order to be successful, products must be relevant and telephone staff should be trained to adopt a personalised approach to customer responses.

Interactive electronic media offers scope for two-way communication. The most likely hardware used is a modem (a specially adapted telephone line linked to a computer screen), in which consumers can pull down a series of instructions on a screen to arrive at a databank of information which can be used to help them make a purchase.

The Internet offers access to a combination of information sources linked globally, allowing easy access to those who hold the technology and pay a subscription (e.g. CompuServe, NISS). Potentially, it poses an opportunity and a threat to many markets. For example, whilst the *Daily Telegraph* can be read from the Internet, does this mean the demand for buying newspapers in the form we are used to will wither?

One major advantage of such a powerful network is that it improves the quality of information by offering quicker access to real-time data. For instance, publishers of travel guides such as *Lonely Planet* now encourage travel writers to send accounts of their latest travel experiences on the Internet. This cuts down the normal lead-time of traditional publishing. The result is an up-to-date account of life in a country – an improved product. Another upshot is that the customer can scan the world for new suppliers on-screen and demand lower prices, so effectively reversing the supply chain.

Currently there are three main limitations in using this mode of delivery:

1. The user or consumer must be selective and discerning because there is much irrelevant (and irreverent!) information that is put on the Internet.
2. It can be especially slow to download because of the amount of usage world-wide, so the convenience factor needs improving.
3. The security in arranging payment for goods needs to be tightened up. Whilst many consumers would be concerned about computer hackers gaining access to their credit card numbers, electronic cash may offer a safer option. By storing digital cash in your account onto the hard disk of a computer, proof of ownership of your account then offers you the facility to withdraw (a kind of virtual hole-in-the-wall cash dispenser).

Generically, home shopping compared to shopping in a retail outlet offers the additional benefits of convenience (no travelling time, no parking problems and potentially no queues). Examining merchandise on-screen or from a brochure in one's own home offers a relaxed atmosphere, in which browsing is not inter-rupted by an aggressive sales assistant. In terms of business hours, home shopping is superior to shopping in retail outlets. When Sunday trading laws were relaxed, many mail order firms extended their accessibility. For example, *Next Directory* have telephone operators ready to take orders between 8.00 a.m. and 11.00 p.m., seven days a week. Other customer service benefits include options in credit facilities and a range of delivery services. Many mail order firms have extended their range of products and services, including insurance and extra care cover on standard guarantees. Advantages to home shopping providers above those of traditional retail outlets include lower costs, such as rents, less inventory tied up in capital (since most suppliers are distributed to order by relationships with manufacturers) and an ability to encourage manufacturers to contribute to the promotional and production costs of the catalogues (such as models, photography or artwork). This is because many branded manufacturers want their goods to be available, which can be a barrier to entry for other competitors. By encouraging customers to endorse the product through tell-a-friend schemes, selling costs can be reduced. Also, recruitment costs can be reduced by hiring from past customers.

With such potential cost savings, it might appear surprising that these are not always passed on to customers. The prices of merchandise in catalogues is often higher than equivalent ranges of merchandise in the traditional retail outlet. One reason is the relatively low penetration rate of people purchasing from catalogues. This is likely to improve in the future as relationships are exploited with their core customers. Apart from the benefits already mentioned, home shopping can be a valuable service to the disabled, the infirm and the housebound. Also, so-called 'taboo products', which cause embarrassment buying face-to-face, appear to be a natural outlet for home shopping. Perhaps it is unsurprising that outsized wedding rings are a common purchase by women from QVC, Britain's first home shopping service, a 24-hour service offered on B Sky B.

Despite the many benefits of home shopping, there are several limitations. Ordering systems are sometimes bureaucratic, particularly on buying for the first time, when much information is requested, often above that of simply screening for bad debts. This information may be used for marketing purposes to assess their customer profiles more accurately. When selling face-to-face, a sales assistant may be granted the flexibility to negotiate merchandise within a range of prices, whereas in catalogue selling prices tend to be fixed from production to selling. This can cause difficulties for a mail order firm if contractual suppliers pass on price increases *after* a catalogue is published for distribution.

Another problem is the additional perceived risk associated with buying goods from a distance (such as from a computer screen or catalogue). This argument has been used in selling certain financial products, such as insurance and mortgages, in which some consumers feel more reassured about speaking with someone face-to-face rather than keying in personal and sensitive information into a computer. Arm's length viewing is not the same as being able to inspect merchandise close-up, e.g. made-to-measure clothes. Whilst an approval service can reduce this problem for tangible products, the intangible nature of many services (for which you cannot experience and examine the total benefits at point of purchase) makes this more difficult. The rate of acceptance of using new distribution channels are therefore both customer- and product category-specific.

The rate of growth in shopping from a computer screen will also depend on how well such organisations can overcome technophobia (the fear of new technology) and encourage the ownership of the necessary technology. Consumers who first experiment with the new delivery channels will be appropriate targets for many financial service organisations. They are likely to be high net worth individuals, and located at the young to middle-aged end of the market. The challenge for the technologically minded marketer is to improve relationships with these innovators by communicating with them interactively and, in doing so, speed up the rate of adoption of the new channels to new users and broaden the overall market.

8.1.3 Deciding the intensity of channel penetration

Why do you think goods like cigarettes and newspapers are stocked *intensively* (in many local outlets), whereas goods like Omega and Rolex watches are only offered in a small number of jewellers? The answer lies in examining the nature of each product and what it stands for. Remember, marketing is an *integrated* discipline. The distribution manager, therefore, has to consider the needs of stockists, as well as the ultimate customers. Items such as cigarettes are *convenience items*, because they are frequently purchased, everyday, low-value items. The major benefit offered by the retailer to the customer must be convenience and accessibility, so an intensive distribution channel makes sense.

Items such as Rolex and Omega watches offer a different set of benefits to the customer. These watches are more than a timepiece to the purchaser – they are an *acquisition*, designed to enhance their self-image. Distribution management must support this by restricting such goods to *exclusive authorised dealerships*, so ensuring strict quality control over retailing, selling and after-sales service. In a similar pattern, car manufacturers often authorise exclusive dealerships to distributors covering a specific area. In many cases, the brand name will be *specified* by the purchaser *before shopping*. Under such circumstances, these products are labelled '*speciality goods*'.

Products between convenience and speciality goods, are known as '*shopping goods*'. These are items that people shop for and conduct extensive search of product information *before* deciding which brand to buy. Since consumers need information on which to base their purchase decisions, the quality of managing the buyer/seller relationship remains important and distribution management will opt for a *selective* level of outlet penetration. The number of outlets is not exclusive, as is the requirement for speciality goods. Table 8.1 summarises the relationship between category of good and level of outlet penetration.

Table 8.1 Relationship between category of good and level of outlet penetration

Category of good	Convenience	Shopping	Speciality
Level of outlet penetration	Intensive	Selective	Exclusive

8.2 Different types of channel members

Once a decision has been made about the length and intensity of the channel, the next decision is to make a selection decision. After having identified a shortlist from trade sources, likely contenders will share some knowledge and experience of your products in your markets. They are also likely to be financially sound, and share an affinity for wanting to do business with you. The basic differences only between agents and distributors are discussed here. The main difference between agents and distributors lies in *who takes title* to the goods. With *agents*, the manufacturer retains title to the goods. This means that policies on branding, packaging, pricing and promotions are set by the manufacturer. Although agents sell on commission, they may hold competing lines of stock. Contrastingly, *distributors* take control of the marketing of their products and so hold title to the goods they sell. Therefore the image of the product is under the control of the distributor. Distributors will not usually hold competing lines.

8.2.1 Traditional retail channel members

Retailing involves all transactions in which the buyer intends to consume for personal or household use. Since retailing has an important impact on the economy, the remainder of this section discusses some major retail store types. (Non-store variations have already been discussed under the section on direct marketing channels.) Major retail stores covered here include supermarkets, hypermarkets, discounters, variety chains and department stores. Supermarkets are large, self-service stores, carrying a wide line of food products. As profits from food are likely to become saturated in the future, there is increasing interest in expanding further into non-food items, such as entertainment, clothes, and health and beauty aids. National chains have central checkout facilities and offer free car parking. Prices tend to be lower than similar products in independently owned supermarkets in town. The top chains in the UK are owned by Sainsbury, Tesco, The Argyll Group and The Asda Group. Hypermarkets are over 100,000 square feet, and offer a greater range in width (product categories) and depth (range of brands within a category) than supermarkets.

Whilst supermarkets are likely to survive on providing value, service and a quality range of assortments, discounters appeal to a different segment of the market who are motivated by low prices, even if this compromises on service. During the UK recession, discounters such as Aldi and Kwik-Save were successful. Using a strategy of selling a restricted range of branded goods, with little service and minimal investment in point-of-sale and promotional display techniques, success is based on volume sales, rather than high margin merchandising.

Variety chains offer a wider variety of merchandise than supermarkets or hypermarkets, but less than department stores. Their appeal is mid-market, characterised by low-cost facilities, self-service shopping, and relies on multiple purchases. Examples include Woolworths and Marks & Spencer.

Department stores tend to be larger and may be independently owned, serving a local town or run as larger chain stores, such as John Lewis. As the name suggests, different categories of merchandise are displayed in separate departments. A common feature is a coffee shop or restaurant on the top floor to attract store traffic through the departments.

8.3 Co-operation in the channel

As the length of the channel increases with the use of more intermediaries, *conflict* between different channel members is likely to increase.

Manufacturers will view their goals as increasing sales and margins on their goods; *retailers* will value more their own store profitability and stock turnover, which are not necessarily compatible. One approach used to improve *relationships* between different organisations at different levels in the channel is to attempt to integrate them. *Vertically Integrated Systems* (VISs) refer to the level of *interdependence* between the various organisations at different levels of the channel. Under a VIS, a single channel member co-ordinates or manages channel activities to achieve distribution objectives cost-effectively. In an *administered VIS*, channel members are independent, but there is much *informal co-ordination*. For example, joint promotional schemes may be funded by both retailer and manufacturer. Small businesses can also take advantage of informal co-ordination: see text box. 'New Partners in Delivery Channels'.

New partners in delivery channels

Small businesses are often unable to identify a marketing solution for their marketing ideas, or indeed have the necessary capital to expand to meet anticipated demand. Networks with brokers allows them to do this. They identify potential partners and offer impartial advice but stand back independently as the business grows. West Country Organic Foods was able to sell fresh organic meat nation-wide to the doorstep of every household within 24 hours. Dominated by supermarkets, an association of organic farmers found difficulty in competing with price (which had to be sustained to meet higher production costs). A network broker gave them the idea of direct mail, since competition in over-night parcel services had reduced delivery charges, and environmentally friendly polystyrene containers kept meat at refrigerated temperatures for 24 hours. Sales may soon extend from households to hotels and restaurants.

Source: Adapted from Roland Adburgham, 'Potential Partners', *Financial Times*, 25 July 1995, p. 8.

The most widespread form of VIS is a *contractual* arrangement, in which relationships between channel members are *formalised by contract*, defining legal obligations for all parties concerned. A *franchise* is an example of a contractual arrangement, under which an independent businessman (or *franchisee*) agrees to abide by the business conditions laid down by a *franchisor* (the organisation with the original business idea). According to the British Franchise Association, business franchises account for nearly 4 per cent of retail sales (compared to about 12 per cent in the US). The franchisee accepts an *exclusive* business deal in a *specified* area (i.e. free from competitive franchisees within the designated geographical area) in return for a capital sum and usually an agreed percentage of sales. The franchisor may start a franchise to raise capital; and it can be an efficient way to grow quickly.

For example, Compass, the catering company, runs a chain of Burger King franchises in leisure centres, railway stations and airports. The Body Shop has over 250 outlets in the UK, which are mostly franchises. When Anita Roddick and her husband first set up Body Shop in 1976, franchising seemed an obvious choice to raise capital. What do franchisors want from their franchisees? They might look for evidence of hard commitment, realistic ambitions, suitable business experience and some evidence of enthusiasm in preparing a business plan.

Entry costs for a franchise might start at £10,000–£20,000, with perhaps additional costs required for stock (if appropriate) and an annual management charge, which may be as low as 1 per cent but which is likely to increase for service franchises such as management consultancy, up to about 25 per cent of turnover.

In return, franchises obtain greater security than starting business from scratch because the business ideas have been tried and tested, although they are tied to a contract (say, 10 years). Within this period they are guaranteed training and product support. There is also the added advantage that most banks will provide more finance from franchise operations than for start-ups from scratch. One potential danger to franchisors is that a franchisee, having learnt the business, may decide they can earn more on their own, and set up as a serious competitive threat upon expiry of the contract.

The *corporate* VIS combines all stages of the marketing channel, from producers to consumers, under a *single ownership*. For example, Esso operate both corporate-owned production facilities and service stations. The ownership of other channel members is perhaps the most effective way to reduce conflict within the channel: see text box 'Advantages of Owning other Channel Members'.

Advantages of owning other channel members

New video-CD systems combine the traditional functions of video cassette recorders and audio compact disc players which can be used to watch films. Sony and Phillips, two of the world's most powerful consumer electronics companies, have joined forces to develop this new generation of compact disc, in which they claim the visual quality is superior to video cassettes, with playing time up to 135 minutes. Toshiba, a main competitor, claims their version is technically superior. Both companies are anxious their version is accepted as the industry standard. If not, the inventor will find it difficult to convince film studios and music companies to record their films, albums or singles on it. Sony learnt this lesson the hard way in the 1980's in the battle over the video system standards with Matsushita, the Japanese electronics group. Despite Betamix being acknowledged as technically superior to Matsushita's VHS, the remaining electronics industry settled for VHS and the film industry followed suit. Eventually it became too difficult for consumers to rent or buy Betamix films. This motivated Sony to take over the Hollywood film studios of Columbia and Tri-Star in 1989, costing 3.4 billion, and CBS Records for 2 billion the previous year. Similarly, Matsushita acquired MCA/Universal Film and Music Group for 6.1 billion in 1990. Both giants argued these acquisitions would enable them to launch electronic products easier in the future if they owned entertainment software in the form of movie and music rights. They could then ensure films and recordings were available in their new formats, making it easier for consumers to buy the hardware.

Source: A. Rawsthorn (1995) 'A Record Fight in Sight: The battle to establish an industry standard for video-CD', *Financial Times*, 21 January, p. 9.

8.3.1 Changing power between channel members

Over the last 30 years, there have been many changes in the way retailers have influenced their power in the distribution chain. The level of retail concentration is particularly intense in the grocery business: the big three multiple chains in the UK, Tesco, Sainsbury and Argyll, hold over 70 per cent of the total market. Their increasing concentration and influence have contributed significantly to the weakening of many manufacturer or national brands. This explains the increasing importance of retailer *own labels*, *private labels* or *own brands*. These are brands identified by a retail or house name (e.g. Tesco or Sainsbury) rather than a manufacturer name. Some guidance on how manufacturers might strengthen their own positions is offered here. The implications of confrontation and co-operation between the channel members of manufacturer and retailer are also outlined.

Several factors have contributed to the retail supermarket concentration of power, as the smaller regional businesses disappeared or were taken over. These include socio-cultural trends, the abolition of resale price maintenance, growth in own labels, economies in volume buying and corporate advertising, and improvements in handling and using information technology for marketing research to improve merchandising and customer service decisions (see Table 8.2). The implication of each will now be explained.

Research has shown that quality and convenience are the two most important factors many shoppers value today, compared to price several years ago. An increase in dishwashers, microwave and in-home fridge/freezers reflects the growing need for convenience. Freezers allow consumers to stock up their food

Table 8.2 Influences strengthening retail power

- Growing need for convenience
- Abolition of resale price maintenance
- Growth in own label contracts
- Savings gained in volume buying and corporate advertising
- Improvements in perceived quality with corporate advertising and innovation
- Improvements in marketing intelligence by using up-to-date stock movements

requirements for perhaps 3 or 4 weeks, with less need to shop so frequently. The multiples of the 1990s, serving an increasing range of non-food items as the potential for future growth in the food market saturates, increasingly offer a one-stop shop, in which the once competing small corner shop is considered less beneficial.

A secondary contributory factor is the abolition of resale price maintenance in the 1960s. This allowed retailers to control the prices of manufacturer brands at point of sale. Own labels, private labels or retail house brands were originally introduced to offer a price differential on the manufacturers' brands. By undercutting on price (owing to alleged savings in packaging and sometimes in product formulation and innovation) they were not considered a serious threat to many of the stronger manufacturer brands, which appealed to different market segments. Weaker national brands were therefore considered most at threat from being removed from multiple shelves. Retailers were keen to stock brand leaders, which promoted store traffic and offered valuable financial returns on their shelf space, but were less favourable towards other brands which increasingly had to trade on price, and being squeezed for margins.

The European grocery market shows a strong relationship between own label share and retail concentration (Fernie, 1994). Over 30 years' multiple growth has shown a prevalence of own label growth. However, the perceived quality of own labels has increased over this time to the equivalent of that of many manufacturer brands. The result is that many own label brands now compete more directly with the best of the manufacturer brands. Many weaker brands have been delisted, or have been given less preferential treatment in terms of shelf space, shelf position or financial terms of business as retailers increasingly are more able than ever before to demand improvements from their suppliers in the bottom line. Improvements in IT using scanner data provide the evidence of poorly trading manufacturer brands, from which retailers can increase their negotiating power.

What accounts for the trading up of own label products? Whilst many manufacturer brands have experimented with tactical price offers at point of sale, the retail multiples have outspent their suppliers in advertising, with the aim of strengthening their brand and corporate images (McGoldrick, 1984). This has had the contributory effect of improving the perceived quality of the store name, and by association, their own brands.

Perhaps unsurprisingly, the multiples appear intent on raising the number of their own brands, although selectively. According to Wileman (1992), the multiple grocers have increased their share of own brands from 21 per cent to 40 per cent between 1981 and 1992 at the expense of their suppliers' brands (down from 76 per cent to 58 per cent during the same period).

8.3.2 Branding strategies in response to power shifts in the channel

What do manufacturers do in response to the increased power by their retailers? They should examine the strengths of their brands relative to others, and consider whether their own position is threatened by own label growth or not. Manufacturers have four branding options at their disposal in dealing with their retailers. They can supply only manufacturer brands, specialise in offering retailer own label brands, practise both (called a dual branding strategy) or decide to rationalise and withdraw from the market or at least from the channel. Some of the major advantages and disadvantages from a manufacturer perspective of the first three options are shown in Table 8.3. In the case of a manufacturer preferring to control branding in terms of packaging, selling and advertising support, a manufacturer will focus on supplying its own national brands. But not all manufacturers will be in such a privileged position to decide this branding

Table 8.3 Supplier advantages and disadvantages of alternative manufacturer branding strategies

Strategy	Manufacturer branding	Own label branding	Dual branding
Advantages	More control over branding policies than for own label contracts	Security of volume, smooth production and cash flows. High volume economies in manufacture	Can be used to fill excess capacity. Experience of own label can help identify special strengths and to defend national brands
Disadvantages	Threats from own label producers and other leading brands	Retailer assumes control over marketing and especially point of sale	Providing own labels may erode strength of manufacturer brands. Additional costs incurred in manufacture, distribution, packaging, inventory and selling
	No guarantee of continuous contract; relationship may be transactional	Discloses potentially sensitive cost information and technical information on product innovation	

strategy. Offering exclusive own label contracts, in comparison, can offer the manufacturer benefits in the security of volume, offering smooth production and certain cash flow and may incur less selling costs in a contractual relationship tied to an own label policy. In the case of a dual branding strategy, a manufacturer agrees to offer a private label contract at the same time offering brands using its own name. The danger is that both brands could be competing for similar shelf space in the same retail chain. A manufacturer with excess capacity might consider dual branding, although Quelch and Harding (1996) suggest they should consider the full costs of own label production, not based on incremental or marginal costs. As the proportion of overall private label sales increases as a percentage of overall sales it makes sense to calculate profits on the basis of full costs. Quelch and Harding refer to the additional manufacturing distribution and inventory holding costs in printing extra labels and packaging when offering additional private label contracts to their existing business. Further dangers in offering either total own label contracts or dual branding strategies include management costs in time lost in renegotiating towards the end of each old contract and their potential renewal or loss of business. Dangers in dual branding strategies involve the possibility that the sales of existing brands will be eroded by additional private label growth, the disclosure of sensitive cost information and technical product innovation expertise transferred to the retailers. All these could strengthen the retail position with future negotiations and should be considered when choosing branding strategies within the channel.

8.3.3 Alternative strategies designed to cope with increasing retail power

Quelch and Harding (1996) suggest that a private label audit should be conducted to ascertain the profitability their private label business makes in the organisation. They suggest that closing down excess capacity may be favourable to adding private label business if the profitability arising from rationalising the range of products (including exit costs) is superior to the lower returns on private labels.

Management should also consider the relative performances of own label success for different product categories. In categories with low private label growth, the manufacturer objectives should be to sustain barriers to entry with frequent technological developments or as low cost producers. For those categories in which private label growth is well established, manufacturers might aim to curtail further growth by lowering costs in the supply chain through demanding minimum order quantities and more efficient trade deals. Leading manufacturers who offer multi-product lines or categories can be more selective in offering trade discounts to those retailers who support their national brands above those of own labels. By examining total sales per retailer, discounts can be customised rather than fixed.

So far branding strategies have been examined from a confrontational perspective (i.e. that one channel member improves their position at the expense of another). But sales promotions that do not compete head-on with normal retail shelf space can be used creatively. Consider the design of custom-built displays such as at end-of-aisles in stores. Alternatively, retailers may be rewarded for increasing sales volume verified by scanner data.

Retailers and manufacturers can co-operate by sharing their goals and learning from each other to develop a stronger attack on other competitors.

8.3.4 Resolving conflict and managing relationships in the supply chain: the case for category management

According to Mitchell (1995), manufacturers are increasingly restructuring their management along category lines rather than individual brands when seeking to gain maximum co-operation from their trading partners. Typically, this involves retailers and manufacturers collaborating on research into consumer shopping behaviour and co-ordinating resources such as advertising, merchandising and promotional offers. The philosophy behind this arises from the fact that a retailer is more interested in maximising the profits from the shelf than a particular brand, so maximising the profitability from a category can serve both groups of needs better. Under the system of brand management, an advertising campaign promoting one brand may simply shift sales from one brand to another rather than alter the sales or profits of the category. Contrastingly, under category management, the store and supplier can redefine the category according to the way the consumer perceives it. This is most obviously achieved by considering end-uses or user occasions. For example, should crisps be placed in the snack section of the store, or next to sandwiches and soft drinks in a consumer-friendly 'lunch-time' category? Should red wine, pasta sauce, garlic and pasta be placed together to promote the joys of Italian cuisine?

Those manufacturers prepared to co-operate with their retailers by offering marketing advice and intelligence are more likely to gain preferred supplier status and probably will be rewarded with better shelf facings and promotional slot benefits.

Those who fail to consider category management may find that they are threatened with delisting as a whole supplier rather than for their individual brands.

Read section 8.3.1, 'Changing power between channel members'.

Q8.2 What are the major advantages to retailers in introducing their own private brands?

Q8.3 In what situations or product categories would it not be appropriate for retailers to introduce their own private brands?

Personal activities

PA8.1 Imagine you are involved in producing a cereal product made from commodity ingredients. Until recently, you have been the leading brand to several multiple retail chains. The price gaps between national and private brands have traditionally been wide, but are closing. One of these now approaches you for a private label contract. What are your options?

Using role play, negotiate your position from the manufacturer's viewpoint, with someone else from the retail multiples' viewpoint.

On the basis of these negotiations, the remainder of the class should discuss who should win and why.

Additional points not considered in the negotiations should then be added.

PA8.2 Choose a distribution channel of your choice and identify the members at each stage of the channel. Then interview one or two members at each stage of the channel to determine their perceptions of potential conflict situations with other channel members. Find out how they proceed to resolve them. Can these channels be classed as administered, contractual or corporate systems?

PA8.3 Choose a product category and store of your choice (for which there are private brands available) and compare and contrast any differences in the prices, the amount of shelf space allocated and the relative shelf position of retail brands and national brands. Record any evidence of sales promotional activity between each brand. What do these differences indicate about the level of retail power compared to their manufacturers in the distribution channel?

Case study: The retail carpet store – are new channels needed?

Carpet retail stores generally follow one of two formats: the discount warehouse or the sample store. Although there are frequent minor variations of these two classifications, these two types are useful models for analysing this industry. There are substantial differences in methods of operation and each type has distinct advantages and disadvantages.

The typical discount warehouse retailer normally occupies a store with over 5,000 square feet of floor space. Name brand carpets are generally not carried.

Most discount stores carry private label carpets displayed in rolls piled into stacks on the showroom floor by type and colour. Normal business hours are usually long, the average store staying open until 9.00 p.m. on weekdays and during the daylight hours at the weekend. Heavy advertising expenditures are common to stimulate a rapid inventory turnover of six times per year or more (i.e. at about an average of every 52/6 or 8 weeks, the stock will have been sold out).

This approach to carpet retailing has several advantages. Products sold to the public are generally available to retailers at a lower price, because they are able to purchase a high volume of full rolls. Since the carpet is a private label, direct price comparison by name brand with other carpet outlets is impossible. Immediate installation is possible because the customer's selection is made from rolls already in stock. This consideration, and the fact that the roll purchased is readily available for inspection, are plus points for consumers.

There are several drawbacks to this type of operation, however. High rents are incurred because of the large area required for carpet display, forcing this type of store into locations less susceptible to drop-in business. High inventory carrying charges are also incurred since the carpet is always on the display floor. Many retailers keep over $200,000 in inventory. The carpets carried also lack the reputation for quality of nationally advertised brands.

The typical sample store carries no inventory. In contrast to the warehouse, the sample outlet displays hundreds of samples by brand name from many mills. Store size is usually less than 1,000 square feet. Hours of operation are usually the same as for the discount warehouse. Advertising expenses are somewhat lower, since rapid stock turnover is not as important and drop-in business is usually higher due to more favourable locations.

The sample store has several advantages over the discount store. Operating costs are typically lower because of the smaller area and lower inventory levels. Advertising costs are minimal. Consumers are offered a wider selection of nationally advertised brands, since the store is displaying only small pieces of carpet. The stores are generally located in high traffic areas such as shopping centres, which are usually more convenient for shoppers.

The sample store has several drawbacks, however. Customers are often reluctant to make a purchase on the basis of a small sample only. Since proprietors purchase only the amount of carpet necessary to install as a result of customer orders, they cannot take advantage of volume cost savings. In addition, once an order is placed, installation may be delayed for days or weeks, depending on the availability of local stocks or the location of the mill.

Carpet consumption in the United States has increased 15 per cent each year since 1960. There is strong reason to believe that this trend will persist.

Many in the industry feel the time is right for a clever entrepreneur to design a new retail distribution system to take advantage of the strengths of each type of store while eliminating some of the inherent disadvantages. Most concede, however, that capital could be a limiting consideration in the design of the new distribution outlets.

Source: 'The Retail Carpet Store' from *Marketing Channels: A Management View* by Bert Rosenbloom, copyright © 1978 by the Dryden Press, reprinted by permission of the publisher.

Q8.4 What are the relative advantages and disadvantages of:
    (a) the discount warehouse?
    (b) the sample store?

Q8.5 Recommend a new channel structure designed to incorporate several advantages of each of the above outlets. What specifically are the advantages of this over the old structures?

Summary

Distribution management plans to ensure the right goods get to the right place at the right time, cost-effectively. This requires the management of distribution channels, ensuring appropriate channels are used. Channel management is about selecting not only the number of levels of channel members within a chain, but also the intensity of penetration at each level. The intensity of penetration is dependent on the type of product being distributed. Convenience goods require extensive distribution because widespread availability is required. Speciality goods require exclusivity to ensure control over marketing. Long channels will involve middlemen, distributors or intermediaries whilst the shortest channel is direct from the manufacturer to consumer. Intermediaries offer a wide range of functions, which should be considered when designing the type of channel structure. Intermediaries can reduce the number of transactions between buyers and sellers, break bulk into saleable units, carry inventory and a range of items or assortment, offer specialist advice, provide market feedback and customised services such as fabrication. Two particular types of intermediary are agents and distributors. Distributors take control over how their goods are sold (price, place, promotion), whereas agents must abide by manufacturers' instructions. To reduce potential conflict in the channel, vertically integrated systems are sometimes encouraged. These may be based on informal co-ordination (administered), formal contracts or ownership between two or more members in the channel. In this way, members can become more motivated to work towards corporate goals.

One contractual arrangement of importance has been that between manufacturers and retailers. The increase in retail power in the UK and in certain parts of Europe has meant that decisions on branding have become more important. This increase in retail power has been catalysed by the abolition of resale price maintenance, the growth in their own label production, increases in perceived quality with corporate advertising and innovation and use of IT to monitor stock movements more closely. This has meant retail own brands are now more than ever competing not only on price but also quality head-on with manufacturer brands. Manufacturers can either control the marketing of their brands by refusing to undertake retail own label production (such as Kellogg's), adopt dual branding strategies (e.g. Heinz) or simply focus on making private labels (e.g. Booker Foods). Each of these will have different implications for management of the supply chain.

The shortest distribution channel is the direct route from supplier to customer. Direct marketing channels are becoming more important because they enable suppliers to evaluate their effectiveness more directly and allow closer contact with their customers, so offering additional opportunities for establishing lifelong relationships. In some cases, such as mail order, costs to the distributor are lower than traditional high street retailing because rents and stocks are negligible. Direct marketing channels include direct selling, home shopping (including mail order and direct response) and tele-marketing.

In addition, there is a growing interest in the Internet, with its potential for interactive response. From this, consumers can scan the globe for the best suppliers. Despite the advantages of direct marketing, ordering can be bureaucratic and customers may be concerned about buying tailor made merchandise from a distance (e.g. clothes that must fit correctly). In the case of home shopping involving IT, technophobia may be a severe obstacle.

References

Adburgham, R. (1995) 'Potential Partners', *Financial Times*, 25 July, p. 8.

Christopher, M. (1994) 'New Directions in Logistics', in James Cooper (ed.), *Logistics and Distribution Planning*. London: Kogan Page.

Fernie, J. (1994) 'Retail Logistics', in James Cooper (ed.), *Logistics and Distribution Planning*. London: Kogan Page.

Houlder, V. (1995) 'Plenty of New Departures', *Financial Times*, 10 August, p. 10.

McGoldrick, P.J. (1984) 'Grocery Generics: An Extension of the Private Label Concept', *European Journal of Marketing*, 18, 1, 5–24.

Mitchell, A. (1995) 'Dangerous Liaisons?', *Marketing Business*, 34–6 (July/August).

Oakland, J.S. and Porter, L.J. (1995) *Total Quality Management*. Oxford and London: Butterworth Heinemann.

Quelch, J.A. and Harding, D. (1996) 'Brands versus Private Labels: Fighting to Win', *Harvard Business Review*, 99–109.

Rosenbloom, B. (1978) *Marketing Channels*. Orlando, FL: Dryden Press.

Wileman, A. (1992) *The Shift in Balance of Power between Retailers and Manufacturers*. Management Centre, Europe, Brussels, June.

CHAPTER NINE

Marketing Communications 1: Advertising and Sales Promotion

Objectives

After studying this chapter, you should:

1. Be aware of many of the factors that affect the success of advertising.
2. Understand the benefits and limitations of advertising and sales promotion as part of the marketing communications mix.
3. Be able to set advertising objectives.
4. Distinguish between consumer and trade promotions.
5. Be able to use promotions strategically, not just tactically.

Introduction

Marketing communications includes making decisions about advertising, sales promotions, personal selling, public relations (PR) and direct mail. It is the fourth area of the marketing mix, also known as the promotional mix (refer to Figure 9.1).

Marketing communications is about how information on products, services, ideas, people or organisations is communicated, and what is communicated. It is one of the most *visible* aspects of marketing. The way information is projected is critical to the image of an organisation. Think about aspects of communications that you find irritating in organisations with which you are familiar – the lack of clear signs and directions in a hospital complex, unclear voice projection through a public address system at an airport or railway station, the apparently indifferent

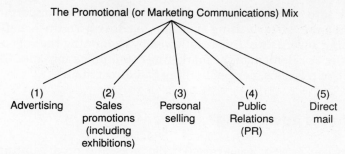

The Promotional (or Marketing Communications) Mix

(1) Advertising

(2) Sales promotions (including exhibitions)

(3) Personal selling

(4) Public Relations (PR)

(5) Direct mail

Key

Advertising   Any paid form of non-personal media presentation promoting ideas, concepts, goods or services by an identified sponsor.

Sales Promotion   Tactical, point-of-sale material or inducements designed to stimulate trade purchases (selling in) or consumer purchases (selling out), in which the promoter has overall control.

Personal Selling   Oral, face-to-face or telephone presentation in conversation with one or more prospective purchasers for the purpose of making sales.

Public Relations   Bridging the gap between the desired attitudes and feelings of specific audiences and their actual attitudes and feelings.

Publicity (as part of PR)   Commercially significant news about a product or service to obtain a favourable presentation of it via a medium not paid for by the sponsor.

Direct Mail   Mailshots targeted at specific groups (sometimes considered part of the sales promotion function).

Figure 9.1 The promotional mix

way you are treated on the telephone by your bank. Consider the disappointment of a promotional offer on goods, say, from a catalogue, when you discover on application (and wasted effort) that the offer has been withdrawn due to oversubscribing.

All these examples have happened to me, and all of them are frequent business problems. The first two relate to public relations (PR), the third to the personal selling function, and the last is a sales promotion problem in underestimating demand. What all these problems have in common is a lack of customer focus; marketing communications should be aimed at addressing the needs of the customer. All four examples highlight the importance of customer service. In the case of advertising, for instance, consumer appeals should be identified and readily communicated. These may either be *informative* (e.g. explaining how to use a new product) or *emotive* (e.g. offering a fantasy and escapism from the harsh realities of life).

Marketing communications covers a wide field and for this module we have split the subject into two chapters. Chapter 9 describes the importance of advertising and the role of advertising agencies, together with the benefits and limitations of using advertising. This is followed by examining the role of sales promotion, another key element of the marketing communications mix. Chapter 10 focuses on public relations, personal selling and direct mail.[*]

9.1 What is advertising?

Advertising is any *paid form*[1] of *non-personal*[2] *media*[3] presentation promoting *ideas/concepts, goods or services*[4] by an *identified sponsor*[5]. Let us examine this definition in more detail.

1. Advertising is *paid for* by an identified sponsor. It should be distinguished from publicity which is not paid for by the sponsor. This distinction is important. A typical advertisement will be creatively managed by an advertiser representing the *sponsor* or client and their agency. The advertiser is responsible for developing a campaign. The agency, which offers specialist services – creativity (developing the message and positioning), media selection and buying, and account management (responsible for co-ordinating the specific account) – will be paid a fee. Traditionally, this has been 15 per cent retained as commission for services rendered. The remainder is handed over to a media space owner in which the advertisement appears. Effectively, two contracts are made, one between the sponsor (or advertiser) and agency, the other between the agency and owner of media space. This is illustrated in Figure 9.2. Although the commission system of remuneration is still common, an increasing trend is to pay a negotiable fee, based on results. A major problem with the commission system is that agencies can receive increased remuneration for recommending to increase the media spend, and this is not always in the best interests of the client.

2. Another characteristic of advertising is that *media* are referred to as *non-personal*, i.e. messages portrayed in the media are not aimed at specific individuals but at mass markets or specific market segments. This means that communication is only directed one way, it does not allow interaction and feedback for the message to be altered and tailored for reaching individuals.

[*]It is acknowledged that future studies on marketing communications are likely to focus more on how all of these elements can work effectively together (referred to as integrated marketing communications, IMC). The importance of this is shown in maintaining a consistent corporate image (p. 269), although for more details in IMC, students should refer to specialist texts.

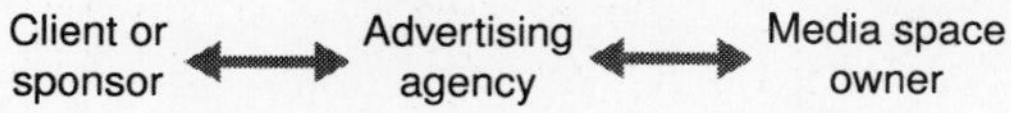

Client or ⟷ Advertising ⟷ Media space
sponsor   agency   owner

Figure 9.2 How the commission system works

3. Media can either be fleeting (such as television, cinema and local radio) or non-fleeting, such as print. This distinction is important because if advertisers need to communicate a complex message (say, how to use a new technology), fleeting media may be less appropriate because recipients of the message are unable to control the pace at which they understand the message. For the same reason, long copy, when needed, is more appropriate for non-fleeting media, such as news-papers or magazines, where receivers of the message can absorb the information at their own pace. Media are also classified according to where they are seen (i.e., as indoor and outdoor media). Outdoor media include advertising on billboards, transport (such as buses and taxis), and other means, such as weather balloons and airships used at shows.
4. Advertising is not only about goods and services. It is also about promoting concepts and ideas. Today, political parties, charities and local government all use advertising as a means of reaching targeted audiences with their vital messages.
5. Finally, the sponsor who is paying for the advertising space, is normally easy to identify.

9.1.1 Advertising is big business

The past and projected advertising expenditures shown in Figure 9.3, indicate that growth in the advertising industry is variable amongst Western European countries, with Germany showing most progress whilst France is relatively static. The highest concentration of advertising agency staff is in Madison Avenue, New York. In the UK, the largest agencies are Saatchi and Saatchi, John Walter Thompson, Ogilvy and Mather. Table 9.1 shows the top thirty based on 1995 declared sales (or billings), sourced from MEAL, in *Campaign*, 1996. MEAL represents media expenditure and analysis, owned by Nielsen, which reports statistical data on advertising expenditure for each market sector. The relative advertising expenditure by main media are shown in Table 9.2.

In terms of overall expenditure, press is the dominant medium, with television second, about half the expenditure of press and with other media relatively insignificant. Figures were relatively static between 1988 to 1993 for each medium, with the exception of cinema, with a relative percentage increase of 50 per cent since 1988. Media expenditure consists of both transmission costs, the cost of media space booked through the media owner (such as newspaper space or air time on TV), and the cost of making each ad, i.e. the production costs. Production costs can vary substantially according to the style of an ad and the

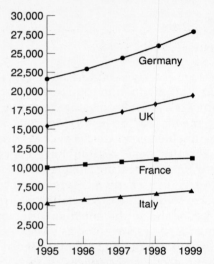

Source: Zenith Media Services Ltd, January 1977,
P127, Advertising Expenditure Forecasts

Figure 9.3 Expected growth in advertising expenditure 1995–9 ($US million at current prices in selected European countries) (Reproduced with permission of Zenith Media Services Ltd)

medium used. For example, using foreign locations or celebrities in TV can increase fees enormously, but as an approximation production costs account for about 15 per cent of overall TV costs, according to the Advertising Association (1994).

Display advertising is reserved for national and local advertisers, whereas classified ads are more likely to be used by individual consumers advertising something to buy or sell. Classified ads are those arranged under sub-headings according to the product or service advertised, e.g. lost or found, or selling a private car. These are often presented towards the back of a newspaper. Display advertising might take up much more space and is most likely to contain pictures or graphics.

Top advertisers, who invest heavily in advertising, tend to be household names, each holding a portfolio of successful brands. Such names include Procter & Gamble, Unilever, Kellogg's, Ford and BT. A typical top 20 ranking would spend over £30 million in advertising. Advertising is clearly an important factor in the success of these brands.

Furthermore, the impact of advertising on our lives can be reflected in the *opportunity to see* or OTS (a variable of advertising used for measuring media advertising, including television). Typical viewing hours for terrestrial (or non-cable) television, are shown in Table 9.3. The total ITV hours watched per day per individual owner is about 1.5, so the television as a medium reaches a large potential market.

Table 9.1 The top thirty Advertising Agencies

Campaign's Top 30 Agencies Ranked by Register-MEAL Billings

Rank 95		Register-MEAL billings (£m) 1995	Declared billings (£m) 1995	Staff 1994
1	Saatchi and Saatchi (excluding K Advertising and Team Saatchi)	260.2	410	530
2	J. Walter Thompson London	258.64	385	400
3	Ogilvy and Mather	255.3	308	308
4	Abbott Mead Vickers BBDO	246.85	259.2	275
5	BMP DDB Needham	227.8	310	330
6	D'Arcy Masius Benton and Bowles	201.09	221.4	310
7	Lowe Howard-Spink	180.07	259.4	N/A
8	Bates Dorland	176.77	235	294
9	Grey Advertising	174.6	301	440
10	Ammirati Puris Lintas	159.38	217.97	N/A
11	McCann-Erickson Advertising London	145.75	337.1	278
12	Publicis	144.22	199	221
13	WCRS	129.76	140.64	175
14	Euro RSCG Wnek Gosper	123.08	141	136
15	Bartle Bogle Hegarty	122.06	171	218
16	Leo Burnett	113.5	203	258
17	TBWA	86.04	130	107
18	Young and Rubicam	82.67	122.05	148
19	GGT Advertising	70.89	115	89
20	M&C Saatchi	65.79	53	N/A
21	Collett Dickenson Pearce	59.05	74.65	135
22	Delaney Fletcher Bozell	52.95	94	71
23	Foote Cone Belding	50.94	73	70
24	McCann-Erickson Manchester	46.76	64	190
25	BST-BDDP	41.71	121	57
26	Barker and Ralston	39.41	38	24
27	HHCL and Partners	38.94	92.52	102
28	St Lukes	37.26	45	48
29	WWAV Rapp Collins	35.49	N/A	210
30	Arc Advertising	33.31	92.7	137

Footnotes: Billings are based on accounts handled on a creative only, creative and planning or full-service basis. Media covered: TV, display press, radio, cinema and outdoor. Outdoor excludes tobacco and London Transport advertising for both 1994 and 1995. Declared billings for 1995 were submitted to *Campaign* between November last year and January 1996.

Source: Campaign report, 1 March 1996, p. 3. © A. C. Nielsen Register-MEAL.
(Reproduced with permission of A. C. Nielsen Register-MEAL)

Table 9.2 Relative advertising expenditure by main medium and by type

Medium	1993 %	1988 %
Press	61.8	64.2
Television, inc. production costs	31.6	30.0
Posters and transport, inc. production costs	3.6	3.4
Cinema, inc. production costs	0.6	0.4
Radio, inc. production costs	2.4	2.0
Type		
Display	74.8	73.6
Classified	25.2	26.4
	100.0	100.0

Source: The Advertising Association, *Advertising Statistics Yearbook 1994*, tables 3.1.1, 3.1.3, 4.1.1 and 4.1.2. (Reproduced with permission)

9.2 Factors affecting the success of advertising

Advertising is all around us and pervasive. We all have strong opinions about what we feel is good and bad advertising. However, as you read this section, you should appreciate the complexities involved in designing advertising in a highly competitive industry.

9.2.1 Advertising must be integrated

It is not sufficient to make advertising decisions in isolation from other business decisions. Designing advertising campaigns requires a multidisciplinary approach, with inputs from many different management functions and levels. Figure 9.4 shows how advertising decisions (effectively components of the advertising strategy) are developed from marketing objectives and more general corporate objectives. This is hierarchical integration: ensuring different managerial levels focus their energies and commitment on the same challenges and problems facing the organisation.

Marketing objectives should always derive from corporate objectives. Corporate objectives are often financially oriented (for example, based on rate of return on investment). The marketing and sales objectives derived from them refer to specific quantifiable goals such as:

- sales volume,
- market share,
- growth rate in sales,
- gross profits in total or by product line per time period.

Table 9.3 Share of terrestrial viewing by channel

Average hours viewing per individual during transmission period

	All ITV	BBC1	BBC2	All BBC	ITV/GMTV	C4	Other
1984	3.3	1.2	0.3	1.5	1.6	0.2	—
1985	3.8	1.3	0.4	1.7	1.8	0.3	—
1986	3.7	1.4	0.4	1.8	1.7	0.3	—
1987	3.6	1.4	0.4	1.8	1.6	0.3	—
1988	3.6	1.4	0.4	1.8	1.5	0.3	—
1989	3.6	1.4	0.4	1.8	1.5	0.3	—
1990	3.4	1.3	0.3	1.6	1.5	0.3	—
1991[1]	3.8	1.3	0.4	1.7	1.6	0.4	0.1
1992	3.8	1.3	0.4	1.7	1.6	0.4	0.2
1993[2]	3.6	1.2	0.4	1.6	1.4	0.4	0.2
1994	3.7	1.1	0.4	1.5	1.6	0.4	0.2

Share of audience

	All ITV	BBC1	BBC2	All BBC	ITV/GMTV	C4	Other
1984	100.0	35.8	10.3	46.1	47.9	5.8	—
1985	100.0	35.0	11.1	46.1	46.7	7.3	—
1986	100.0	36.5	11.0	47.5	44.6	7.8	—
1987	100.0	37.4	11.6	49.0	42.6	8.5	—
1988	100.0	38.1	11.0	49.1	41.9	9.0	—
1989	100.0	38.9	10.6	49.5	41.9	8.7	—
1990	100.0	37.7	10.1	47.8	43.4	8.9	—
1991[1]	100.0	34.2	10.1	44.3	42.2	9.7	3.8
1992	100.0	33.7	10.5	44.2	40.7	10.1	4.8
1993[2]	100.0	32.3	10.7	43.0	39.9	11.2	5.9
1994	100.0	29.7	10.8	40.5	43.2	10.8	5.4

Notes: Average viewing figures for 1984–85 should be used with caution due to changes in the measurement technique used to produce the data.
[1] Aug.–Dec.
[2] Jan.–Aug. Calculation methodology changed in August 1991.
Source: BARB, London.

If the main marketing objective for your particular organisation is to develop market share in the domestic market, there is little point in concentrating all the advertising investment in foreign markets, since the operations would be incompatible.

This compatibility, or *integration*, is also important across departments. Like any investment, there must be a commitment to advertising. Finance, for example, would need to co-operate by pledging support for advertising, once an investment decision had been agreed. The problem in arriving at a consensus about advertising decisions is that professionals often differ, as a result of their background and training. To illustrate how perceptions affect commitment, some professionals might describe a glass of water as half full, others as half

Source: Davies (1993).

Figure 9.4 The advertising plan

empty. One account gives a more positive description than the other. Many accountants would consider advertising as a cost, a burden to an organisation. Marketers therefore must have *highly developed interpersonal* skills to justify the existence of advertising as an investment for the future.

A third aspect of integration, apart from hierarchical and departmental components, is that of fostering a *balanced marketing mix*. This means that advertising decisions should not be made in isolation from the overall marketing strategy for pricing, distribution and product design. Consider your frustration if you are not able to obtain a brand or product shortly after it has been advertised. This is wasted advertising. Such advertising might actually make you aware of a latent need, so you buy a competitor's product. This highlights the need for integration between advertising and distribution.

As another example, it would be pointless to spend vast sums of money on advertising a product that is badly made, poorly designed and distributed through channels that offered no selling support or advice and after-sales service. Not only would the advertising investment be redundant, but costs might escalate, so forcing higher prices on to price-sensitive consumers patronising such distribution channels. Conversely, if a product is well designed in premium packaging and distributed in up-market department stores, inferior advertising is also wasted. Advertising alone is clearly not enough. Advertising benefits that cannot be delivered are also counterproductive.

9.2.2 Advertising must focus on its intended target audience

Referring to Figure 9.4, you can see that the first stage of the advertising strategy is to make decisions on targeting and segmentation.

Once target segments have been prioritised, advertising objectives can be formulated. One difficulty here is ensuring that the advertisements designed are properly focused and *do not aim at too many audiences*. If they do, it would suggest the variables used for identifying segments should be re-examined. It is also important to recognise the limitations in using advertising, if the targets are *too small* or *too difficult to reach cost-effectively*. If the target is very small, it is likely that alternative promotional forms should be considered, such as sales promotions, personal selling or PR. For example, Rolls-Royce have used sponsorship of the arts to reach the affluent social class A (3 per cent of the population) since although they are geographically diffuse, 50 per cent of them attend the opera.

9.2.3 Advertising must consider positioning

As we discussed in chapter 4, positioning is about how the consumer, rather than the advertiser, perceives the brand, product, organisation or concept being advertised. Using radical advertising which conflicts with current consumer perceptions may therefore be a risky strategy. Advertising convention conforms to the stereotypical association of promoting beers on heritage and tradition, whilst the emphasis on computers is their state-of-the-art modernity. Imagine reversing this association.

Life styles can also help to position brands, such as participating in the latest sports or using the latest media. A recent television campaign for the new Fiat Bravo and Brava shows teenagers examining these models from what appears to be a site on the Internet. This was designed to encourage viewers to associate Fiat products with high-tech automative machinery, at the cutting edge of technology. This is a positive selling benefit. Although it would be expected that many viewers would not know how to use the Internet, what was important was that they understood the image.

For advertising to be effective, the positioning of the message must be:

1. relevant to the target audience,
2. well understood,
3. (preferably) unique.

If all three are satisfied, this combination is called a *unique selling proposition* (USP). 'Polo – the mint with the hole' demonstrates that a product need not be technologically advanced to hold a unique position in the mind of the consumer. Nevertheless, the claim should be an accurate reflection of what the product or service can do.

Advertising by the Co-operative Bank demonstrates the power of finding a unique selling proposition even when a firm has neither the resources to fight head on with major banks nor a similar identity. Market share of the personal banking sector slipped back to just over 2 per cent in 1991. An agency was appointed which discovered that because the bank's deposits come from local authority and trade union sources, it had an unwritten ethical code, never having lent money to unsound organisations politically or environmentally. Since the bank has positioned itself as the ethical bank, there has been an increase in current account openings and a decrease in closures. More upmarket customers have also been attracted.

Since running this campaign the Co-operative Bank have claimed they will offer £10 to anyone experiencing an error in opening a current account or an error on their statements (conveying trust in their professionalism).

In refining the positioning, tracking consumer understanding is important. Advertising copy may not be suitable or appreciated by the target audience, for example, when technical *features* are over-emphasised instead of product *benefits*. Copy includes both the design of the ad in writing and its visual components, if relevant. Under-utilising a product in an advertisement may reduce its visibility. A common problem facing management is how to explain the major benefits of something new which is unfamiliar to the target audience. Often, the benefits of new products can be understood by demonstrating a use for them graphically. Pictures can be useful to emphasise a benefit, particularly if contrasted against a familiar object associated in the opposite direction. The benefit of 'spreadable' butter is easy to understand in Plate 9.1 because familiar objects of diamonds *symbolise* hardness against the softness of Anchor Butter.

Consumers may admire creative execution, but this will serve no purpose if they are left wondering what the ad is all about. '*Video vampires*', as they are called, may win creative awards but not market share. Some commercial advertising over-emphasises institutional information, which may appear trivial and irrelevant to the target audience.

Relevance is also transient – it varies over time. Look at the Gartmore advertisement (Figure 9.5). This was placed in the financial section of the quality press and shows an effective way of reaching readers who are most likely to be in need of such services. This is another approach designed to reduce waste.

9.2.4 Determining the appropriate objectives

A critical aspect of any advertising plan (Figure 9.4) is to determine what

Plate 9.1 Anchor Butter advertisement (Reproduced with permission of Saatchi and Saatchi advertising)

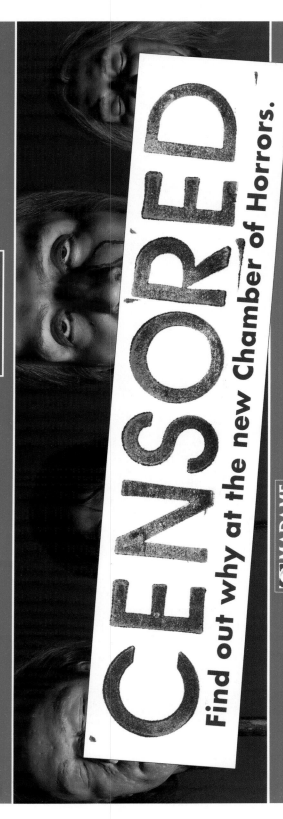

Plate 9.2 Madame Tussaud's advertisement: 'Severed Heads' and 'Censored' (Reprinted with permission of JWT Co Ltd and client)

Figure 9.5 Gartmore advertisement (Reproduced with permission)

objectives should be addressed. There are two main types of advertising objectives. One of these is based on *hard data*, which are either based on sales achieved or the number of enquiries made. The other set of important advertising objectives are based on *communication effects*, which typically lead to sales being made. The impact and effectiveness of an ad campaign should not always be measured in sales terms. Indeed, *rarely does one ad exposure induce sales*. What advertising does frequently is to *build up* favourable associations, images and an identity towards a brand, organisation, idea or concept (see Table 9.4 for a check list of possible advertising objectives).

Various *models of hierarchical effect* have been presented (for example, Colley, 1962; Lavidge and Steiner, 1961). These models assume that the viewer processes the information conveyed in ads *sequentially* through a series of stages. A general model is described in the form of an *advertising hierarchy* (Figure 9.6). In the advertising hierarchy shown, awareness is assumed to precede comprehension, preference and purchasing behaviour. This basic model assumes that communication objectives (awareness, understanding or preferences) need to be achieved first in order to create favourable conditions for selling to take place. In

Figure 9.6 The advertising hierarchy

other words, objectives are *prerequisites* before ultimate purchase is a realistic objective.

Consider how you might apply the model to a commercial situation. Using advertising with the intention of creating an immediate purchase may not be realistic. Advertising is unlikely to be effective if a campaign focuses on the wrong objectives. For instance, it is wasteful to try to create a sale through advertising if the target audience do not understand the product benefits first.

Whilst the model can be usefully applied to many purchases which are planned for, such as high outlay items, the model does not reflect habitual or impulse purchasing behaviour. With impulse behaviour, for instance, a good is purchased without prior planning and forethought, in which the cognitive stages of the model (awareness and understanding) are bypassed before purchase, only to become more important as the product is actively consumed through meaningful experiences. Habitual behaviour suggests the consumer purchases on autopilot. Competitors would need to develop marketing strategies that offered sufficient incentives for the habits to be broken. Another criticism of the standard hierarchy of effects model is that it ignores the indirect effects of advertising which can play a significant role in promotion.

Importance of indirect communication effects of advertising

Advertising can be measured in terms of its direct effects (or main effects) on performance (considered above) and its indirect effects. As markets become increasingly competitive during a period of escalating promotional costs, management will be assessed for the total effectiveness of a campaign on their firm's market performance. Park, Roth and Jacques (1988) assert that advertising has multiple effects on such performance. They believe that measures need to be developed in order to evaluate the indirect effects of communications, which they consider to be often overlooked or undervalued. Indirect effects include stimulation of word-of-mouth communications, both between consumers or final end-users and between intermediaries, or intermediaries and final users.

Table 9.4 Types of advertising objectives

Design objectives for closing an immediate sale	**Invest in building a long-range consumer franchise**
Offer a special reason for buying now (perceived value, incentives, closing down sale and so forth).	Build consumer and trade confidence in company and brand which helps to generate demand.
Use a command to instruct consumers to buy.	Help to improve bargaining position of the advertiser with the trade.
Remind consumers to buy.	Make it easier to launch new brands or trials by establishing a quality association with the organisation.
Design objectives to encourage consumers to move closer to a sale, by developing favourable brand conditions	**Develop sales objectives**
Create an impact and hence 'top of mind' awareness for the product or brand, especially when consumers are considering to buy.	Offer a reason for trying brand (e.g. trial offers). This could also be targeted to non-users.
Generate recognition of brand features (e.g. colour, pack, logo, style).	Maintain current customers.
Create 'brand image' or favourable emotional disposition towards the brand.	Encourage competitive users to switch brands.
Implant positive associations with the brand, such as relevant and unique benefits.	Increase frequency, usage or user occasion, attempting to convert light buyers to regular buyers.
Combat or offset competitive claims.	Educate about new developments relating to brand (e.g. new stockists, new uses of the product, new products and deals).
Clarify any misinterpretations of brands, possibly through repositioning.	
Develop the indirect effects of advertising	**Position the organisation with a clear, strong identity, based on**
Improve the morale of the workforce, especially those closest to customer contact (e.g. sales or branch staff). This will help to improve retention and staff performance.	Quality or reliability of service (eg Amex).
	Corporate citizenship (e.g. The Body Shop).
Stimulate media chatter, so improving brand familiarity.	Technical, progressive, forward looking (e.g. Audi, BMW).
Forge favourable alliances with the government and the media.	
Develop goodwill amongst investors and shareholders.	
Impress and harness confidence with the trade, so encouraging greater order sizes, preferential shelf space and active reselling.	
Help create confidence in sales staff and create a foot-in-the-door technique in personal selling.	

Word-of-mouth communication involves communication that is disseminated by the public at large – it is not marketer-controlled. Another is the enhancement of the firm's name and reputation. Another effect is to measure the increase in sales motivation arising from their awareness of advertising which promotes the products they represent. Collectively, these can serve to retain and recruit top sales staff.

Advertising that deliberately uses sensationalism can create additional impact and attention through word-of-mouth. For example, a poster ad for 18–30 Holidays featured the reference headline 'Beaver España', which created a buzz of publicity in newspapers and consequently reached audiences further afield than their prime prospects. This extended the life of the campaign, using a relatively modest budget. An ad for Madame Tussaud's featuring its Chamber of Horrors section was originally deemed gruesome by the Advertising Standards Authority, and was subsequently banned. It reappeared a year later (Plate 9.2). The banning caused a stir, gaining much media attention.

One indirect effect of the previously described Co-operative Bank campaign (section 9.2.3) is the improvement in employee morale, which helps service providers improve their relationships with their customers. Some examples of indirect effects are provided in Table 9.4. Particularly important are those which enhance the corporate image of a company and help the sales staff to sell their products.

9.2.5 Advertising must be well executed

In choosing an execution, the advertiser is choosing the means to communicate the main appeal of the advertised brand or product. A list of possible executions is shown in Table 9.5. There are no hard-and-fast rules on which execution to use for a given solution, although you should recognise that some types of execution are more suitable for particular market situations. For example, the advertising objective of *credibility* might be achieved by using a test result, a demonstration or by showing how the product or brand in question provides a solution to an every day problem (sometimes referred to as *slice of life ads*). Slice of life ads often under-emphasise the brand name, compared to repeat assertions, and so might be more suitable for brand leaders or for those brands with a high market share. If sponsors feel that their product is difficult to distinguish from the competition, or it is considered to be in a relatively unexciting product area, curiosity and humour might achieve *impact* and *attention*.

Executional decisions are not just about choosing between the options in Table 9.5. Once selected, the issue of implementation (refined to the level of exact graphics and wording, colour and size), is also an executional matter. The importance of execution is highlighted by Davidson (1972). Whilst using advertising on inferior products is wasteful, using inferior advertising is possibly even worse. Clutter is a particular feature of poor execution.

Table 9.5 A typology of executions

Title	Examples
Evidence/reason why	Argument
	Question and answer
	Often verified by demonstration or logic
	Scientific test
	Comparative test
Demonstrator	Spokesperson/testimonial
	Celebrity
	Reference group
	Trade association
Repeat assertions	Jingles
	Themes
Curiosity/exploration	News
	Ambiguity
	Provocation
	Mystique
	Fantasy
	Suspense
Mood/slice of life	Descriptive/problem-solver
Humour	Surprise
	Entertainment

Source: Davies (1993).

Cluttered daily messages compete strenuously for concentration. The 'clutter' approach suffers from trying to cram too much information into too little space. There is a danger that none of it will be read, since the ad fails to create impact. They can be used selectively if targeting price sensitive customers, or when introducing bargain sales into stores. (See Figure 9.7, for Wickes stores.)

9.2.6 Consider the market conditions in which you are advertising

The type of advertising used will be influenced by the stage at which a product has reached in the product life cycle (PLC). Since market conditions and the *degree of competition* will vary over the product life cycle, it follows that advertising should *serve different purposes across the market life of a product*. At the pre-launch stage, before a new product has reached the consumer, it is necessary to advertise in the *trade press* to reach stockists with the objective of *persuading* them to build up inventory.

If the product is radically new, using advertising alone is unlikely to be adequate – some form of investment in personal selling, together with trade promotions may be necessary. (See the next chapter for fuller details.) Personal

Figure 9.7 Wickes advertisement (Reproduced with permission of Wickes Building Suppliers)

selling may be appropriate where the benefits of the new product are hidden, not obvious or likely to need elaborate explanation to ensure correct usage. Thus *two-way communication* may be necessary.

Once the product has been introduced to the market, *informative advertising* aimed at consumers is appropriate. At this stage, creating an awareness of product benefits, explaining how to use it, and informing of potential stockists will probably be critical to ensure the product takes off into the growth stage, with mass market appeal. Proven market acceptance will attract competitors, but they can be frustrated by stimulating a *brand personality* for the product which is both relevant and distinctive.

For example, Volvo, associated for many years with safety and reliability, were conscious of their over-reliance on a narrow model range, which appealed to the family segment but which was considered rather dull by other segments. To inject a more adventurous, yet safe personality in to their brands, they have used shock executions in their commercials. These have attracted a wider market in appealing to both younger pre-family and older post-family buyers. Resembling mini feature films, each ad conveys a dramatic story using a first person commentary set against a tense soundtrack. One film showed a stuntman driving a Volvo Estate across an exceptionally narrow railway bridge. Another featured the perils of a tornado researcher.

As the product enters maturity, the market reaches saturation. Price as a promotional tool might be used to motivate alternative market segments that have yet to enter and try the product. Alternatively, the product might be increasingly refined (such as a new improved formula of a car design) in which case this feature needs to be promoted to gain maximum advantage. In many cases, advertising serves to *reinforce* or *remind* customers of product benefits to retain loyalty.

In the decline stage, advertising serves to *reassure* consumers about the product. *Replacement sales* may be an important feature. In order to survive, the organisation might focus on a *niche* market such as targeting bargain hunters before total divestment takes place.

9.2.7 Consider the process in the setting of budgets and the size of the company

Advertising budgets should be determined by what is considered sufficient to achieve the advertising objectives. In practice, they are sometimes determined by a given volume of sales, which follows that a firm with falling demand will inevitably be allocated a smaller budget next year than perhaps it deserves. Another problem is that the actual budget set for the next trading year represents no more than a statement of intent at the time it is allocated. It may not be what is actually received by marketing. The advertising budget is a relatively easy target in a drive for cost-cutting in poor trading conditions, particularly because revenues derived from it have not been traditionally easy to justify. One solution is to make marketing and advertising management more accountable for their actions, and to encourage both financial and marketing managers to work in cross-functional teams to share in each other's viewpoints.

You should appreciate that advertising is *comparatively less effective for smaller brands*. The cost can be spread across a higher volume for larger brands. Consider the cost per unit sale of a £2 million advertising campaign with an alternative 10p price cut for two brands A and B (Table 9.6). Since the sales of B are smaller, the cost of advertising per unit is more expensive, and is financially less effective compared to a 10p price cut.

Another related problem for the advertiser of smaller organisations is that they tend to have *lower budgets*. Since the production costs for some media may be prohibitive, this might restrict the creativity of a campaign. For example, a high turnover (perhaps over £50 million) would be necessary for a sustained television campaign. Any organisations shifting their allegiance to cheaper media (e.g. radio) might need to sacrifice some quality in their creativity. For some markets, in which television might be the best medium for advertising (e.g. instant cameras, in which demonstration could be shown to good effect), limited budgets might cause severe problems. A smaller budget will also hamper media objectives from being achieved. Apart from media considerations affecting the creative output as mentioned above, a smaller advertising budget means either a cut in *quality and/or quantity of exposures*.

9.2.8 The client/agency relationship

For a campaign to be developed effectively requires commitment from both client and agency. Because advertising is about communication, it is essential there is a *healthy rapport* between the sponsoring client and their appointed ad agency for necessary interaction to take place. To some extent, an agency can only be as good as the *ad brief* that is devised by the client. Typical questions that may need answering at the beginning of a campaign are shown in Table 9.7.

How much structure and detail a client gives, and how many mandates they require will vary for different campaigns. Mandates might include observing strict deadlines, tight budgets and specific advertising aspects, such as product appeals or media required. Failure to adhere to mandates may result in penalties, or even in switching accounts to another agency.

Table 9.6 Comparison of costs/unit sale of advertising and sales promotions

Brand	Net sales (millions)	Cost/Unit 2m ad campaign	10p price cut
A	100	2p	10p
B	10	20p	10p

Table 9.7 Examples of questions asked for in an advertising brief

Client-specific requirements	Possible solutions
The target audience To whom is it talking?	
What is it intending to achieve? What should they think when they see it?	
What supportive evidence is there?	
Alternative appeals that might be used	
Type of market/product	
Type of media	

9.3 Regulation in advertising

All non-broadcast advertising media is self-regulated by the Advertising Standards Authority (ASA). Non-broadcast includes all print media, direct mail, cinema, cassettes and teletext. Television and cable ads are regulated by the Independent Television Commission (ITC), and for radio by the Radio Authority.

All broadcast ads are vetted by the Broadcasting Copy Clearance Centre, whereas only a sample of non-broadcast ads are examined by the equivalent body (the ASA) to ensure they conform to particular standards which aim to protect both other advertisers and consumers. The copy clearance of the Radio Authority is voluntary, and organised by the radio stations themselves.

All non-broadcast ads must adhere to the British Code of Advertising Practice, (CAP) and all televised ads to the ITC Code of Programme Sponsorship. Outdoor advertising also must adhere to CAP and the ASA. Broadly, all bodies require that ads adhere to their codes of practice to ensure ads are legal, decent, honest and truthful. Additional restrictions apply to the advertising of charities, alcohol, health claims, direct mail, and children.

Claims must not be misleading (subject to the Misleading Advertisements Regulations 1988). In the case of television, the licensees or television companies are responsible for the ads they show on air. Advertisers using superiority claims about their products should ensure that they are capable of objective assessment, and can provide evidence to support their claims. When Tesco advertised their 'New Deal Pricing Scheme' on television, announcing they '. . . actually lost money' on certain items, Asda objected because they felt it inferred that the items advertised were sold below cost (i.e. they were perceived as loss leaders). Despite Tesco defending their claim, explaining that this was meant to suggest they were not making as much profit as they previously had on these items, the ITC agreed with Asda that it was misleading. The ITC instructed the television companies not to repeat the ad without appropriate changes.

Certain procedures should be followed if you, as a consumer, decide to make a complaint. The advertising regulatory bodies first encourage you to deal with the sponsor direct. If you are not satisfied with the response, you may then write to the relevant regulatory body. You should supply the name of the sponsor, where and when the ad was seen, and the nature of the complaint. The regulatory body must decide if you have a justified case for complaint. Only a fraction proceed further. A regulatory body has the power to amend or withdraw an ad, if they feel their code has been violated.

Many complaints from the public are based on perceptions of offensive ads. The regulatory bodies such as the ASA comprise a multidisciplinary team of academics, advertisers, industrialists and consumers. The 'jury' should not be considered biased in favour of one party or another. Having acknowledged this, few complaints made by the public are upheld in their favour, with something approaching less than 5 per cent upheld in whole or in part. Combined with the extra publicity that apparently offensive ads can create, you can begin to appreciate why creating controversy and 'media chatter' is big business in the advertising world. (Sources: ASA, Advertising Standards in Europe, July–August 1995; ITC (1993) *Code of Advertising Standards and Practice*, May; ASA (1994) Annual Report; and ASA (n.d.) *Advertising under Control*.)

9.4 Choosing the media

Once the advertising strategy has been decided, the next step is to decide the media plan. This involves both choosing and scheduling the appropriate media. The sequence in choosing appropriate media is shown in Figure 9.8. Our attention will be restricted to choosing media, since scheduling is a very specialist area. First, the media class is decided. This involves choosing amongst broadcast and non-broadcast media. This is determined by two main criteria: the budget available for a campaign (since the cost of some media may be prohibitive for a small budget), and the requirements of the advertising strategy. An advertising strategy that requires high-impact imagery (perhaps necessitating strong visuals) would require a visual medium such as television or cinema. Conversely, an advertising strategy that requires an informative and complex message works best in print. Providing suitable media classes have been selected, media vehicles can then be shortlisted. Once again, creative considerations are important. For example, in advertising personal computers, there are various specialist magazines available, which can attract the target audience with little wastage. In contrast, personal computers priced for a mass audience might be better promoted in the national press, in which volume sales are an important marketing objective. Once a shortlist has been identified, the actual vehicles can then be determined from using a range of measurement techniques.

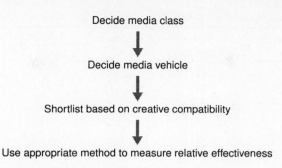

Figure 9.8 Decisions in choosing media

9.4.1 Methods used in measuring media vehicle effectiveness

A common method of measuring media effectiveness is by cost per thousand. For press or magazine advertising, it is necessary to know the cost of insertion for each page displayed, or part thereof, for colour, or black and white. It is also necessary to know the circulation for each vehicle. Circulation refers to the number of buyers of a media vehicle. Both display costs and average circulation figures for a variety of print media can be found in the reference book *BRAD* (*British Rate and Data*). Cost per thousand is then determined by the ratio:

$$\text{CPT} = \frac{\text{cost of insertion in vehicle}}{\text{circulation of vehicle}} \times \frac{1000}{1}$$

The cost per thousand criterion provides the cost of reaching 1,000 buyers of the vehicle medium. This is more beneficial to an advertiser than simply selecting vehicles on the basis of rates per page because circulation figures vary enormously between different media vehicles. Table 9.8 lists various insertion costs and circulation figures for computer journals targeted at either the consumer or organisational market.

Using the cost per thousand method should be treated with caution. First, it informs you of the cost of reaching 1,000 buyers, not necessarily those who are readers. Since the number of readers per buyer can vary a lot between journals and magazines (owing to their availability at clubs, doctors' and dentists' waiting rooms, hairdressing salons, and in the home) the cost per readership would be an improvement on the cost per circulation as a measure of alternative media effectiveness.

This can be further refined. It is unlikely that everyone who has an opportunity of reading will be a member of the target audience. Unless they are, some wastage will occur. Whilst *BRAD* does offer circulation figures based on ABC1 profiles, this will not always be the target audience for some products and would

Table 9.8 Circulation and costs of display advertising

Home computer specialised journals	Issue frequency	Circulation[1]	Page rates[2] £ Mono	Page rates[2] £ Colour
Mean Machines Sega	M†	45,156[1]	1,395	1,880
PC Review	M†	43,984[1]	900	1,400
Trade computer and professional journals				
Computer Shopper	M†	150,124[1]	1,655	2,365
Computer Weekly	W	115,659[2]	3,824	5,126
Computing	W	116,335[2]	3,759	5,019

Sources:
1. ABC data (various dates, as follows): † six months data only, UK; [1] January to June 1995; [2] January to December 1994. (Reproduced with permission of ABC Ltd)
2. *BRAD* (August 1994) single insertion rate. (Reproduced with permission of EMAC Business Publications Ltd, London)

Example of cost per thousand criterion, based on colour page:

$$\text{CPT of } \textit{Computer Weekly} = \frac{£5,126}{115,659} \times \frac{1000}{1} = £44.32.$$

*Permission to reproduce from EMAP Publications, London.

then require an adjustment. Bear in mind that the ABC1 audiences provided are only estimates, based on a sample of viewers. Since they are retrospective, they do not guarantee future audiences on which costs are based.

A further criticism of the cost per 1,000 criterion is that circulation or readership figures do not represent the amount of exposure given to an advertisement. The problem in estimating the quality of exposure is difficult. Some readers will read magazines or newspapers thoroughly, whilst others scan or browse, skipping ads deliberately. Most will vary in how much concentration they give different ads under different circumstances. To cope with these difficulties, media research can be conducted to identify the percentage that have read a particular journal, a particular page and those who can remember details of a particular ad (used as a measure of their concentration or exposure quality). Thus:

$$\text{Refined cost per 1,000 (of reaching readers who are sufficiently exposed)} = \frac{\text{cost of insertion of ad}}{\text{circulation} \times \text{readers per circulation} \times \text{\% sufficiently exposed to ad}}$$

The term 'sufficiently' relies on the judgement of the advertiser in determining what is required for a particular campaign.

The Broadcaster's Audience Research Board Ltd was set up in 1980, and is designed to offer a single system of broadcast audience research in the UK. Television can also be evaluated by the cost per thousand method, but instead of using circulation figures, audience size is used. This requires estimating the percentage of homes using television, which will be influenced by the time of the day and the popularity of programmes, which ultimately determine the viewing figures from which media rates are charged to advertisers. In order to provide an estimate of who is watching what at particular times of the day, a small sample of viewers are provided with meters in their own homes. The results are then grossed up to provide viewing rates. Each viewer is allocated a switch or light which, when activated, should indicate they are watching television. Viewing habits are recorded by the meter. The system relies on the conscientiousness of each viewer to provide a full record of their viewing habits. Samples are often small or distorted. Once again, the quality of the ad exposure can be questioned.

Research has suggested that the majority of viewers do multiple tasks whilst watching television. Lee and Lee (1995) recommend measures should be devised to record their physical proximity to their sets, and their mental and physical involvement with other activities. Television, together with radio, may be used as a background noise for many, and the television may be switched on without being watched. Although diaries can be used to record their activities or 'quality of viewing', it still relies on complete reporting by the respondents, which is unlikely to be totally accurate.

Cost of television breaks, or spot times, are divided into peak and non-peak rates, depending on estimates of the targeted viewing figures. Cost will also be influenced by special events (such as scheduling a series of ads during the World Cup), and special requirements (such as requesting the first or last position of a commercial break, or fitting in with the content or target audience of particular programmes). Discounts are available for volume purchases. The skill of the media buyer working in an agency is to obtain the most effective package of spots at minimum cost for their clients. When deciding the timing and media space required, the media planner will estimate the number of exposures required to reach a given percentage of the specified audience effectively. It is often considered that several exposures are required to achieve maximum effectiveness. The cost per thousand criterion is also used for radio ads and the diary method is used to estimate audiences of different channels.

For outdoor media, such as public transport, cost per exposure is used. A recent development in poster site evaluation is to offer travel survey and visibility tests to provide clients with more accurate data on their poster audiences (Summers, 1996).

Case study: A sticky problem

The sales of a household cleaning fluid designed to remove limescale in kitchens and toilet surfaces is currently restricted by several problems. The target audience (typically working women) do not believe that limescale is a problem to them, as part of their routine cleaning regime. Furthermore, many women believe there is little point in expending effort trying to remove stubborn stains which progressively tarnish working surfaces. Generally, hard water areas suffer most from limescale deposits.

Research has revealed some intriguing findings about consumer behaviour. First, the majority of working women take a great pride in keeping their homes clean. Secondly, any sign of uncleanliness is considered a failing in their duty as a 'proper housewife'. However, other women share similar problems with limescale, and this appears to reduce the seriousness of their problem.

This limescale brand also suffered from low recall levels compared to other brands. It was believed this arose from frequent creative shifts in brand positioning, low share of voice, inconsistent media scheduling and the difficulty in developing a brand personality in a market considered intensively competitive and commoditised.

You have been hired as an advertising consultant to:

Q9.1 Clarify the advertising and marketing problems and justify how advertising may salvage the brand.

Q9.2 Develop a new campaign, including advertising objectives, appeals and executions that will make it difficult for competitors to copy any success enjoyed.

Q9.3 Outline options for continuity of brand success beyond the campaign.

9.5 Sales promotion

Sales promotion is a general term used for a wide range of promotional tools not formally classified as advertising, personal selling or public relations. Promotions can be targeted at a company's own sales force, distributors or retailers, or to the final consumer to encourage buying (Figure 9.9).

9.5.1 Types of sales promotions: consumer promotions

We begin by examining a variety of consumer sales promotions. These may be either *price-related promotions*, usually based on a prime motive, or *non-price-based promotions* (designed to encourage usage and to enhance brand equity, i.e. add value to the promoted brand or service). (Refer to Table 9.9.)

Note that *samples* or *trial packs* are ideal for introducing new products. (For example, when the washing powder Radion was first launched, trial packs were made available; refer to Figure 9.10.) Ensure there is no confusion between

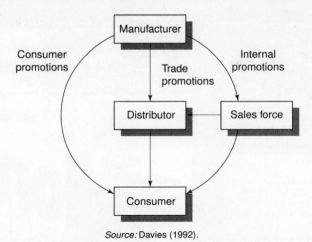

Source: Davies (1992).

Figure 9.9 Different targets for sales promotion

Table 9.9 Taxonomy of consumer sales promotions

	Generic title	**Examples**
Price-related trial promotions	Sampling	Free samples
		Trial-size samples
		Demonstrations
	Coupons	Redemption offers
		Refunds or rebates
	Price offs	Bonus factors
		Flashpacks
Non-price (mainly usage) promotions	Warranties	Money back guarantees
	Premiums	
	Contests and sweepstakes	
	Continuity programmes	Stamps
		Collector items

Source: Davies (1992).

samples and *free gifts* or *premiums*. Free gifts are offered, either in-store, inside or on-pack, or by mail drop. The advantage of free gifts or premiums (in which a part payment may be made by the consumer) is that awareness can be promoted through the name. Examples include Whiskas (cat food) calendars showing various poses of cats, and the collector items of vintage cars offered by Nabisco (breakfast cereals). The ideal gifts and premiums are those that offer opportunities for display. Their high visibility can encourage word-of-mouth referral, so increasing brand awareness. Gifts may also be offered in the industrial market to

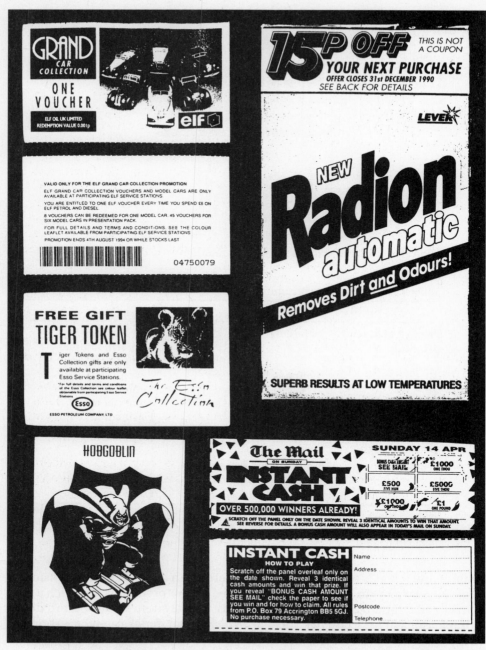

Figure 9.10 Examples of sales promotion (Reproduced with permission of Elf Oil UK Ltd; Esso Petroleum Company Ltd; Lever Brothers Ltd; Quaker Oats Ltd; *The Mail on Sunday* (Associated Newspapers Ltd)

reinforce a favourable image, in which there is a *considered fit* between the image of the gift offered and that intended to the promoting organisation. For example, Brush Transformers offer Parker Pens as free gifts to their corporate clients to convey a quality image.

Another consumer promotion which you are likely to be familiar with is *redeemable coupons*. Coupons are collected and redeemable for gifts. Examples include the promotions run by Elf and Esso oil companies, in which a number of coupons can be redeemed either to build up a car collection or select gifts from the Esso Collection (Figure 9.10). They are often used in fiercely competitive markets, designed to encourage loyalty until expiry of the promotion. The problem is that the consumer may be rather more loyal to the promotion than the intrinsic value of the brand promoted. Coupons, therefore, rarely strengthen brand loyalty. Moreover, if the redemption offer is stimulated on price, consumers may actually *attribute inferior quality* to the brand, and so reduce brand equity. The same can be said for using other price-related offers such as *flashpacks*. These are star-shaped signs with a price offer, usually offered on commodity items. They may increase *impulse buying* but rarely long-term brand loyalty.

Discounts can sometimes be useful in price promotions. Utilities such as Water Boards often offer discounts to consumers if they pay in lump sums instead of on an instalment basis. This is cost-effective when dealing with a captive market, providing the extra returns based on interest invested on early receipt is more than the discount allowed. Building societies have also targeted their discounting incentive on first-time house buyers in a housing recession. Here the consumer is effectively 'locked in' through high *switching costs*.

Another option is to offer *deferred payment schemes*. These are suitable for consumer durables, where the outlay may be considerable. Like the availability of credit options, deferred payments may widen the market. Instalment plans allow consumers to budget for their payments. British Gas and the Electricity Boards often promote their appliances on this basis.

Although a substantial amount of money spent on promotions is price-based (Petersen, 1980) there is a variety of other promotions which do not focus on price as an incentive. Amongst these are *competitions* and *continuity programmes*.

Whilst the cost of coupons to the promoter or sponsor depends on the redemption rate, which is difficult to forecast accurately, competitions offer the sponsor the advantage of deciding the cost from the outset, which is based predominantly on the prize money. Competitions can offer the consumer the chance of winning a significant prize. Major competitions may therefore lure consumers who would normally ignore smaller offers through collecting coupons.

Competitions are legally distinguished from draws and lotteries – competitions require a significant degree of judgement or skill. This difference allows sponsors to charge for entering such competitions. Another advantage of competitions is that sponsors may gain significant *media coverage* by releasing the results. Sometimes the competitions are combined with a questionnaire, identifying consumer intentions.

For example, in return for a test drive and the chance to win a special prize, drivers might be asked to complete demographic details of age, occupation, numbers of children and behavioural data such as car ownership and registration data. Promotions can therefore become part of an organisation's future *market intelligence gathering*, and reveal a lot about a product's key positioning.

Companies often request participants to develop a *catchphrase* or *slogan* as part of a competition. If slogans are intended to say something about a given brand, analysis of consumer responses by skilled psychologists might uncover key perceptions of the brand. Winning slogans may also be used as future advertising material. They are likely to communicate directly with the target audience since they have been written in their language. An example is the catchphrase 'Once driven, forever smitten', which was developed from a competition for Vauxhall Motors.

Another popular promotion, designed to increase loyalty, is frequently used in fiercely competitive markets such as newspapers. A week's scratchcards may be supplied on a single purchase of a newspaper, with the intention of encouraging repeat purchases of newspapers for the remaining week. Refer to Figure 9.10 (*The Mail* example). Scratching out the panel reveals several cash amounts. A winner has to reveal three identical values on a panel to win that amount. The secret to encourage repurchase is to ensure each panel reveals a daily bonus cash amount, which is only made known on buying the daily issue of the newspaper. Psychologically, consumers may become hooked on this because once they have bought a single copy, they feel they might be losing out.

Ongoing or long-term promotions such as *continuity programmes* are designed to foster loyalty by developing high switching costs. Profiles Points are offered by Barclaycard (a major UK credit card) on every £10 spent using the card, which can be redeemed for a variety of gifts. Barclaycard holders are encouraged to use their card more frequently than other credit cards which do not offer such an incentive. Importantly, once the saving habit towards a gift has begun, the cost of switching over (in using a competitor's card) is no contribution towards a gift. This represents a high switching cost.

The *quality of the promotion* offered can also be significant. It can enhance perceived quality by *reinforcing* or *transferring* distinctive *associations*. These associations must be relevant and distinctive for the target audience to be motivated in participating. For example, Figure 9.11 shows a Flora promotion, which aims to reinforce their health-oriented credentials by associating themselves with the London Marathon by sponsoring the British Heart Foundation. Sponsorship is the financial support of a business activity, individual or organisation in order to achieve a positive image. Similarly, the quality or fit of the promotion is exemplified with Barclays Profile Points, associated with gifts such as exotic travel, and provides offers to take part in the latest sports, matching the sophistication of the target groups. Opportunities for pampering such as 'Tone up Time' and 'Dine with style' can capture an experience which helps reinforce and maintain enthusiasm in the scheme, and so help increase brand usage.

Figure 9.11 Flora advertisement (Reproduced with permission of Van Berghs Foods)

Trading stamps are designed to increase store loyalty rather than brand loyalty through the collecting habit. Fictitious or *trade characters* may bring a brand to life or personify it. Davies (1992) suggests that the key to sustaining a competitive advantage with sales promotions is to ensure that a *planned stream of promotions reinforce each other* and are consistent with the firm's *intended positioning*. Trade characters like the cuddly Honey Monster, which is appealing to kids, have been retained by Quaker Oats Ltd for a continuous series of promotions for their Sugar Puffs brand of breakfast cereal. Such presence keeps the name active in the minds of the target audience, particularly when the character resembles the product visually. If the trade character does not resemble the product, the feelings associated with it must be positive, such as the Hobgoblin character, which appeals to kids (again, by Quaker Oats Ltd, Figure 9.10). In another example, Mr Sheen, a trade character sporting flying goggles and moustache, used by Reckitt & Colman for wax polish, is associated with speed, spirit, warmth, reliability and panache, according to consumer research. In this case, the name is effective because it combines the qualities of being shiny and clean (i.e. SHINY and CLEAN = MR SHEEN).

Other consumer promotions involve using reciprocal deals. An example would be getting members of the public to use their own home as a selling environment in return for a discount on purchases. Suitable products might be double glazing and conservatories, in which *signals of value* are conveyed to consumers by:

- promoting the ability to see and inspect the product *in situ*;
- promoting the salesperson's 'purchase' as an endorsement of quality and value;
- informing consumers they are not paying for expensive showrooms and professional sales staff;
- demonstrating, through physical evidence, the extent to which the *in situ* product has been customised to the physical surroundings of the house.

An example of a promotional tie-in, designed to improve the performance of two or more companies, is provided by Esso and Cadbury in their Snack and Shop advertisement (Figure 9.12). This is intended to improve sales for both companies and help establish increased purchases of non-petrol goods at petrol stations. The skyscrapers shown in the ad feature a range of goods, so improving awareness of what can be purchased from Esso shops.

Other schemes involve getting closer to the consumer through *relationship marketing*. Some car manufacturers, such as BMW, offer *club schemes* to their customers, which adds an identity to the status-conscious, which can also help reduce *cognitive dissonance* after purchase. *Factory visits* offer the chance for consumers to be in close contact with senior management, which can provide valuable feedback for improving future offerings.

Spend a few pounds at an Esso Snack & Shop and you could spend a few days in New York.

Spend at least £3.00 in one of our shops, including a block of Cadbury's chocolate plus anything else you choose, and you and a partner could be heading for a shopping trip to the Big Apple. Alternatively, you could find you've won a trip to The Mall of America, Paris, London, Edinburgh or even a family trip to Cadbury World.

 **Snack & Shop**

See full terms and conditions in participating stores. While stocks last. No purchase necessary. Product range and prices may vary. Promotion ends 8th May 1996.

Figure 9.12 Esso advertisement
Source: Permission granted by Esso Petroleum Company Ltd and JWT Co Ltd.
Photographer: Gary Bryan.

9.5.2 Trade promotions

The major aim of trade promotions is to motivate the trade to carry a particular product line or brand, and so *push* the merchandise through the channel (Figure 9.9). One strategy designed to achieve this is to offer an abundance of point-of-sale material designed to attract attention to specific brands, especially if it lures consumers to promotional offers. Whilst many trade promotions are similar to those targeted at the consumer or end-user, such as cash discounts for prompt payment or deals on bulk purchases and competitions aimed at dealers, several are different.

Retailer trade promotions, for example, may be demanded by the large multiple chains because of their buying power. In grocery retailing, for instance, 60 per cent of the possible consumer market is denied to food manufacturers unless they conform to retail specifications. These specifications include slotting fee allowances, product support packages, advertorial, deferred payment schemes and trade return sales policies. *Slotting allowances* are preliminary listing fees demanded by retailers in consideration of allocating shelf-space for a new brand. If the manufacturer requires a *special display position* or *premium space* requirements, more up-front money is demanded. In addition, a manufacturer may need to help in sharing the costs of the retailer's advertising and sales promotions, in-store. *Advertorial* offers the chance for the manufacturer's brand to be endorsed in the store magazine *disguised as publicity* (although the manufacturer would pay for this service). Retailers may also ask for *extended credit* and a *returns policy*. A returns policy reduces the risk to the organisational buyer. If the goods do not sell within an agreed date after purchase, the buyer is entitled to return goods. This is particularly pertinent for *weak brands*, which have yet to prove an impact in the marketplace, and *slow-moving lines*. New products, which need high awareness for market acceptance, may need to be promoted in this way.

Retailers will want to stock high branded goods with a proven track record, since such products might increase store traffic and loyalty. In this case, the *balance of power* shifts to the manufacturer who may demand *minimum order quantities* purchased.

9.5.3 Problems in implementing trade promotions

Those in charge of implementing trade promotions need to ensure that their distributors understand fully how they may benefit. For example, a manufacturer offering rebates based on purchases made may need to clarify whether purchases relate to single retail branches or to total branch purchases. There is also the possibility that sales staff may push only those items on promotion, so effectively cannibalising others in the product line. Care is therefore required in *briefing* the sales force.

9.5.4 Internal promotions: dealer staff incentives and recognition awards

Incentives may be offered to staff, based on performance. Sales staff, for instance, may be offered special incentives for exceeding their personal sales targets. These incentives can be directly *financial* or *non-financial*, such as in dining out in a top restaurant with senior management to provide an ego boost. To maintain motivation, it is important that incentives are *varied periodically*. The *criteria* on which incentives are based should also be revised regularly, otherwise it is likely the same people will continue to win such awards, causing divisions within the ranks and/or possibly demotivation.

Summary

Advertising is a one-way form of communication, aimed at a specific audience, through the use of appropriate media, financed by a recognisable sponsor. Ads are usually developed by approaching agencies who may offer skills in creativity, media selection and account management. The importance of advertising can be reflected by the top 200 advertisers most of which are household brand names.

The success of advertising can be attributable to many factors. Ideally, advertising strategy should be planned, in which decisions are derived from the marketing plan (objectives and strategies). Advertising strategy includes making decisions on targeting and segmentation, formulating ad objectives, creating a positioning format, and deciding what appeals and executions to use.

Within the advertising *plan*, the main reasons why ads fail are:

- poor integration with other decisions at the marketing and corporate level; and
- poor integration with other departmental objectives.

Within advertising *strategy*, reasons for failure include:

- poor integration of marketing strategy;
- poor targeting (too small to be cost-effective, too difficult to reach effectively or aiming at too many audiences);
- focusing on the wrong advertising objectives;
- conveying a poor positioning strategy such as:
     overemphasising technical features (irrelevance),
     underemphasising product visibility (incoherence),
     overemphasis on institutional data (irrelevance);
- not conveying an easily understood message;

- not conveying uniqueness, where possible;
- poor choice of appeals and execution, such as:
    using the 'clutter' approach,
    overelaborating the 'attraction' factor at expense of achieving ad
        goals;
- setting inappropriate objectives at the current stage of the product life
    cycle;
- size of budget in terms of:
    cost per unit,
    not gaining sufficient exposure, so affecting either frequency or
        reach objectives; and/or
    a poor agency/client relationship.

Advertisers should also abide by the expectations of fair competition outlined by the regulatory bodies referred to in their Code of Practice. These expectations are that all ads must be legal, decent, honest and truthful. Thus ads should not be designed to mislead the public nor cause grave offence.

Apart from creative decisions, the choice and scheduling of media need to be decided. Media choice can be divided into classes (e.g. print, broadcast or outdoor) or vehicles (e.g. in terms of print, different publications of newspapers or magazines). Whilst choice of class is determined partly by the creative requirements of the campaign and the size of the budget, selection of vehicles requires some approximation of audience size and, if possible, their quality of exposure or level of concentration. Media rates are determined by the reach (the numbers of a qualified audience who are exposed at least once) and the frequency of exposures offered. Different vehicles are often compared on a cost per thousand basis.

Sales promotions are either targeted at the consumer, the trade or internally to motivate staff. Although the traditional view of promotions is for tactical gain (e.g. in the shift in the timing of sales rather than increasing overall sales), they can be used *strategically* if the focus is on *objectives other than price*. These non-price-based promotions can be used to create brand awareness, offer perceived quality which may sustain premium pricing, increase loyalty by increasing switching costs and possibly provide cost leadership and valuable marketing research for future planning. Awareness may be created by parading premiums which cannot easily be copied, such as an *Observer* or Guinness sweatshirt, serving as a proxy advertisement. Competitions and games offer the opportunity of involvement long after the product has been advertised and consumed, so giving periodic reminders. When reinforcing perceived quality, the promotion must be carefully selected. Ideally the promotion and the brand, or third party promotions must complement each other. Also each new promotion must be carefully chosen to support previous ones to sustain a consistent positioning. Furthermore, sales promotion should be properly integrated with other elements of the marketing mix to be most effective.

References

Aaker, D., Batra, R. and Myers, J. (1992) *Advertising Management.* Englewood Cliffs: Prentice Hall.

Advertising Association (1994) *Advertising Statistics Yearbook*.

Colley, R.H. (1962) 'Squeezing the Waste out of Advertising', *Harvard Business Review*, 40, 5, 76–8.

Cummins, J. (1989) *Sales Promotion.* London: Kogan Page.

Davidson, H. (1972) *Offensive Marketing.* London: Cassell.

Davies, M.A.P. (1992) 'Sales Promotions for Competitive Strategy', *Management Decision*, 30, 6, 5–10.

Davies, M.A.P. (1993) 'Combinations of Message Appeals for Campaign Management', *European Journal of Marketing*, 27, 1, p. 46.

Lavidge, R.J. and Steiner, G.A. (1961) 'A Model for Predictive Measurement of Advertising Effectiveness', *Journal of Marketing*, 25, 6, 59–62.

Lee, B. and Lee, R.S. (1995) 'How and Why People Watch T.V.: Implications for the Future of Interactive Television', *Journal of Advertising Research*, November/December, 9–18.

Park, C.W., Roth, M.S. and Jacques, P.F. (1988) 'Evaluating the Effects of Advertising and Sales Promotion Campaigns', *Industrial Marketing Management*, 17, 2, 129–40.

Summers, D. (1996) 'Displaying the Results', *Financial Times*, 11 April, 9.

Zajonc, R.B. (1968) 'The Attitudinal Effects of Mere Exposure', *Journal of Personality and Social Psychology*, 9, 2, 2, 1–24.

CHAPTER TEN

Marketing Communications 2: Public Relations, Personal Selling and Direct Mail

---

Objectives

After studying this chapter, you should:

1. Understand the benefits and limitations of the following aspects of the marketing communications mix:
   public relations,
   personal selling,
   direct mail.
2. Be aware of the main aspects of a public relations plan.
3. Be aware of the diverse range of activities in personal selling.
4. Understand how to prepare a sales presentation, overcome objections and monitor sales performance.
5. Appreciate the basic rules for designing an effective mail shot, with a view to improving response rates.
6. Understand the importance of planning and developing a database for selective and precise targeting.
7. Know how to build a suitable mailing list for direct marketing purposes.

10.1 Public relations

Public relations (PR) is the third aspect of the marketing communications mix. It involves developing and maintaining harmonious relationships and attitudes with any people connected directly or indirectly with the business. The targeted audiences (or *target* or *client publics* as they are often called) may include not only consumers and customers, but employees, management, distributors, shareholders, the media and the government. PR is about the image-building of institutions, statesmen or symbols, in which gaps often have to be bridged between desired and existing attitudes held by various publics. This is managed through the selection and channelling of information and messages to the various publics. These publics (shown in Figure 10.1) must be prioritised in order of importance, since once information is released, there will be a natural tendency for it to filter through other publics in some predictable pattern. It is for this reason that *media relations* are often crucial because they have such a powerful influence over what and how information is conveyed to many other of the target publics. Thus targets should be prioritised on the basis of their impact upon achieving or obstructing objectives, and ultimately how they affect the performance of an organisation. For smaller companies, serving local markets, maintaining good relationships with local buyers and suppliers may be of utmost importance, whereas for a multinational, whose markets are global, governmental relations may have a significant impact on its international trade.

We begin this section by examining the development of a PR plan (Table 10.1). There are five main stages to remember:

1. identification or problem (or opportunity);
2. identification of the target publics;
3. revising your objectives after assessment of the feelings of each of the targeted publics compared to your original objectives;
4. implementation;
5. monitoring and control.

The first two stages are often considered together. You might identify the target publics by using a checklist, such as the one shown in Figure 10.1. A press cuttings agency might be commissioned to collect everything that is printed about a company or subject, and this could be analysed for possible problems (or opportunities) with target publics.

Midland Bank carefully selected to whom it would donate on commercial grounds to achieve positive PR. Its chosen targets were youth, the disabled and the elderly. Around half of its new account holders were young people, so this target made sense. The forthcoming Disability Discrimination Act was considered to add presence to supporting the disabled, and targeting the elderly was considered a unique selling proposition (since they tend to be ignored by most business groups).

Problems may become apparent from making an assessment of the feelings of each of the targeted publics. A list of strengths and weaknesses exposed by each public might suffice here. Thirdly, you need to compare this assessment of the current feelings surrounding the company, product or person under examination against your original objectives. If the existing attitudes are positive, can these be

INTERNAL   EXTERNAL

Employees	Customers
Management	Distributors
Blue-collar staff	Suppliers
Subsidiaries	Shareholders
	Media and the press
	Consumer groups
	Government
	(Other) nations

Figure 10.1 Various target publics

Table 10.1 Stages in a PR plan

Stages	How?
Identity problem (or opportunity)	Press cuttings, news. Ask/interview publics who interact with business, sales feedback, examine changes in company performance
Target publics	Identify those with greatest opportunity to achieve or obstruct achievement of objectives, e.g. opinion leaders, influentials
Setting revised objectives	Maintain positive attitudes, change negative attitudes, convert hostilities to tolerance, educate the uninformed
Implementation	How to achieve the objectives Decide communications strategy: who is involved, when, and with what message
Monitor and control	Measure results either by: (a) Published sources, e.g. ratio of positive/negative articles written per publication/reporter/targeted public (b) Unpublished sources: conduct primary research, e.g. attitudinal survey into intensity of feelings towards product or company, benchmarked against competition

maintained or are there potential threats? If attitudes are predominantly negative, can they be changed and altered within budget? Achieving the change may incur considerable cost and may indicate that objectives need to be revised.

Next, objectives need to be achieved. This requires setting a communications strategy: who is involved, when and with what message. Once objectives are implemented, PR must be monitored to ensure it is working. This can be done by measuring the impact of coverage of published material such as the ratio of positive/negative articles written or broadcast per subject, per publication, per reporter and per targeted public, and so on. This should be supplemented by primary research. The intensity of feelings should also be recorded and compared relative to competition. The nature of the messages that need to be conveyed to your target groups or public will vary according to the company and its type of business. For example, Bass Brewers with the help of a PR agency have identified eight measurable messages that need to be put forward. They should be perceived as innovative, having a rich tradition, well managed, a good employer, a good neighbour (charitable in looking after people), the most successful brewer, and looking after licensees and customers (Miles, 1995). You might consider which of these are most pertinent for each of the groups (publics) in Figure 10.1. Events such as exhibitions can also be evaluated by measuring the visibility of brands or logos present, and the degree of exposure or opportunity to see by members of the target audience.

The stages above are the rudiments of a PR plan (refer to Table 10.1). Let us return to the target publics (Figure 10.1). You will notice that there are two types of targeted publics – *internal* publics that work in the firm on a regular basis, and those *external* to the firm, but having some connection. When designing a PR plan, it is important that you are able to identify the most *critical groups* in your business. Consider why employees might be important. Sales assistants are closest to our customers, yet they are often treated badly and considered unimportant by other sections of the workforce. Sales staff are at their most productive in dealing with customers when they are able to express their personality in a positive way.

In an advisory capacity, sales staff are also invaluable, yet they are unlikely to work wholeheartedly for a company and project this enthusiasm in a selling role if they are not themselves identified and treated as another form of customer.

Let us turn our attention to the external customer. Relationships with existing customers can be renewed with regular updates about new products and services. For instance, car dealers regularly send mailshots to their clients with newsletters. This makes customers feel that the organisation is caring and responsive. Canon (UK) Ltd encourages a continuing interest in its cameras to its customers by offering (i) a colour magazine on useful hints and latest developments, (ii) advice by phone, (iii) workshops and seminars, and (iv) an opportunity to sell photos to its customer magazine. Collectively, this encourages consumers to upgrade their cameras and equipment as they improve, so contributing to profitability. Shareholders, another group, are interested in the latest trading figures. *Investor relations* is important to enhance the future financial stability of a business.

Before continuing reading, you might focus on the other internal and external publics that relate to your business, or one that you are familiar with. Try to prioritise your targeted publics against your required PR objectives. This will indicate who is important and why.

To set appropriate PR objectives, you should identify the causes behind negative attitudes and the symptoms. Negative attitudes might be caused through *ignorance* manifest in *confusion*, *suspicion*, *hostility*, *fear*, *lack of credence* or *indifference*. Each symptom needs to be treated differently in the way the targeted publics might be educated. For example, private health insurance has been treated with hostility by some potential consumers because they believe it is a substitute for the NHS. By identifying the underlying cause of the symptom, it is possible to reply with the appropriate form of communications. In this example, PR can be used to justify, through gentle persuasion, that private health care is a *supplementary* option (so nullifying the perceived threat).

Many PR activities involve convincing a public that a company is 'on their side'. For example, British Nuclear Fuels Ltd (BNFL) have a major task in persuading members of the general public that nuclear fuel is safe. They have achieved some success by giving priority to schoolchildren, since youngsters are particularly receptive. BNFL holds seminars in schools, stressing that nobody can escape radioactivity and demonstrating the truth of this statement by monitoring the radioactivity in a piece of blackboard chalk with a Geiger counter. Families have been targeted with a different PR strategy. Works visits have been offered at the BNFL Exhibition Centre at Sellafield. Such perceived openness tends to fortify *credibility* in their message.

Sometimes firms need to provide *tangible evidence* that they are doing something to change for the better. As a result of industrial action following privatisation in 1987, British Telecom (UK telephone system) was described by the *Financial Times* as 'Britain's most hated company'. The public linked inadequate payphones with irresponsibility but they were *unaware* of the severity of vandalism. Many of the old coin-operated public telephones in red boxes were subsequently replaced with card phones based on electronics, which are more secure from vandalism. The new kiosks constructed from smoked glass offered a tangible way of showing how quickly the service was being improved. Additional publicity was gained by national newspaper coverage. Attitudes improved significantly amongst the general public.

This demonstrates that a company's image (as viewed by consumers) may be very different from reality. An important aspect of PR planning is to monitor *image* constantly. An obvious example is airlines, which are very sensitive about news reports on air crashes, since they can affect the whole market. In general, PR executives need to be able to anticipate disasters in order to develop *contingency plans* ahead of time (*proactive PR*). It is much more difficult to react smoothly to events if no contingency plans exist. This was shown clearly by Exxon, the US oil company which was responsible for a major oil spillage off the coast of Alaska several years ago – complacent and slow reaction cost the company dear. US senators were shown on television cutting up their Exxon cards, and many of their products were boycotted. To prepare for a crisis it is useful to have a control team trained to deal with them. Typical members would include experts in insurance, legal affairs, public relations and quality control. A control room with hotline access and fax availability for the sole use of the crisis is also required. It is also important to respond quickly, to be seen to be responsive. Communicating through the media by issuing press releases to announce firm actions makes a company look strong. According to a media relations manager of Shell UK, if a company communicates nothing, it is probably communicating badly.

The UK Post Office ad (Figure 10.2) shows an emotional appeal based on PR. It recognises the importance of being *seen* to be responsive to consumer demands, stressing service and commitment. The text box 'The Need for an Improved Corporate Image' stresses the importance of communicating positively with your 'publics'.

The need for an improved corporate image

A survey by an international consultancy revealed that responses to different publics or audiences (such as a complaining customer, a potential employee, a fund raiser for charities, a personal investor) varied in promptness, tone, accuracy and completeness both across companies and significantly across departments within the same organisation. This would suggest that, whilst firms are attending to the direct effects of advertising and promotions, their total effectiveness is undermined by the indirect effects of word of mouth, resulting in an unsatisfactory corporate image that could harm their reputation. Most organisations need to respond more positively to these people.

Source: H. Aldersey-Williams (1995) 'Letters that Say a Lot', *Financial Times*, 19 October, p. 15.

10.2 Personal selling

Personal selling is the fourth element of the marketing communications mix. The emphasis of personal selling relative to other elements depends on:

1. the type of market.
2. the stage in the buying process;
3. whether a firm focuses on 'push' or 'pull' strategies.

The Post Office believes the best way to improve results is to publish them.

The Post Office can't just say it's going to provide an even better service.

It has to deliver. And it has to be seen to be delivering.

So, we're putting posters in all main post offices which set out

> **HOW QUICKLY WE DELIVER YOUR MAIL**
> First Class Letter deliveries next working day.
>
> RESULTS
>
> TARGET

our targets for letter delivery and show whether or not we're meeting them.

These figures will be independently audited and up-dated every quarter. So, you'll always be able to see at a glance how prompt and efficient our service is.

We will also be showing you how quick and efficient our counter service is. Currently it's

> **HOW QUICKLY WE SERVE YOU**
> People served in under five minutes.
>
> RESULTS
>
> TARGET

faster than the average bank, building society or supermarket.

And we'll soon be doing the same for parcel deliveries.

But, if you have any questions, you'll always know who to direct them to.

We're introducing name badges for staff who meet you, the customer.

Making ourselves more approachable is just one of the

many ways we are further improving our service which, according to independent research, is already the most efficient in Europe.

To tell you all about the other things we're doing, we've published a booklet titled 'Putting the Customer First'. It's a small book but it speaks volumes for the depth of our commitment.

For your free copy, write to the Post Office, FREEPOST BF 12, Kempston, Bedford MK12 7YF.

Or, pop into any main, high street post office, and see the results of our efforts for yourself.

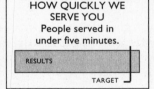

NAME OB2
(Block Capitals)
ADDRESS ....
....
.... POST CODE ....

THE POST OFFICE
FREEPOST BF 12, Kempston, Bedford, MK12 7YF

Figure 10.2 Post Office advertisement combining PR and advertising (Reproduced with permission of the Post Office)

In general terms, advertising and sales promotion play a more important role in the marketing of consumer products; personal selling features more prominently in organisational markets. The reasons for this arise from the differences between organisational and consumer marketing, outlined in chapter 5. But do not dismiss the role of advertising in organisational markets: it can be very useful for supporting the sales task. For instance, it can help build a reputation of a company and its products through corporate advertising, create awareness to prospects, and help educate about the technical features of new products.

Recall the advertising pyramid or the hierarchy of effects model of sequential communication objectives (see Figure 9.7). Evidence suggests that, for a given outlay, advertising and publicity are most effective in creating awareness and comprehension. Personal selling is relatively more cost-effective at the conviction and (purchase) action stages. This explains why each element of the communications mix should work together; cold canvassing is far more effective if the prospect is already aware of a company and its products.

There is a much greater emphasis on personal selling and trade promotion if resellers in the channel can be persuaded to stock a given product (called a *'push' strategy*). Contrastingly, advertising aimed at the consumer can create consumer demand, so 'pulling' the product through the channel (a *'pull' strategy*).

Because of the importance of integrating advertising with personal selling, sales staff should be fully briefed about current advertising campaigns. Only then can they reinforce the benefits of such advertising in the sales presentations they make to their clients.

10.2.1 Sales tasks

Sales tasks involve:

- prospecting for potential customers,
- maintaining company records as part of marketing intelligence,
- providing advisory support to customers and the sales presentation itself (which includes problem recognition and needs analyses),
- dealing with objections,
- negotiation,
- closing the sale.

Prospecting may be done:

- through existing customers by quoting them as a reference to their friends or colleagues, so reducing perceived risk to the buyer (see text box on 'Two Cases of Direct Selling' on p. 273),
- through trade directories such as *Kompass* or *Dunn and Bradstreet*,

- by inquiries through off-the-page advertising (enabling consumers to buy goods directly from an advertisement) direct mail and exhibitions,
- by cold canvassing (selling direct to a prospective customer, perhaps by telephone or door-to-door, without the initial interest coming from the prospect),
- by scanning the trade or business sections of the general press for signals in market trends.

In addition, press cuttings agencies can provide clippings of all the news about nominated companies. The trade press is invaluable for many organisational markets. For example, marketing magazines often publicise companies who are looking for new agencies – of obvious interest to ad agencies seeking to win new business.

Salespeople should be encouraged to use their strategic positions (in being close to the customer at point of contact) for channelling up-to-date marketing information back to marketing departments. This serves as a valuable ingredient for future strategic planning. This might include recent developments of new products of competitors, feedback from distributors and any changes in the distribution channels used.

To achieve their sales targets, salespeople are responsible for managing their own time. Sales representatives may spend significant amounts of time travelling to reach prospects within their allocated territories. It follows that decisions on how to route their calls, and the call frequency of prospects can affect selling costs significantly. It is therefore sensible to grade customers according to their potential. Such delegation of responsibility may encourage some salespeople to use 'friendliness of buyer' or 'ease of sale' as the sole criteria for making decisions on visit frequency, rather than using sales potential as the basis. IBM (computer systems) have been associated with 'providing solutions to problems' as their mission rather than being in the business of computers. Certainly the salesperson who *learns solutions* to common problems and provides appropriate advice to customers builds an effective barrier to any competition.

10.2.2 Preparing for the selling process

The selling process itself includes a number of stages. Initial impressions should be positive – salespeople should be well-groomed, courteous and business-like. Secondly, sales assistants should be adequately prepared. Ideally, they should know at least as much as the buyer. The first point of contact is to establish the buyer's problems and needs through the skilful use of 'open' *questions*, inviting a detailed response. A common mistake is for retail salespeople to start a conversation with 'Can I help you?' inviting a terse but predictable 'No thank you, I'm just looking.' Table 10.2 shows some of the wide variety of questions which may be used.

Two cases of direct selling: party selling and network marketing

You've probably heard of party selling from home, in which an agent sells goods to a group of friends and neighbours in the comfort of their homes. Names which you may be familiar with are Tupperware (e.g. plastic bowls and lunch boxes) or Anne Summers (lingerie). The advantage of this method to the organisation is that pressure from friends and neighbours can be very influential in persuading guests to buy something.

OK for low value items, in which everyone has a bit of fun, but not suitable for consumer durables, you might think. But think again. Marketing opportunities are borne where a current problem is identified and solved using new or borrowed techniques. Habitech is a business, selling personal computers from home, in which 'technology partners' or reps, are self employed, bring their own equipment for demonstrations and gain about 5% commission on say £1700 of multimedia. It is the start of a new wave of business – the *'home technology'* party. Why does it work? Because a significant amount of consumers are repeatedly irritated at the lack of, or poor, sales advice given by retail assistants. The problem is compounded if the average 'punter' doesn't know precisely what they want, and lacks the confidence to pry and probe. The result: a lost sale, or an inappropriate one, resulting in a dissatisfied customer. One of the keys in the latest direct selling operation by Habitech is that their equipment is installed on behalf of the customer.

Typically, equipment is first demonstrated at school and upon a purchase being made, the rep will make a home visit, install and offer advice on the basic operations. Further after-sales service is provided in a telephone helpline, home repairs and regular updated information on new products. Advantages to the company is that there are few liabilities with little stock held at any time. With few overheads, the firm can afford to price hardware cheaper than the high-street, with software at competitive prices.

A second example of direct selling demonstrates the incredibly fast growth that can be achieved. Nu-Skin sells skin care products around the world, using network marketing techniques and the Internet. In network marketing, self-employed distributors are appointed often working part-time, to sell to their friends, colleagues or general public. Incredibly, Nu-Skin has recruited about 30,000 active distributors in Europe in the last six months. Agents are only paid for the sales they, or the colleagues they have recruited make, not simply for recruiting other agents in to the company. Had the company rewarded on the basis of recruitment alone, there is a danger that some would be left with unsold stocks. Nu-Skin is prepared to improve the image of direct selling by acting responsibly and agreeing to buy back any unsold stocks (from agents) for 90% of the original selling price. Such a 'sale or return' policy protects against agents over-estimating their need for stocks.

Sources: Diane Summers (1996) 'Computer Party', *Financial Times*, 14 March, p. 18; Peter Marsh (1996) 'Grand Design for Network Selling', *Financial Times*, 4 April, p. 13.

Having identified the needs and problems of the buyer, a sales person is better able to persuade the buyer that the solution can be delivered. This must be conveyed through benefits that are meaningful to the consumer, and must therefore be communicated in their language (not the technical jargon of features). To confirm understanding, a series of check questions may be prompted.

It is likely that the buyer may still feel uneasy about making a firm commitment, perhaps due to perceived risk in trying something new and making a change. This risk can be reduced through offering proof of endorsements from current customers, volunteering to offer demonstrations, inviting prospects to be involved in trying out the products, offering extended guarantees (or even returns policies) and offering a range of incentives on trial orders. (These ideas were developed in the chapter on promotions.)

One of the biggest problems facing sales staff is how to deal with objections. A number of techniques are shown in Figure 10.3.

Whichever method is chosen, sales staff should try to listen without interrupting to gain a full understanding of what the problem is. One technique is to *agree* with the buyer before putting forward an *alternative point of view*, so gaining rapport. For example, if a buyer questions the cost of a new packaging material compared with the competition, the salesperson may agree but then

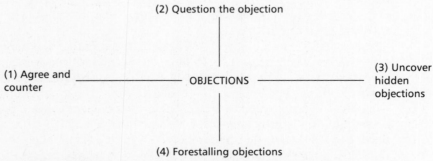

Figure 10.3 Techniques for overcoming sales objections

Table 10.2 Types of question used in personal selling

Type of question	Objective	Example
Tie down question	Used for confirmation or to commit a prospect to a position	You want the programme, don't you?
Leading question	Direct or guide a prospect's thinking	How does that coat feel on you?
Alternative question	Used to elicit an answer by forcing selection from two or more alternatives	Would you prefer the red or blue model?
Statement/question	A statement is followed by a question which forces the prospect to reflect on the statement	This machine can spin at 5,000 rpm and process 3 units per minute. What do you think of that productivity?
Sharp angle question	Used to commit a prospect to a position	If we can get it in blue, is that the way you would want it?
Information-gathering questions	Used to gather facts	How many people are you currently employing?
Opinion-gathering questions	Used to gather opinions or feelings	What are your feelings concerning the high price of energy?
Confirming questions	Used to elicit either agreement or disagreement about a particular topic	Do my recommendations make sense?
Clarification questions	Reduce ambiguities, generalities and non-committal words to specifics	When you say . . . exactly what do you mean?
Inclusion questions	Present an issue for the prospect's consideration in a low-risk way	I don't suppose you'd be interested in a convertible hard-top, would you?
Counter-biasing	To obtain sensitive information by making a potentially embarrassing situation appear acceptable	Research shows that most drivers exceed the speed limit. Do you ever do so?
Transitioning	Used to link the end of one phase to the next phase of the sales process	In addition to that is there anything else that you want to know? (No) What I'd like to do now is talk about . . .
Reversing	Used to pass the responsibility of continuing the conversation back to the prospect by answering a question with a question	(When can I expect delivery?) When do you want delivery?

Source: De Cormier and Jobber (1993).

suggest how this packaging material is more cost effective (perhaps by being stronger yet lighter), so reducing breakages and physical distribution costs. This is called the *'agree and counter'* method. Another technique is to question the objection, particularly if its nature is general. If the buyer does not like the quality of a product, for instance, the *specific objection should be clarified*, which may turn out to be trivial and can be easily overcome. Another technique is to ask questions in the event of silence by the buyer, to uncover their *hidden objections*. If the buyer appears unwilling to reveal their real objections, questions must be asked to invite hidden objections, such as 'Is there anything so far that you are not sure about?' Some sales staff are skilled at *forestalling* objections by anticipating and raising them as part of their sales presentation. The timing of the objection is then controlled. It is most useful when sales staff are faced with the same objection being raised by different buyers. Perhaps buyers are continually raising the issue of lack of experience to one of the newest companies in the packaging industry. Sales staff may forestall the objection with something like 'As one of the newest companies in the industry we are highly innovative and can respond quickly by exploiting new packaging materials and processes'. The possible objection is then turned into a strength.

In some selling situations, the sales team may have *discretion* on the terms of the sale. Sellers may therefore *negotiate* prices, delivery times, the specification of the product (e.g. whether it is fabricated or not), the price (including installation and maintenance contracts, as with computer hardware), methods of payment (on despatch, receipt or by credit terms) and trade-in terms if appropriate. Concession depends upon an accurate assessment of power between the buyer and the seller, influenced by the depth of information held by each party (i.e. a buyer needs to know the *seller's cost structure* to negotiate a cheaper price, a seller would like to know how much the buyer *needs* the item, and how much they are willing to pay, together with *how many alternative suppliers* there are).

The final act in the sales presentation is to *close the sale*. The first technique is the *trial* or *assumptive close*, in which a question may be raised as if the sale has already been made. The salesperson may raise details about delivery dates, for instance, after hearing the buyer extol the virtues of the product. Notice that the presentation may continue even if the timing is premature. Another technique is to *summarise the main benefits*, so reminding the buyer, before asking for a sale. In the last resort, a *concessionary close* should be made, such as an extra discount, but concessions should not be given away without careful consideration by sales-people, since they could adversely affect gross margins.

10.2.3 Sales force planning

To make the best use of the salesforce, it is necessary to:

1. specify standard of performance (goals) and tasks to be achieved (the means),

2. delegate and select appropriate personnel to fulfil task objectives,
3. guide and train where necessary,
4. measure standards achieved (against set objectives),
5. compare variances and evaluate,
6. prescribe appropriate action. This would include sales reorganisation to achieve maximum sales effectiveness, alternative incentive schemes and management of personnel on an individual or team basis.

This last section of the personal selling function examines an important aspect of sales management, sales performance evaluation and control. We will therefore look in detail at points 4–6.

Performance standards may be set by:

- inputs = desired indicators of effort expended
- outputs = desired levels of achievements and various sales management ratios (inputs/outputs)

Inputs include the 'call rate' or 'call norm', the calls made per year and the calls per active account. Example of output ratios are given in Figure 10.4.

It is important to analyse ratios in *combination* rather than in isolation. A selection of investigative procedures is given in Table 10.3.

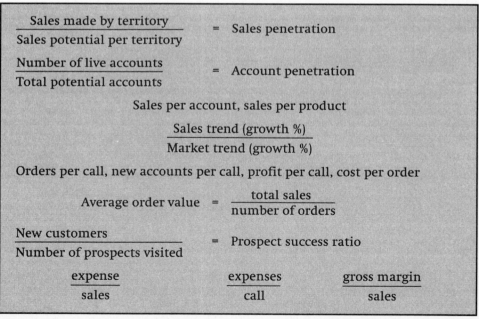

Figure 10.4 Examples of quantitative output ratios for measuring sales performance

Table 10.3 Examples of investigative procedures in ratio analysis

Problem	Reason	Investigative ratios	Action
Too many calls	Calling on 'marginal players'	Low orders/call Low orders/hr/day	Investigate sales call reports Educate to prioritise custom and be more discriminating
Too few calls	Little selling time. Disorganised workload, poor planning, idleness	Low calls/day (may be high orders/call)	Counsel
Too few orders	As 1: Poor selection of calls: market saturation, poor selling, poor region	Low orders/ call Low orders/hr/day	Check area potential; if OK, then counsel
Too many expenses	Needless distance/call Poor journey planning Careless discount policies, too lax in 'give aways'	High miles/call Low calls/day Low gross margin/sale	Train in time management and routing journeys Counsel Indicate significance of gross margin on profitability

Performance standards should be compared to what is expected, based on historical data (industry/trade norms, territory norms and sales representative opinion), the state of development in the market, the nature of competition and extent of market saturation. Performance indicators should be split by product, brand, and whether the product and customer is new or established (to assess level of effort expended). This quantitative analysis should be combined with a qualitative analysis. The attitude of a salesperson can be assessed by examining their:

- relationship to other staff,
- client/supplier feedback perhaps measuring level of satisfaction with customer service such as:
    promptness in dealing with enquiries,
    eagerness in handling delivery problems,
    proficiency in advising customers on problems and/or product usage.

Sales management should make their own judgements through:

- field sales visits to assess ability to overcome objections and close sales,
- level of product knowledge and competitor knowledge,
- willingness to attend sales meetings, seminars,
- honesty in completing all reports methodically.

Factors contributing to poor performance might be related to:

- level of experience,
- domestic problems (marriage, family),
- health,
- indolence.

The sales manager must use intuition and experience to determine the necessary remedial action.

In some cases all that is required is a pep talk to 'recharge the batteries' or to restore confidence in the field. In other cases, problems may hide more deeply rooted motivational problems. The skill of the sales manager is then to decide an appropriate combination of motivational tools to rejuvenate their sales representatives' enthusiasm. The text box demonstrates why motivation of the sales force is a common problem facing sales management.

Difficulties in maintaining sales motivation

The challenge for most management is to enforce and retain a motivated sales team. However, few marketing managers who are often responsible for the sales function have any significant field sales experience. This suggests they are unlikely to understand the difficulties facing the sales function. In some fields like the direct selling of life assurance or double glazing, the level of rejections may greatly outnumber the successes, so motivation may be difficult. Furthermore, the salesperson may be geographically apart from supervision and his other peers, so that they feel isolated and/or neglected. Motivational strategies are therefore required to take account of the needs of the salesforce. In addition to this, the flatter structure in many organisations (as layers of management have disappeared as part of a cost-cutting exercise arising from the recession) have resulted in less career opportunities for some employees. This can have a detrimental effect on morale. Whilst the salesperson should have a certain quota of self-motivation and drive, it is the job of the sales manager to ensure this drive and determination to succeed is channelled in the right direction.

Even the high-performing salesperson can sometimes experience motivational problems. Beyond a certain level of financial reward, it may be necessary to reward them in alternative ways. Expressing their valuable contribution in the company and providing recognition for their efforts in front of others may help. Possibly offering them a chance to develop in other aspects of the selling task (training new recruits, prospecting, market research, new product proposals) or even job rotation in which they may be temporarily moved to a different job, could be the stimulus they need (e.g. allowing an opportunity for a fresh challenge in a new sales territory).

The Jackson & Kline case study is designed to apply your knowledge to sales promotions. Study the case, then answer the following:

Q10.1 Recommend and justify suitable consumer and trade promotions aimed at the domestic and commercial markets respectively.
Hint: Think of channel objectives, and how these can be achieved by using promotions.

Q10.2 How else might the manufacturer motivate the channel?
Hint: Think of the role of personal selling in channel design.

You should be able to generate at least ten ideas relating to promotions.

Case study: Jackson & Kline Ltd

Jackson & Kline Limited (JKL) were established almost 100 years ago in the UK to produce high-quality door locks. They steadily expanded and today have a very good reputation for their wide range of door locks, handles, hinges, knockers, letter boxes and numbers. All these products are made from the highest quality materials such as brass, stainless steel and alloy steels, conveying a traditional and solid image. The central importance attached to consistently high quality and craftsmanship is, they believe, the main reason for their success so far. During the past two or three years they have detected a definite market trend towards higher security locks for both homes and commercial premises. This trend is confirmed by the significant increases in burglaries and insurance claims for stolen property. Advertising campaigns by the police and government departments have increased awareness of the need to increase the security of premises.

JKL, believing that high-security door locks would fit very well with their traditional and reliable image, have developed a completely new range of such locks, suitable for domestic and commercial premises.

They expect that the demand for their new range will be primarily as replacements for existing locks, as people attempt to increase the security of their premises. However, they also recognise that there may well be a useful, though smaller, market for them as original equipment fitted to new property.

JKL consider that the market is now in the growth phase, with demand, which started some three years ago in socio-economic groups A and B, now coming from a much wider cross-section of the population. It is, nevertheless, evident that large sections of the population are still most unlikely to be interested in such products. The usual channels of distribution for JKL's products provide a comprehensive coverage of the market and include wholesalers, builders merchants, traditional hardware stores, special locksmiths and DIY retailers.

A number of competitors have already developed and are marketing high-security door locks – JKL are anxious to launch their products as soon as possible. It is now necessary to resolve some important marketing questions to ensure the successful introduction of the new products.

Source: CIM examination question. Permission granted from Chartered Institute of Marketing, Cookham.

10.3 Direct mail

Direct mail should be distinguished from direct selling – it is important that you do not get these terms confused.

- *Direct mail* involves mailshots aimed at individual households (*en masse* or selected) through the post or to businesses.
- *Direct marketing* involves selling goods directly to the public, which includes direct mail *and* other techniques, for example, mail order and telephone shopping (but not personal face-to-face selling).

Direct mail is increasing in popularity as a means of promoting goods and services. In the UK alone, there were 2.1 million direct mailshots sent out in 1991.

10.3.1 Reasons for growth of direct mail

The growth of direct mail can be accounted for by the following factors:

- Accountability/measurability,

- Demassification/selective targeting,
- Cost-effectiveness.

Accountability/measurability

Compared with other means of promotion, such as advertising, it is possible to measure more precisely how successful direct mail is. Direct mail can be assessed on the basis of percentage of responses or enquiries against *versioned copy* or *split-run* tests. A split-run test involves using varied mailshots on the target audience, usually only changing one variable at a time. For example, the difference between two batches might be a slight copy change. Alternatively, one of two batches might have an incentive, the other not, to discover whether incentives pull more responses.

Marketing service managers are normally responsible for promotional budgets and must justify their expenditure. It is therefore not surprising that mailshots are becoming more popular as an element in the marketing communications mix.

Demassification/selective targeting

During the 1980s, there was a widening gap between people on lower and higher incomes. This polarisation of markets (or *demassification* according to the Henley Centre for Forecasting), requires more selective targeting. Aiming for a mass market may miss both high- and low-income targets; more precise targeting can address the needs of specific market segments. We have seen this in retailing with the success of discount stores at one end of the market (such as Kwik Save and Aldi) and the middle-market multiple chains at the other (such as Sainsbury). Both sets of stores have different objectives aimed at different customer profiles.

Direct mail is particularly suitable when markets are polarising because consumers can be targeted more directly than advertising. Customer purchase histories can be built up on databases. The stored data can then be retrieved and merged with other data, providing a powerful tool to identify likely prospects for new merchandise. *Merge purge* allows the fixing of two or more data lists without duplication. 'Junk mail', with which you will be familiar, is simply direct mail poorly targeted.

Cost-effectiveness

Targeting can potentially be more precise than advertising. There is less chance of promoting to people who are not interested in the offers, and so less wastage. Production costs of mailshots have reduced significantly with the development of desk top publishing. Advances in technology have decreased the cost of laser printers dramatically – a modern laser can print 7,000 mailshots per hour. EPOS (electronic point of sale) technology provides another access to customers' purchasing histories. This information can also be sold to other firms for direct mail, or other purposes. Additionally, joint mailings by several firms are often used to reduce distribution and postage costs.

10.3.2 Direct mail design: content and presentation

AIDA model objectives

The effectiveness in using direct mail depends how the AIDA model objectives are achieved (see Figure 10.5).

Imagine you are the recipient of direct mail at home. The first objective of the direct mail must be to encourage you to *open* the letter. This can be achieved through creating awareness of any benefit on the envelope or through the window. The Post Office suggests that up to 90 per cent of mail is opened; so around 10 per cent of your mail is thrown away, unopened. Once opened, the next obstacle is to get you to *read* it. Many letters fail here to stimulate interest quickly. It is suggested that unless interest is obtained within 8 seconds, it is unlikely that more than the title of the letter will be read. Think back to the number of times you have discarded mail at home or in the office without reading all the fine details. Getting you to read the complete message requires good copy. It should be punchy and well punctuated. It should lead you through the positive arguments of why the product/service or idea is precisely for you. Somewhere in the letter, the product has to be suitably differentiated from the competition for you to create a preference for it. So the copy must also be persuasive, reinforced by credibility.

Getting you to *respond* is often enhanced by using '*reply facilitators*'. Examples include incentives conditional on speed of reply, partially completed application forms and freepost reply envelopes.

Response rates must then be *transformed* into conversion or actual sales rates. Finally, post-purchase *relationships* should be encouraged with judicious use of purchase histories and database management.

Developing a relationship with you requires identifying what motivates you. For example, is it necessary to offer incentives, or are you more impressed by the core value of the product? Is price a critical feature? What about quick delivery – is this necessary to seal a sale? Is it necessary to offer numerous assurances from previous buyers? Do you respond best to emotive or rational appeals? These questions convey some of the complexities in the design of effective direct mail.

The example shown as Figure 10.6 demonstrates the efficient use of a series of *amplifiers* by a retail chain introducing a store card to existing customers. Notice the significance of the PS as an opportunity for reminding about an offer of an incentive.

Amplifiers and filters

Direct mail compilers must recognise and overcome several hurdles in communications. The task is to ensure the letter and its contents perform at each stage of the buying sequence, using the AIDA model as a check. For example, there is no point in spending a vast sum on excellent letter copy if the outer envelope is not opened. One way of predicting the success of mailshots is to examine the number of net amplifiers compared with filters as shown in Table 10.4.

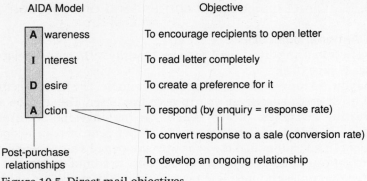

Figure 10.5 Direct mail objectives

Table 10.4 Examples of amplifiers and filters

Amplifiers	Filters
Incentives to read	
Clear benefits in title	Unclear benefits
Little effort in reading	Much effort required
Credibility	
Offer: tangible cues	Evidence of biased results
testimonials	Dubious endorsements
testing	
sources of information	
independence	
Reply facilitators	
Postage paid	Difficulties in how to reply
Reduce effort in replies	No incentives
Trial purchase	

Amplifiers encourage recipients to move down the hierarchy of effects (or AIDA model) positively; that is, any questions the reader may have are answered positively. Filters pose unsolved queries to the reader, and so effectively are like obstacles or objections in a sales conversation. The outcome is therefore the net result of amplifiers over filters (Vögele, 1992).

Question	*Answer*
Amplifier	$\Sigma(\text{yes}_1 + \text{yes}_2 \ldots \text{yes}_n)$
Filter	$\Sigma(\text{no}_1 + \text{no}_2 \ldots \text{no}_m)$
Result =	$\Sigma(\text{yes}) - \Sigma(\text{no})$

i.e. the sum of the amplifiers less the sum of the filters determines the likelihood of the mailshot being a success.

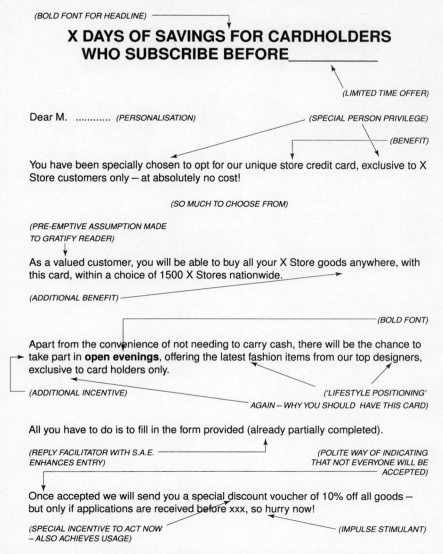

Figure 10.6 Suggested copy layout for mail offer promoting a retail store card

10.3.3 Example of mailshot design: Reader's Digest

Figure 10.7 shows part of the contents of a Reader's Digest mailshot, designed to encourage consumers to try an annual subscription. It demonstrates how different parts of the design help to achieve different communication objectives. The mailshot consisted of a 16-page booklet, a 'mystery gift' sachet, some postage stamps, a leaflet showing a testimonial, and a 'yes' and 'no' envelope.

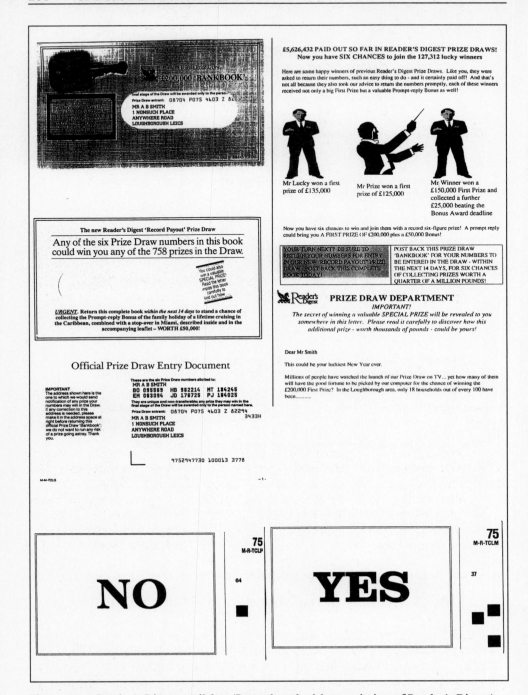

Figure 10.7 Reader's Digest mailshot (Reproduced with permission of Reader's Digest)

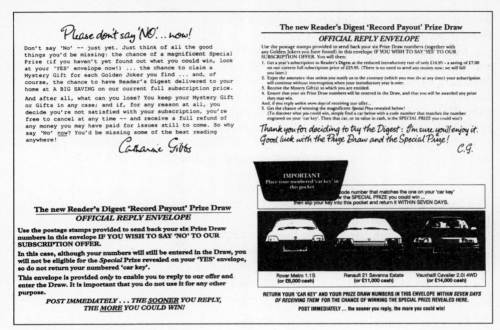

Figure 10.7 *Continued*

Let us start with the *incentives to read*. A personalised approach, addressing the reader directly, as shown on the front of the booklet, helps to give a customised appeal. This is superior to using 'Dear Sir or Madam', which makes the reader feel less important.

A common feature of many promotional strategies of mailshots is a variety of incentives offered. In this Reader's Digest offer, the incentives include a prize draw, a mystery gift and a bonus prize conditional on prompt reply.

The *key* on the front of the booklet announces the opportunity of winning a special prize and helps to lure the reader into the text. The key acts as a mechanism to get readers to participate in some activity (i.e. the number on any key must be matched to the number of one of three cars that might be won, but only if taking out a subscription, in which case the reply is sent in the 'yes' envelope shown). This particular prize is therefore *conditional* upon a positive response.

Should the reader use the alternative 'no' envelope provided, additional text on opening up the envelope attempts to convert the undecided or wavering consumers to take positive action and subscribe (see Figure 10.7).

Credibility is enhanced throughout the mailshot with a series of testimonials, particularly of peer groups drawn from the target audience. Series or lottery numbers (such as at the top of a letter) or on the prize draw also help. *Exclusivity* is maintained throughout the text, informing the reader that since only 20 per cent of households are selected, this creates a greater chance of winning. The perception here can be powerful.

Reply facilitators in this offer included conditional offers for prompt replies, some postage stamps for free reply, and partially completed application forms (with the name and address of the receiver already typewritten on the application forms.) Under the 'no' envelope was a reference made to the refund upon cancellation. This reduces perceived risk in responding favourably, and is another reply facilitator. Refer to Table 10.4 for a list of examples of amplifiers and filters.

You should now be able to answer the following questions next time you receive some direct mail correspondence. Ask yourself:

1. Who is the target audience for this product, service or ideas? Have you been correctly targeted? If not, why not? How could targeting be perfected?
2. What are the specific benefits being offered in the mailshot?
3. What evidence is provided that offers differentiation from the competition? Why is the product, service or idea so special, or has it failed in your estimation? How would you improve it?

Q10.3 Think creatively about the ideal characteristics that products, services or ideas should have which makes them appropriate for direct mail. Make a checklist of characteristics.

Q10.4 Using the AMEX card offer (Figure 10.8) consider:

1. the incentives used to encourage the target market to read the material
2. the strategies used to gain credibility
3. the reply facilitators (to encourage response)

Make notes under each of these headings.

10.3.4 Building a mailing list

We have already indicated the importance of databases for building up information on consumer purchasing patterns to improve targeting. But how are mailing lists evolved? There are three main ways for finding information from which to build lists. These are by using:

- internal lists,
- response lists,
- compiled lists.

Figure 10.8 American Express Cardmembership mailshot (Reproduced with permission of American Express Europe Ltd)

Internal or *house lists* are developed from the company's customer files or potential customer files (often called 'prospects'). *Response lists* are built up from the customers of competitors. *Compiled lists* involve some common characteristic. Examples of each are shown in Table 10.5.

Based on these tables, what kind of data are mail order companies likely to have about their customers, and why?

For a start, they will need to screen prospects for bad debts. They may use a credit agency for this, which may already hold data on the prospects. These data include previous transactions in dealing with credit, including other mail order firms, and any past purchase history with the company in question. This information is used to build up a picture of the prospect and an assessment of the likelihood of their paying within the credit period allowed. A decision can then be taken as to whether they are allowed credit, and if so, how much. When the prospect buys say, a suit from a catalogue, the purchase record is added to the database and can be used for future marketing purposes.

Purchasing patterns may be divided into recency of purchase, order value, frequency of order and brand loyalty. Clearly a customer who is a heavy user and loyal to a particular brand, is a better future prospect than those customers who have failed to buy within the last two years (sometimes deemed as inactive or dead accounts).

Table 10.5 Sources of data for mailing lists

| Source of information | Internal lists | |
	Data	Segmentation
Sales records	Name	Ethnic origin
Call sheets	Title	Sex
Purchase orders	Address	Area/region
Enquiries:	Source of original sale	Media
Telephone		
Trade shows		
Private label retailer		
Credit cards		
Business information		
Reply cards in trade magazines		
Sales promotions		
Contest entries		
Sample offers		
Direct response		
Advertising in media		
	Product type	Usage and
	Length of time on file	behavioural patterns
	Date of last purchase offers	
Census data	Address	Spatial/
	Street name	geodemographic
	County postcode	

Table 10.5 *(continued)*

Response lists

Source of information	Data
Magazine subscribers	Recency of sale (fmcgs)
Mail order buyers	New buyers (hot line lists)
Enquiries	Active buyer (current buyers within
Club members (e.g. BMW)	12 months)
Donors (e.g. charity)	Lapsed buyers (bought within 12–24 months)
	Inactive buyers (bought over 24 months ago)

Compiled lists

Sources	Data
Kompass *Kellys* *Sells*	Companies by product/location
Computer Users' Yearbook *Yellow Pages*	Business and professional lists: addresses and telephone numbers
Electoral Roll (local library archives) Can be used in connection with CACI or MOSAIC* using ACORN (43 million adults)	Geodemographic segmentation: names and addresses (and postcodes can be linked to ACORN) see appendix
List broker or List manager	Class of list members (purchaser, subscriber or enquirer) indicating: Recency of list, Recency of purchaser

Notes:
*MOSAIC is a system devised for segmenting markets based on 58 types of multi-factorial data
based on:
- Housing size and quality: council, flat, bedsit, terraced, semi or detached.
- Housing age: pre-war, inter-war, post-war, newly built (since 1981).
- Status: reflecting spending power measured by class and occupation (e.g. professional or unemployed) and congestion (e.g. number of dependants).

Summary

The personal selling function is a two-way form of communication. This means that the effectiveness of sales staff relies in part on the training and ability to put together a good sales presentation. This includes the pre-planning of likely customer problems and needs, overcoming possible objections and being able and willing to close a sale.

Other functions of the salesforce involve prospecting potential customers, keeping up-to-date with company records, providing advice to customers and distributors. Sales management is about getting the best out of the salesforce. This can be achieved through adequate planning of targets, allocation of territories, setting sales objectives, motivating and training the sales staff. An important aspect of this is the setting of appropriate control standards for evaluation and appraisal. A variety of qualitative and quantitative analysis should be used in combination before making recommendations. Performance indicators should be analysed by product line, region, and age of account. Follow-up field visits or interviews may be necessary to identify the exact cause of any symptoms shown.

Direct mail is becoming a more popular form of marketing communications because it enables marketers to be more accurate in targeting, enhanced by advances in technology. There is a premium on more selective targeting because of a polarisation of markets. The need for cost-effectiveness has been heightened by the previous recession.

The effectiveness of direct mail, as a means of enhanced positive response, depends on the design both in terms of content and presentation. A good heuristic is to use the AIDA model of communication objectives as a checklist for assessment. Post-purchase relationships are also important to build up loyalty value. This requires a database of past purchase behaviour, together with a zealous attention to detail. A good predictor of mailshot success is to identify the net number of amplifiers over filters, roughly equivalent to positive over negative features respectively.

A suitable database from which to improve targeting of mailshots starts within the company: drawing, collecting and collating internal data. This is then combined with data collected outside, such as competitor purchaser lists and other geodemographic data. Only by using a combination of factors about consumers, rather than studying them in isolation, can a more accurate prediction develop about how consumers might purchase. The mailshot manager therefore has to apply complex segmentation techniques (refer to chapter 4 for more details).

Public relations involves establishing and maintaining a favourable relationship with groups of people considered influential to a business, called target publics. Messages from these target publics can have an influential effect on the future success of a business. More control over how these messages are spread can be achieved by using a PR plan. The PR plan consists of:

- identification of the critical target publics,
- assessment of the current mood and feelings of the targeted publics,
- a comparison of this assessment with the company's objectives,
- implementation and monitoring.

Targeted publics are both internal and external. Internal publics include employees. External publics may involve customers, suppliers, shareholders, the media, government agencies and consumer groups. Targeted publics should be prioritised according to how critical they are to the business.

Next, for each critical target public, the intensity of their feelings must be grouped. In particular, it is important to isolate the causes behind negative attitudes and symptoms. These can then be compared to intended company objectives and a PR programme developed to rectify any problems. Strategies might involve providing tangible evidence to improve perceptions of responsiveness, or encouraging toleration and sympathy from a target public. Once the PR programme has been implemented, it needs to be constantly monitored. A company cannot afford to be complacent, since a slow reaction to adverse publicity or a public scare can be extremely costly.

References

De Cormier, R. and Jobber, D. (1993) 'The Counselor Selling Method: Concepts and constructs', *Journal of Personal Selling and Sales Management*, Fall, XIII, 4, 39–59.
Lancaster, G. and Jobber, D. (1994) *Selling and Sales Management*. London: Pitman.
Miles, L. (1995) 'Measures for Measures', *Marketing*, 22 June, XIII and XV.
Vögele, S. (1992) *Handbook of Direct Mail*. Englewood Cliffs: Prentice Hall.

CHAPTER ELEVEN

International Marketing

Objectives

After studying this chapter, you should be able to:

1. Understand why international trade can be an important strategy for many products and markets.
2. Know the stages of an international marketing plan.
3. Know what criteria to use as the basis for target market selection.
4. Understand why the marketing mix may need to be adapted for foreign markets.

Introduction

International marketing means any marketing activity that extends across national or domestic boundaries. This includes:

- export marketing in which the international marketing is largely handled by another party;
- manufacturing activities abroad involving joint ventures or direct investment abroad with up to 100 per cent equity stake.

International marketing is more complex than domestic marketing because of the special circumstances associated with a foreign environment. Consider, for example, a much quoted international success – McDonald's fast food chains.

Whilst their hamburgers are popular in many parts of the world, they were not an automatic success in Rome, where the slower pace of Italian eating habits conflicted with the notion of fast food. In other countries such as Japan, the basic hamburger product had to be modified to account for different taste requirements.

The importance of international marketing is underlined by the significant number of multinationals, such as IBM, Nestlé, Ford, Coca Cola, BP, Black & Decker and Caterpillar, who all derive over 50 per cent of their sales from overseas. A leading US multinational oil company, Exxon, obtained about 75 per cent of its profits from abroad.

If we are enthusiastic about finding new markets for our existing products, or adapting them to suit local conditions, we must know the best way of approaching this. In the *international marketing plan*, we must decide:

- Whether or not to use international trade,
- Marketing screening (i.e. of potential countries),
- Market selection (i.e. of shortlisted countries),
- Method of entry (i.e. distribution strategy used),
- Marketing mix policy (i.e. whether to standardise the mix across each country or customise the mix for each country).

This chapter focuses on the international marketing plan. The reasons for deciding whether to move into international markets include the level of domestic saturation, the theory of comparative advantage and economies of scale associated with greater production.

Once a decision has been made to move into international markets, potential countries must be screened. As you learnt from chapter 2, environmental factors can influence marketing decisions greatly. Since these factors may vary significantly from country to country, it is important to screen on the basis of economic and technological development, political stability and cultures. Ideally, cultures should be closely comparable to the domestic market because the closer they are to those in the domestic market, the lower the costs involved in adapting the product internationally. The selection decisions can be helped by referring to booklets on many countries, issued by the British Overseas Trade Board. These offer guidance on how to conduct business for each country.

Once the target market countries have been chosen, the next decision is to design the method of entry, selecting an appropriate means of distribution. In general terms, more direct methods of entry require higher capital investment, but give *more control* over how the product will be marketed. If the firm sells to a foreign buyer or to an international trading company, as a means of export, there is much *less control*. Marketers must find the correct balance between investment outlay, financial risk and control over how they wish the product to be marketed.

The final decision of the marketing plan involves deciding the extent to which the elements of the marketing mix are standardised or customised (adapted) for each target market country. Decisions on the marketing mix, which were explained in chapters 5-8, need to be made in an international context. For example, the ingredients of Pepsi-Cola are marginally different in other European countries from Britain. The product is sweeter in Britain to cater for our specific palate – the product element of the marketing mix has been adapted. Similar standardisation/adaption decisions must be made for the other elements of the mix: price, distribution and marketing communications.

11.1 Whether to use international marketing

The first decision is to decide whether, or when to move international. This is governed by several factors, including saturation, comparative advantage and scale economies of production.

11.1.1 Saturation

As domestic markets become more and more saturated, manufacturers may either develop their products (perhaps with improved technologies) or look for new markets abroad. This situation faces many British manufacturers. The ownership and use of televisions in Britain suggests that television manufacturers and distributors are faced with saturation, as 92 per cent of Britons own a colour television, and 41 per cent a second set. It may be easier for them to target foreign markets, where ownership is currently unsaturated. The screening process (outlined in more detail at the next stage) would involve both the ability and willingness of consumers to purchase, matched against the willingness of the manufacturer to conduct business in each potential target country.

11.1.2 Theory of comparative advantage

This assumes that by specialising in the production of a good at which the nation is most efficient, the nation can increase its welfare by international trading. Consider the labour cost (in hours) of producing two goods: cloth and grain for two countries A and B as follows:

Labour cost of production per unit

Country	Cloth	Grain
A	10	20
B	20	10

The cheapest for A to produce is cloth, so it should specialise in making cloth. For the same number of hours it takes A to produce 1 unit each of cloth and grain (30 hours) it could make 3 units of cloth. Similarly, country B could make 3 units of grain in the same time (30 hours).

Using international trade allows each country to specialise in what it is most efficient at making, giving mutual gain. If A only produces cloth and B only makes grain, A and B can then trade with each other 1 unit of each of their respective goods, providing:

> 2 units of cloth and 1 unit of grain to A
> 2 units of grain and 1 unit of cloth to B

compared to 1 unit of each made for both countries if there is no international exchange of trade.

11.1.3 Economies of scale in production

The Boston Consulting Group have shown that reductions in costs of up to 20–30 per cent can be achieved, each time output is doubled. This is known as the *experience curve*. These reductions are attributable to more experience of being in the market (having learnt from mistakes made in the domestic market), bulk purchase discounts and the possibility of spreading fixed costs over more units of production. For many foreign markets, products will require adapting to become acceptable. How far they need adapting, together with the choice of entry method, will influence the total costs of doing business in foreign markets.

11.1.4 Mediating factors affecting demand

Several factors influence the level of demand for foreign products in a home market. International marketing may be able to turn an apparent threat into an opportunity. Consider the expansion of foreign cuisine in the British restaurant market. Several factors have influenced this. Diffusion or spread of new ideas and products has been influenced by:

- higher standards of living, a greater accessibility to a wider range of media, giving variety and exposure to new products;
- lower cost foreign travel, encouraging a willingness to try new things. In 1994, a typical UK economy return fare from London to New York was 1.11 times an average week's wage, compared to 8.07 times in 1964. (*Source*: BA archive.)

Geographical mobility offers a greater awareness of alternatives, so encouraging a more discerning consumer, and the consequence of wider competition.

11.2 Screening criteria

In screening foreign markets, those with greatest potential are shortlisted for further consideration. To be selected for a shortlist, markets must hold particular qualifications. They should have a high potential for profitability. Expected methods of conducting business should not be incompatible with what the organisation can adapt to. There should also be an expectation of security of earnings. Various economic, socio-cultural and politico-legal indicators offer clues as to the likely risks and benefits in entering foreign markets.

11.2.1 Economic indicators

The size of the potential market should be sufficient to support economies of scale. Since it is more costly to reach foreign markets than the domestic market (owing to additional changes required) there is a 'critical mass' below which the market is deemed unsuitable. A firm might consider exporting to gain cost leadership if the economies of scale more than offset the additional costs incurred through trading internationally. See how the market size of the Single European Market opens up new trading opportunities.

Impact of the Single European Market

The goal of the Single European Market in 1993 was to avoid the threats of national protectionism which traditionally had plagued business between European countries. This protectionism often came in the form of tariffs (usually taxes on imports at border points) or quotas (restricting the amount of imports in to the domestic market). With a general reduction in cross-border checks enjoyed by members of the European Union (EU) the net effect is to speed up the distribution of goods, with a consequent reduction in distribution costs. Secondly, legislating for a set of pan-European manufacturing standards has resulted in many manufacturers being able to supply the entire EU with a single set of production facilities (such as motor vehicles or pharmaceuticals). This enables manufacturers to produce greater production runs to serve the needs of the EU and should bring down unit costs for members. With less legal restrictions regarding product specifications, this will encourage more partnerships between different companies, in which knowledge transfer should help to provide greater consumer choice and quality.

Source: European Marketing Data and Statistics (1996).

More specific measures of potential market size include Gross National Product (GNP) and standard of living, measured by distribution of wealth, disposable income, appliance ownership, quality of the labour force, working patterns and population density.

GNP (per capita) is defined as the value of goods and services produced by each nation (per average person). It does not consider the *distribution of wealth*, which might vary enormously between countries with a *bimodal distribution of income*, characterised by a very poor and a very rich group, with little or no middle class. According to the Human Development Report (1996), the wealth of the world's 358 billionaires exceeds the combined annual incomes of countries comprising of nearly half the world's people. Thus GNP can only be used as a crude indicator of market potential. Wealth should be measured by *disposable income*, since the cost of living/or high taxes may erode a standard of living.

A better measure of market potential might be to relate earnings to the *buying potential*. For industrialised countries, *house prices to earnings* might be used as an indicator of living standards, as a house is for many consumers their biggest asset and investment. The rule is that, as the house prices/earnings ratio becomes more than 3.5,there is progressively little income left for luxury items and the standard of living becomes reduced. Table 11.1 shows that the house price/earnings ratio in Japan is over twice that in the United States. Not surprisingly, many Japanese properties are often handed down from generation to generation without the need to make formal purchases.

Another measure of living standards is the *hours required to purchase*. This can vary enormously across different countries and so is an important index. For example, a joint of beef in Eastern European countries might cost several weeks' wages.

Marketers may use a profile of selected consumer items as an index of market potential. For example, a manufacturer of dishwashers may be interested in knowing the penetration of freezers, if it was known there was a high correlation of ownership between the two items. (N.B. This might be expected, since they are both relative luxuries and are both time saving devices.) Also of importance are the relative strengths of currencies and inflation. These are covered under the marketing mix (section 11.6) because they have particular implications for pricing.

Table 11.1 House price/earnings ratios

USA	3.0
UK	3.6
France	2.7
Japan	6.5

Source: Far Eastern Economic Review (1985).

11.2.2 Socio-cultural indicators

Size is ultimately linked to *population growth*. Although demographers expect the world population to decline in absolute numbers by 2090, the variation between continents reveals some common patterns emerging. Population trends (to predict future growth) can be measured by *fertility rates*. Fertility rates are declining in industrialised countries (owing to more effective contraception, the increased female labour force, higher divorce rates, and delayed marriage and child rearing). Interestingly, Holland is the most densely populated European country, perhaps attributable to the labour force of women being rather low (Catling, 1993). In general, alternative markets need to be sought to those in which fertility rates are in decline. Although the ability to buy is greater in the traditional industrialised nations of North America, Israel, Japan, Australia and Europe, their collective share of the world's population is projected to decline as shown in Table 11.2. This share is largely offset by Africa. Hence the need for the more developed, industrialised countries to find new markets.

Kenya is the fastest-growing country by percentage increase, with the population predicted to quadruple by 2025. The total fertility rate (average number of children a woman will bear) is considered an indicator of market potential. 2.5–5.0 is a good range. But Kenya has a poor market potential for investment, since the average Kenyan women rears 8 children. This level of fertility strains existing limited resources, i.e. Kenyans find it difficult to buy more than the basic necessities, to feed, clothe and provide shelter for their young,

Another factor affecting market size is *mortality rates*. According to the World Health Organisation, life expectancy is little above 40 years in the poorest countries, whilst in the richest it approaches 80. This is largely attributable to

Table 11.2 World population projections (percentages) to 2025

	1900	2000	2025
World LD	76.91	79.2	83.2
World MD*	23.1	20.8	16.8
	100.0	100.0	100.0
Africa	11.9	13.5	17.6
America	13.7	13.5	12.7
Asia	58.9	59.2	58.5
Europe and former Soviet Republic	15.0	13.4	10.7
Oceania	0.5	0.5	0.5
	100.0	100.0	100.0

Source: World population projections 1992–3, Bos, E., Vu, M. T., Levin, A., and Bulatao, R. A., The International Bank, extracted from Table 1, p. 2, Washington D.C., Johns Hopkins University Press. (Reproduced with permission of the World Bank)
* Comprises Europe, former Soviet Republic, North America, Australia, New Zealand, and Japan.

poor health standards in the Third World, which also inhibit an individual's ability to work and reduces earning capacity. The Third World has the highest percentage of 15-year-olds, owing to the high mortality rates, which is a considerable drain on local resources.

Culture was discussed in chapter 5. It is about the core values and customs of a society. Management are far more likely to communicate in an acceptable way if they are aware, and are sensitive to, these values and customs. This is of particular relevance when conducting sales visits in a foreign market. To avoid offence, it is useful to study the *conventional methods of conducting business* for each country. For example, as you can see from Figure 11.1, it is customary in China to present visiting cards when negotiating or trading, and to translate names in Mandarin, not Cantonese. Cultural analysis of this kind is required to understand not only behaviour between nations, but within. In China, the family name is always written first, so someone introduced as Mr Ralph Cooper might well be addressed as Mr Ralph. When negotiating, it is imperative to be aware of cultural differences. In Indonesia, for example, when assessing someone's knowledge of a product or a market, locals are more likely to reply positively, even if they know little about a product or market. It is important to Indonesians that they do not lose face. To do so might cause offence and reduce the chances of winning a contract.

One of the most important aspects for understanding a given culture is to study its value systems. In Japan, it is common for workers to stay at work until after their boss has left, which might be late at night. This is considered a mark of respect. It is also customary for management to stay at work until late in the evening, although some of this time may be spent entertaining rather than strictly working. Japanese business people also dress conservatively and may disapprove of visitors who are casually dressed.

Interpersonal relationships can be improved with a knowledge of acceptable body language. For example, whilst a nose tap in Britain indicates secrecy or confidentiality, in Italy it is interpreted as a friendly warning. This could be highly useful for sales staff. How conversation is conducted is particularly important. The physical distance considered acceptable between individuals talking during normal conversation varies enormously. In Latin American countries, the distance is much closer than in the UK. Many nations are far more tactile in their conversations than the British and sales staff should be aware of this to assess the correct personal selling approach.

The tone used in personal selling should also be adapted for different markets. Effective selling in Japan requires an awareness that politeness, harmony and beauty are valued, not aggression and outspoken comments. A successful salesperson there would not criticise the competition as this would be considered discourteous. Sales staff should ensure they are liked personally. Similarly, advertising commercials should be directed at positive feelings rather than negative statements about individuals or competitors. Attacking a competitor in advertising should be avoided. An aggressive pitch is, therefore, likely to fail in Japan, even if it is based on an accurate, rational argument.

Photography
No difficulty is put in the way of visitors who wish to photograph places of historic or scenic interest. Visitors who are interested in photographing other subjects are advised to consult their hosts. It is forbidden to photograph military personnel, vehicles or installations. The latter especially are not always readily identifiable, and it is advisable to check first if in any doubt.

Social customs and etiquette
Chinese names   In China the family name is always mentioned first. Thus Mr Deng Heming should be addressed as Mr Deng.

Visiting cards   It is customary to present a visiting card. It is an advantage to have them printed on the reverse side in Chinese; this can be done in London or in Hong Kong, but be sure to insist that personal company names are transliterated into Mandarin and not Cantonese.

Dinner parties   The Chinese are very hospitable to visitors, and it is quite normal for a visitor to be entertained to a dinner (banquet) in a restaurant during his stay by, for example, the organisation which is sponsoring his visit.
   Dinner usually begins at about 18.00–18.30. It is customary for guests to arrive punctually or a little in advance of the time stated, and to leave shortly after the meal is finished, which is generally by 20.00–20.30. The host normally bids his guests welcome with a toast at an early stage of the meal, and the chief guest will normally reply with a similar toast after a short interval. At the end of the dinner the guest should make the first move to depart, but it is not unusual for the host to do so. It is not customary to linger at table once the meal is over.

Source: HMSO. Crown copyright is reproduced with the permission of the Controller of Her Majesty's Stationery Office.

Figure 11.1 DTI export advice (China)

Marketers must also be sensitive to the *languages* spoken and written in the targeted countries. The way a language is decoded has special significance for buyer behaviour. One exporter to a Middle Eastern country advertised a detergent, featuring dirty clothes piled to the left of the poster and clean clothes stacked to the right. Since the nation were accustomed to reading from right to left, the intended message was inverted: the brand of detergent appeared to make the clothes dirty. Refer to the text box about the effect of language on lost business in France.

French buyers expect delivery dates to be honoured and for trade literature in their own language. The DTI acknowledges that British business is lost because of incoming telephone calls in French never getting past the switchboard. Recruiting a multilingual receptionist may be a solution.

Source: DTI (1989) *Hints to Exporters* (France).

The level of sophistication in which the language can be read, written and spoken will affect many marketing decisions. Consider the waste of using print media in Brazil or Mexico with their nation's high rate of illiteracy. There, highly visual media are most apt, such as colourful posters and television.

The use of *colour* in marketing communications is also culture-significant. European packaging manufacturers would be quite happy to use white as a background colour, or as the main colour of text, but white indicates mourning in the Far East. Packaging designers and, in particular, brand mark designers (i.e. those designing the non-verbal part of a brand such as the logo) must therefore take great care in identifying such differences. The same care is required when naming brands for global use. A *brand name* which appears appropriate in the domestic market may be difficult to pronounce in another language, too close to the name of a foreign brand, or simply associated with something that works against its acceptance in other countries: product names sounding distinctly American may not be widely accepted in Iran. In extreme cases, *translations* can be highly embarrassing for brand managers. Consider the Vauxhall Nova car, which means 'it doesn't go' in Spanish.

Communications indicating the country of origin can help position a brand strongly, simply and straightforwardly. This is because certain products are associated as being country-specific, with an intended indication of quality. Thus the United States is associated with hamburgers, Coca Cola and popcorn. The text box shows how influential perceptions of country of origin can be.

Perceptions of country of origin

Perceptions of the value of country of origin are not only product-specific but culturally specific. This is important when building global brands because an individual company needs to consider how or to what extent its national heritage should feature in its labelling, packaging and branding for positioning. A Wolff Ollins survey interviewed 200 directors of leading international companies about the image of various countries abroad and their association with certain products. Whilst Germany was associated with durability and technical prowess and high quality by over 90 per cent, none felt German goods had emotional appeal, and 84 per cent said they were expensive.

Most recognised Germany as associated with automobiles (85 per cent) and state-of-art engineering, but only 3 per cent with consumer goods and 10 per cent with chemicals. In the UK, highest recognition was given to financial services (41 per cent) followed by tourism (13 per cent). France was overwhelmingly associated with consumer goods and Japan with electronics. Americans have a considerably higher opinion of American products than consumers in the rest of the world, according to Roper Starch in another survey. Seventy-eight per cent of Americans thought they made the best jeans, compared to 59 per cent elsewhere and 61 per cent thought they made the best moderately priced cars compared to 16 per cent elsewhere. A similar survey by Bozell and Gallup found the Japanese even more confident than the Americans about their national produce. Self-perception of quality appeared lowest in the UK and Taiwanese consumers in this survey, with only 27 per cent of those from the UK rating domestically produced manufactured goods as excellent or very good, whilst the corresponding figure in Taiwan was 16 per cent. The exact ranking of quality appears to follow a pattern of geographic proximity – in which Japan ranks highest in Asia, Germany leads in Europe whilst the US is considered best in the Americas.

Source: Adapted from Diane Summers, 'When it's All in the Label', *Financial Times*, 3 August 1995, p. 14.

11.2.3 Political and legal indicators

Political stability should be used as a screening device for evaluating suitable target countries. General indicators about political instability that may rule out a country for consideration include threats to democracy (perhaps through a civil war or military takeover). History suggests this is most likely when one or several of the following can be identified:

- tense relationships existing between sub-cultures or religious groups in multicultural societies;
- countries holding vast reserves of natural wealth which are strategically important for world order, e.g. the Middle East;
- countries that are characterised by wide variations in standards of living between different groups or societies;
- governments that are particularly unpopular and where a low level of electoral support is combined with a belligerent electorate;

- countries with high international debt and an unstable economy (e.g. high inflation).

In addition, the existing political and social relationship between governments should be considered before making a shortlist. The current relationship a country holds with the governments of surrounding countries should also be screened for compatibility. Another factor to consider is the consequences of significant political changes by a collective group of countries that may have repercussions in economic opportunities or threats for a number of neighbouring countries. The effectiveness of the economic reforms arising from the unification of Germany in 1990 (which moved ownership and control away from the state in Eastern European countries towards private businesses, relying on market forces) may well depend upon the commitment given to it by its people – see text box below.

East meets West

With the unification of Germany, the degree of change required to create successful economies which can trade in similar ways to Western Europe is still a long way ahead.

The economic fortunes of Eastern Europe are mixed. Several countries have suffered further economic decline since reforms were implemented, whilst others have improved their positions. Many of these countries share differences in opinion regarding the pace of future reforms in order to bring about market economies. Drastic changes, some argue, would lead to dangerous social, political and economic tensions. Protectionism, uncertainty, political chaos and weak leadership continue to be serious barriers. Consequences arising from the opening of the Berlin Wall offer many opportunities to the West. What is abundantly clear is that there is ready demand for branded goods from Western Europe and elsewhere, in which locals are ready to sacrifice paying higher prices for them compared to locally produced goods. There is the ready supply of cheap labour in Eastern Europe, offering the possibilities of partnerships. Conversely, exports from these countries are likely to reduce prices of many goods to Western Europe. There is also a greater access to more reliable marketing statistics from Eastern Europe which were previously difficult to obtain.

Aside from political hurdles, there are legal barriers to consider. Regulations may arise from changing political circumstances. With the growing influence of Moslem fundamentalists, Malaysia, with a significant Moslem population, banned ads showing women in sleeveless dresses or showing underarms. There may also be *restrictions on trade* such as *quotas* (a strict limit set by the government in the number of imports it allows onto its market) or *tariffs* (effectively a tax on imports, making foreign made goods less competitive than those made domestically). There are also a number of *non-tariff barriers* to consider. Governments can set their own standards which may favour domestic companies. For example, Japanese regulations on car emissions from exhaust fumes are among the most rigorous in the world.

The unification of Europe permits theoretical free trade between Member States making it the largest single market of close to 400 million people, but it is not a truly homogeneous market. Consider the psychological barriers. Nationalism is likely to prevail despite the possibility of an eventual centralised economy with a single currency. The British government has raised doubts about a single currency and political union. It is likely, therefore that several administrative barriers will remain, whilst some legislation is in the process of standardisation. For example, several laws on labelling requirements are in the process of being standardised across Member States – see text box.

Psychological obstacles towards full economic union

Speculation rests on whether a single European currency will be created in the long term, with the hidden agenda (perhaps) of political union. But this relies on Member States placing mutual trust in the 'European-mindedness' of their European neighbours. Unfortunately, few of the EU's 373 million citizens consider themselves to be purely European. In a poll by the EU, citizens from twelve Member States were asked whether they considered themselves in the near future to be identified in purely national terms with their own country, or whether they were European. Nearly one-half of Britons, Danes and the Greeks consider themselves to be nationalistic, and even one-third of Germans, Dutch and Spanish.

Those most pro-European were from Belgium and Luxembourg, but only one tenth of these felt purely European (*The Economist*, 1995a). Thus it would appear there are still significant psychological barriers to trade amongst European countries. Perhaps a contributory factor towards nationalism is some of the obscure rules that are made by the bureaucrats from Brussels. For example, determining whether fruit and vegetables are of merchantable quality and acceptable for retail sale. In the case of the Nordic climate, many of their strawberries are smaller than the required size to meet EU standards.

11.3 Selecting target countries

After screening potential countries against set environmental criteria, the next stage is to make a selection from the shortlist. This will involve screening the shortlisted countries on the basis of how each of the economic, socio-cultural, politico-legal and technical factors will affect changes in the marketing mix from those used in the domestic market. To start, a qualitative assessment of changes should be acknowledged and tabulated (as in Table 11.3). This is then transferred into a quantitative measure in terms of how much each aspect of the mix has to be altered from that offered to the domestic market. Figure 11.2 shows ten cost increments for each element of the marketing mix. Assuming each increment is of an equivalent cost, the profile of countries shown provides a cost of 38/4 or 9.5 for UK, 27/4 or 6.75 for France, 33/4 or 8.25 for Germany and 26/4 or 6.50 for Italy. Thus, of the four countries, Italy would appear to be most similar to the home market (whatever that might be), incurring an additional cost of 6.50 units, in which distribution channels would hardly need changing (requiring a minimal change) but price and product would need changing a lot. On this basis, the most costly country to target would be the UK, requiring vast changes from the home market.

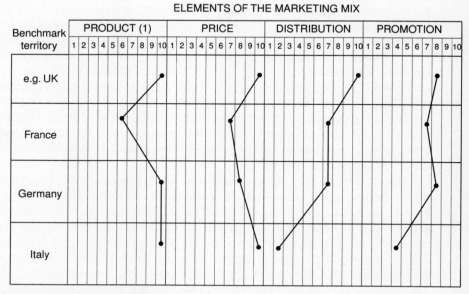

Source: Adapted from Majaro (1977).

Figure 11.2 Quantitative measurement of marketing mix changes

Table 11.3 Qualitative assessment of change in international markets

Product:

Market Country:

Environment	Product	Price	Distribution	Promotion
Culture				
Economy				
Technology/ industrial development				
Politico-legal				

11.4 Deciding method of entry into selected target countries

Once you have decided on your selected countries for international marketing, the next stage is to decide how to enter them. Indirect or direct methods may be used.

Indirect methods involve selling the goods (or services) in the domestic market to a buyer who has the aim of marketing them in another country. All necessary export procedures and documentation are handed over to a third party. Examples are foreign buyers making overseas trips at exhibitions. Alternatively international trading companies, such as the Hudson Bay Company, may be used. These typically hold a large portfolio of goods and have an extensive international network of contacts with foreign buyers. The disadvantage in using such indirect methods is that the manufacturer has little or no control over how these goods are marketed abroad. Moreover, the level of commitment in selling particular products may be rather limited. The main advantage of indirect methods is the minimum effort, risk and cost. Whilst the main expenses might involve adapting packaging or labelling to suit local legal or customary requirements, there is no direct investment in the country.

If more control over price, promotion and after-sales service is required, more direct methods are advised. These include using your own nominated agents (who cannot take title to goods, and are paid on commission and so may be more motivated to shift your stock). Other direct methods involve using licensing, joint ventures and foreign direct investment (FDI). Licensing involves authorising a firm to use your idea, product or process for a fixed period. One disadvantage is selling an idea to a competitor, once the licence has expired. Licensing also offers quick entry into a new market without incurring trade barrier expenses (such as tariffs or local taxes on goods imported) and may be desirable if the licensor (granter of the licence) has limited capital for expansion overseas.

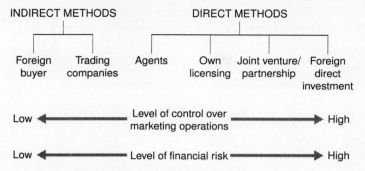

Figure 11.3 Entry decision-making

If a country is associated with high political instability, a licence may be preferred to joint ventures or more committed forms of direct investment.

Manufacturing abroad (in the form of a joint venture with an existing foreign firm) or alone can avoid customs duties but suffers from high financial risk. Large amounts of capital are likely to be tied up, and fixed assets may be open to threats from a future hostile government. The advantages of direct investment include having more control over how the product is marketed at point of sale, which may be beneficial to a company that values its international reputation for quality. Figure 11.3 summarises the main advantages and disadvantages of each method of entry.

The choice of method of entry will be influenced by the infrastructure and general conditions underlying alternative distribution channels in potential target countries – see text box.

In Spain, personal contact is very important, and regular visits are required, if appointed agents are used. A partnership with a Spanish company might be a preferred alternative to manufacturing under licensing in Spain because royalties on sales are low. Also, the timing of entry could influence the success rate. Commercial activity throughout the mainland is very slack during the hot summer period from July to early September.

Source: DTI and Foreign and Commonwealth Office (1989), *Hints to Exporters Visiting Spain*.

11.5 Adapting the marketing mix policy to local needs

Products may need to be adapted to suit the requirements of foreign markets. The extent of the environmental changes present in the chosen foreign markets will influence the extent to which products are standardised or adapted (Figure 11.4).

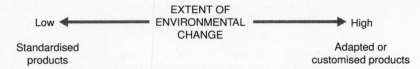

Figure 11.4 Selection of the appropriate marketing mix

Factors which influence product adaptation include the physical environment, the stage of industrial development, cultural factors, industry conditions, competition, legal constraints and economic factors such as exchange rates, currency strength and inflationary pressures.

In terms of the physical environment, climatic conditions will affect what and how products are used. For example, chocolate will melt in very hot weather and must be kept refrigerated. With respect to stage of industrial development, developing countries may require less sophisticated versions of products to those geared to Western society, because of varied and patchy spending power. Due to the relatively higher costs of labour in developed nations, time-saving devices of value will be needed which will be redundant in the cheaper labour markets of many Third World nations. Limited end-user skills may restrict markets for high specification products. Cultural factors have already been covered earlier, and you should be aware of their importance. Industry conditions include the stage of the life cycle for each market. This will influence the degree of competition, and the price elasticity of demand. Competitive factors include their strategic impact upon sales. They may have a significant effect on how much you need to spend on promotions in gaining sufficient share of voice or in gaining favourable relationships with distributors. Legal constraints can also affect the marketing mix policies decided.

For example, UK electrical appliances will need to be fitted with different types of plugs for continental Europe. Communications will have to be adapted if the end-uses of a product between countries are different. For example, the purpose of a bicycle in the UK might be for leisure, whereas in India it would be the main method of transport for many, so informational appeals would need to vary. Similarly distribution strategies may require adapting. Once the method of entry has been decided for each selected market, a decision has to be reached about whether intensive, selective or exclusive channels are used. The relative standard of living for each selected market will influence how products are classified: as speciality, shopping or convenience goods. Thus luxury products may require exclusive or selective channels, and the luxury label will depend upon the rate of economic prosperity a given country has reached.

There are several advantages to be gained from adopting standardisation policies:

1. Bulk purchasing and sourcing offers greater opportunities for larger discounts.

2. Stock-holding costs can be lowered because under customised policies, more variations of products would need to be kept. The cost of producing spare parts is also cheaper for the same reason, so enabling a uniform customer service to be achieved.
3. Research and development is likely to be lower if it is known that international tastes are similar and market homogeneity is possible.
4. Additional staff training (e.g. in educating salesforces about adaptations in foreign markets) is not required.
5. The risk of failure in entering a foreign market is much reduced if it is known that the product does not need changing significantly to be acceptable there.

There are certain strategies that can be used to accommodate standardisation policies and enable a firm to communicate effectively as a global brand. If there are problems of illiteracy or translation difficulties, avoid text and use illustration/visuals that are familiar to just about everyone. For example, British Airways, in conjunction with Saatchi and Saatchi, have used the Manhattan Skyline in 45 countries with only a voice-over change. A second option is to use trade characters. The Marlboro cowboy provides international recognition which has made it the World's No. 1 best seller of cigarettes. A third option is to identify international market segments, in which common appeals cut across national boundaries. For example, the needs of youth markets are remarkably similar across countries, that has helped to make Levi's a dominant brand in the world. Whilst a company may be able to standardise its product, communications and distribution policies, keeping prices similar for each market is difficult. The next section explains some of the economic factors that influence international pricing issues.

11.6 Economic factors affecting pricing in international markets: exchange rates, currency strength and inflationary pressures

11.6.1 Exchange rates

When a company buys a good from a foreign market it first needs to buy the foreign currency before it can buy the good. Since the relative value of currencies fluctuates, there is the possibility of losing money. When a currency rises in value, it is said to appreciate, if it falls it is said to depreciate. The strength of a currency is measured in terms of its exchange rate, i.e. the ratio that measures the value of one currency relative to another. If the currency in the domestic market rises, the prices of domestic goods become more expensive relative to foreign imports, and this has an adverse effect on demand for exports. This means domestic businesses have greater difficulty in selling their goods abroad. As demand slumps, jobs may be lost in the domestic market, and unemployment rises. Conversely, for example, if the value of the British pound falls relative to the Japanese yen (say, it is devalued) more British pounds are required to trade for an equivalent amount of goods before the devaluation. This means Japanese imports to the UK are more expensive and British goods become cheaper to Japanese buyers. This might help British export trade with Japan and encourage more Japanese tourists to visit the UK whilst these conditions prevail. These effects of currency fluctuations on the demand for imports and exports are summarised in Table 11.4.

The future direction of exchange rates can be predicted by examining the relative price differences in buying a similar basket of goods in different countries. One currency is chosen as the standard against which all others are benchmarked. For example, if the McDonald's Big Mac is used as the good, and the US dollar the currency benchmark, it can be assumed that over the long run, a dollar should buy the same amount in all countries (*Economist*, 1977). A working example illustrates this point. If the price of a Big Mac in the States is $2.40, whilst the price in Sweden is $3, the Swedish price is over-valued by 3/2.40 or by 25 per cent. If the Big Mac is a fair reflection of a typical basket of goods, then the Swedish Kröne could be considered to be currently over-valued.

11.6.2 Currency strength

The strength of a currency is determined by its supply and demand. This in turn is influenced by the expectations of inflation by international traders, specu-lators, investors and the role of governments. If international traders expect inflation in the domestic market to exceed that of our trading nations, then domestic goods become progressively more expensive. Consequently, domestic consumers will demand more foreign goods, thereby increasing the supply of the domestic currency to the foreign exchange market. Therefore, with high inflation in the domestic market, the international value of the domestic currency will fall with increased supply. Thus high domestic inflation is one of the major causes of a depreciation in the exchange value of a currency.

Table 11.4 Effects of currency value changes on demand for domestic goods, imports and exports

	Currency change on goods in domestic market	
	Rises	Falls
Relative price of domestic goods	More expensive relative to imports	Less expensive relative to price of imports
Demand for our goods abroad	Reduced	Improved

11.6.3 Dealing with inflationary pressures

For much international trade, two currencies between the buyer and the seller are involved. There is a risk that the rate of exchange between the two currencies will change between the signing of the contract and subsequent receipt of the foreign currency (settlement date). We have already noted that inflation may influence this.

When exchange rates are expected to shift before settlement date, the firm selling may decide the amount of currency it requires for payment (i.e. by setting a fixed price) irrespective of the spot price (or value of that currency if purchased now at current exchange rate values). Effectively, the supplier is negotiating a guaranteed exchange rate for some time in the future.

Alternatively, an escalation or fluctuation clause allows for relative movements within a predetermined limit. If these are exceeded, the contract can be amended.

With high inflation rates, the purchasing power of a local currency is progressively eroded. If payments are late, a firm must take action to protect itself from potential losses. This can be achieved by constantly adjusting price movements to achieve constant margins. Alternatively buyers can be encouraged to pay immediately with substantial discounts or by levying penalties on those who fail to pay within agreed periods.

11.6.4 Methods of quoting prices for export

In export marketing, the method chosen to quote prices varies world-wide. Owing to these variations it is necessary for a foreign buyer to know what exactly they are paying for. The common terms used for quoting prices are included in INCOTERMS, a booklet of terms and definitions, obtained from the International Chamber of Commerce. These include:

> *c.i.f. (cost, insurance, freight)*: This is an inclusive price, which includes the product (cost), all transportation and insurance to the point of unloading from the vessel at a named destination (i.e. often foreign port).
>
> *f.o.b. (free on board)*: This includes the price of placing the shipment onto a specified vessel, but further transportation is the buyer's responsibility.
>
> *ex factory*: This applies to a price for products at the point of origin, in which the buyer incurs all transportation charges.

Exporters should use the export pricing process to match buyer requirements, where possible. Whilst American firms attach a great deal of importance to proper presentation, including sales literature of a product, they also prefer to be quoted in imperial measures in their own currency and quoted either ex-works unit price (i.e. basic price to US importer) or c.i.f. US port price (with a separate quotation for direct shipment to the West Coast if an agent is required there). However, quoting in a foreign currency rather than the domestic currency incurs risks in exchange rate fluctuations. Solutions to this problem have been suggested.

11.7 The future of international growth

Traditional world trade has come from four broad geographical areas. The Americas, the Asia/Pacific Rim, Europe and the Rest of the World (*The Economist*, 1991). If governments in emerging or developing markets continue to encourage free market reforms, growth is likely to outpace developed countries by twice as much over the next decade (*The Economist*, 1995b). Emerging economies include many South American countries, Mexico, India, China, Thailand and Taiwan, plus several Eastern European nations including Poland, the Czech Republic and Hungary. Those emerging markets likely to sustain most wealth are those that encourage high savings and investment, low trade barriers, a well-educated labour force, and sound, low inflationary policies.

According to the East Asia Analytical Unit of the Department of Foreign Affairs and Trade, Australia, Asia is likely to dominate the twenty-first century trade, with world trade between China and Japan increasing from 13 per cent in 1993 to 28 per cent by 2015. However, economic progress could be hampered by political disputes over territorial ownership.

Case study: A timely reminder – all that glisters is not gold

The practice of wearing wrist watches dates back only to the First World War when they were introduced for timing military operations. Today, the wrist watch is accepted as a jewellery item, being part-functional and part-symbolic, in so far as people may be judged on the basis of what they wear on their wrist. Whilst the status of a watch-owner is conferred by the reputation of the manufacturer, its name is also influential in determining the potential as an investment. Limited editions from established Swiss manufacturers are particularly popular and are often tied to special events such as the 25th, 50th or the 100th anniversary. If a watch bears a unique number in the production-run, then it can quickly trade at a premium to its original selling price.

The term 'Swiss made' is associated with a minimum quality of craftsmanship, reliability and discrete fashion which is not 'over the top'. Consequently, the words are fiercely protected as a trade name. Watches only qualify if they contain at least 50 per cent Swiss-manufactured components by value, and must have been assembled in Switzerland.

Since the Second World War, the number of watch manufacturers has declined, whilst unit output has risen. Volume manufacturers are still found in Russia, India, China, Hong Kong, Japan and Taiwan, using the technology of the 'quartz revolution' developed in the early 1970s, which badly affected the Swiss watch trade. Although nowadays a watch purchased for £1 can be as accurate as one costing £10,000, the average selling price of watches is rising quite dramatically. Recently, the Swiss have experienced their margins eroding in export markets because of the strength of the Swiss franc.

Competition from the Far East is likely to intensify as the global assembly point for watch-making in Hong Kong improves its position with the growing demand from neighbouring China. To facilitate trade, China is also relaxing its import tariffs on watches this year.

Other problems that the Swiss watch industry must contend with are the excess world supply and the unfair trading practices such as counterfeiting and the parallel market. Good counterfeits are the real menace, because they appear to be the genuine article unless closely inspected. Classy fakes, presented in high quality 18 carat gold cases, are a real threat to prestigious manufacturers such as Rolex and Cartier. Many of the counterfeits originate in China and South Korea, but may also come from Spain and Italy, where the relaxing of border controls between Member States of the European Union offers an easier life for potential smugglers. The World Trade Organisation, together with numerous other international bodies, are attempting to reduce the flow of world trade in counterfeit products. Parallel importing refers to products that are made and assembled elsewhere, predominantly in low wage economies, which subsequently emerge in the domestic market at a significant price advantage.

The Société Suisse de Microéléctronique et de d'Horlogérie SA (SMH) now controls the world's biggest group of watch brands. In response to the flood of inexpensive Japanese quartz watches that appeared in the 1970s, the Swatch watch was created, its biggest selling line. Buyers are attracted by the constantly updating of inspired youthful designs to fit in with active life styles. The sports watch is still preferred by a large contingent of younger buyers.

Source: Adapted from M. Balfour (1996) 'Watch and Clock Industry', *Financial Times* Survey, 18 April, pp. I–III. (Reproduced with permission)

Q11.1 What are the main market segments for wrist watches?

Q11.2 What are the threats to the Swiss watch industry?

Q11.3 How can the Swiss watch industry respond to threats identified in Q11.2?

Case study: World Wide Publishers

World Wide Publishers, a long-time leader in the US greeting card industry, began its international operation in the 1930s when a sales-man began selling its line of products in Canada. Realising the potential greeting card market in Canada, the form soon established a subsidiary to handle the Canadian operation.

Shortly after the success in Canada, another subsidiary was established in Leeds. The English operation was very successful and the World Wide name was considered to have an excellent reputation in the English greeting card industry.

In the late 1950s, World Wide investigated the feasibility of entering the continental European market and engaged a Swedish marketing consultant firm to do research on the question. As a result of its favour-able finding, World Wide formed three separate subsidiaries in France, Germany, and Italy.

In the United States, everyday cards and seasonal cards each account for 50 per cent of the total greeting card volume. Notepaper, party goods, and various sundry items are also handled by World Wide, because of the similarity in the channels of distribution used for both these products and their well-received card line.

The German subsidiary began with a limited line of studio (contem-porary) cards and gift-wrap paper. Such a limited line of products, of course, involved a smaller capital investment by the parent company and a smaller staff to operate the firm.

The procedure used by the German subsidiary to produce cards was to copy successful cards marketed by the parent firm in the United States. The designs were a replica of the US cards with a German translation of the text printed on the card. Often a text would lose something in the translation. For example, a card that was humorous in English would not always be funny in German. Also, because of cultural differences between the two nations, a text appealing to Americans would not necessarily appeal to prospective German customers. The net result was that greeting card sales in Germany were significantly less than originally anticipated.

There were also marked differences in product design and quality. Traditionally, the German greeting card was either of the single fold or postcard variety (refer to Figure 11.5). A great deal of workmanship went into the design of these cards, but seldom was any text or message required since it was customary in Germany for buyers to write their own message on the inside or back of the card.

World Wide introduced *sentiment* (a technical word used by the industry to connote written verse) to the German greeting card market. A prepared verse on the inside of the card was something new and

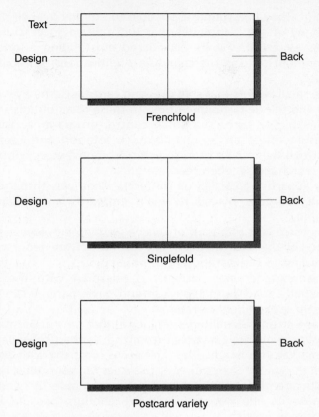

Figure 11.5 Types of postcard

different in this market. World Wide also introduced the Frenchfold type of card.

In addition to product innovations, World Wide established an entirely new approach to greeting card merchandising in Germany with the introduction of the American type floor-stand rack, which holds 120 cards.

Prior to the innovation of this floor-stand rack, merchandising of greeting cards had been carried on in a haphazard manner. A counter between 1 and 2 metres in length usually held all the cards in the store. The lower-priced cards were piled in a bin in the centre of the counter. All the cards were individually wrapped in cellophane, with the more expensive cards laid out flat at the ends of the counter. These were often under glass and had to be asked for specifically.

The management of World Wide considered the innovation and implementation of their merchandising programme in Germany to be very successful. They had found it possible to employ in their German subsidiary many of the techniques that had proved successful in the United States, where they were considered outstanding in quality of product (*sentiment*) and in merchandising innovations, particularly at the retail level.

The main retail outlets that sold greeting cards in Germany were the chain stores and the department stores. To these retail outlets the firm introduced its highly successful stock control programme. This programme was in effect an automatic stock rotation and reordering system that freed the retailer from concern about inventory control and selection of merchandise when reordering.

The only advertising carried on by World Wide was through trade journals. The company placed its main emphasis and reliance on personal selling.

The sales force was made up of twelve German employees trained and supervised by the sales manager. The territories were geographically divided according to the distribution of population.

The sales manager was formerly a salesman with the parent company. He had a solid German background, as his parents had lived in the country. He spoke fluent German.

There was a strong US military presence at that time in Germany but this market was completely divorced from the German subsidiary. The US military market was handled by the parent company with products shipped from the United States directly to a sales representative based in Germany. Management felt the subsidiary was unable to handle this market because its line was not extensive enough, nor did it have facilities to print in English.

The company believed its pricing policy to be competitive despite the fact that its prices were slightly higher than those of German manufacturers. Most of World Wide's line was priced at DM1.00 or less. It was discovered that the cards priced at DM1.40 and at DM2.00 did not sell well in the German market. Management attributed its slightly higher price line to the fact that the cards offered by local German competitors were smaller and had little or no verse.

The retailers' mark-up in both Germany and the United States was 100 per cent. For example, a card selling for 50 cents cost the retailer 25 cents.

When approaching retailers with their line, World Wide was faced with two obstacles. The first one was that German manufacturers always supplied with each card a tissue envelope with a coloured lining. World Wide, however, supplied a regular white envelope without coloured lining or tissue.

The second obstacle that World Wide ran into was the long-established practice of the German firms of wrapping their cards individually in cellophane. This was done because traditionally greeting cards had always been a low turnover item at the retail level, and the cellophane protected the inventory while it was in stock. World Wide packaged their cards, with individual, white envelopes in lots of 6, 12, or 24, depending on the card, and wrapped them in a brown envelope. The retailer removed the cards from the brown envelope and displayed them on the rack.

To overcome the German traditions, World Wide told greeting card retailers that it was introducing *sentiment* into the market and therefore the cards had to be read and could not be wrapped in cellophane.

World Wide felt that the envelope was not as important as the card and stressed the idea that it was putting more quality into the card rather than the envelope, which was thrown away after opening.

Later, the line was expanded to incorporate a variety of everyday (birthday, anniversary) and seasonal (Christmas, Easter) cards. The line was not as extensive as the US line, but was considered adequate by management for the German market.

Sentimental design and text were never a big seller and long flowery verses did not sell in Germany. Verses had to be kept to a minimum of one or two lines to be at all successful.

The firm continued to employ native, German-speaking translators to translate the text of cards selected for presentation to the German market. Since it was important, however, that the cards be adequately adapted to the German language and cultural sensitivities after translation, particularly in an industry where, in the words of one World Wide executive, '*Sentiment* is our most important product', a more selective means of choosing which American cards to use was a constant challenge and a constant opportunity.

Despite the high levels of prosperity characterising the market areas serviced by the German subsidiary, its sales did not achieve the desired volume nor even the desired rate of growth. The high administrative and initial start-up costs incurred to launch the German subsidiary and required to continue the product and merchandising innovations that had been introduced by it were of increasing concern. Company executives believed that the introduction of sentiment and of effective merchandising practices and controls at the retail level to the German greeting card industry had been steps in the right direction. They also believed, however, that factors other than product design and retail merchandising methods were operating in the German greeting card market to limit prospects of any immediate increase in the rate of sales growth.

Germans do not send each other as many cards as Americans do because they are by custom and tradition a very formal people. As a result, card sending is more of an occasion, a fact which might relate to the preference for and frequent insistence upon individually wrapped cards. Analyses of the German market did suggest, however, that there had been a gradual shift to the informal, partly due to contacts the German people have had with the many Americans living in their country.

The company re-examined the many factors present in the German greeting card market and the opportunities for further progress and contribution in it. A number of possibilities were considered, among them negotiating a sale of part of the German subsidiary to a German publishing company. Under the proposed terms of sale, the company would recoup a significant proportion of its unamortized administrative and initial costs. World Wide executives felt that the German firm had a good reputation, was familiar with the market and temperament of the German greeting card purchaser, and could easily carry on the operations of the firm. The German firm would continue to use the American cards, for which World Wide would receive a royalty, and there would be a sharing of profits and expenses at a ratio not yet worked out.

Source: Adapted from V. Terpstra (1987) *International Marketing*. Orlando, FL: Dryden Press.

Q11.4 Explain the socio-cultural factors that vary in Germany from the domestic market.

Q11.5 What implications do these factors have on adapting the marketing mix? Explain your answer.

Summary

International marketing is marketing across national boundaries. It is often attractive to manufacturers whose domestic markets are approaching saturation. International marketing is also useful because it can reward a firm with economies of scale and it offers greater efficiency for those countries being able to specialise in what they can make most productively (theory of comparative advantage).

Once a firm has decided to move internationally, a marketing plan must be developed. This consists of market screening to develop a shortlist of potential countries, market selection (after assessing costs involved in adapting the marketing mix elements from the domestic market), method of entry (such as using direct or indirect methods of distribution) and a marketing mix policy (deciding the exact nature of customisation of the mix elements for each targeted country).

Market screening criteria are used to assess the viability of a marketing strategy. These involve economic, socio-cultural, politico-legal and technological criteria. This chapter has considered the first three in some detail. Economic criteria that require consideration include the size of the potential market, the distribution of income and the relative standard of living. Socio-cultural criteria require examining conventional methods of conducting business, value systems, body language and the written language with implications for translation. Political criteria include the degree of political stability and the relationship of the domestic government to current and possible future governments of all the assessed countries for selection and their surrounding countries. Aside from this, there may be legal restrictions on trade such as a set quota or tariffs imposed on trade.

Once a shortlist of potential countries has been identified, they are then assessed on the basis of comparative costs of adapting each mix element to suit the special requirements of each country. Those countries whose environmental criteria vary little from the domestic market will be most suited for selection, because the mix elements will only need to be adapted slightly.

It is then necessary to decide the method of entry for each selected country. Whilst indirect methods offer little financial risk, there is less control over how the products are marketed at point-of-sale. Indirect methods include using foreign buyers at international fairs, and international trading companies. Direct methods offer more control over how the product is sold but may involve more financial risk. Examples include licensing and joint ventures.

Finally, the international trader must decide the exact degree to which each mix element is customised for each selected foreign market. Legal differences may involve product specification changes. If the reason for use varies, communications will require adapting, and so on. Figure 11.6 provides a summary of the elements of the marketing mix which may need changing as a result of the

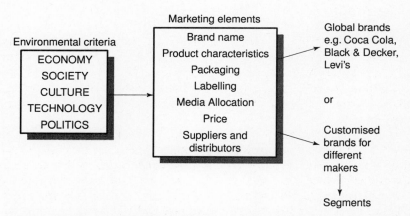

Figure 11.6 Factors affecting standardisation vs. customisation strategies

environmental criteria. Another way of understanding this is to consider how each environmental factor will affect buyer expectations, and how these expectations might vary for different geographical markets.

References

Catling, C. (1993) *Insight Guides, Holland*. Singapore: Houghton Mifflin.

European Marketing Data and Statistics (1996) 31st edition. London: Euromonitor.

Hennessey, J. (1992) *Global Marketing Strategies*. New York: Houghton Mifflin.

The Economist (1977) 'Big MacCurrencies' (12 April), p. 107.

The Economist (1991) 'The World Economy' (5 January), p. 22.

The Economist (1995a) 'More-or-less European Union' (26 August), p. 40.

The Economist (1995b) 'Rising Markets, Sinking Feeling' (13 May), pp. 109–10.

The Human Development Report (1996). Oxford: Oxford University Press.

Majaro, S. (1977) *International Marketing: A Strategic Approach to World Markets*, 1st edition. Allen and Unwin, p. 60.

CHAPTER TWELVE

Services Marketing

Objectives

After studying this chapter, you should be able to:

1. Understand the special problems in the marketing of services, in particular the difficulty in controlling consumer evaluation.
2. Identify opportunities for alleviating these problems.
3. Understand the significance of search, experience and credence qualities.
4. Appreciate the extension of the marketing mix for services.

Introduction

The characteristics of services have been recognised as different from goods (Sasser *et al.*, 1978). Along with these characteristics are special problems associated with services, which offer an additional challenge beyond that of marketing physical goods. According to Bateson (1989), the service sector now accounts for the bulk of new employment in most developed economies and has fuelled the economic growth of the past two centuries. Hence the marketing of services deserves special treatment.

This chapter begins with some of the reasons for service growth, then discusses how services may be categorised, identifies special problems associated with services and finally examines several strategies to deal with them.

12.1 Reasons for service growth

General economic prosperity leads to an increased demand in services, such as entertainment, health care, personal care, travel and financial services. There is also an increased tendency for consumers to search for products and services which reduce time to complete tasks, or alternatively to contract them out to others. For example, there is a steady, although seasonal, demand for cutting lawns in the United States. The growth in home shopping offers a useful service to professionals who have difficulty in shopping in normal business hours and avoids the time taken in travelling to and queuing in a traditional retail store. Incidentally, this lack of time during normal working hours has also contributed to the growth and success of sandwich bars as more people resort to quick snacks at lunch-time.

In Europe in particular, fewer working people are increasingly supporting more non-working or retired people (Handy, 1991). Although this might increase the opportunity for a ready market for recreational and leisure services it has an increased burden on health services.

As more markets face saturation there is a greater need for more repair and maintenance services. There is also an increasing importance of business services, such as after-care in car fleet and computer sales.

Finally, it has been suggested that there are very few 'pure' products or services but that one or other predominates (Shostack, 1977). The upshot of this is that, for most things sold to consumers, there is a dimension of customer service. Figure 12.1 shows a continuum for different types of products and services ranging from those with few service dimensions towards the left, whilst those towards the right are increasingly considered as services, in which the service elements may be critical in terms of how they are perceived or evaluated by consumers.

However, you should appreciate that even for items such as clothing or jewellery, customer service can be critical. You might stop here and consider why this might be so. Imagine a situation in which you have to take back an item of clothing because it doesn't fit properly. You might expect a refund or an alternative size. The range of options available to satisfy your problem is wide, but it is *how* you perceive you are treated that is critical. Zemke and Schaaf (1990) advocate that, wherever a marketer is faced with a problem, they should treat it as an opportunity to advance beyond satisfying the consumer. Thus a complaint can be considered as feedback, and offers the chance to develop a relationship with the customer beyond simple redress. You might, for instance, be given a voucher in recognition of your inconvenience in addition to a normal refund, or replacement. The philosophy and practice of paying great attention to detail in customer complaints is referred to as *symbolic atonement*. It matters, and it has proved to increase loyalty because the marketer is perceived as being professional, responsive and, above all, caring. Thus the retailer, in this case, is investing time and money (because it costs time to train staff adequately to deal with complaints)

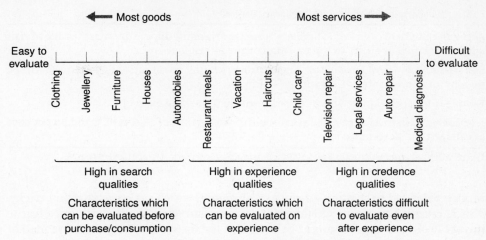

Figure 12.1 Continuum of evaluation for different types of product

in the long-term potential market value of the consumer. Over the course of a life-time, this consumer might buy £30,000 of clothes, so the investment could be very worthwhile if this treatment increases store loyalty.

Symbolic atonement reflects the art of good customer service. It is unfortunate that many businesses do not treat their customers in this way. It is a pity because, as Tom Peters suggests, superb service is becoming a requirement for survival under fast and changing, quality-conscious, increasingly competitive markets. Table 12.1 shows how targets can be set to measure customer responsiveness, one aspect of customer service.

12.2 Categorising services according to ease of evaluation

We shall now turn to Figure 12.1 once again, since this model is essentially one of evaluation.

Products and services can be categorised according to their ease of evaluation. Evaluation can be ascertained prior to, during and after purchase. These are referred to as search, experience and credence qualities respectively (Nelson, 1974; Darby and Karni, 1973).

Goods and services high in search qualities enable consumers to evaluate with confidence before purchase. Typically they are tangible goods, which can be inspected for purchase, such as the hallmark of a gold ring which will indicate its authenticity and purity. In the case of buying a house, the buyer can use the services of a surveyor who will issue a report on its condition and market value. For many services such as surveying, consumers are unable to inspect the exact

Table 12.1 Targets for measuring responsiveness

Appointments to visit customers in their own home: On arranging appointments, the time of visit will be specified as either in the morning or the afternoon.

Customer calls to Severn Trent offices: Any customer calling on an office with a query will be seen by an appropriate person within 5 minutes.

Writing to the organisation: Aim to respond within 5 working days.

Telephoning: Aim to answer general calls within an average of 15 seconds, and 90 per cent of calls within 30 seconds.

Source: Adapted from Customer Service Information, Severn Trent Water (1996–97), p. 6.

service provided to them in advance of purchase, which makes evaluation tricky. This is referred to as *intangibility*. How can the surveyor instil confidence in the buyer? Proforma reports might be available for inspection, to gain some idea of what to expect. The surveyor is attempting to make the service tangible.

Many services are also high in experience qualities, which can only be evaluated with confidence at the time of service delivery. Typically, this would include restaurants, vacations and child care services. There are several reasons attributable for experience qualities.

As offerings become more service-oriented, the role of service staff or contact staff dealing with consumer requests become more important in influencing the final outcome or quality of the service. In reality, each service offering is unique because both the provider and the consumer can and do provide a unique contribution.

First, the integrity and competence with which service staff conduct their duties will vary between individuals. Their performance will also vary over time. Consider a hospital doctor whose performance is likely to be strained from tiredness towards the end of a long shift. Consider also a waiter who has been reproached by an angry customer. How will he or she react to their next customer? The implications of this apparent variability or *heterogeneity* for management are significant. Management must ensure that a consistent standard of customer service is maintained. If standards fluctuate, the organisation is likely to suffer from confused positioning and a lack of customer confidence. This will have a significant effect on overall profitability because customers are far more likely to talk about negative experiences than positive ones. If consumers have had bad experiences, negative word-of-mouth communication can be a significant barrier in developing a strong corporate reputation for a service.

Second, you should recognise that as a consumer you also influence the service that is offered to you. The significance of this is that you are partly responsible for the service you receive. This characteristic is referred to as *joint production with consumption*.

This characteristic becomes a problem if consumers, as in many service situations, are unsure what they need. The emphasis is then on the service organisation training their staff to help guide consumers to articulate their needs, with the aim of selecting appropriate services. A poor judgement of consumer needs by service providers is likely to lead to consumer dissatisfaction. The importance of this judgement can be illustrated in financial services. In a LIMRA survey (Fletcher, 1994), 69 per cent of consumers understood little or nothing about the life assurance industry. This has contributed to many customers taking out the wrong policies. The recent adverse publicity arising from the mis-selling of many life assurance services accounts for the poor image associated with the industry (*Business Review*, 1994).

If consumer demand is less than the capacity available at the service delivery, then potential sales are lost. This *perishability* problem is another feature of services. For example, an airline loses money on a poor booking for an off-season flight, whereas at peak times in the year it might be full. In order to encourage more purchases during off-peak times, it might offer heavy discounts that cover or contribute towards the fixed costs of its operations.

Services high in credence qualities refer to those that cannot be evaluated confidently, even with experience. Typically, they include professional services such as legal advice, car repair services and medical services, in which most consumers would have difficulty in assessing exactly what they are getting in return for their money. It is here that the value of the service is most difficult to discern. In some cases, integrity of the service provider may not always contribute to positive feelings and so the marketing of such services requires the utmost care.

Imagine the situation if you were told you would lose a legal battle in court, or that your car, involved in an accident, was irreparable, or that you were diagnosed with a terminal illness. How would you react to the solicitor, garage mechanic or medic respectively? Although they are acting with integrity, accurate information in the latter case may not always be in the consumer's best interests because consumer reaction may cause anguish and destroy any remaining quality in life. The point is that the service provider must understand each consumer as an individual in order to find out what should be offered in their best interests. Training courses can help here in developing interpersonal and counselling skills.

12.2.1 Perceived risk

The marketer of physical goods holds an advantage over those who deal in services because consumers can inspect and, in some cases, sample before purchase. This reduces the amount of perceived risk in making the wrong choice, in which there might be performance risk (product does not meet expectations), financial risk (not perceived value for money or considered to provide poor return on investment) or social risk (considered embarrassing to use in front of one's peers).

In the case of financial services, for instance, not only is it not possible to sample before purchase, but the exact value gained by a purchase is not always immediately available and is difficult to measure even after purchase. Many investment products, for instance, are complex insofar as performance (return on investment) may be rather uncertain and should be considered in years rather than months.

12.3 Service strategies

Davies (1996) has developed a list of strategies designed to deal with the service problems associated with intangibility, complexity, uncertainty of performance, joint production with consumption, heterogeneity and perishability, through examining search, experience and credence qualities (Table 12.2). Although the analysis focuses on financial services, it is widely applicable to other services.

Thus intangibility can be reduced by using strong messages in advertising and publicity in order to support a clear position and provides additional search qualities. Tangible cues can be offered based on performance, reliability, innovativeness or expertise. For example, in the case of personal equity plans, the credibility gained through experience of investment managers is often discussed in promotional material. Although this in itself does not predict future performance, it acts as a tangible cue or information on which readers might assess alternative investments. If there is a criterion on which the service excels but is not considered important or valued by consumers, it is possible to educate them by raising its salience with 'a reason why' message or by providing evidence. Independent evidence from third parties is best if it is available. There is a wide variety of promotional techniques available to reassure consumers of service quality. In the case of experience qualities the main problems are associated with joint production with consumption and heterogeneity. Service providers can set appropriate objectives to deal with these problems. They might encourage consumers to develop more confidence in their own ability to make choices. Alternatively, service staff need to manage the service encounter, and this requires suitable recruitment, training and remuneration schemes in order to develop a high level of inter-personal skills in managing the interaction.

In the first case, developing consumer autonomy requires screening and simplifying communication to ensure it is user-friendly. Promotional support can be offered explaining the procedures in buying or selling a house or starting your own business in the form of a set of guidelines. A common cause of dissatisfaction has been where consumers are confused about what they have been charged for.

It is perhaps significant that this has also arisen in the business-to-business sector, in which clients raised concerns over a lack of clarity in the bills delivered to them by their advertising agencies (Osmond, 1992–93). Referring to the consumer market, you might have noticed that companies such as British Telecom and the regional electricity companies have re-designed their bills, in order to show how they calculate their charges, so reducing customer hostility.

Table 12.2 Problems and possible strategies for dealing with different information qualities

Information quality	Search	Experience	Credence
Problems	1. Intangibility 2. Complexity 3. Uncertainty of performance	1. Joint production with consumption 2. Heterogeneity	1. Intangibility and deferred benefits 2. Heterogeneity 3. Perishability
Global objectives	Make evaluation easier, lower perceived risk, develop/restore trust		
Objectives	Extend search qualities	1. Encourage consumer independence from service provider 2. Manage service encounter	1. Reduce credence qualities 2. Manage service encounter
Strategies	Offer tangible cues • Positioning using relevant criteria through: • Performance • reliability • innovativeness • expertise Suitably present appropriate position • Raise salience of criteria • Offer 'reason why' a criterion is best • Match intensity of message to competitive standing	1a. Offer user friendly advice • Use cognitive scripts guiding expectations • Simplify charges • Offer support materials e.g. videos 1b. Maintaining consistent message 1c. Ensure service is easy to use 1d. Focus on key customers, demarket others	1a. Reinforce claims through consistent positioning using: • Physical environment • Corporate livery 1b. Encourage serving same customers 1c. Develop relationships through: • Responsiveness • Offer integrated services
		2a. Boost morale to retain staff and improve performance using internal marketing and suitable remuneration schemes. 2b. Ensure ready access to information: • Point of sale • Personal advisers • Hotlines 2c. Training in interpersonal skills	
			3. Anticipate changes, offer flexibility in services.

Source: Davies, M.A.P. (1996).

If services are difficult to evaluate after experience, they suffer from problems associated with intangibility and deferred benefits, heterogeneity and perishability. Service providers could aim to reduce these credence qualities by reinforcing the existing positioning. This can be achieved by ensuring the location, layout, size and decor of all the physical facilities used to conduct the service support the intended position. This can be extended to the corporate livery (clothing, signage and business correspondence). For example, a management consultant should be seen to be successful, so the car he or she drives and the clothes worn should reflect this. If the positioning of the service is intended to be prestigious, publicity should be presented on quality paper and the type of office furniture should be appropriate to match customer expectations.

Consistency can also be maintained by retaining the same service providers to deal with a group of clients. This would reduce problems associated with heterogeneity. Relationships can be lost and won by being responsive to future requests and developing opportunities for add-on services. Offering a package of services together reduces the need for a consumer to shop around and offers additional convenience. This has been developed in the housing market. Faced with a saturated mortgage market, many building societies have had to extend their range of services to retain existing customers. Some societies have extended a range of benefits to their house insurance contents as competitors increasingly tempt consumers either on entry prices or discounts for low claims. Some now offer annual travel insurance as an integrated package designed to increase switching costs.

Offering a package of services can also be used to reduce threats from aggressive competitors. For example, British Telecom have had to become more service-oriented with threats from competitors (such as Mercury) by offering an augmented array of service benefits to their customers such as a 'call return service' in which previous unattended phone calls are stored. These numbers can be traced, with the data and time of the call by dialling a special number. Returned calls are then charged at normal rates, offering a cheap answerphone service.

Another aim, if faced with credence qualities, would be to manage the service encounter. Offering ready access to information such as personal advisors and hotlines can reduce any lingering doubts about the quality of service and help to secure customer loyalty.

12.4 The extended marketing mix of services

Having discussed the special characteristics of services: intangibility, inseparability or joint production with consumption, heterogeneity and perishability, it is not enough to make decisions on the product, price, place (distribution) and promotions. It is necessary to consider an additional three factors: physical evidence, people and process. Thus, the marketing mix of services is now recognised to consist of the 7 Ps, in contrast to the 4 Ps of physical goods. Why?

Consider the intangible nature common to all services. Since services touched, seen or inspected, nor indeed sampled before purchase, in contra~ sample of a convenience product or a test-drive of a car, say, the need to provid~ some *physical evidence* is of paramount importance in supporting product positioning. Physical evidence is about paying attention to the tangible clues that offer support or represent an appropriately intended ambience. Thus a restaurant such as McDonald's Golden Arches is sensitive to issues such as cleanliness and litter surrounding its restaurants. If the marketing management get this wrong, negative publicity could act as a hygiene factor against McDonald's or even against fast-food in general. The physical evidence that enables consumers to evaluate the ambience of a restaurant might be the outside decor, the type and layout of furniture, lighting, menu displays and uniforms of staff. This is especially important in the absence of previous experiences.

You will recall from chapter 4 that developing a consistent positioning for a good is important. For services this can be difficult because of the service variability or heterogeneity of staff. Although it is acknowledged that people are also involved in the marketing of physical goods, people become a more important component in the marketing mix for services. This is because consumers become an integral part of a service when it is produced (i.e. consumption and production can take place together). Thus if a patient is ill at ease during a medical consultation, the consultant's job is made more difficult. However with the right training, a consultant might reduce the tension in the patient and put his or her mind at ease. The result should be a better experience for both consultant and patient.

For many employees who have daily contact with customers (e.g. waiters, shop assistants, receptionists) the personal interaction between customer and employee can dramatically influence the perceptions of a company and its services. Unfortunately, many employees who have such daily contact with customers are not always treated with the best of intentions by management and this results in an indifferent attitude towards their jobs, which is then mirrored in the way they greet potential clients. Sound recruitment, retention and motivation policies can help resolve this problem.

When employees are treated as internal customers, this is sometimes referred to as internal marketing. Hopefully investment in training and a suitable reward structure for recognition will develop employees to reach their full potential and enable them to be co-operative and understanding when engaged in client contact (Figure 12.2).

The final mix element is *process*. This is how consumers are treated at the place of purchasing and consuming the service (or service encounter). It involves the process of transaction including ease of payment. For example, what is the speed at which consumers can be served? How many can be served at the same time? Will peak times result in queuing, and will this affect the perceived quality of the service adversely? Are there special groups that need to be served faster who will pay a higher price for it? It is recognised, for instance, that some airlines have

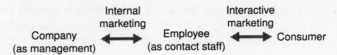

Figure 12.2 Relationship between employers, employees and consumers

developed premium-priced services designed to cater for the busy, time-conscious executive, in which they can avoid the crowding and waiting that appears commonplace at major airports.

The process is concerned with customer service levels. There is a trade-off between high customer service levels and the higher costs of providing them, which usually means these costs are passed onto their customers. There is a need to ensure the customer service/price ratio is appropriate for the market.

Case study: The Euro Disney encounter

Euro Disney opened in the summer of 1992. Since Florida's Disney World and Epcot attracted many visitors from Europe, it appeared that locating a theme park in Europe would be a sensible choice. However, its specific location within France, 32 km east of Paris, has proved to be rather less than spectacular.

The French weather, particularly north of the Loire, is decidedly more fickle than Florida. Many Continental Europeans have an aversion to queuing (unlike their American counterparts) and tend to be rather less well disciplined in standing in line. Somehow consumers are more receptive to a theme park concept providing entertainment in the form of fun, mystique and fantasy in the outdoors if it is accompanied by warm sunshine.

Perhaps Disney did not clarify its marketing concept for the European culture. When Euro Disney first arrived, Parisians were hostile to the Americanism of Mickey Mouse and all it stood for, with some French intellectuals branding it as 'a cultural Chernobyl'.

Whilst prior experiences had shown that Americans and Japanese adopt new products quickly, the French were far more reserved. Significantly, 95 per cent of Continental Europeans and French had never been to a Disney Park and so awareness was low. Boosting attendance amongst the French is problematic. Whilst most nationalities treat the park with the enthusiasm of an assault course, staying until the close, the French are perplexingly casual sometimes, turning up towards closing time or leaving early if the weather deteriorates. They are also unpredictable, making planning for unexpected increases in demand a difficult burden to cater for.

Disney have been disciplined in attempting to transfer core Disney values and themes in to Europe. Nowhere in the Disney park can you see the outside world, with not a glimpse of litter, delivery vans or stacks of deliveries. The world of Disney appears to be timeless and self-sustaining.

A more sinister discipline appears to be the recruitment and training policies of how its contact staff deal with the public. Their list of don'ts is long. They're not allowed to smoke, chew gum, wear flashy jewellery, tint their hair an unnatural shade, possess a visible tattoo, appear fat or smell of sweat. Their code of conduct is stricter than the Mormons, with no long hair and no facial hair. Even the executives appear to be cloned to the rule book.

The world of Disney is further regimented with its own language. Thus shops are referred to as 'retail entertainment centres', waitresses are 'quality hosts', employees are 'cast members' and queues are endowed with the title of 'pre-entertainment areas'.

Since the opening of the theme park, Disney have been refining their product. Early visitors complained of few Disney characters, so these were increased. The shortage of rides and other shows is also being extended. Visitors can now not only meet Mickey Mouse but see where he lives.

The question is: Is it worth it? If consumers are going elsewhere, what are they spending their leisure time on?

Source: Adapted from: Bill Bryson (1993) 'Of Mice and Millions', *Observer Magazine*, 28 March, 16–23. (Reproduced with permission)

Q12.1 What marketing problems does Euro Disney face beyond those expected of a physical goods manufacturer? Why are these problems significant for Euro Disney?

Q12.2 How does Euro Disney offer search qualities to develop consumer confidence in the Euro-Disney product?

Q12.3 How does Euro Disney use experience qualities to support its intended service positioning?

Q12.4 In terms of the marketing mix of people, physical evidence and process, do you believe Euro Disney got it right? If not, why not?

Summary

The marketing of services poses several challenges beyond those of marketing physical goods. These are intangibility, heterogeneity, inseparability and perishability. Intangibility of many services means that goods cannot be sampled in advance. With a lack of search qualities, they can sometimes be evaluated only on experience or in some cases not easily even after experience (in which case they hold credence qualities). Physical evidence can sometimes be used, along with tangible cues, in order to help create a position for a service to stand out from the remaining competition. This can potentially reduce the perceived risk of purchase and help to reassure customers of the type of service offered.

A second problem is heterogeneity because employees vary in their performance and can significantly influence the type of service offered. Recruitment, training and recognition awards can help to ensure consistent staff behaviour. It is also possible that consumers can affect both the type and quality of the service they receive (i.e. inseparability). Thus the type of haircut a person can have is constrained somewhat by the hair (or lack of it!) they already have, and what suits them best is somewhat influenced by the shape of their face and head.

Perishability is the last problem in which a service cannot be inventoried for a later sale – if not sold today, that sale is lost for ever. Owing to the higher costs imposed on services when in low demand, resources need to be matched to fluctuating demand patterns. Accurate forecasting and flexible pricing are therefore important concerns in services marketing.

Owing to the nature of services, the marketing mix can be extended to include people, physical evidence and process. Thus managing people, setting an appropriate physical layout to support the intended positioning and offering appropriate options in how consumers receive and participate at the service encounter are important. This needs also to be harmonised with decisions made in the core product, the price, the place and the promotion (i.e. the traditional marketing mix variables). Thus the marketing mix of services is acknowledged to encompass 7 Ps.

References

Bateson, J.E.G. (1989) *Managing Services Marketing*. Orlando, FL: Dryden Press.

Business Review (1994) 'Public Confidence Slumps after UK Pensions Scandal', August.

Darby, M.R. and Karni, E. (1973) 'Free Competition and the Optimal Amount of Fraud', *Journal of Law and Economics*, 16 April, 67–86.

Davies, M.A.P. (1966) 'Image Problems with Financial Services: Some Considerations for Improvement', *Management Decision*, March, 34, 2, 76–81.

Fletcher, F. (1994) 'Tracking Public Opinion for the Life Insurance Industry, Year 1993', *Great Britain Report*, LIMRA International Europe Ltd.

Handy, C. (1991) *The Age of Unreason*. London: Business Books.

Nelson, P. (1974) 'Advertising as Information', *Journal of Political Economy* (July–August), 81, 729–54.

Osmond, J. (1992–93) *ISBA/ARM Press Inquiry*, Stage 1, September 1992 and Stage 2, January 1993.

Sasser, W.E., Olson, R.P. and Wyckoff, D.D. (1978) *The Management of Service Operations*, Boston, MA: Allyn and Bacon.

Shostack, G.L. (1977) 'Breaking Free from Product Marketing', *Journal of Marketing*, 41, 73–80.

Zemke, R. and Schaaf, D. (1990) *The Service Edge*. New York: Plume (The Penguin Group).

Multiple Choice Questions

Chapter 1

1.1 Marketing is about:

(a) promoting goods and services;
(b) the ability to plan for the future to gain more control over environmental uncertainty;
(c) the need to develop relationships with customers over time;
(d) satisfying and maintaining consumer needs profitably;
(e) developing and maintaining mutual exchange relationships with consumers in order to achieve organisational goals.

1.2 An organisation that believes it is in the telephone business rather than a means of delivering communications and information, and subsequently only invests in designing improvements in telephones, is:

(a) sales-oriented;
(b) production-oriented;
(c) marketing-oriented;
(d) market-oriented;
(e) design-oriented.

1.3 The components of a market orientation are:

(a) customer orientation only; that is all that matters;
(b) a customer orientation and a competitor orientation;
(c) a competitor orientation only, since it is only necessary to match your competitors;
(d) a customer orientation, competitor orientation and interfunctional co-ordination;
(e) developing a long-term vision for the organisation.

1.4 Strong brands tend to have superior financial performance because:

(a) they have been around longer;

(b) marketing investment has been heavy and sustained;
(c) they are promoted better than weak brands;
(d) they tend to have higher customer loyalty and so enjoy significant trade leverage;
(e) perceived risk in usage is lower.

1.5 A product that can enjoy a sustained premium in price above rival brands reflects:

(a) brand commitment by marketing management;
(b) quality packaging and advertising;
(c) continuous research to ensure a superior perceived value by customers;
(d) good fortune: the organisation will soon suffer as market forces change;
(e) a high-risk strategy in the face of lower priced competitive products.

Chapter 2

2.1 Phases in the marketing planning process include:

(a) the marketing audit only;
(b) setting objectives, strategies and tactics;
(c) analysis of the competitive position, SWOT analysis, managing objectives, implementation of strategy and evaluation and control;
(d) internal and environmental resource analysis;
(e) revising objectives based on a SWOT analysis.

2.2 The selection, investment and withdrawal of products from the business is known as:

(a) competitive analysis;
(b) the internal audit;
(c) portfolio analysis;
(d) shareholder analysis;
(e) the marketing audit.

2.3 Shareholders within the external audit include:

(a) customers, buyers and shareholders;
(b) employees, customers and distributors;
(c) suppliers, buyers and employees;
(d) buyers, distributors and management;
(e) shareholders, management and suppliers.

2.4 Future manufacturer policies on 'lookalike' brands is most likely to be influenced by:

(a) economic forces;
(b) social forces;
(c) cultural forces;
(d) legal forces;
(e) technological forces.

2.5 Organisations which keep abreast of changes in the external environment which may affect their future by formally monitoring opportunities and threats is called:

(a) environmental scanning;
(b) marketing planning;
(c) marketing analysis;
(d) marketing auditing;
(e) SWOT analysis.

2.6 The most complete influences on buyer behaviour are:

(a) inflation, interest rates and wage rates;
(b) consumer confidence and expectations of their future standard of living;
(c) availability of goods and intensity of competition;
(d) existing purchases and future buyer wants;
(e) disposable income, availability of and attitudes towards credit, and willingness to spend.

2.7 A future economy is characterised by a working minority supporting a non-working majority. This minority is likely to favour:

(a) mass unemployment;
(b) luxury markets;
(c) products which are capital intensive;
(d) products designed to save time;
(e) more products provided by the state.

2.8 A supermarket decision to increase the number of smaller units of pre-packed food is most likely to arise from:

(a) technological forces;
(b) social forces;
(c) legal forces;
(d) economic forces;
(e) political forces.

2.9 The most influential environmental factor in shortening product life cycles arises from:

(a) technological forces;
(b) social forces;
(c) cultural forces;
(d) economic forces;
(e) political forces.

2.10 The competitor profile analysis (Figure 2.4) indicates that:

(a) Competitor B is more successful than A;
(b) Organisation A is in a stronger position than competitor B;
(c) Competitor B is in a stronger position than organisation A;
(d) Competitor A is more likely to succeed than B because it is not very weak on any critical factor;
(e) It is impossible to predict the likely success from either organisation from the information supplied.

2.11 Obstacles to sustaining a differential advantage include all of the following except:

(a) ease of imitation;
(b) patents;
(c) moving targets;
(d) higher expectations and a growing sophistication of user needs;
(e) availability of new technologies.

2.12 Sustaining a competitive advantage can be achieved through all of the following except:

(a) ongoing training, recruitment and motivation of staff to enhance customer service levels;
(b) focusing on activities that influence customer value;
(c) achieving a distinctive, well-known and respected corporate personality;
(d) by developing caution and restraint, in taking time to solve customer problems;
(e) to adopt a continuous organisational learning culture, in which competitive success can be acknowledged and used as a platform for inspiration, ideas and know-how.

Chapter 3

3.1 Using accounting records for marketing research purposes is an example of:

(a) internal secondary data;
(b) internal primary data;
(c) external secondary data;
(d) external primary data;
(e) second-hand data.

3.2 Assessing combinations of packaging attributes can best be derived from using:

(a) focus groups;
(b) conjoint analysis;
(c) the tachistoscope;
(d) projective imagery tests;
(e) semantic differential scales.

3.3 Secondary data cannot be obtained from:

(a) trade journals;
(b) government sources;
(c) international sources;
(d) surveys;
(e) computerised retrieval data bases.

3.4 Test marketing is an example of using:

(a) continuous data;
(b) observation;

(c) experimentation;
(d) survey research;
(e) syndicated research.

3.5 Marketers at General Motors wanted to determine the effects of an advertising budget increase on sales of Cadillacs. In setting up the experiment, the independent variable would be:

(a) sales;
(b) price;
(c) advertising expenditure;
(d) production cost;
(e) wholesale purchases.

3.6 Consumer panels offer all the following data except:

(a) family size;
(b) brand special offers;
(c) brand loyalty;
(d) type of retail outlet;
(e) trade purchases.

3.7 A toy manufacturer wishes to find out the opinions and behaviour of its target audience: 2–3-year-olds. The best way of evaluating their behaviour on a limited budget is by:

(a) attitude survey;
(b) focus group discussions of their parents;
(c) observation;
(d) test marketing different products;
(e) past sales.

3.8 The first stage in designing a marketing research plan is to:

(a) write a report;
(b) clarify the marketing problem;
(c) interpret the research findings;
(d) decide the research questions or hypotheses;
(e) present the findings.

3.9 Willingness to answer a questionnaire will be positively affected by questions which appear:

(a) controversial;
(b) irrelevant;
(c) confidential;
(d) to reflect on the consumer's knowledge of the subject;
(e) socially embarrassing.

3.10 Questions used in a questionnaire can be clarified to improve the design by all of the following, except by:

(a)   using filter questions;
(b)   avoidance of leading questions;
(c)   gearing the questions to the language of the target audience;
(d)   pre-testing;
(e)   probing for responses.

3.11   The presentation of a questionnaire can be improved to aid clarity by all of the following, except by:

(a)   the use of consistent instructions;
(b)   colour coding to help guide the reader through the questionnaire;
(c)   a logical sequence of events/issues/or questions;
(d)   restriction to closed questions;
(e)   pre-testing.

3.12 An organisation with clear research objectives wishes to reach and assess the changing attitudes of a consumer market which is widely dispersed geographically. It has a limited budget for research, has a tight deadline and wishes to select its members randomly to achieve this. The total sample size is to be 5,000. The best possible method of data collection is:

(a)   focus groups;
(b)   telephone survey;
(c)   personal survey;
(d)   mail survey;
(e)   desk research.

3.13 A research agency acting on behalf of a publisher conducts a stratified random sample of its readers' views about its editorial policy on its best-selling magazines. The sample is stratified according to their relative proportions within different age bands. The split is 20 per cent of readers below or at the age of 15, 35 per cent between the ages of 16–35, and 45 per cent the remainder. If 700 16–35-year-olds are selected, what was the original sample size?

(a)   200
(b)   1,000
(c)   1,400
(d)   20,000
(e)   2,000

Chapter 4

4.1 A direct mail organisation investigates past purchase and loyalty patterns to determine its future target segments. This form of segmentation is called:

(a)   psychographics;
(b)   demographics;
(c)   niche marketing;
(d)   benefits;
(e)   behavioural.

4.2 Positioning, in communications, refers to:

(a) corporate image;
(b) management perceptions of customer feelings about a product, brand or organisation;
(c) consumer perceptions of a product, brand or organisation;
(d) customer preferences;
(e) consumer expectations of a brand, product or organisation.

4.3 A product which offered similar needs to everyone, which could not be easily differentiated by any means, will most likely serve a:

(a) heterogeneous market;
(b) mass market;
(c) concentration segmentation strategy;
(d) multi-segment strategy;
(e) segmented market.

4.4 An organisation recognises it is profitable to serve the needs of three different groups with three different pricing, promotional and distribution strategies. The organisation is practising a ___ strategy:

(a) concentration segmentation;
(b) undifferentiated;
(c) multi-segment;
(d) mass marketing;
(e) homogeneous.

4.5 A niche strategy is best used when the market is characterised by:

(a) intense competition, with a large market size, in which end-user wants are varied and complex;
(b) weak competition, with a large market size, in which end-user wants are varied and complex;
(c) intense competition, with a small market size, in which end-user wants are varied and complex;
(d) weak competition, with a small market size, in which end-user wants are varied and complex;
(e) intense competition, with a small market size, in which end-user wants are similar but complex.

4.6 A college lecturer buys a personal computer with the intention of running a small consultancy business from home. The lecturer is involved in the:

(a) organisational market;
(b) not-for-profit market;
(c) consumer market;
(d) reseller market;
(e) institutional market.

4.7 A financial services organisation uses postal codes combined with housing areas and merges these with details of households, such as numbers and ages of children living at home. The organisation is most likely using:

(a) age and geographical segmentation;
(b) ACORN and age;
(c) social class and age;
(d) social class and family life cycle;
(e) ACORN and family life cycle.

4.8 A restaurant decides to offer a pick 'n' mix, self-service, mixed menu choice, rotated every month, to meet the needs of its core profile of customers. This variation is most likely to appeal to the:

(a) fulfilleds;
(b) believers;
(c) experiencers;
(d) achievers;
(e) makers.

4.9 Organisational segmentation might involve all of the following, except:

(a) SIC codes;
(b) size of turnover;
(c) social class of purchasing officers;
(d) spatial segmentation;
(e) behavioural segmentation.

4.10 In industrial marketing, the seller needs to plan for purchases, arising from all of the following features, except:

(a) the high potential outlay of each purchase order;
(b) the level of purchasing experience of the buyer;
(c) the number of decision-makers influencing the purchasing process;
(d) the age of the purchasing officer;
(e) any existing loyalty to the current organisation supplying the order.

4.11 A lottery organisation decides to use complex segmentation in its promotions by combining three segmentation indices: volume usage, population density and gender. Volume usage is split into heavy, moderate and light users, and population density is subdivided into city centre, urban, suburban and rural. The total number of possible segments the lottery organisation might choose to target is:

(a) 27
(b) 12
(c) 18
(d) 24
(e) 3

4.12 A brand follower A is mapped in perceptual space by two salient attributes, X and Y. A scores equally on both attributes, although currently the target audience rate attribute Y greater than X. A is shown to be some distance from the ideal position B, but it cannot reposition itself closer to B on account of its weak product development capabilities. It is, however, potentially strong in external communications. The brand leader, C, is close, but not on, the ideal position. A is best placed to:

(a) Introduce an improved product;
(b) Introduce a fighter brand D, which would be close to the ideal, but away from A;
(c) Shift A towards the ideal position C;
(d) Move the ideal position closer to A by raising the salience of X;
(e) Accept its current position or divest out of the market.

4.13 Perceived purchase risk can be reduced by all of the following except:

(a) lowering prices;
(b) no-quibble refunds;
(c) extending warranties;
(d) endorsements;
(e) strong brand positioning.

4.14 An organisation has a strong consumer position but has low sales. This might be attributable to all of the following, except:

(a) low awareness;
(b) low availability;
(c) low share of voice (proportion of advertising spent compared to competitive advertising spend);
(d) negative word-of-mouth communication;
(e) poor terms of sale.

Chapter 5

5.1 All the following explain the importance of studying consumer behaviour by marketers except one. Which?

(a) Many brands are not sufficiently liked to stimulate purchase.
(b) Consumer behaviour affects us all daily.
(c) Consumer behaviour is dynamic.
(d) It is difficult to predict consumer responses with certainty.
(e) Consumer behaviour includes an analysis of both psychological or mental influences and overt behaviour.

5.2 Consumers are least likely to brand switch if they are:

(a) offered special deals;
(b) inspired by novelty-seeking behaviour;
(c) exposed to advertisements for competitive brands;
(d) satisfied with their existing brand;
(e) given new advice from friends or sales assistants.

5.3 All of the following influences are psychological components except one. Which?

(a) perceptions;
(b) personality;
(c) family influences;
(d) attitudes;
(e) learning.

5.4 Self-concept is an important feature for:

(a)   expensive items;
(b)   conspicuous consumption goods;
(c)   impulse items;
(d)   convenience items;
(e)   fast-moving consumer goods.

5.5 Behaviour will most likely reflect prior attitudes when:

(a)   consumers have reservations about their immediate purchase;
(b)   there is memory relapse;
(c)   the time spent between evaluation and purchase is short;
(d)   there is a strong influence to conform to a group;
(e)   situational factors affect ultimate purchase.

5.6 When a brand is associated with an intended stimulus through repeated marketing exposure, it is known as:

(a)   rehearsal;
(b)   classical conditioning;
(c)   operant conditioning;
(d)   time proximity;
(e)   concrete imagery.

5.7 Memory is least retained by using:

(a)   jingles;
(b)   rehearsal;
(c)   limited storage capacity;
(d)   concrete imagery;
(e)   pictures.

5.8 A readiness to act in a specific way, based on prior knowledge, feelings and a behavioural component is called:

(a)   emotion;
(b)   perception;
(c)   motive;
(d)   value;
(e)   attitude.

5.9 Apathetic shoppers are motivated by:

(a)   empathy;
(b)   sentiment;
(c)   perceived value for money;
(d)   time proximity;
(e)   time utility.

5.10 When there is a gap between your current position and an ideal situation it is known as:

(a)   problem recognition;

(b)   information search;
(c)   evaluation;
(d)   purchase;
(e)   post-purchase evaluation.

5.11 External search is least likely when:

(a)   buying convenience items;
(b)   buying high outlay items;
(c)   buying items which incur considerable perceived risk (in case of making a poor choice);
(d)   marketing information is easily available;
(e)   members of the family offer friendly advice.

5.12 The main behavioural goal of post-purchase for convenience items is to encourage:

(a)   brand-switching;
(b)   brand loyalty;
(c)   trial purchase;
(d)   positive associations with the brand;
(e)   attitude change.

5.13 Cognitive dissonance about a brand is least resolved when:

(a)   paying attention to competitive advertisements;
(b)   rationalising that the brand is not important;
(c)   paying attention to leaflets and publicity about the brand;
(d)   rationalising that the criteria used for making brand comparisons are unimportant;
(e)   feeling that the source of competitive information is unreliable.

5.14 Supermarkets display elaborate lighting around their meat counters, which intensifies its redness. This is an example of exploiting:

(a)   personality traits;
(b)   motives;
(c)   attitudes;
(d)   time proximity;
(e)   evaluation.

Chapter 6

6.1 Characteristics of asset-led marketing include:

(a)   quick payback, low investment, low risk and using the market as the starting point;
(b)   quick payback, high investment, low risk and using the market as a starting point;
(c)   quick payback, high investment, low risk and using the assets of the company as a starting point;
(d)   quick payback, low investment, low risk and using the assets of the company as the starting point;
(e)   none of the above.

6.2 Delivering a quality/value association in the marketing mix means:

(a) identifying and matching the needs and motives of consumers with an appropriate level of price and non-price factors;
(b) being able to predict when consumers are likely to trade up and down according to market conditions;
(c) segmenting the market on price;
(d) always offering a high quality product to everyone;
(e) always trading on value in a recession.

6.3 The stage of the life cycle when competition will be most intense is generally:

(a) introduction;
(b) growth;
(c) maturity;
(d) decline;
(e) none of the above.

6.4 Product extension strategies are most likely at:

(a) introduction;
(b) growth;
(c) maturity;
(d) decline;
(e) all of the above equally.

6.5 Persuading resellers to allocate shelf space for a product are most intensively conducted at:

(a) introduction;
(b) growth;
(c) maturity;
(d) decline;
(e) all of the above equally.

6.6 Advertising expenditure is at a minimum at:

(a) introduction;
(b) growth;
(c) maturity;
(d) decline;
(e) all of the above equally.

6.7 The second stage in the new product development process is referred to as:

(a) business analysis;
(b) product development;
(c) screening;
(d) test marketing;
(e) ideation.

6.8 Break-even analysis is normally conducted at:

(a) business analysis;

(b) product development;
(c) screening;
(d) test marketing;
(e) ideation.

6.9 Prototypes are typically developed at:

(a) business analysis;
(b) product development;
(c) screening;
(d) test marketing;
(e) ideation.

6.10 Market launching of new products to a small group to assess acceptability is called:

(a) concept testing;
(b) product testing;
(c) test marketing;
(d) product development;
(e) product screening.

6.11 Growth strategies of the firm involve:

(a) market penetration;
(b) new product development;
(c) market development;
(d) diversification;
(e) all of the above.

6.12 The Boston Share Growth Model:

(a) is a prescriptive rule for managing the marketing mix of new products;
(b) is a prescriptive rule for managing the investment and withdrawal of new and established products;
(c) offers guidance on how to identify marketing opportunities for a range of products;
(d) offers guidance on managing the investment and withdrawal of new and established products;
(e) is a prescriptive tool on how to identify marketing opportunities for a range of products.

6.13 Problem children are:

(a) leaders in high growth markets;
(b) leaders in low growth markets;
(c) followers in high growth markets;
(d) followers in low growth markets;
(e) all of the above.

6.14 Contributory factors that help to explain why cash cows generate a surplus of cash over expenditure are:

(a) leaders usually have a good reputation in the market;
(b) leaders tend to have better trade leverage than followers;

(c) leaders suffer from less brand switching than followers;
(d) competitors have withdrawn from the market;
(e) all of the above.

Chapter 7

7.1 Inelastic demand to price changes is characterised by:

(a) a downward sloping demand curve;
(b) a horizontal demand curve;
(c) price-cutting activity;
(d) familiarity with price points;
(e) convenience goods.

7.2 Elastic demand is most likely for:

(a) unsought goods;
(b) luxury goods;
(c) innovators;
(d) KVIs;
(e) customised services.

7.3 Skimming prices is most suitable at the ___ stage of a product life cycle:

(a) introduction;
(b) growth;
(c) maturity;
(d) decline;
(e) none of the above.

7.4 A penetration pricing policy is superior to skimming in offering:

(a) high payback;
(b) less risk to innovators;
(c) high margin sales;
(d) a ready mass market;
(e) more flexibility to change prices.

7.5 Price competition is *most likely* under conditions of:

(a) a small number of suppliers able to differentiate their goods or services;
(b) a large number of suppliers able to differentiate their goods or services;
(c) desensitising customers to price;
(d) a large number of suppliers offering similar goods and services;
(e) a small number of suppliers offering similar goods and services.

7.6 To fill seats near to take-off time, airlines offer discounts. This is a case of:

(a) transfer pricing;
(b) team pricing;
(c) bait pricing;
(d) differential pricing;
(e) marginal cost pricing.

7.7 Bus operators in Atlantic City lure consumers to casinos by offering free rides and/or money vouchers to spend inside. This is practising:

(a) transfer pricing;
(b) team pricing;
(c) bait pricing;
(d) differential pricing;
(e) marginal cost pricing.

7.8 A car manufacturer offers a range of prices consistent to market expectations for different market segments. This is an example of:

(a) transfer pricing;
(b) team pricing;
(c) bait pricing;
(d) differential pricing;
(e) marginal cost pricing.

Chapter 8

8.1 Stockholding costs may be reduced by all the following, except:

(a) reducing wastage;
(b) obsolescence;
(c) modularisation of stocks;
(d) using intermediaries when appropriate;
(e) producing economic production runs.

8.2 Three manufacturers are served by a wholesaler who, in turn delivers to five retail buying centres. Previously, each manufacturer distributed directly to the retail centres. The number of transactions saved by using the wholesaler is:

(a) 8
(b) 7
(c) 15
(d) 23
(e) 9

8.3 A manufacturer is most likely to distribute direct:

(a) if intermediaries are appropriate;
(b) if far from the market;
(c) if the producer wishes to have minimal control over the terms of sale;
(d) for low margin products;
(e) for highly perishable products.

8.4 Examples of direct marketing include all of the following except:

(a) teletext;
(b) off-the-page advertising;
(c) the Internet;
(d) vending machines;
(e) direct selling.

8.5 Advantages of the Internet include all of the following except:

(a) quicker access to real-time data;
(b) an alternative to conventional shopping for all goods;
(c) global sourcing;
(d) convenience in transactions;
(e) a supportive medium for reaching groups who are not heavy users of alternative media.

8.6 Advantages of mail order include all of the following except:

(a) lower inventory costs;
(b) lower recruitment costs;
(c) flexibility in deciding when to buy;
(d) a range of credit facilities and methods of payment;
(e) lower prices to customers.

8.7 Marketers who wish to speed up the rate of consumer acceptance of new technological channels of distribution need to:

(a) target the innovators;
(b) reduce the costs of using channels through technological innovation;
(c) reduce technophobia through education and training;
(d) a and b only;
(e) a, b and c.

8.8 Goods that are considered for purchase by specific brand name, before shopping is conducted, are referred to as:

(a) selective goods;
(b) shopping goods;
(c) premium goods;
(d) speciality goods;
(e) convenience goods.

8.9 A convenience product which is purchased on a routine basis is likely to have which of the following marketing mixes:

(a) low price, selective distribution and minimal sales support at point of sale;
(b) low price, intensive distribution and substantial sales support at point of sale;
(c) low price, intensive distribution and minimal sales support at point of sale;
(d) low price, exclusive distribution and minimal sales support at point of sale;
(e) low price, selective distribution and substantial sales support at point of sale.

8.10 The issue about taking title to goods is strategically important because:

(a) stakeholders need peace of mind;
(b) the title owners can set their own prices;
(c) the title owners have a stake in how the good is distributed to the customer;
(d) the title owners may have complete control over the marketing of their products;
(e) it is required for legal reasons.

8.11 Stores which offer mid-market appeals but compromise on service, relying on multiple purchases per shopping visit, are known as:

(a)   variety stores;
(b)   hypermarkets;
(c)   discounters;
(d)   department stores;
(e)   franchises.

8.12 A relationship between two distributors who hold much informal co-ordination of activities, but remain independent, is called a(n):

(a)   franchise;
(b)   administered VIS;
(c)   corporate VIS;
(d)   exclusive dealer arrangement;
(e)   partnership.

8.13 An independent business person who agrees to pay a fee or commission on sales in return for a proven management idea, support and advice within an exclusive territory, is referred to as a:

(a)   franchise;
(b)   franchisor;
(c)   franchisee;
(d)   network broker;
(e)   corporate VIS.

8.14 Factors that have contributed to the increasing threat by many own label brands on the impact of top manufacturer brands are:

(a)   an increase in price-led promotions by many manufacturers;
(b)   the strength of corporate advertising to enhance store reputation;
(c)   an increased leverage by supermarkets as their concentration of ownership has increased;
(d)   greater retail awareness of customer account and brand performances arising from using information technology;
(e)   all the above.

8.15 A manufacturer should be wary of pursuing own label contracts because:

(a)   they may erode sales of its own brands;
(b)   there is the additional burden of renegotiating new business as an old contract expires, coupled with the uncertainty of the new terms and conditions;
(c)   there may be disclosure of sensitive cost information;
(d)   expertise in product innovation may be transferred to the retailer;
(e)   all of the above.

8.16 Retailers who seek to maximise returns on a shelf in collaboration with their manufacturers are most to be practising:

(a)   creative merchandising techniques (e.g. end-of-aisle displays);
(b)   using slotting allowances;
(c)   using category management;
(d)   using each other as a source of advice, not conflict;
(e)   meeting regularly to discuss business operations and ironing out any problems.

Chapter 9

9.1 Which of the following is the correct answer? The promotional mix does not include:

(a) public relations;
(b) personal selling;
(c) direct mail;
(d) pricing;
(e) sales promotions.

9.2 When presentations are made about a product or service in the media not paid for by the promoted organisation, this is known as:

(a) advertising;
(b) sales promotions;
(c) public relations;
(d) publicity;
(e) word of mouth.

9.3 Examples of communication effects do not include:

(a) preferences;
(b) brand recognition;
(c) sales enquiries;
(d) understanding;
(e) credibility.

9.4 All the following media may be suitable for presenting complex messages except:

(a) newspapers;
(b) consumer magazines;
(c) television;
(d) direct mail;
(e) trade press.

9.5 Communicating a unique selling proposition must satisfy all the following requirements except:

(a) relevance or target salience;
(b) clarity;
(c) accuracy of claim;
(d) uniqueness;
(e) image differentiation.

9.6 Towards the decline of the PLC if the firm is not considering immediate withdrawal of investment, the most appropriate form of advertising to existing users is likely to be:

(a) comparative advertising (or positioning);
(b) persuasive advertising;
(c) reassurance advertising;
(d) informative advertising;
(e) corrective advertising.

9.7 The best form of promotions to educate sceptical consumers about a new product would be:

(a) price offers;
(b) free samples;
(c) prize draws;
(d) premiums;
(e) collectors' items.

Chapter 10

10.1 Tracking the ratio of positive to negative articles written about different organisational issues is designed to evaluate:

(a) investor relations;
(b) employee relations;
(c) media relations;
(d) supplier relations;
(e) all of the above.

10.2 It is often necessary, but not sufficient, to change aspects of an organisation to achieve PR objectives. When information about a sensitive issue is likely to be leaked and transferred to the general public, the way this information is spread can be somewhat controlled by prioritising different groups or publics. The most important public to monitor first is usually:

(a) distributors;
(b) shareholders;
(c) the media;
(d) consumer groups;
(e) the government.

10.3 Personal selling is most effective at the ___ stage of the communication process:

(a) awareness;
(b) interest;
(c) understanding;
(d) preference;
(e) conviction.

10.4 Sales prospecting involves all of the following activities except:

(a) referral from past customers;
(b) off-the-page selling;
(c) cold canvassing;
(d) scanning market opportunities in the business press;
(e) overcoming objections.

10.5 The first point of contact in the sales presentation is to:

(a) reduce perceived purchase risk;
(b) deal with objections;
(c) negotiate the terms of the sale;

(d) establish customer needs;

(e) persuade the potential buyer a solution is available.

10.6 A salesperson is most likely to raise objections as part of their presentation if:

(a) they wish to gain credibility;

(b) they wish to develop trust in their relationship with the buyer;

(c) they face the same objections by different buyers;

(d) they wish to gain rapport with their customers;

(e) they need to deflect the conversation from different objections that may be raised.

10.7   Output ratios which may be used by sales management include all of the following except:

(a) average order value;

(b) the 'call rate';

(c) account penetration;

(d) cost of sales;

(e) prospect success ratio.

10.8   Too few calls may be symptomatic of all the following except:

(a) a disorganised workload;

(b) poor planning;

(c) calling on 'marginal players';

(d) idleness;

(e) focusing on a few customers.

10.9 Direct marketing includes all of the following except:

(a) interactive television;

(b) direct mail;

(c) personal selling;

(d) mail order;

(e) teleshopping.

10.10 Growth in direct mail can be attributable to all of the following except:

(a) considered more easy to measure than alternative forms of communication such as advertising;

(b) consumer groups are becoming more diverse in terms of incomes;

(c) there is now a greater accessibility to consumer data on databases and from purchased lists;

(d) lower postal rates;

(e) there has been a reduction in production costs of mailshots arising from technological improvements.

10.11 The second objective in designing direct mail is:

(a) creating a preference;

(b) opening the letter;

(c) developing an ongoing relationship;

(d) responding to the appeal(s);

(e) reading the letter.

10.12 Amplifiers designed to stimulate credibility include all of the following except:

(a) partially completed application forms;
(b) testimonials;
(c) independent testing statistics;
(d) photographs demonstrating benefits;
(e) a personal message from the chairman or some other senior representative.

10.13 Sources of information for internal lists include all of the following except:

(a) sales records;
(b) all charity donors;
(c) off-the-page enquiries;
(d) credit cards;
(e) enquiries at trade shows.

Chapter 11

11.1 The first stage in an international marketing plan (after having decided to use international trade) is to:

(a) shortlist a selection of target countries;
(b) decide a method of entry;
(c) conduct market screening;
(d) decide a marketing mix policy;
(e) deciding whether the mix is standardised or customised for the target countries.

11.2 A firm is least likely to move internationally if:

(a) the demand in the domestic market is saturated;
(b) research shows there are greater opportunities abroad;
(c) competition abroad is intensive and hostile;
(d) the experience curve can be exploited with the market size abroad;
(e) GNP is similar to the domestic market.

11.3 Specific economic criteria which influence potential market size include everything below except:

(a) disposable income;
(b) labour quality;
(c) distribution of wealth;
(d) inflation;
(e) price elasticity of demand.

11.4 Specific socio-cultural criteria which influence potential market size include everything below except:

(a) population growth;
(b) life expectancy rates;
(c) general standard of education;
(d) diversity of cultures and languages in a country;
(e) GNP.

11.5 When conducting sales visits in a foreign country, it is necessary to be aware, and adapt to local:

(a) methods of conducting business;
(b) value systems;
(c) tones in sales presentations;
(d) customs in working habits;
(e) all of the above.

11.6 Protectionism involves barriers which protect local trade. This does NOT include:

(a) standards set by governments (such as laws on packaging or labelling);
(b) tariffs on imports;
(c) nationalistic pride;
(d) state-controlled practices, such as the state ownership of manufacturers or wholesalers;
(e) quotas.

11.7 Current advantages to members or customers of the European Single Market include all of the following except:

(a) greater choice and quality of products;
(b) less protectionism, so enabling better links with trading partners;
(c) economies of scale in production;
(d) a single European identity of all members;
(e) ease of mobility of labour, as trade restrictions are overcome.

11.8 The fastest growing country by percentage increase is:

(a) Kenya;
(b) India;
(c) China;
(d) Indonesia;
(e) United States.

11.9 If a company wishes to have a minimal presence in a foreign country, yet wishes to have some control over marketing operations, and wants to expand fast with limited capital, the most apt method of entry is a(n):

(a) foreign direct investment;
(b) joint venture;
(c) licensing;
(d) foreign buyer;
(e) international trading company.

11.10 The method of market entry which is at greatest risk from political instability in the foreign market is by (a):

(a) distributor;
(b) licensing;
(c) joint venture;
(d) foreign direct investment;
(e) trading company.

11.11 A weakened currency in the domestic market suggests that:

(a) imports are less expensive;
(b) domestic goods become more expensive to foreign buyers;
(c) potential tourists to the domestic market will be discouraged to visit;
(d) relative demand for our goods abroad improves;
(e) unemployment is likely to rise.

11.12 In order to ensure a seller does not lose revenue from fluctuating exchange rates, it may decide to:

(a) negotiate an advanced guaranteed exchange rate;
(b) include an escalation clause in the contract;
(c) constantly adjust price increases to achieve constant margins;
(d) levy penalties on firms who default on early payment;
(e) all of the above.

Chapter 12

12.1 A retail organisation trains its salesforce in how to deal with customers. However, some of its salesforce use their own discretion in dealing with customers with negative consequences, such as keeping customers waiting in long queues. This behaviour represents:

(a) heterogeneity;
(b) perishability;
(c) inseparability;
(d) intangibility;
(e) none of the above.

12.2 Services which are difficult to evaluate even after purchase experience would typically be:

(a) medical care;
(b) clothes;
(c) vacations;
(d) restaurant meals;
(e) furniture.

12.3 Paying great attention to 'correct' customer complaints is referred to as:

(a) sympathy;
(b) symbolic atonement;
(c) recognition;
(d) responsiveness;
(e) dedication.

12.4 A customer choosing the wrong service, arising from a lack of judgement, on behalf of both customer and salesperson, reflects:

(a) heterogeneity;
(b) perishability;
(c) inseparability;
(d) intangibility;
(e) none of the above.

12.5 A product considered to embarrass in front of one's peers is characterised by:

(a) financial risk;
(b) performance risk;
(c) social risk;
(d) imporisk;
(e) economic risk;

12.6 Service providers can stimulate customers to develop more confidence in their own ability to make purchase decisions by improving all of the following communication methods except:

(a) using cognitive scripts;
(b) simplifying charges;
(c) offering promotional support;
(d) maintaining a consistent message;
(e) offering incentives.

12.7 McDonald's sensitivity to litter-free zones around its restaurants is a reflection of managing the ___ of the extended marketing mix:

(a) product;
(b) place;
(c) physical evidence;
(d) process;
(e) people.

12.8 Service quality concerned with customer service levels refers to the ____ of the extended marketing mix:

(a) product;
(b) place;
(c) physical evidence;
(d) process;
(e) people.

12.9 Internal marketing involves improving all of the following activities except:

(a) motivating staff;
(b) internal communication processes;
(c) training schemes for staff;
(d) remuneration schemes for staff;
(e) interactive marketing.

12.10 Rufus Hackerbond wishes to hire a solicitor to help protect his reputation against an alleged computer fraud. He has never consulted a solicitor before and is uncertain how to choose one who will give him the best prospects of clearing his name. This difficulty facing Rufus is best described as:

(a) heterogeneity;
(b) perishability;
(c) inseparability;
(d) intangibility;
(e) none of the above.

Glossary

ACORN	An acronym for A Classification Of Residential Neighbourhoods, in which consumers may be classified according to the type of residential area they live in.
Adaptive management	Ability to adopt new policies, ideas, processes or products to meet changing circumstances.
Ad hoc research	The reverse of continuous research; that which is commissioned to solve a unique problem.
Advertising	A paid form of non-personal communication about products, organisations, people or ideas, delivered to a target market through a mass medium.
Advertising brief	Checklist of requirements developed by client in order to guide an agency about its needs. There are often several briefs (e.g. a creative brief for the advertising strategy and a media brief for the media strategy).
Advertising objectives	The goals of advertising; what it is meant to achieve. Often considered in terms of various models of hierarchical effect.
Advertising plan	The result of integrating the components of the advertising strategy and the media strategy.
Advertising research	The testing of copy effectiveness or some other aspect of a campaign (this may be conducted either before public launch or after it has been launched) usually in relation to that aspect's ability to achieve prespecified objectives (e.g. 40 per cent awareness within 6 months).

Advertising Standards Authority	A body that aims to ensure all non-broadcast advertising is legal, decent, honest and truthful in the interests of competition, consumers and the wider public.
Advertising strategy	Advertising decisions encompassing targeting and segmentation, advertising objectives, appeals and executions.
Advertorial	Promotional coverage of manufacturer brands in retail magazines disguised as publicity.
Agent	A marketing channel member who permanently represents either buyers or sellers and in return receives a commission.
AIDA model	An acronym for Awareness, Interest, Desire and Action to describe the collective marketing communication objectives that need to be achieved in order for products to be promoted successfully.
Analysis and interpretation	The presentation and interpretation of results statistically or by other means to help extract conclusions.
Asset-led marketing	A practice in which company assets are considered as central to the marketing strategy.
Assimilation	A situation in which brands are positioned closely to each other.
Attitude	An overall predisposition to act in a specific way, based on knowledge and feelings towards a given object. In a marketing context, this would be the likely reaction towards the marketable object or stimulus.
Attitude scale	A means of measuring attitudes towards an object, dimensions of an object, or a series of statements relevant to an object or activity, in which numbers are assigned to a series of prespecified responses for analytical purposes.
Attributes	Product characteristics which describe tangible or abstract characteristics.
Augmented product	Supportive or non-core aspects of a product, such as delivery arrangements, warranty details, payment terms and maintenance.
Bait pricing	Luring customers with a tempting low-price offer, only to lock them in with higher-priced complementary products or services.
Balanced marketing mix	Ensuring that each marketing mix element contributes positively towards supporting a unified product concept. Also referred to as integrated marketing mix.
Bargaining power	Negotiating power of stakeholders determined by their relative size and numbers.

Behavioural segmentation	Segmentation based on a study of how people behave using purchase or usage behaviour.
Benefits	Desirable consequences (or outputs) of using and/or consuming a product or service.
Benefit segmentation	Dividing groups within a market on the basis of the specific benefits they seek.
Brand	A collective term that identifies and distinguishes an organisation's products from the competition by the name, design and/or logo.
Brand cannibalisation	A marketing problem in which increased sales of one brand causes a reduction in sales of another in the product mix.
Brand equity	A series of assets associated with the brand that may add or subtract from its value.
Brand follower	A brand whose share position is below that of the brand leader.
Brand leader	A brand whose market share position is first in its sector or given product category.
Brand manager	A person responsible for the overall performance of a brand using the marketing mix.
Brand mark	Any aspect of the brand other than the name, i.e. design and logo.
Brand name	The spoken part of the brand, i.e. the letters, words and numbers.
Break-even point	Refers to the amount of a product that needs to be sold, below which the firm makes a loss and beyond which the firm makes a profit. Costs per unit are higher on a smaller sales turnover owing to the ratio of fixed to total costs being higher.
British Code of Advertising Practice	A set of rules that all non-broadcast ads must adhere to.
Business analysis	Estimating the financial viability of a product through break-even analysis and effects on other products.
Business confidence	A general feeling of well-being about one's standard of living, or more generally about the state of the nation, the economy or a sector of industry, which will affect a willingness to spend.
Buyer behaviour	The study of how, why, and when consumers buy, involving the study of psychological and environmental influences upon the decision-making process leading to purchasing and beyond.
Buyer power	The combined effect of an ability and willingness to spend.
Cash cows	Typically these products are characterised by a high market share (leaders in the market) but are set to decline (in terms of the life cycle). High market share is associated with high margins, and a declining

	overall market is also associated with lower costs of marketing, so cash cows can generate sufficient cash to fund other products.
Centralisation	An organisation in which decision-making and authority is restricted to senior management, with scant delegation to lower levels within the hierarchy.
c.i.f.	A pricing quotation which indicates an inclusive price for cost of goods transported, insurance and freight charges to a named destination.
Circulation	Number of buyers of a media vehicle.
Classified advertising	Advertising arranged under subheadings according to the product or service promoted.
Client publics	Stakeholders, as target prospects, used in public relations. Also known as target publics.
Closed question	A question associated with a prespecified set of response options.
Closing	The final stage in the selling presentation before the actual sale is made, in which the salesperson asks the prospect to buy the product. Also referred to as the close.
Cognitive age	The concept of how old a person feels and how they conform to a particular age group.
Cognitive dissonance	Anxiety arising from a mismatch between attitudes and (purchase) behaviour, say, when expectations have been disappointed after buying a product.
Commercialisation	The final stage of the new product development process in which plans are fine-tuned to full-scale launch.
Commodity products	Characterised by little or no perceived differences between products.
Communication	A sharing of meaning through transferring information, either through personal or non-personal means.
Communication effects	Communication objectives (as distinct from sales-related objectives). It includes awareness, interest, desire and action, and credibility.
Competitive advantage	In terms of Porter, to achieve a business advantage over competitors by one of four generic strategies.
Comparative advertising	A form of competitive advertising in which the sponsor makes a claim against a named or implied competitor based on one or more attributes, benefits or values.
Competitive analysis	Identifying the relative strength of competitive activities and their current and likely effect upon performance.
Competitive forces	Accredited to Porter, the threat of new entrants and substitutes, the bargaining power of buyers and

suppliers and the existing relationship between competitors.

Competitive orientation   An assessment of competitive activity in order to respond effectively and maximise competitive advantage.

Competitive pricing   Pricing which matches or takes account of the pricing of competitive products. The implication is that other factors (e.g. costs) are considered less important.

Competitive strategy   The strategy an organisation adopts in order to offset the competition. This arises from an assessment of the impact or potential effects of competitive activity. In terms of Porter, the impact of the competition is assumed to be influenced by the bargaining power of suppliers, the bargaining power of buyers, the threat of substitute products and the threat of new entrants.

Competitor profile analysis   As part of the audit, competitors are compared by relevant criteria, considered critical for success.

Compiled lists   A database comprising lists of potential customers who share some characteristics with current or past customers.

Complex segmentation   Dividing markets into segments by using two or more variables to refine and discriminate between the needs of different groups of buyers. Also known as multi-variable segmentation.

Concentration segmentation strategy   A market segmentation strategy in which an organisation focuses its attention and expertise on a single market segment through a single marketing mix.

Concept testing   Inviting reactions from consumers to a product idea or concept to assess the product's market acceptability.

Conjoint analysis   A research technique that examines bundles of attributes to interpret more clearly their interactive effects, with a view to improving the marketing mix for a given product. It is based on a trade-off analysis.

Consumer market   Buyers who intend to consume for their own private consumption, perhaps for their own pleasure or for their household, but not with the intention of making a profit.

Consumer panel   Consumers who agree to keep records of their attitudes and/or purchases for market research purposes, in return for a fee.

Continuity programme   An ongoing sales promotion method designed to foster loyalty by developing switching costs. Usually it consists in awarding points or coupons on

	purchases. Accumulated points/coupons can be redeemed for various gifts. Also known as loyalty bonus.
Continuous data	Data collected on an ongoing basis, often by agencies with the intention of selling to clients of commercial organisations. Examples include purchasing habits of fmcg's often collected by a consumer panel.
Convenience products	Frequently purchased and usually inexpensive items that are bought with little mental effort on the part of consumers.
Core product	The main benefit to be gained from a product, and hence the likely motive for purchase.
Corporate image	The corporation as seen by one of its client publics.
Corporate strategy	A plan of action that guides and unifies how resources in each business function, including marketing, will be utilised in reaching the goals of the firm.
Cost leadership	A strategy which allows a firm to maintain leadership in the industry on the basis of low costs incurred in its business operations (e.g. supply, manufacture, marketing).
Cost per thousand	A method for measuring the relative value of alternative media vehicles based on the cost of reaching one thousand prospects.
Cost-plus pricing	A method of allocating a percentage to the predetermined costs borne by the seller.
Credence qualities	Qualities of services that cannot be assessed even after purchase and use.
Critical success factor	Factor considered crucial to the success of an industry.
Culture	Everything around us that has been influenced by human beings. It therefore includes not only objects but ideas and concepts as well.
Customer orientation	A marketing philosophy that offers an appropriate marketing mix which satisfies the needs of its target consumers by creating and sustaining superior value.
Customised product	Policy in which products are adapted to suit the various needs of different foreign markets.
Cycle of virtue	A customer orientation designed to perpetuate loyalty and from which profits allow continual investment in a customer orientation.
Data collection	A stage in the market research process in which a decision is reached about how and what data are to be collected to help solve a marketing problem. Data collection can involve primary or secondary

research. Data can be collected by survey, observation or by experimentation.

Decline	Stage of the product life cycle in which sales fall rapidly and profits are eroded.
Demographics (or demographic variables)	Personal characteristics of individuals, such as age, sex, nationality, occupation, social class and family life stage.
Department store	A retail store format organised into separate departments for different categories of products; characterised by a wide product mix.
Dependent variable	A variable affected by a relationship with another, or several other variables; e.g. sales (dependent variable) may be affected by the decisions taken by the firm, actions of stakeholders, the economic climate and the weather.
Derived demand	Demand for industrial markets which arises from the demand for a consumer market.
Desk research	The art of sourcing and making use of published data; it may entail interviewing business contacts.
Devaluation	When a currency falls in real value or buying power compared with another.
Differential pricing	Offering a similar product to different groups of customers or segments at different prices with the purpose of reducing sharp changes in demand.
Differentiation	A generic strategy by Porter in which products or brands are successfully distinguished from competitive alternatives in order to achieve superior value and gain a distinctive competitive advantage.
Direct channel of distribution	Distribution channel selling products directly from the producer to the consumer or end-user.
Direct mail	Mailed promotional material sent direct to a company or home address of a target prospect. Also known as mailshot.
Direct marketing	A form of communication direct to the end-user to promote a product other than by face-to-face personal selling. This might include using mail, off-the-page selling, telephone or electronic means.
Direct method (of foreign market entry)	A method of entry in which investment by an organisation is either direct export or direct investment abroad in manufacture (say, setting up plant abroad). Direct export involves the manufacturer performing the export tasks in-house, with their own export department.
Discretionary market	Non-essential products. Its demand is likely to be affected by economic conditions.
Disposable income	After-tax income. Note this is different from discretionary income, which is residual income available for spending or saving after basic

	necessities (i.e. food, clothing, general living requirements) have been purchased.
Distribution	The management of ensuring products are available and readily accessible.
Distribution research	Research examining channel design including supplier requirements, customer service levels and potential site locations.
Distributor	An intermediary who takes control of the marketing of their products by holding title to the goods offered.
Diversification	A growth strategy in which sales are increased by developing new products in new markets.
Dog	Product characterised by a low market share with declining market prospects. Dogs are a drain on the firm's cash and so should be seriously considered for divestment or elimination.
Dual branding	A manufacturer policy in which national and private (retail) brands are offered under the same product category.
Economic factors (or forces)	Factors that determine the size and intensity of demand for products, including competitive forces.
Economics of scale	The condition in which costs per unit are reduced as the operations of a business are increased (such as with greater purchasing orders or longer production runs).
Electronic point of sale (EPOS)	The use of information technology which can scan cash transfers from consumer to retailer, and store valuable customer purchasing data. These data can be used to build up local store shopping profiles in terms of purchasing habits, and hence to improve merchandising, customer service levels and the timing of promotional offers.
Emotional need (or emotional appeal) or emotive needs or appeals	Psychological appeal (such as enhancing self-image or self-gratification) or social need (such as popularity or respect amongst peers).
Environmental scanning	The process of monitoring and detecting politico-legal, economic, socio-cultural and technological changes in the environment.
Environmental influences (on buyer behaviour)	Social or situational factors that exert influence on purchasing behaviour.
Environmentalism	The awareness of, interest in and reaction to environmental policies of business.
European Union	An economic alliance of countries in Europe, whose members agree to share common policies such as harmonising trade regulations in order to reduce legal and economic barriers between members.
Exclusive distribution	A distribution policy which uses only one type of

	outlet or channel member within a given market coverage.
Experience quality	A quality of services that can only be assessed after purchase and use.
Experimentation	An investigative method in which two or more groups are given identical offerings except that one independent variable is different. This allows testing of the impact of this variable on a dependent variable.
Exploratory studies	Research conducted in order to investigate further into a given problem or hypothesis.
External audit	An audit involving the macro-environment and the company stakeholders.
External data	Data collected from outside the organisation.
Fad	A temporary and unstable upswing in demand created by a particular group whose fashion needs may be intense.
Family life cycle	The stages of a person's life marked by significant family circumstances (e.g. marriage/size of household, employment and retirement) which have a bearing on net income over expenditure.
Filtered question	Question which offers a range of responses which direct the future sequence of questions asked in a survey, designed to restrict questioning to those aspects of the survey which are relevant to the respondent.
Fixed cost	Cost incurred which is not affected by the number of units produced.
f.o.b.	Free-on-board destination. A pricing quotation which indicates that the producer pays for the shipping charges of merchandise delivered to the customer.
Focus group	A form of qualitative research in which a small group (or groups) of people is recruited to discuss specific marketing issues. An example would be to discuss attitudes towards a new product proposal. Feedback allows the firm to refine the proposal. Future decision-making arises from the interpretation of what consumers have said.
Foreign direct investment (FDI)	Method of foreign market entry in which investment is made in manufacturing operations within a foreign market.
Franchising	A contractual agreement in which the supplier of an idea (the franchisor) offers to sell their business idea to an independent business (the franchisee) in an exclusive area, in return for a fee and usually some commission on sales. The franchisee receives ongoing support and after-sales service.

Geographic segmentation variable	A variable which affects market behaviour by area such as urban compared with rural areas, or by comparing the characteristics of different regions or nations.
Government market	Demand for goods purchased by local or national government with the intention of providing a better standard of living for the nation.
Green issues	Includes all policies relating to environmental concern.
Growth stage	A stage of the product life cycle in which sales rise rapidly and profits reach a peak owing to market acceptance.
Heterogeneity	A problem in services marketing in which standards of service delivery vary both according to the moods and temperament of the service provider throughout their workload and between the abilities and aptitudes of each service provider.
Heterogeneous needs	Needs which are diverse, calling for market segmentation.
Hierarchical effects (of advertising)	Models assuming that advertising works sequentially and that consumers process information (and derive meaning from it) through a series of stages.
Home shopping	A variety of retailing that does not involve traditional outlets, but reaches consumers in their own homes.
Hypothesis testing	A stage in the market research process. Involves the construction of research questions in which guesses are made about relationships between two or more variables.
Ideation	A stage of new product development in which ideas are created as a potential source for new products. When refined and developed, these ideas can help to achieve the objectives of an organisation.
Impulse buying	Unplanned purchase behaviour in which a trigger to some marketing stimulus (e.g. price offer, packaging) compels consumer to buy something immediately.
Income	The amount of money received through wages, investments, pensions and benefit payments.
Independent Television Commission	A regulatory body that screens broadcast media in order to protect the public, consumers and competition from unfair practices, indecency and impropriety.
Independent variable	A variable that is not affected by the values associated with other variables in a test design.
Indirect effects (of advertising)	The side-effects of advertising, relating to the way it affects stakeholders of an organisation other than the direct effects on the target audience.

Indirect methods (of foreign market entry)	An organisation which restricts its operations to the domestic market and does not actively participate abroad. By selling to a foreign buyer or export or import house, the marketing activities in the foreign market are then decided by the new owners.
Industrial market	A market in which purchases are made either for resale, for direct use in producing other products, or for daily use in business operations. Also referred to as an organisational market.
Inflation	A condition in which price levels change faster than incomes, so eroding the purchasing power of the currency.
Information search	Information which is gained either from the memory (internal search) or the market-place (external search) in order to help evaluate and screen alternative marketing offerings.
Informative advertising	Advertising that communicates facts about a product's functional benefits, how to use it or where to find it.
Innovation	The commercial development of ideas, processes or products new to the market.
Innovators	Part of society that influences the degree of market acceptance for a product owing to their early adoption of a new product.
Inseparability	*See* joint production with consumption.
Institutional market	A market in which the objectives of the organisation are to offer charitable, educational or community-conscious benefits and are not principally reliant on making profits.
Intangibility	A characteristic of services in that they cannot be examined and inspected before purchase in the way that tangible products can.
Integrated marketing mix	*See* balanced marketing mix.
Intensive distribution	A form of distribution which ensures that a product is stocked in as many outlets as possible.
Interactive marketing	Non-personal marketing which allows two-way communication (from both seller and buyer), in which the consumer has the opportunity to respond with a view to customising their requirements or by offering direct feedback.
Interfunctional co-ordination	Co-ordination of the resources of an organisation to help create superior value to customers.
Intermediaries	Channel members who perform a variety of functions (e.g. holding stocks) on behalf of other members in the chain such as manufacturers and end-users.
Internal audit	An audit of the internal activities and decision-making processes of the firm analysed per product per market.

Internal data	Data collected from within the organisation.
Internal lists	Lists of names and addresses of customers or target prospects compiled as part of a database.
Internal marketing	A philosophy and set of managerial activities (such as training, motivation) designed to treat all employees as internal customers to enable and encourage them to represent a chosen marketing strategy of the firm.
International marketing	Marketing activities conducted in more than one country.
International Trading Companies	Organisations with extensive market coverage that offer indirect export of goods. They may carry competitors' products.
Internet	The largest connection of computer systems in the world which enables information to be passed between server (the provider of information) and client (the party requesting information).
Intervening variables	Variables that influence the likely response when subjected to a stimulus.
Introduction stage	The first stage of the product life cycle on launching a product on the market. At this stage, profits are negative owing to the initial costs incurred before and during launch.
Joint production with consumption	A characteristic of services, in which a consumer is directly involved in the production process at the same time as consumption. Also known as simultaneity or inseparability.
Joint venture	A partnership between a domestic firm and foreign firms and/or governments.
Junk mail	Direct mail which is discarded because it is perceived to be irrelevant, and so has been poorly targeted.
Kelly Repertory Grid	A rating method for evaluating salient or relevant attributes by using showcards of brands.
Known value items	Items of merchandise which, because of their frequent purchase, are highly price sensitive.
Learning	The act of modifying behaviour (or attitudes) based on the rewards and benefits of previous experiences.
Legal forces	Legislation which controls marketing decisions and activities.
Licensing	A business arrangement, which allows the owner of a business idea (or licenser) to expand rapidly without incurring risks of direct ownership in another business by selling it to a purchaser (or licensee) who pays commission from sales.
Life cycles	The duration of a product in the market.
Life values	The expected commercial value of customer patronage, projected from past purchase behaviour.

Loss leaders	Products priced with the intention of attracting additional sales (and hence incremental profits) from other goods.
Loyalty bonus	*See* continuity programme.
Mail order retailing	A type of non-store retailing that uses direct mail advertising and catalogues to promote merchandise.
Mailing list	Addresses of target audiences or prospects which can be compiled or bought from data brokers for the purposes of direct mail campaigns.
Mailshot	*See* direct mail.
Manufacturer brand	A brand identified with the producer at point of sale. Also referred to as national brand.
Marginal cost	The incremental or additional cost borne in producing an extra item of output.
Market	A group of individuals or organisations which have the ability, willingness, need and authority to purchase products in a given product class or category.
Market development	A growth strategy designed to sell current products in new markets.
Market orientation	Involves adopting a customer orientation, a competitive orientation and interfunctional co-ordination in order to maintain and sustain customer satisfaction and profitability.
Market penetration	A growth strategy in which sales are increased by expanding with current products in current markets.
Market research plan	Structure of research stages designed to ensure research objectives are achieved within budget and deadline.
Market segment	A group of individuals or organisations who, by sharing one or more characteristics, have similar product needs.
Market share	The sales of an organisation relative to the sales of the total industry, often expressed as a percentage.
Marketing audit	The first stage of a marketing plan. A thorough review of the external and internal market positions of an organisation relative to its objectives.
Marketing communications	The communication of information for marketing purposes. Collectively, this involves using advertising, sales promotions, public relations and personal selling.
Marketing concept	A managerial philosophy that requires an organisation to develop and maintain an appropriate strategy through a co-ordinated set of marketing decisions (product, price, place and promotion) in order to both meet and satisfy the needs of its customers and achieve its own objectives.

Marketing environment	The environment that surrounds the stakeholders in a business, involving politico-legal, economic, socio-cultural and technological factors.
Marketing intelligence	All data collected for marketing purposes.
Marketing management	A process of planning, implementing, monitoring and controlling marketing activities in order to help achieve marketing objectives.
Marketing mix	Core decisions which are taken by management regarding the product, its pricing, place and promotion. An extension is to include people, process and the physical environment, especially in the marketing of services.
Marketing myopia	Accredited to Levitt, refers to defining businesses too narrowly and thereby ignoring key opportunities and threats.
Marketing objectives	Quantifiable goals which marketing management aim to achieve within a specified time and which guide the future direction of a firm.
Marketing plan	A written document setting out the future strategy of an organisation, which helps to implement and control marketing activities.
Marketing planning	The process of auditing, monitoring and controlling the performance of an organisation with a view towards implementing a revised strategy.
Marketing research	A part of marketing intelligence that examines marketing problems and activities with the aim of improving marketing decisions.
Marketing research process	The formal stages in designing and implementing marketing research, from problem definition to presentation of findings and recommendations.
Marketing strategy	A plan involving the design of an appropriate marketing mix for each market considered worth targeting.
Mass marketing	Aiming a marketing mix at everyone without segmenting the market. Also known as undifferentiated marketing.
Maturity stage	A stage in the product life cycle in which the sales curve peaks and begins to flatten whilst profits continue to decline.
Media	The collective name for a medium, or choice of transmission for a campaign (such as the choice of print, television, radio, cinema, posters, etc.)
Media class	Types of media available, such as broadcast (TV, cinema), versus non-broadcast.
Media plan	A plan that involves both the selection and scheduling (or timing) of each media vehicle for a given advertising campaign.
Media relations	The relationship between an organisation and the media.

Media research	Research conducted to establish the best package of media classes and/or vehicles.
Media scheduling	The decision-making process involving the timing and frequency of advertisements in various media.
Media selection	The decision-making process involving the selection of media classes and media vehicles.
Media strategy	Advertising decisions encompassing media objectives, media selection and media scheduling.
Media vehicle	Examples of media within a class, identified by a particular owner.
Monopolies and Mergers Commission	A body set up to ensure that there is healthy competition in the interests of consumers.
Motive	A force that drives an individual towards personal goals.
Multi-attribute utility	Method of evaluation in which alternative products are ranked for satisfying various criteria which, in turn, are weighted by the relative importance attached to each criterion.
Multi-segment strategy	A market segmentation strategy in which an organisation targets more than one segment, each with its own distinctive marketing mix.
Multi-variable segmentation	*See* complex segmentation.
National brand	*See* manufacturer brand.
Nationalism	A state of mind in which behaviour is driven first and foremost by the interests of a country.
New product development	A process for developing new products from scratch, involving six stages: ideation, screening, business analysis, product development, test marketing and commercialisation. It is also a growth strategy.
Non-price competition	A policy for emphasising non-price factors, such as product benefits, perceived quality, promotion, packaging.
Non-price factor	Element of the marketing mix that attracts custom by reliance on intrinsic product quality and promotional factors (without using price as a main motive).
Non-store retailing	Retailing that does not involve visiting a store.
Objections	Consumer misgivings or anxieties about a product or service which create obstacles towards sales staff achieving a sale. Sales staff therefore need to be aware of the different types of objection in order to prepare for them and to ask pertinent questions to find out what consumers really think.
Observation method	A research technique which examines the visible behaviour of people of interest (e.g. hidden store cameras can track the store movement of customers to assess the effectiveness of merchandising displays or locations).

Omnibus survey	Continuous surveys used to examine a series of topics. Since they are of interest to a wide audience, client companies ensure specific questions are asked which relate to their interests, and buy that part, so keeping commissioning costs to a minimum.
Open-ended question	Question which invites as wide a range of responses as possible. There is no prespecified response option.
Opportunity cost	The value of benefits forgone arising from choosing one alternative over another.
Organisational culture	A set of values, beliefs, attitudes and norms that permeate an organisation and influence the kind of behaviour and decision-making that is acceptable within it.
Organisational market	*See* industrial market.
Own label	Brands which are identified by the retailer's name. These are also owned and controlled by the retailer. Also known as private brand, private label or house brand.
Packaging research	Research conducted into either the aesthetics and visual attraction of packaging as a promotional tool or its efficiency in terms of physical distribution (space utilisation, ease of stacking and usefulness in storing provisions).
Pareto analysis	Applied to buying patterns: a relatively small group of buyers makes up a significant number of sales.
Payback (period)	Time in which it takes to recoup the original investment in, say, a new product.
Penetration price	A low price designed for quick market acceptance (penetration) to gain volume sales.
Perceived risk	The apparent risk to the consumer associated with the purchase or as a consequence of using a product or service.
Perception	The process of interpreting information from which the receiver makes sense of their world.
Perceptual mapping	A process in which consumer perceptions of a variety of brands are measured on two or more attributes or benefits. These perceptions are visually displayed to describe their strategic positioning.
Perishability	A characteristic of services in that unused capacity to consume services in one period cannot be stored for use in a later period.
Personal selling	A personal form of marketing communications which aims to inform and persuade customers to purchase products. A key requirement is to push the benefits.
Personality	A unique collection of traits or characteristics, both physical and mental, from which an individual is identified.

PEST	Acronym for Politico-legal, Economic, Socio-cultural and Technological forces which may alter the ability of the firm to achieve its marketing objectives.
Physiological need	Biologically driven need (e.g. the need to eat, drink).
PIMS	Acronym for Profit Impact on Market Share. A research programme which studies the relationships between numerous marketing variables on performance (e.g. quality and market share on financial performance).
Point-of-sale materials	Displays and signs which are designed to offer information and cause impact at point of purchase which can influence both retailers to stock a particular product and consumers to consider buying.
Political forces	Decisions and rules taken by governments which can influence both domestic and foreign trade practices.
Population	All individuals who are of interest to a research study.
Positioning	How consumers rate a product relative to competitive alternatives. The rating is based on salient or relevant attributes, benefits or values to the consumer.
Post-purchase evaluation	Any evaluation of a product or brand made after purchase.
Post-test	Evaluation of an advertisement after it has been launched to the target market.
Pre-launch	The stage prior to the introduction of a product in the market-place.
Premiums	Items that are offered free on pack, inside pack or after a number of qualified purchases or redeemed for coupons. Also includes items that are offered at a lower than normal price.
Prestige pricing	Supporting a prestigious quality image by using high prices.
Pre-test	Evaluation of an advertisement before it is shown to the target market.
Price	The value placed on what is exchanged.
Price bundling	Offering an inclusive price for a range of functions.
Price elasticity of demand	How much demand changes in response to price changes.
Price inelastic demand	Demand is relatively unaffected by changes in price. Specifically, a change in price will bring about a less than proportional change in quantity demanded.
Price skimming	A policy in which the highest possible prices are charged to those who most need the product.

Price/volume chart	A mechanism for monitoring changes in demand at various price points in order to maximise contribution.
Pricing research	Research that enables a firm to judge changes in price on market demand.
Primary data	Unpublished marketing data designed to solve a particular problem of an organisation. This is derived from conducting research.
Problem child	A product characterised by low market share and facing a growing market. It is likely to absorb much management time and cash, hence continued investment in it should be selective. Also known as question mark.
Problem definition	The first stage of the marketing research process, in which the boundaries of the problem require to be clearly defined. If they are not, the results of the research are most likely to be invalidated.
Producer markets	Demand for goods purchased with the purpose of making something of commercial value.
Product development	A stage of new product development in which price, distribution and promotion are used in concert with the business concept in order to prepare the product for testing.
Product life cycle	Each product is assumed to move through several stages from launch to decline. Its importance to an organisation is that strategies need to be altered according to which stage a product has reached.
Product mix	The total combination of products available from one firm.
Product portfolio	In terms of the Boston Growth Matrix, this is the balance of cash generating and cash absorbing products to ensure a healthy future of new products. Without such a balance, there will either be too few new products (so reducing the survival chances of the firm) or too few cash resources (signalling a financial disaster).
Product features	Technical characteristics of products which do not readily convey consumer benefits.
Production orientation	An organisation geared to improving production efficiency without researching consumer needs.
Prospecting	Targeting people as potential customers for personal selling.
Psychographics	A form of segmentation based on a study of consumer lifestyles, often analysed and classified into different groups on the basis of consumers' activities, interests and opinions.
Psychological factors (of buyer behaviour)	The collective influence of personality, self-concept, learning and memory, attitudes, perceptions and motives on buyer behaviour.

Psychological pricing	A pricing method that uses emotional appeals to encourage purchase.
Public relations	The management of responses and feelings of client publics towards an organisation and its products. Client publics include not only customers or suppliers, but any group or individual who participates in the activities of the organisation as a stakeholder, such as shareholders, special interest groups and government officials.
Publicity	Newsworthy communication about a product, organisation or individual that is non-personal and covered in print or broadcast.
Pull strategy	Marketing efforts designed to create consumer demand for a given product.
Purchasing power	A buyer's income, credit and wealth available for purchasing products.
Push strategy	Marketing efforts designed to persuade the trade to stock a given product.
Qualitative research	Information which explains or contributes towards a richer understanding of marketing perceptions or behaviour which cannot readily be quantified. Responses from research may explain how or why individuals behave or react in the way they do towards particular marketing practices.
Quality	In a marketing context, the ability to satisfy the specific needs of consumers.
Quantitative research	Responses from research which can be presented and analysed numerically. Typically this involves large sample sizes.
Question mark	*See* problem child.
Quota	In international trade, the maximum amount that is legally allowed into or out of a country, designed to protect the local economy.
Quota sampling	A form of non-profitability sampling in which a predetermined group or quota is selected by interviewers on the basis of holding specific qualifications, e.g. a sample of working mothers living in the South East.
Random sampling	A form of probability sampling, i.e. in which each member of a population has an equal chance of being selected in the sample.
Rate of return on investment (ROI)	Specifically, in accounting terms, ROI is the net profit/capital employed expressed as a percentage, in which capital employed is the total assets of an organisation less the current liabilities. It is one of the key accounting ratios which expresses the financial health of an organisation.

Rational needs	(Or rational appeals). Benefits based on some performance-related criterion.
Reactive marketing	Responding to marketing problems as they arise without prior planning or research.
Readership	The number of viewers who have an opportunity of exposure to a given media vehicle.
Recall score	A rating of advertising or brand strength which measures the ability to remember an ad, brand or some dimension of them.
Reciprocal agreement	A business understanding in which two stakeholders in a business agree to buy from each other, typified in industrial markets.
Reference group	A group which influences the values, attitudes or behaviour of individuals by readily identifying with them. Examples might include friends, members of the family or workgroups.
Regulatory forces	Rules which arise from government which restrain the marketing activities of organisations and result in sanctions if broken.
Relationship marketing	Developing relationships with business partners or customers on the basis that it is in their interests to cooperate rather than confront and exploit each other. From a seller perspective, the motive is to develop customer commitment and loyalty.
Reminder advertising	Advertising that serves to jog the memory about a product or service.
Repeat patronage	Consumer repurchases of a brand or product.
Reply facilitators	Direct mail tactics designed to reduce the effort or increase the reward in responding to an offer.
Reseller markets	Demand for goods purchased with the intention of selling through a distributor.
Response lists	A database comprising competitors' customers.
Retail audit	A form of continuous data collection of retail stock records, purchases and sales.
Retailer	An organisation which purchases products to resell to consumers as a business.
Sale of Goods Act 1979	Legislation designed to protect the consumer from deceptive trade practices.
Sales performance analysis	The process of using qualitative and quantitative sales-related data to analyse the business in order to interpret the underlying causes of strengths and weaknesses and develop appropriate action for improvement.
Sales performance input ratios	Desired indicators of effort used to create sales.
Sales performance output ratios	Desired indicators of sales achievement.
Sales orientation	A preoccupation with increasing sales as the major driver for increasing profits.
Sales promotion	A form of marketing communications which is

	aimed at resellers or consumers (or internally within an organisation) to persuade them to buy (or sell) promoted products.
Sample	A group of individuals selected from the population who are used for research studies and from whose results interpretations are generally made about the wider population.
Screening	A process of new product development which ensures that only those ideas that fit in with organisational objectives are considered for development.
Search quality	A service attribute which can be examined prior to purchase; it tends to be the most tangible.
Secondary data	Published information used for a different purpose from that for which it was first intended.
Segmentation	Process of identifying groups of members and whose needs are similar to each other within a group but different from members in other groups.
Segmentation strategy	Deciding the means of segmentation: either a multi-segment or a concentration segmentation strategy.
Segmentation variable	A personal or behavioural characteristic of individuals, groups or organisations that forms the basis of dividing markets into segments. A subset would be demographic variables.
Selective distribution	A level of distribution in which selective outlets are chosen to cover a market area.
Self-actualisation	The highest need in Maslow's hierarchy, referring to self-fulfilment, contentment.
Self-image (or self-concept)	How a person views himself or herself.
Selling	*See* personal selling.
Selling in	Selling to the trade.
Semantic differential scale	A rating scale bounded by bipolar adjectives in which the direction of attitudes and their intensity of direction can be measured.
Shopping goods	Strongly branded goods sought by name.
Simultaneity	*See* joint production with consumption.
Situational factors	A set of unique circumstances that face consumers when making a purchase decision. Examples include the relationship with any sales staff, distractions at point of sale and the atmosphere and congestion of a retail environment.
Slotting allowances	Preliminary listing fees charged to manufacturers in order to get their new products stocked or placed in preferred shelf positions.
Social class	A social ranking in society determined by the income of the chief earner of the household.
Social factors (of buyer behaviour)	The collective influence of culture, social groups and the family on buyer behaviour.

Socio-cultural factors	The impact of society, or individuals, and culture upon buyer behaviour.
Sponsorship	The act of supporting a business activity, person or product with funds by a donor or sponsor in order to achieve a positive image by association with it.
Stakeholders	Parties who interact with the operations of an organisation, such as buyers, suppliers, distributors, competitors and shareholders.
Standard Industrial Classification or (SIC) codes	A classification system of industrial organisations and services determined by what they produce. A coding system is used.
Standardised products policy	Policy of ensuring that products are not altered specifically for a foreign market. If research shows that needs are similar to the domestic market, this is a sound policy.
Star	A product characterised by a high market share in a growing market. These are tomorrow's breadwinners.
Stimulus	An object or idea that causes a response (in terms of attitudes or behaviour) generated through our senses, i.e. through taste, hearing, sight, smell or touch.
Strategies	Means of achieving objectives by using the marketing mix, geared to the needs of a target market.
Stratified random sample	A sample whose members are subdivided by one or several characteristics, in which members are randomly selected on the basis of their relative proportions in each subdivision.
Supermarket	A self-service store carrying a wide range of food items, together with some non-food items.
Surveys	A method of data collection in which respondents of interest are interviewed either by mail, telephone or face-to-face to identify some aspect of their behaviour, feelings or opinions.
Sustaining competitive (or differential) advantage	To continuously hold a competitive advantage (likely to be involved in hard-to-copy products or services).
Switching costs	Rewards forfeited or costs incurred (in time or money) by buyers when switching from one brand to another.
SWOT analysis	An acronym for Strengths, Weaknesses, Opportunities and Threats, which are analysed per product per market. Strengths and weaknesses refer to current internal decision-making in an organisation. Opportunities and threats refer to the future marketing environment.
Symbolic atonement	Creating opportunities to engender greater goodwill from consumers by paying particular attention to their grievances.

Symbolism	Act of conveying meaning with an object or activity.
Synergy	A concept in which the overall achievement of a strategy is worth more than the combined individual efforts of each decision leading to it.
Target audience	A specific group or segment of the market at which a marketing strategy is aimed. Also known as target market.
Target market	*See* target audience.
Target pricing	A form of pricing in which prices are decided by competitive and market factors before a product is produced.
Target publics	*See* client publics.
Targeting	The process of identifying and selecting the best segment or segments in which to focus the marketing activities and efforts of the firm.
Tariffs	Taxes on imported products, designed to protect the local economy.
Team pricing	Pricing for a range of goods to ensure consistency in prices for products offering varying degrees of quality and or functions.
Technological factors	The advance in progress of technical knowledge and science that affects a nation's future standard of living and demand for products and services.
Test marketing	A cost-effective introduction of a product to a smaller area than the intended market in order to gauge the reaction towards market acceptance or experiment with variations in the marketing mix before deciding the final strategy for a full-scale launch. The testing in a restricted area may act as an insurance policy in case the product is a failure.
Time proximity	The association of particular products or activities together in time.
Total quality management (TQM)	A managerial practice that encourages everyone within an organisation to think of ways of improving quality at every level of activity in order to serve customers better.
Tracking	Monitoring changes in a dependent variable over time (e.g. consumer attitudes towards brand attitudes).
Trade characters	Fictitious characters used in marketing communications in order to develop a personality for a brand.
Trade promotions	Sales promotions targeting the trade.
Trademark	A symbol that identifies and protects the legal owner of the brand from others who might use or imitate it.
Transfer pricing	The pricing options open to a division or unit of an organisation selling to another. The choice of

adopting a price to the outside market or a cost-plus derived price (i.e. below the price to the open market) will depend upon the state of demand in the market.

Undifferentiated marketing	*See* mass marketing.
Unique selling proposition (USP)	A brand characteristic considered to be unique, relevant and physically distinctive to a defined target audience.
Unsought good	Product bought in an emergency, or unplanned for.
Value analysis	Examining and streamlining the component parts of a product in order to offer the customer improved value.
Value chain	The required activities that a firm performs which add value to achieve its business objectives.
Values	States of feelings more general than benefits. Benefits tend to be more product-specific.
Variable cost	Cost that varies with production.
Variety store	Store which sells a wider variety of merchandise than a supermarket, but less varied than a department store's.
Vendor rating	A formal means of rating all suppliers on similar criteria.
Vertical marketing systems	A marketing channel in which a single channel member manages the activities of everyone within the channel. Also known as vertically integrated systems.
Wastage	Promotional material geared to an audience that is unlikely to be in the market for the promoted product.
Wholesaler	An intermediary that offers a cost-effective service of extended market coverage to producers or other channel members by buying and holding their stock for resale, together with transporting, fabricating, sorting and breaking its bulk.
Width (of product mix)	The number of product lines an organisation has.
Willingness to spend	A positive mood towards spending.
Zone of acceptance	The range within which prices may be accepted at various quality associations by different sectors of the market.

Subject Index

Organisation and Brand Index